Marxism and the

Marxism and the Critique of Value

Neil Larsen, Mathias Nilges, Josh Robinson, and Nicholas Brown

M·C·M′
CHICAGO·ALBERTA

Published by MCM' Publishing
Chicago 60608
www.mcmprime.com

Library of Congress Control Number 2013950962

For Robert Kurz, 1943-2012

Contents

Introduction

Marxism and the Critique of Value is the first broadly representative book-length collection in English translation of work from the contemporary German-language school of Marxian critical theory known as *Wertkritik*, or, as we have opted to translate the term, value-critique or the critique of value.[1] The critique of value itself is understood in these pages as having begun with Marx, who initiated a theoretical project that was as philosophically radical as its implications were revolutionary; an incomplete project that has been taken up only fitfully by Marxism after Marx.[2] In Marx's critique of political economy, value and other categories attendant on it are shown to be concepts both fundamental to the functioning of capitalism and fundamentally incoherent, riddled with contradictions as pure concepts and productive of crisis as actually existing concepts operative in the day-to-day reproduction of social life under capital. While this "esoteric" Marxian critique has been rediscovered from time to time by post-Marxists who know they've found something interesting but don't quite know which end is the handle, Anglophone Marxism, for reasons that will become clear in the course of this book, has tended to bury this esoteric critique beneath a more redistributionist understanding of Marx, imagining that there could be a positive Marxist science of the economy, a science that would be oriented toward devolving surplus value to the labor that creates it.[3] But what if the value relation does not constitute itself in contradiction to labor, but rather encompasses labor as precisely another of its forms of appearance — if labor is, to paraphrase and echo what is perhaps Norbert Trenkle's most direct challenge to "traditional Marxism," itself always already a "real abstraction" no less than the commodity form? What then are, for a critical thought still faithful to Marx, the implied forms of revolutionary practice and agency?

The introductory remarks that follow are intended principally for readers with little to no previous knowledge of *Wertkritik*. The nearly universal absence of English translations that has prevailed up until now — over a period of nearly three decades, in effect an entire generation — has resulted in a virtually total absence of *Wertkritik* from Anglophone critical theory — even as one of those spaces marked "terra incognita" on the maps drawn up by the conquerors and colonizers of the first phases of the capitalist world-system. Given this absence, the need for a minimum of historical and bibliographical information can hardly be more urgent — even as the context would itself demand to be contextualized, ad infinitum. The bulk of this introduction will consist of a series of interpretive summaries of the thirteen texts selected for translation and conforming to a loosely thematic sequence.[4] These summaries, making up the most practical segment of the introduction, are intended only to orient the reader toward the esays themselves. The best introduction to *Wertkritik* as a theoretical orientation is the essay that begins this collection, Norbert Trenkle's "Value and Crisis: Basic Questions." There the reader will find a concise presentation of the "what and why" of value-critique (originally presented as a lecture for this purpose in 1998) that would render an elaborate summary of fundamental tenets here superfluous.

Although its precise origins in the West Germany of the 1970s and 1980s remain a matter of some dispute, *Wertkritik*'s emergence as a well defined and systematic direction within German-speaking Marxian critical theory is made clear by the sheer mass, range, and depth of the *Wertkritik* archive, which consists of thousands of pages distributed across publications ranging from short newspaper columns to lengthy journal articles to monographs. Yet it may come as surprise to Anglophone readers to learn that *Wertkritik* in this systematic sense designates in practice the accumulated work of probably no more than thirty or forty individuals making up two presently non-cooperating theory-oriented collectives, the central core of whose members have for years lived and worked in and around the northern Bavarian city of Nuremberg and whose main activity has been to produce two roughly annual journals — *Krisis* and *Exit!* — with *Streifzüge*, a Vienna-based, loosely *Krisis*-allied, more pamphletary publication, making up a third venue.[5]

A smaller number of individuals closely involved in the production of one or the other of these periodical organs have published book-length works as well, most notably and prolifically in the case of *Wertkritik*'s most prominent author and foundational thinker, the late Robert Kurz. Until his untimely death in July 2012, Kurz wrote voluminously, publishing theoretical essays regularly in *Krisis* and then, after 2004, in *Exit!*; contributed regular, short newspaper columns in the left-wing German press (and a monthly column for the *Folha de São Paulo*, the major Brazilian daily); and authored a number of book-length works as remarkable for their uncompromising but innovative theoretical tenor as they are for their relentlessly polemical militancy. Probably the best known of these is *Schwarzbuch Kapitalismus*, Kurz's *Black Book of Capitalism*, a massive and truly paradigm-shattering reconstruction, from its beginnings to its present-day crisis, of the history of the capitalist mode of production.[6] Meanwhile, other, somewhat younger value-critical theorists, most notably *Exit!*'s Roswitha Scholz and *Krisis* editors and stalwarts Norbert Trenkle and Ernst Lohoff, have published a stream of profoundly original book-length works.[7]

Those who imagine themselves at the vanguard of critical theory, Marxist and otherwise, within the privileged zone of today's unquestioned, convertible currency of a lingua franca, often share an unspoken article of faith according to which one can trust that someone, somewhere will see to it that translations of anything of vital significance will sooner or later find their way into theoretical circulation. When one considers that few of the value-critical theorists publishing in *Krisis*, *Exit!*, or *Streifzüge* are employed as academics, it might appear understandable that the still predominantly university-based audience for contemporary shifts and discoveries in Marxist critical theory would take little notice even of an undertaking as enormous and electrifying as Kurz's *Black Book of Capitalism* — despite the rumors that German investment bankers and chief executives are worried enough to have been among the more loyal, if clandestine, readers of Kurz's journalistic columns. Is the absence of *Wertkritik* from Anglophone discourse an exceptional, even scandalous state of affairs? Or is such absence rather inevitably the case whenever something genuinely new or simply chronically excluded from the awareness of any cosmopolitan stratum of intellectuals is "discovered"? The editors of this volume do not pretend to any superiority of judgment. We have, nevertheless, undertaken the work of preparing this volume in the conviction that the contribution of *Wertkritik* to Marxist and critical theory generally is of such importance that its absence from contemporary Anglophone debates is remarkable and possibly symptomatic: a perhaps inadvertently enforced exclusion from a theoretical-critical field of vision, and the removal of what it excludes to a location at which what has for unknown reasons failed to become present for theoretical and critical awareness is presupposed as, by virtue of its contingent absence, necessarily absent, even excluded a priori from such theoretical and critical awareness. There are, of course, important exceptions.[8] But English-speaking Marxists have tended to acknowledge the existence of the esoteric Marx as it were only on Sundays, quite as if the inner dynamic of the value form and an understanding of the historical unfolding of events down to the present moment had nothing to do with one another. And perhaps that fact, as much as the hitherto extremely sketchy dissemination of the crisis theories linked to German-language critiques of political economy, from Henryk Grossman, Paul Mattick, and Alfred Sohn-Rethel, via the origins of the *neue Marx-Lektüre* in Adorno's classroom in the 1960s, up to and including both the contemporary manifestations of the new reading of Marx and present-day value-critique, explains why the latter has remained mostly unknown ground for Anglophones.[9]

The difficulty of finding value-critical material in English serves as an exacerbated model for the rest of the non-German-speaking world.[10] English-language translations of the occasional short article by Robert Kurz or Anselm Jappe (as often as not thanks to the opportune discovery of Portuguese, Spanish or French translations from the original German) have cropped up now and then on the blogosphere or, if one knew enough to look, in citation indices. And (thanks to the tireless efforts of Joe Keady) a more consistent stream of English renderings of, for the most part, excerpts from the works of Trenkle and Lohoff now appear on the new, online-formatted *Krisis*. But true to a longstanding intellectual import pattern in the English-speaking world, French remains the quasi-official foreign language of new radical theory — with Italian now sharing the domestic market for exotic wares. Interestingly, the single most important exception to this linguistically imposed localism has been, since the mid-1990s, the still comparatively small but energetic and sustained study of *Wertkritik* that can be found in and radiating out from the University of São Paulo, thanks ultimately to the efforts of Roberto Schwarz, one of Brazil's foremost Marxist literary, cultural, and social theorists, whose influential review of the Portuguese translation of Kurz's *Der Kollaps der Modernisierung (The Collapse of Modernization)* sparked the intense Brazilian interest in value-critique.[11] There followed the inauguration of Kurz's column for the *Folha de São Paulo*. With this, shorter writings by Kurz and other well-known value-critical theorists and authors began to appear in Portuguese translation as well. This then made possible the at first spontaneous, now organized publication of translations of the periodical literature of value-critique on websites (including Portugal's *obeco*, on which virtually everything published in issues of *Exit!* appears practically overnight in highly competent Portuguese translation) that are the work of independent radical theory circles, one of which formed in the city of Recife, a relatively peripheral city in the far Northeast but one with an august radical tradition.[12] So much for the notion that theoretical vanguards travel first from metropolis to metropolis!

The phenomenon of so-called "anti-German" communism requires some careful mention here. With its origins in the critical Marxist currents that rejected the Leninism and Mao-Stalinism of the fragmented cadre-organizations and groupuscules known as the *K-Gruppen* (so called because the first initial of most of their organizational abbreviations was K for *kommunistisch*) in the late 1970s and 1980s, the "anti-German" German trajectory can be credited with having played an important role in the rediscovery of a range of non-orthodox Marxist traditions, including the first generation of the Frankfurt School (Adorno in particular), the council communists, Alfred Sohn-Rethel, and Hans-Jürgen Krahl. Influenced by their rediscovery of the anti-nationalism of Rosa Luxemburg and Karl Liebknecht (and later that of the left-communists), anti-German communists controversially turned away from the reflexive support for movements of national liberation that was near-compulsory among the West-German radical left of the 1970s.[13]

This anti-national orientation entailed a complex relationship to the nationalist anti-Zionism that since at least 1967 had been the default position on the Left in both East and West. This stemmed in part from critical reflection on the latent antisemitism that sometimes hides behind criticism of Israel, not the only state with a record of violent and criminal discrimination. But it also went hand in hand with a new understanding, strongly influenced by Moishe Postone's "Anti-Semitism and National Socialism," of eliminationist anti-semitism.[14] The rethinking of the politics of antisemitism and anti-Zionism that took place in the German-speaking radical Left during the course of the 1990s was closely related to the kinds of attempts, carried on and further developed by *Wertkritik* in ways visible in some of the essays collected in this volume, to understand, to analyze, and above all to criticize the capital relation. In particular the "anti-German" tendency led, among other things, to the rejection of two kinds of position that are still popular among large parts of the self-styled radical left. The first is the criticism of the role played by finance capital with respect to the so-called real economy of industrial capital. This criticism, frequently heard in the wake of the financial crisis of 2007-8, both ignores the force of the Marxian insight that finance capital is itself dependent on the production of surplus value, and can at times come disturbingly close to mirroring the National Socialist objection to "parasitic" (international, Jewish, exploitive) capital in favor of "productive" (national, German, autochthonous) capital. The second is the anti-Americanism masquerading as opposition to capitalism that would later characterize large sections of the anti-globalization movement, manifesting itself in a hostility to symbols such as Coca-Cola and McDonalds.

What is clear in the case of both of these phenomena — and what *Wertkritik* drew from its own complex origins in the political debates and divisions of the era, and despite later criticisms voiced against the "anti-German" tendency as it began itself to take on more and more openly reactionary and even pro-U.S. imperialist positions — is that they are not, appearances notwithstanding, critiques of capitalism at all. The first explicitly appeals to industrial capitalist production (and in doing so erases all class distinctions in the industrial production process), while the second is an argument in favor of local and often smaller-scale production, an argument which is frequently imbued with anti-American *ressentiment*, and which neglects the capitalist compulsion to valorize value on an ever larger scale. Along these same lines, objections to the actions of the players in the game of "casino capitalism" are misdirected insofar as they see these individuals as responsible for the system within which they act rather than recognizing that the systemic consequences of the compulsion to the valorization of value constitute the sphere within which casino-agency is produced. In doing so, such objections misconstrue financial speculation and public borrowing as causes of the crisis, when in fact they are merely responses to — and more specifically, processes of deferral of — the crisis of exchange value in which capital, which can no longer attain valorization in industrial production, seeks greater returns elsewhere, by means of the inflation of speculative bubbles.[15]

And as a final observation here: given *Wertkritk*'s key contributions to crisis theory, its relative absence within Anglophone economic and political discourse has become especially crippling since the outbreak of the current severe and historically unprecedented crisis of global capitalism in 2007-8. The considerable upsurge of interest in Marx that has been one result of the current crisis — in particular in Marx's theory of capitalism's "tendency to self-destruct," as favorably mentioned by Wall Street's and the *Financial Times*'s most listened-to doom-mongering mainstream economist, Nouriel Roubini, in August, 2011 — has in turn given rise to a plethora of theoretical and political debates in Left-leaning, Marxism-friendly alternative media in North America concerning the nature and outcome of the Great Recession, as the global economic downturn in the wake of the financial crisis of 2007–8 seems to have come to be called, at least within the U.S.[16] But what has been missing in this literature has been an analysis that reaches deep into the structure of Marx's mature critique of political economy and at the same time beyond the limitations of what Kurz refers to as the exoteric Marx: the points and aspects within his work where Marx is concerned with and oriented toward the modernization and development of capitalism, from the historical perspective of his existence in the nineteenth century.

Not surprisingly, and despite the impressive exploratory range of *Wertkritik* across the at times seemingly endless matrix of social relations mediated through the value abstraction, especially as the latter sinks ever more rapidly and deeply into the array of symptoms that mark what is possibly the terminal crisis of the value form itself, many problematics remain unexplored. Prominent among these, for reasons perhaps not difficult to discern when one considers that they tended to dominate the critical theory of the Frankfurt School from which *Wertkritik* has had, ironically, to distance itself in order to make full use of its ties to precursors such as Adorno, are the spheres of culture and the aesthetic. But the question of the emancipatory in its immanent relation to the crisis of commodity society may be what finally eludes the critique of value even as it bores its way ever further into the depths of a future as though from front to back. If the associated producers no longer appear as capitalism's gravediggers, who takes their place? At times *Wertkritik* refuses to consider that its take on this question requires, at the very least, evidence that the old notion of a political subject, whatever its composition, is worse than its lack — evidence that the current moment coyly witholds. But if one is to find such an immanent ground of emancipation, even if its traces are as yet absent from them, one must start by looking hard into the new and at times uncannily dark illuminations in the mirror held up to our own contemporaneity by the essays that follow.

Marxism and the Critique of Value

Norbert Trenkle's "Value and Crisis: Basic Questions," the first text in this collection, sets forth in condensed form the central tenets of the critique of value.[17] The first, which makes clear *Wertkritik's* origins in the Western Marxism stemming from Lukács's *History and Class Consciousness* and its Frankfurt School offshoots, is the critique of the naturalization of social relations, according to which the fundamentally social categories of commodity-producing, capitalist society — value, commodity, money — appear, in Trenkle's words, "reified and fetishized, as seemingly 'natural' facts of life and as 'objective necessities'" (1). It is the misrecognition of these categories as transhistorical, as 'second nature,' that masks the internal contradictions of capitalist society, contradictions from which stems the latter's inexorable tendency toward crisis. Thus it is that, for Trenkle, the critique of value is "essentially a theory of crisis" (13).

The point at which value-critique differs sharply from both what it refers to, following Postone, as "traditional" or workers'-movement Marxism as well as from a more "traditional" critical theory becomes most apparent is the concept of labor, which is understood not as a universal precondition of human existence or as a point of departure for the analysis of commodity society, still less as a basis for the construction of a new, liberated society, but as an "oppressive, inhumane, and antisocial activity that both is determined by and produces private property" (2). Labor, which only comes to exist as such as the result of a violent process of appropriation that separates workers from the means of production and existence, is a "specific form of activity in commodity society," whose highest end is the valorization of value (4).

In the critique of value, labor is made the object of theoretical critique, falling, along with the more familiar, "traditional" manifestations of the value-form under the aegis of what Alfred Sohn-Rethel termed a real or "actually existing abstraction," a "process of abstraction that is not completed in human consciousness as an act of thought, but which, as the a priori structure of social synthesis, is the presupposition of and determines human thought and action" (7). Trenkle takes issue, however, not only with the claim of Sohn-Rethel but also of Michael Heinrich, both of whom situate the real abstraction in the sphere of circulation and more specifically the act of exchange. For Trenkle and *Wertkritik*, in contrast, commodity production is not distinct from or opposed to circulation, but always mediated through it: the production of commodities for the sake of their exchange value itself always presupposes the sphere of exchange: "every process of production is from the outset oriented toward the valorization of capital and organized accordingly" (9). This reconsideration of the fundamental categories of the economic sphere of commodity-producing society has radical and profound consequences for the relationship between value-critique and classical economics. For if value is no longer seen as reducible to an empirical category that can be positively determined by calculating the number of hours of socially useful labor that are embodied within any particular product, but a fetishistic result of the internalization of processes of dispossession, then the Marxist attempt to solve, for example, the so-called transformation problem, to explain how a commodity's price can result from its value and to account for any divergence between them, is revealed to be a category mistake. All attempts to formulate a critique of capitalism from the standpoint of labor or to found a society on the principle that the price workers should be paid for their labor should justly be determined by its (notionally calculable) value will necessarily reaffirm the fetish on which capitalism is based rather than moving beyond it.

Along with these more axiomatic arguments, Trenkle's brilliantly concise outline of value-critique also sets forth the "basic finding of crisis theory," namely that "since the 1970s, as a result of the worldwide, absolute displacement of living labor power from the process of valorization, capital has reached the historical limits of its power to expand, and thus also of its capacity to exist" (13). It is this, in turn, that makes up the central claim of the second essay of this dossier, Robert Kurz's "The Crisis of Exchange Value" ("Die Krise des Tauschwerts") which has perhaps the strongest claim to be regarded as the founding document of value-critique. The essay was first published in 1986 in Issue 1 of the journal *Marxistische Kritik*, of which seven issues were published between 1986 and 1989 before it was renamed *Krisis* for the publication of Issue 8/9 in December 1990 after the fall of the Berlin Wall.

Marxistische Kritik was itself described in the editorial of its first issue as in certain respects a successor of *Neue Strömung* [*New Current*], a journal of radical-Left theory that had been made up of people with a wide range of revolutionary Marxist political backgrounds, former members of groups ranging from the *K-Gruppen* (which at one point in the 1970s were estimated to have had about 15,000 members among them), to Trotskyist organizations that trace their heritage back to the opposition that formed in the KPD in 1928 under Heinrich Brandler and August Thalheimer, and the *operaismo*-influenced *Autonome* and squatters' movement that had its origins in the Extra-Parliamentary Opposition of the late 1960s. According to contemporary reports, this constellation necessitated considerable discussion over a period of two years before it was possible to overcome the conceptual differences that resulted from such relatively heterogeneous and contrasting traditions, clearing a path for *Wertkritik* both to begin publishing a theoretical organ of its own and, as part of the same process, to begin to develop along increasingly systematic and rigorous lines.

It is perhaps a legacy of these discussions that Kurz's essay advances a position that more than a decade later would be described in the editorial to *Krisis* 12 as "completely naïve, seen from our current perspective." While it was clear at the time that Kurz's reading of Marx's account of relative surplus value implied "a fundamental turn against the primary current of all previous Marxist theory," the essay was still predicated on a "traditional" Marxist affirmation of the working class as revolutionary subject that will no doubt come as a surprise to anyone whose first point of contact with value-critique was the 1999 "Manifesto against Labor." In the concluding section of "The Crisis of Exchange Value" Kurz insists that he does not "in any way wish fundamentally to belittle the role of the subject: any true revolution must proceed by means of the subject of a social class and its political mediations" (73). At this point the critique of commodity society and of value and the doctrine of a revolutionary struggle for state power led by the working class were still living side by side in a state of peaceful co-existence. Three years later, this position would be fundamentally rethought in a process that finds what is perhaps its first explicit manifestation in the publication of Robert Kurz and Ernst Lohoff's essay "The Fetish of Class Struggle" in *Marxistische Kritik* 7.

"The Crisis of Exchange Value" nonetheless contained the core of what would develop into the collection of ideas that are represented by the texts translated in this dossier. The essay's opening criticizes the belief of what he refers to as "the Marxist Left" that the "law of value" is merely a "formal law of the social allocation of resources that can be influenced politically," and argues that as long as value is allowed to hold sway as an element of second nature, such a Left will not be able adequately to understand the developments in the productive forces that characterized the twentieth century (18). Kurz takes issue with the "petrified historical interpretation of Marx" in which the concepts of "productive labor" and "productivity" fail to take into consideration the distinction between use value and exchange value (20). From the perspective of use value, productive labor is any form of useful activity; from that of exchange value, it "refers exclusively to the abstract process of the formation of value" (21). While it is the case that in simple commodity production the two are more or less identical, under the industrial capitalist mode of production they begin to diverge.

Kurz analyzes this divergence with particular attention to the category of relative surplus value, the term Marx gave to the decrease in the ratio of necessary to surplus labor achieved by means not of the absolute extension of the working day but of increases in productivity such that the same magnitude of labor power can produce a greater mass of commodities, or the same mass of commodities can be produced by a lesser magnitude of labor power, lowering production costs, and making capitalist enterprises more competitive on the global market. Kurz claims that "[c]apital has no interest in and cannot be interested in the absolute creation of value," but is concerned merely with the proportion of this new value that can be appropriated as surplus value (47). However, this increase in productivity results in a decrease in the mass of value in every individual commodity, since less labor time is required for the production of the same unit produced. "With the development of productivity, capital increases the extent of exploitation, but in doing so it undermines the foundation and the object of exploitation, the production of value as such" (47). The substance or content of value is eliminated, but capital must ensure that its forms of circulation persist. "This must lead to catastrophic social collisions" (54). Kurz thus identifies an absolute, immanent limit to capitalism, and claims not only that capital and its advocates are necessarily blind to the tendency toward the reduction of value-production, but also that the Marxist Left has failed adequately to address much less to refine its understanding of this problematic. For Kurz writing in the mid 1980s, the crisis dynamic has already begun: each additional increase in productivity and each further rationalization driven by the need of individual capitals to maintain competitiveness on the world market only add nails to the coffin of the self-valorization of value. Capitalism has, in this sense, and if the theory holds true, entered upon its final crisis.

Despite the foreboding predictions of barbarism in this context, Kurz's strongest attack is directed not against capital and its advocates, but against the failure of the Left to recognize the dynamic of the crisis. From Engels, Kautsky, and Luxemburg's presentation of Marx's theory of crisis as a theory purely of overproduction or underconsumption to Bernstein's rejection of Marx's theory of collapse altogether, Kurz accuses the historical Left of remaining fixated on the fetishistic, surface-level categories of capital and of thus failing to consider the divergence of contemporary capitalist production from simple commodity production, and the role within this divergence of relative surplus value. Even the ultra-left, Kurz argues — here with respect to Grossman and Mattick — confined themselves to a "value-immanent" critique that remained within the surface categories of market circulation, a claim that will strike readers familiar with Mattick's *Marx and Keynes* or his introduction to *Fundamental Principles of Communist Production and Distribution* as curious. "It thus becomes clear," Kurz nonetheless insists, "that Marxist crisis theory, so far, has in fact not moved beyond a value-immanent mode of observation, and has not seized on the elements of a logical-historical explosion of the value relation as such are included in Marx's work" (71).

Claus Peter Ortlieb's "A Contradiction between Matter and Form: On the Significance of the Production of Relative Surplus Value in the Dynamic of Terminal Crisis" begins from a distinction that, though misunderstood almost as often by Marxists as by non- and anti-Marxists, is fundamental to Marx's analysis of the dynamic of capitalism. As Ortlieb reminds us (following Moishe Postone), no less a figure than Habermas has been led disastrously astray by confusing value and wealth. The former is the legible form that the latter assumes under capitalism; wealth does not for all that disappear in its conceptual nor indeed in its actual distinction from value. Two identical coats, for example, always represent precisely twice the material wealth of one; they will keep two people warm instead of one. But the two coats do not represent twice the value if they were made in a process more efficient than that used to manufacture the single coat.

Although under capitalism the increase in wealth is only accomplished by means of the production of value, there is nonetheless not only a distinction but also a discrepancy between the two. In spite of all the cycles of expansion and contraction that have characterized the history of capitalism, the productivity of labor has increased over time in a unidirectional movement within the development of modern capital. Ortlieb's argument, like Kurz's, hinges on Marx's distinction between absolute and relative surplus value: once the mere intensification of the working day or suppression of wages has reached a natural or legislated limit, the development of capital can henceforth only be accomplished by means of increases in the productivity of labor — that is, by means of decreases in the use of labor relative to output — a decrease which at the same time reduces the value of the product of labor. As local gains in productivity diffuse across the economy, the value of particular goods tends to decrease even as the wealth produced in particular processes tends to increase. For this reason new markets and new products must constantly be found in order to absorb the labor thrown off by increased productivity in existing processes.

While Ortlieb demonstrates that we have reached a point where such continued expansion at the required rate is unlikely — and it is worth noting that economists as solidly establishment as Larry Summers, Secretary of the U.S. Treasury under Bill Clinton, have been led recently to speculate about "secular stagnation" — he does not rule it out: his analysis of the "terminal crisis" is a tendential matter, not a punctual prediction. In any case, for Marxist analysis the "terminal crisis" is no way triumphal, since its issue, barring political intervention, would not be a liberated society but rather universal unemployment and destitution. Moreover, Ortlieb points out that the continuing "resolution" of this process by means of economic growth runs up against an environmental limit, the origin of which is none other than the same contradiction between wealth and value: while environmental factors like a more or less stable global range of temperatures clearly count as wealth, they cannot be accounted for as value, and "if the destruction of material wealth serves the valorization of value, then material wealth will be destroyed" (112).

How, Roswitha Scholz's essay "Patriarchy and Commodity Society" asks, might we formulate a Marxist-feminist theoretical framework that is able to account for the current crisis and other developments since the end of actually existing socialism? The answer is what Scholz theorizes under the name "value dissociation theory." The beginnings of such a critique are rooted in the fundamental assertions of value-critique to which Scholz adds what she calls a "feminist twist," but which amounts to a framework that does nothing less than foreground the centrality of gender relations in the development of capitalism (125). As is the case for value-critical approaches generally, Scholz begins with the assertion that the object of critique should not be surplus value itself (or its production via labor) but rather the "social character of the commodity-producing system and thus [...] the form of activity particular to abstract labor" (125). Traditional Marxism tends to foreground only one facet of what should rather be understood as a complex system of relations, ultimately privileging analyses of the unequal distribution of wealth and exploitive appropriation of surplus value over the level at which a more fundamental critique should begin. It is precisely this narrow concentration and focus of traditional Marxism that Scholz breaks open. Indeed, she claims, today the Marxism of the workers' movements has exhausted itself and has effectively absorbed all the basic principles of capitalist socialization, the categories of value and abstract labor in particular.

Yet, Scholz argues, the critique of value, which argues against this absorption, is itself found wanting insofar as its hitherto inadequate attention to gender means that even an analysis that begins with a fundamental critique of the value form misses a key basis of the formation of capitalism. The immense significance of Scholz's contribution for *Wertkritik* proper cannot, therefore, be understated in this regard, as the recent critical production of the *Exit!* group adopts Scholz's emphasis on value dissociation and the importance of examining the gendered dimension of the value form. The analysis of value dissociation attempts to capture this previously missing basis and aims to foreground all those elements that can neither be subsumed by nor separated from value — all those characteristics, in other words, that value can neither contain within itself nor eliminate entirely. In a logical operation that builds upon Adorno's notion of determinate negation, Scholz argues that "capitalism contains a core of female-determined reproductive activities" that are necessarily "dissociated from value and abstract labor" (127). The provocative claim that masculinity should be understood as "the gender of capitalism," then, can be understood as Scholz's attempt to foreground the instrumental function of capitalist gender relations in the development of capitalism itself (130). The gendering and subsequent dissociation of an entire range of broadly reproductive activities, therefore, ought not to be considered a side-effect of capitalism and its value form, but rather as a necessary precondition of value, which makes it necessary to speak of the emergence of a commodity-producing patriarchy that determines the historical development of modernity and postmodernity. Indeed, the universalization of gender relations under the principle of value dissociation as part of the development of the capitalist value form reveals itself to be an instrumental aspect of the rise of modernity. Gender without the body, then: gender whose being derives neither from biology nor from "culture," but rather from the value form in its dissociated development. But gender that is still gender: it is no coincidence that the crash of 2008 is followed not only by an unemployment crisis but also by intensified anxieties about gender norms, as evidenced in the U.S. by a brutal anti-feminist backlash and renewed assaults on reproductive rights.

   Such an understanding of the gender relations that structure the social dynamism of capitalism also highlights the shortcomings of the theoretical paradigms that predominate within contemporary gender studies. Deconstruction and the wide field of identity-political and even identity-critical paradigms share a problematic understanding of causality that obscures the necessary connection between gender and value, namely value dissociation as the principle that structures gender relations. The assumption, in other words, that cultural meaning attaches itself to a previously existing gendered social division, misses the fundamental importance of value dissociation for the development of capitalism in the first place. It is thus neither to be considered a consequence of capitalism nor even to be likened to the non-identical as analyzed by Adorno. Rather, Scholz stresses, value dissociation is a precondition for the formation of capitalism. Ultimately, value-dissociation theory allows for important metacritical historicization that reveals, for instance, the ultimate complicity of the deconstructivist paradigm with postmodern forms of capitalism and its social logic. "Consequently, it is not only unnecessary but in fact highly suspect to suggest that we must deconstruct the modern dualism of gender" (135). While the U.S. technological sector will gladly recognize fifty-one genders, such a recognition does nothing to disturb the overwhelming dominance of men in that sector by every metric at every level, or to disrupt the prejudice the women who work in that sector face daily. An examination of the changes in the form of capitalism from the perspective of value-dissociation theory reveals that critics such as Judith Butler "ultimately merely affirm [...] postmodern (gender) reality": postmodern capitalism's "double socialization" of women in the context of diversity politics and of the structural and logical centrality of difference is a key aspect in what we must understand as "actually existing deconstruction" (135).

   Norbert Trenkle's "The Rise and Fall of the Working Man" provides a provocative companion to Scholz's essay. For Trenkle, as for Scholz, any examination of the ongoing economic crisis in general, and of the crisis of labor in particular, must include an examination of its gender dimension. "The crisis of labor," he argues, must also be seen as "a crisis of modern masculinity" (143). Like Scholz, who insists that the emergence and development of capitalism cannot be understood without accounting for its gendered social dimension, Trenkle foregrounds the dialectical connection of modern masculinity with the logic of modern real abstraction of labor (while the focus on both subjectivity and labor significantly differentiates Trenkle's from Scholz's approach). The attachment of masculine power to the logic of labor power places the working man in a perpetually precarious situation. Since power is bestowed upon him externally — and as this power is connected to the business cycle (and thus beyond the influence of individuals) and therefore carries within itself at any given point the potential for devaluing specific forms of power and labor — it must therefore be aggressively defended and renewed. In consequence, modern man is not characterized by the dominant cultural images of muscular, physical power as such but instead by the ultimate privileging of the will, by the exercise of discipline and self-restraint over the body that puts the emerging masculine subject totally in the service of a system that rests upon the fundamental desensualization of life as the basic precondition for its labor processes. Indeed, Trenkle argues, an examination of the relation between the capitalist form of labor — its real abstraction — and its corresponding form of masculinity reveals that both the body and the material existence of the commodity are nothing more than a necessary evil in a system that is primarily aimed at the generation of money out of money, in the context of which materiality becomes nothing else than a mere representation, a "body" that in the end is nothing but an abstract content postulated by the form of the valorization of value.

But Trenkle's essay also foregrounds an even more fundamental aspect of a value-critique of capitalism: the relation between capitalist form and its corresponding social dimension. After all, Trenkle argues, the establishment of "this historically unique form of social activity and relation was not possible without the creation of a particular human type" (146). This particular human type reveals itself to be nothing else than the "male-inscribed modern subject of labor and commodities, whose central essential characteristic is that the entire world becomes to him a foreign object" (146). In a logical operation similar to Scholz's assertion of the dialectical connection of the modern form of value and the feminine-inflected characteristics that are dissociated from value (and that precisely via this operation become its basic precondition), Trenkle stresses that the emergence of the modern working man should not be regarded as a mere consequence of capitalism. Instead, he insists, modern subjectivity itself is constructed according to the compulsory push toward this form of subjectivity without which capitalism (and its value and commodity form) would not have been able to develop in the first place. This form of subjectivity must be regarded not as a matter of passive subjugation but of active complicity in the development of capitalism. While the development of this form of masculinity must, of course, also be analyzed diachronically in its relation to a long history of paternalism that precedes capitalism, its role in capitalism is unique insofar as "the abstract and objectified relation to the world" with which it is associated "becomes the general mode of socialization" (148). The valence of feminine identity, then, differs in comparison with Scholz's model. For Trenkle, the construction of modern feminine identity takes the form of the construction of a social other, a counter-identity that first and foremost serves to stabilize and ground the parameters of the male subject of labor — without, however, neglecting the role the division of genders plays with respect to the division of labor and capitalist enterprise in general. Ultimately, the purchase of Trenkle's argument for the current moment is its ability to account for the rise of masculine-inflected aggression (including racist and sexist violence) that for Trenkle must be understood as directly related to the changes and crises of the current form of capitalism, which inevitably brings with them a crisis of masculinity.

In the first part of "Off Limits, Out of Control: Commodity Society and Resistance in the Age of Deregulation and Denationalization," Ernst Lohoff shows that what in the U.S. appear as "liberal" and "conservative" politics are in fact two sides of the same coin. The liberal side regards the remains of the welfare state as "off limits" and fights rearguard actions against its dismantling and commodification. The other, conservative side regards the welfare state as "out of control" and seeks to dismantle and commodify it. Both camps regard the gulf separating them as essentially political, rather than driven by an underlying economic crisis, and neither questions that the role of the state itself is to guarantee conditions for the the reproduction of capital that cannot be met by capitalism itself. Lohoff points out that the asocial sociality that characterizes capitalism — a social formation that is thoroughly integrated and integrating, but that functions, paradoxically, through atomization and competition — can only be brought under control by the state: "The asocial character of commodity society imposes on the latter, as still another of its essential aspects, the formation of a second, derivative form of wealth," namely the state (157). But from the perspective of commodity society, this derivative form of wealth (infrastructure, social provision, public education — in sum, all material wealth that is not directly commodified) appears rather as consumption. The symbiotic character of this relation then depends on the state plausibly serving its integrative function, a state of appearances that wanes as the explosive increase of permanently "superfluous" human material begins to fall under the jurisdiction of the state. That is, at the moment that "labor society" as such enters a crisis. The crisis itself is offset by two mechanisms — speculation and finance on one hand, and privatization on the other — and it is this latter mechanism that prompts the debate: "off limits, or out of control?" Lohoff argues that the answer is neither: instead of concentrating our political energies on the state as the flipside and guarantor of commodity society, we should think material wealth as such outside of the money nexus, which is to say outside both the state and the commodity relation. This is easy to say (if not so easy to think), at the level of philosophical critique. But can it translate into a practical politics? The second half of the essay is devoted to thinking through what a counter-politics that aimed at a non-commodity society would look like from within commodity society, and the first maxim is that rearguard defenses of the state cannot be the answer. "The question of legitimacy ought rather to be addressed offensively from the outset" (172-3). If commodity society can no longer afford social security, this is an argument against commodity society, not against social security. The answer to commodity society's principle of equivalence is then free access, a slogan that organizes Lohoff's vision of a counter-politics.

Kurz's "World Power and World Money" is an attempt to think through the causes and consequences of a looming global economic crisis that was then only in its initial stages. Kurz traces the origins of the crisis to the Reaganite policy of "weaponized-Keynesianism" — massive, debt-financed military spending — that, on Kurz's account, stabilized the world dollar economy and established the dominant global flows of debt and goods that would persist until the onset of the crisis (192). These phenomena are often recognized on the Left as well as on the Right, only in inverted form: greedy bankers and American imperialism, rather than a crisis-induced flight to finance and the arms dollar as the "overarching common condition of globalized capital" (198). Popular slogans such as a more democratic globalization or a return to Fordist employment patterns are therefore not likely to be effective. The closing pages, focusing on the ultimate issue of the current crisis, are necessarily exploratory; speculating on the fate of the oil regimes in the event of a world depression, Kurz does not rule out the danger of an irrational "flight forward" into globalized civil war (199).

Norbert Trenkle's "Struggle without Classes" is perhaps the most striking contemporary manifestation of value-critique's rejection of class struggle that began with the publication of Kurz's and Lohoff's "The Fetish of Class Struggle" in 1989.[18] In the earlier article they had argued that the claim that the working class represents an "ontological opposition to the abstract logic of the valorization of capital," that the workers' movement is the gravedigger of capital, should properly be considered as a form of thought that is immanent to a society based on value, an ideology of modern capitalism. A subject capable of overcoming modern capitalism, they argue, "cannot arise from the affirmation of the category of the worker, but only from the crisis, the crisis of value." They accuse traditional Marxism of mistaking the classes, a "secondary, derived category," for what are the genuine foundations of society, and of reducing the analysis of the value form to a "merely definitional and uncritical trailer to the 'true' theory of capital," and thus of replacing Marx's critique of political economy with an affirmative vulgar socialism.

Trenkle insists that the notion that the antagonistic character of class struggle can point to a future beyond capitalist social relations is an illusion, but nonetheless affirms its historically important role in the constitution of the working class as a subject conscious of its ability to act in pursuit of a social mission. In this essay, however, he addresses the consequences of what might be thought of as the converse process, which following Franz Schandl he terms "declassing," in which four principal trends are identified.[19] First, direct production is increasingly replaced in the labor process with functions of surveillance and control, functions which have been internalized by the individual worker, both in the "horizontal hierarchies" of large companies and the precarious conditions of freelance and self-employed labor (204). Second, responding to the demand for flexibility, workers cease to identify with a single function of the labor process. Third, there develop more, and more distinct, hierarchies among workers, particularly with regard to distinctions and divisions between permanent employees and temporary, part-time, and agency workers. Fourth, there emerges as a consequence of long-term unemployment a new underclass that is primarily defined by the fact that its members are not required by the valorization process.

Trenkle rejects the trend, particularly in the anti-globalization movement and its aftermath, to see this underclass as a "precariat," the contemporary embodiment of working-class, revolutionary subjectivity. That is, while the early value-critical texts on this thematic rejected class struggle on the basis of the co-determination of labor and capital as mutually dependent aspects of commodity society, Trenkle questions whether the category of a class subject is valid under the conditions of contemporary capitalism, suggesting that appeals to the working class now involve the extension of the concept to refer not merely to those workers whose surplus labor turns the wheels of valorization, but to all who are dependent on wage labor, or even all those whose labor power, following Marcel van der Linden, "is sold or hired to another person under economic or non-economic compulsion," a more or less universal and to that extent meaningless category (qtd. 209). Indeed, this also allows all conflicts to be reinscribed as class struggle and permits the inclusion of reactionary movements such as ethnic nationalisms within the category of anti-capitalist struggles.

Trenkle not only offers an analysis of the fragmentation of capitalism as nothing more than "the intensification of the logic of capital in the stage of its decomposition," but also discusses the possibility of forms of resistance to this fragmentation and to the tyranny of the commodity-form (219). This is best seen as a growing tendency of the *Krisis* group and the Göttingen-based group *180°* to investigate forms of value-critical political (or, since it rejects the foundation of politics that is the value form, anti-political) praxis. He insists that struggles such as those of "the Zapatistas, the autonomous currents of the Piqueteros, and other grass-roots movements" must not be romanticized or idealized, but identifies them as sites where we might find "approaches and moments which point to the perspective of a liberation from the totality of commodity society" (221). This tentative discussion of praxis is perhaps a point at which value-critique could constructively be brought into contact with Marxist currents outside the German-speaking world. Value-critique has up until now neither engaged particularly thoroughly nor been received by elements of the contemporary ultra-Left that insist both on the importance of struggle and on the abolition rather than the affirmation of the proletariat. This essay may provide the starting point for such confrontations.

In "Violence as the Order of Things," Ernst Lohoff takes up a series of fundamental questions about violence in the present moment. Given that, with the supposedly final and complete triumph of free-market capitalism and its associated secular-Enlightenment catechism of "Liberty, Fraternity, and Equality" over its erstwhile Cold War rival all the underlying sources of violent conflict and war ought to have been extirpated as well, how is one to explain the violence with which we are confronted almost daily? How can such epidemic violence be understood as anything other than a paradoxical aberration in the face of an otherwise irreversible march toward world peace? What can be the sources of the violence we see emerging today on all sides? Must it not be categorically different from the more familiar forms of violence that marked previous moments in history?

Counter to the dominant narrative that traces the gradual disappearance of violence in tandem with the subsumption of the state under market forces, Lohoff's essay illustrates the ways in which capitalism and the rise of Western liberalism are inextricably and indeed constitutively bound up with violence. This relation is, according to Lohoff, particularly marked in the post-1989 era in which we are supposedly witnessing a transition into a peaceful world of globalization but which is instead defined by growing forms of violence that are the result not of momentary aberrations but of the violent core of capitalist modernity, itself pushed to a moment of crisis. Lohoff's essay traces the history of this violent core that, he argues, lies at the very heart not only of capitalism but also of Enlightenment thought. Thus, any genuinely genealogical tracing of the forms of violence that define our present moment must begin from a clear understanding of the historical changes — in a word, the crisis — affecting that same commodity form.

Lohoff returns to the writings of Hobbes, Hegel, and Freud to show that the Western ideals of Liberty, Fraternity, and Equality are not pathways toward peace but instead directly linked to merely temporary suspensions of violence that mask the more fundamental relation: the violent core of the commodity subject and of commodity society. Such a change in perspective, Lohoff argues, allows us to highlight the ways in which war and violence have not been so much eradicated as instead sublimated, controlled, and instrumentalized, that is, brought under the rule of the modern state, the formal genesis of which parallels the rise of commodity society. This brings about the need to reconsider the work not only of Hobbes but also of Hegel. Indeed, from this perspective, according to Lohoff, Hegel emerges, surprisingly, as an apologist and propagandist for rising commodity society to the extent that his theoretical model of consciousness rests upon a logic of violence: the famous need to wager one's life that is central to Hegel's account of self-consciousness. Lohoff's essay concludes with a forceful critique of a contemporary capitalist and free-market ideology that does not, by means of its gradual dissolution of the state and thus of the state monopoly on violence, herald an age of peace, but instead brings once more to the forefront capitalism's paradoxical but no less essential defining social relation, "asocial sociality." Only this time Enlightenment's gradual ideological sublimation of the commodity form's "violent core" from Hobbes, say, to Rosseau, Kant, and Hegel, from the *Leviathan*'s deterrent threat of a pre-atomic mutually assured destruction, to the more compassionate faith entrusted to the "volonté generale" (equipped with a guillotine) of the *Social Contract*, to Kant's purely rationalized "categorical imperative" (always back-stopped by the sovereign state of exception commanding obedience to enlightened despotism) begins to play out in reverse.

Like Lohoff, Kurz traces the linkage between the dark underbelly of Enlightenment thought and the rise of capitalism. In his essay "The Nightmare of Freedom," he turns more specifically toward the ways in which concepts such as freedom and equality have not only shaped liberalism (a well-known story) but also Marxism and anarchism, traditions in which these concepts and their attachment to the development of Enlightenment thought occupy a much more uncomfortable position, and indeed have often been explicitly disavowed. Kurz finds in Marx a persuasive account of how freedom and equality emerged not simply as lofty ideals, but rather under precise material conditions that assigned to these concepts a specific material and historical function. Indeed, as Kurz shows, the dominant form of equality (a far from homogenous concept) in modern Western thought is the equality of the market. The freedom to buy or sell on equal ground and by equal means becomes the dominant form of fulfilling and retroactively defining equality and equality's aims. Under capitalism, all customers are equally welcome, the marketplace is the realm of mutual respect, and the exchange of commodities is an interaction free from violence. Yet, Kurz argues, it is important in this context to return to Marx's forceful critique of this line of argumentation, which reminds us that the market sphere constitutes only one small facet of modern social life, and that a more profound understanding of these relations begins with the insight that exchange and circulation are secondary to the more fundamental relations of capitalist production. And once we regard capitalist society from the perspective afforded by this more primary relation, the well-worn theory that, like "bourgeois democracy," principles such as equality, freedom, and non-violence must inevitably suffer betrayal at the hands of the capitalist social relations (that are nevertheless their historical conditions of possibility) is disclosed, more precisely, as itself a thoroughly bourgeois ideology. As Kurz illustrates, it is just this seemingly paradoxical opposition that is constitutive of capitalism: the unfreedom within capitalist production is systemically bound up with the narrative of freedom and equality that underlies the ideology of the market — a tension that, as Kurz argues, becomes even more acutely pronounced under neoliberalism.

What becomes visible here is neither simply an illustration of the limits of discussions that focus on trade and circulation (over and against production or the constitution and reproduction of capitalism's value form), nor an analysis that foregrounds the violent dialectic of freedom and unfreedom that lies at the heart of capitalism. Instead, the account of the paradoxical ways in which Enlightenment ideals are integrated into the logic of capital demonstrates that freedom as it is understood even by discourses that understand themselves as emancipatory is nothing more than a necessary element of capitalism's valorization machine. Specifically, this means that we should regard the sphere of circulation and the market not only as a "hypocritical sphere of freedom and equality" (which it of course is), but more importantly as "a naked function of the end-in-itself of capitalist valorization" (288). In this sphere, where abstract value "realizes" itself as money, the freedom that constitutes the logic of free trade is indispensable. Utopias based on a liberated exchange relation, like the LETS (Local Exchange Trading Systems) championed by Kojin Karatani, realize the logic of capital rather than oppose it.

In "Curtains for Universalism," Karl-Heinz Lewed brings a startling perspective to the characterization of political Islam. The initial and obvious object of critique, the "clash of civilizations" hypothesis, is hardly taken seriously by anyone on the Left, but Lewed begins with it in order to lay bare the deeper dimensions of his analysis. So, for example, Lewed reminds us that, far from representing the resurgence of an archaic form, Islamic fundamentalism takes shape at the local level as precisely the brutal repression of archaisms, here in the form of longstanding local Islamic traditions that must be suppressed in the name of a standardized system of law and jurisprudence. Furthermore, Lewed not only debunks the widespread (and often murderously aggressive) belief that "Islamism" is the atavistic expression of a hostile and "foreign" culture or civilization. On the contrary, Lewed argues that Islamism is in fact nothing other than a form of appearance of our own "civilization," rendered superficially "exotic" by ideologies of culturalism. That is, more accurately put, Islamism is disclosed as simply one possible variation on a form of civilization required by the saturation of social relations by the market, that is, by the value relation. To be specific, this saturation necessitates a dialectic of universal and particular such that the generalized pursuit of particular interests cannot dispense with a universal framework to preserve the appearance of a universal redress of interests. But this system of social mediation is itself administered by individuals with particular interests. Such a dialectic proves to be irresolvable in the long run but not uncontainable: the ideological force that keeps the whole dialectic in check is the promise of national progress. The classical anticolonial movements develop on this basis: the colonial sovereign power operates in its own interest rather than that of the colonized territory, which is to say that the local economy, although universal in form is dominated by the particular interest of a foreign power. The strategies of recuperative modernization (*nachholdende Modernisierung*) pursued by the newly independent postcolonial states, once they fail to deliver on the promise of national progress, are assailed on precisely the same basis: governing elites, charged with guaranteeing universal progress, proceed instead to channel the wealth of the new nation back into the service of their own particular needs.

Islamism represents a "solution" to this ideological dilemma, a solution which, since it patently has neither grounds from which to think through, nor any interest in thinking through, the problem of a neo-colonial formation in relation to a critique of the value form, can propose no way out of it, presenting instead a hypertrophied, transcendentally guaranteed version of political universalism. In a reading of a key text by Osama bin Laden, Lewed shows that it is shot through with the rhetoric and logic of Enlightenment politics. Universality, since it can no longer be guaranteed by the sovereign, can only be guaranteed transcendentally, through a religiously-inflected universal law. With this we return, ironically, to Kant, who perceived that the guarantee of universality could only be transcendentally postulated and not empirically established through contract: "The metaphysics of the divine law of the Islamists should, therefore, be seen within the horizon of modern bourgeois relations, as formulated by Kant in *The Metaphysics of Morals*" (318-9). It should be emphasized, then, that the political crisis represented by Islamism is the form of appearance of a much more general phenomenon. In understanding Islamism as a cultural matter rather than as the local expression of bourgeois politics as such, the "Enlightened perspective of today... hides the problem of its own foundations" (319).

In Kurz's examination of the ongoing global economic crisis, assembled from interviews conducted for the Internet magazine *Telepolis* and the Portuguese internet organ *Shift*, published by Zion Edições, he not only engages in detail with the economic crisis itself but takes this examination as an opportunity to illustrate the general stakes of a critique of the value form at this moment in history. The result is a programmatic and methodological essay that at every moment parallels the illumination of the object of inquiry with an analysis of the theoretical model with which the operation is carried out. The current global economic crisis constitutes for Kurz the moment at which a range of fundamental contradictions that underlie the valorization of value under finance capital come to a head. Far from being an isolated incident, the current crisis should be more accurately understood as the consequence of the gradual, disproportionate growth of the cost of the necessary mobilization of real capital (material capital) in relation to labor power as a by-product of the increasing integration of science as a productive force with capitalist production in the aftermath of the third industrial revolution, the restructuring of production in the wake of the development of microelectronics. Financing this structure required the massive mobilization of anticipated future profit in the form of credit, whose direct consequence was a series of financial bubbles that, once burst, triggered the recent crisis. Yet, Kurz argues, the problem is to be located at a more fundamental level than that imagined by those who merely point toward the seeming irrationality of finance bubbles, since such bubbles are not aberrations confined to the discrete sphere of finance but rather constitute a symptom of the underlying global economic system that developed into a "deficit economy" (332). The growing gap between the future profit necessary to justify present credits and the profit actually generated ultimately led to a situation in which the "valorization of capital was virtualized in the form of fictional capital that could no longer be matched by the actual substance of value" (335). Even the neoliberal revolution could only strategically defer but not resolve the fundamental contradictions of a deficit economy. Examining the problem from this perspective also illustrates the contradictions underlying current attempts to address the crisis in the form of state-sponsored bailout and stimulus programs that merely displace the problem from one sphere of credit to another while also actively counteracting the logic of the stimulus interventions by the simultaneous implementation of austerity measures. In fact, Kurz predicts, the irrationality of the contradictory state-sponsored measures underlying all current attempts to resolve the crisis — the simultaneity of stimulus and saving programs — does little to change the more fundamental contradictions (the global economy and its logic of value and credit will remain confined to the circulation of deficits), and will likely lead to a further amplification of contradictions that will result in a second wave of the global economic crisis.

Solutions to the current problem, therefore, do no lie in illusory attempts at recreating "good" (most frequently state-controlled) forms of capitalism — as proposed, for example, by calls for a return to Keynesianism. Instead it is necessary to forward a radical critique of the value and commodity forms themselves that is not limited by the desire to leave intact the fundamental principles of capitalism, a limitation that will reduce all attempts at resolving the crisis to mere crisis management and will result in a further intensification of contradictions. Such a critique must centrally include the transition from workers'-movement Marxism to what Kurz calls, in reference to Lukács's early work, "categorical critique" — a critique that does not seek social emancipation based upon the persistent ontologization of the concept of labor but instead seeks to address capitalism's "basic forms" (349). Indeed, categorical critique and the corresponding new global social movements for which Kurz calls (calls which are accompanied by a radically revised concept of revolution) aim at the contestation of what he calls, using the concept and term first introduced by Alfred Sohn-Rethel, the dominant "social synthesis":

the negative totality of the specific form of socialization determining the present historical moment, which can only be surpassed by means of a total social revolution that begins in theory as in practice with a categorical critique of the internal barriers of contemporary capitalism, namely the reliance upon abstract labor, its form of the valorization of value, and its corresponding gender relations.

We turn finally to Kurz's essay "The Ontological Break" in which he explores what is widely understood to be one of the defining problems of theoretical thought and political discussion today. The debate over globalization appears to have reached a moment of exhaustion — why? The reasons for this exhaustion are not linked to what some may understand as the end of globalization. On the contrary, Kurz suggests, the social process underlying globalization is still in its incipient stage. Rather, it is critique that has run out of steam. The dominant approach to globalization is to examine it against the backdrop of national economies. Yet, Kurz suggests, even as critique points toward the end of national economies and the nation state, the reaction to such proclamations is regressively contradictory: the end of the nation state appears merely to reaffirm the commitment to the nation state, to previous modes of economic and social regulation, and to modes of analysis that remain rooted in the logic of nation states and politics. This problem emerges, Kurz suggests, because within such a hermetically sealed form of thought there exist "no immanent alternatives to these concepts because, just like concepts such as labor, money, and market, they represent the petrified determinations of modern capitalist ontology" (357-8). The main task of critique today, therefore, is to explode the entire epistemological construct by radically historicizing its underpinnings — that is, to return the focus of critique to the precise historical fields within which our concepts of sociality emerge and within which they acquire meaning, force, and necessary historical limits. The endpoint we have reached, therefore, is that of a form of thought, of a range of linked historical concepts. Whenever such a moment of exhaustion is reached, it also carries with it a distinct crisis of theory and critique, for the replacement of the fundamental categories of thought or their revision appears unimaginable, and the endpoint appears untranscendable. Yet, Kurz shows, such a moment of exhaustion must be rigorously historicized with the aim to reveal it not as an endpoint proper, but rather as the endpoint merely of a historically specific form of thought. In order for us to develop forceful accounts and critiques of globalization, Kurz therefore argues, we must bring about nothing less than a profound and complete ontological (and consequently epistemological) break — a break, that is, with those forms of thought that, once dominant, have now run out of steam.

Such a break might begin with Kurz's suggestion that the perceived crisis of critique we are experiencing contains a misrecognition: "contemporary analysis asserts more than it knows. With its insight into the loss of the regulatory capacity of the nation state and of politics, it involuntarily comes up against the limits of modern ontology itself" (359). Yet the aim radically to re-evaluate the very categories within which critique has played itself out, categories that emerged under historically determinate conditions between the sixteenth and the eighteenth century, is blocked by what Kurz calls an "ideological apparatus, which is as constitutive of modernity as the categorical totality of its social reproduction" (360). This ideological apparatus is, Kurz's essay shows, nothing other than Enlightenment thought itself. Additionally, he argues, it is important to foreground the fact that modernity was determined by large-scale conflicts between liberalism, Marxism, and conservatism, conflicts that "always addressed specific social, political, juridical, or ideological matters." Yet these conflicts "never addressed the categorical forms and ontological modes of sociality," the precise terrain on which the categorical break that can reinvigorate contemporary critique must take place (365). Kurz's essay outlines the forms such a break and its subsequent modes of critique may take, modes of critique that are aimed at nothing less than the constitution of a new society of critique, a "common [...] planetary society" (372).

It is the possibility of such a common planetary society — of life free from mediation through the categories of value and labor — toward which the critique of value is oriented. We present these thirteen texts not merely because we are of the opinion that value-critical voices and arguments — along other recent and contemporary work from the *neue Marx-Lektüre* not represented in this volume — can make a significant theoretical contribution to the interpretation and analysis of the ongoing crisis. For the critique of value has profound consequences for both theory and practice, and urgently raises the question of the form(s) that an emancipatory response to the crisis might take. As the renewal of the remorseless critique of everything that exists — the remorseless critique of the mediation of everything that exists through the categories of labor and value — the critique of value both demands and makes possible the instantiation of a means of struggle, of action, of practice that not only goes beyond the constraints of the capital-labor relation, but also aims at the emancipation from value of all aspects of life.

Work on the publication of this book has from the outset confirmed and re-confirmed the impossibility of such a project without the support of an informal collectivity that has, over the years ultimately needed to reach this goal, grown both outwards and inwards, and that has sometimes seemed to shrink and weaken only to prove itself to be just as firmly in place. Offers of help in all aspects of the work have frequently appeared before those of us who had necessarily to stay with the preparation of the book without let-up were even quite aware that we needed it. To the translation work undertaken by the co-editors themselves, many, many others contributed, including especially: Jon Dettman, Ariane Fischer, Elmar Flatschart, Joe Keady, Matt McLellan, Sina Rahmani, Emilio Sauri, Imre Szeman, Geoffrey Wildanger, and Robert Zwarg. Our gratitude to the authors of the texts themselves could hardly be overstated, but for their ex cathedra help we are especially indebted to Elmar Flatschart, Anselm Jappe, Wolfgang Kukulies, Karl-Heinz Lewed, Moni Schmid and Roswitha Scholz, and above all to Claus Peter Ortlieb of *Exit!* and Norbert Trenkle of *Krisis* with whom we have been in regular communication throughout this long editorial process, and without whose co-operation — not to mention that of the many other German and Austrian friends and comrades who answered more and less trivial questions on our behalf at their request — this project would scarcely have been possible. And finally we wish to express special thanks for the many kinds and many hours of dedicated assistance provided to us by Joe Atkins, Aaron Benanav, Brett Benjamin, Mark Bennett, Jasper Bernes, David Brazil (together with the California, East Bay chapter of the Public School), Nora Brown, Pat Cabell, Maria Elisa Cevasco, Joshua Clover (together with the many students and other readers of *Capital* and crisis theories — including early draft translations of this volume — who sepnt many rewarding hours together in multiple indepedent group study formations under the auspices of the Program in Critical Theory at the University of California, Davis), Kfir Cohen, Sean Delaney, Tanzeen Dohan, Eef, Anna Björk Einarsdottir, Maya González, Christian Höner, Laura Hudson, Fred Jameson, Tim Kreiner, Felix Kurz, Alexander Locascio, Duy Lap Nguyen, Erin Paszko, Jen Phillis, Michel Prigent, Ricardo Pagliuso Regattieri, Pedro Rocha de Oliveira, Gwen Sims, Magnús Snaebjörnsson, Chris Wright, and Michelle Yates. Unnamed here, for the simple fact that they are so many, are the 'enemies of utopia for the sake of its realization' — those students, colleagues, activists, and hard-thinking individuals and groups of all kinds who helped with or simply took an interest in this project out of a common desire to understand the crisis-driven, moribund, and lethal capitalism of our present day — to understand it precisely so as to hasten its destruction.

This project could not have been completed without support from the Alexander von Humboldt-Stiftung; the LAS Award for Faculty Research at the University of Illinois at Chicago; the Killam Research Fund at the University of Alberta; St. Francis Xavier University and the University Council for Research at St. Francis Xavier University; the Arts and Humanities Research Council; the Deutscher Akademischer Austauschdienst; the President and Fellows of Queens' College, Cambridge; the Peter Szondi-Institut at the Freie Universität Berlin;

the School of English, Communication, and Philosophy, Cardiff University.

For all our gratitude to the great many who have helped us, responsibility for all errors remains of course with the translators and editors. And we are confident that despite our best efforts there will still be a great many errors to be found. Anyone who has paid critical attention to translations of theoretical work will be aware that they are all in some way flawed — and yet the vast majority are nonetheless good enough. However, the possibilities enabled by online publication will allow us to correct with relative ease many of the errors that we find and that are drawn to our attention. We invite readers to participate in a process of open peer review, and to send notice of any errors and inconsistencies of translation, or other errors or inaccuracies, to corrections@mcmprime.com before June 30, 2014; the gamma or definitive edition will be published in summer 2014.

- *The Editors*

Notes

1. We use "Wertkritik," "value-critique" (and variations, e.g., "critique of value," "value critical," and so on) to refer specifically to the theories represented in the output of the journals *Exit!*, *Krisis*, and *Streifzüge*. (Since its founding in 2004, *Exit!* has tended, following the work of Roswitha Scholz, to refer exclusively to *Wertabspaltungskritik*, or the "critique of value-dissociation" — a term that effectively labels the same systematic theoretical and critical standpoint, although *Exit!* would argue that their theoretical understanding of it differs from that of the post-2004 *Krisis*.) This is to an extent a label of convenience that goes back to before 2004, up until which time most of the figures associated with *Wertkritik* in Germany were to a greater or lesser extent affiliated with and in many cases involved in the production of the "first" *Krisis*, of which, between 1986 and the end of 2003, twenty-seven issues had been published, the first seven under the title of *Marxistische Kritik*. The publication of *Krisis* 28 in 2004 marked the beginning of a resolution, however unsatisfactory, to a conflict-ridden and at times highly polemical public split in the pre-2004 *Krisis* that saw two of its central figures, Robert Kurz and Roswitha Scholz, along with others including Hanns von Bosse, Petra Haarmann, Brigitte Hausinger and Claus Peter Ortlieb, found the journal *Exit!* as an alternative project, which began publication later in that same year.

    We are of course aware that this term, as well as references in English to "value-critique" or "critique of the value form," can and often are taken to refer much more broadly to works of Marxian critical theory and of advanced Marx scholarship written mainly in German and as well as in some fewer cases to works and authors writing in English, French, Portuguese and a scattering of other languages. Principal among these works are those of Hans-Georg Backhaus, Helmut Reichelt, and some others who, influenced by such seminal works as Roman Rosdolsky's landmark study, *The Making of Marx's* Capital (first published in English in 1977), began the task of a serious re-examination of Marx's theory of value (and his critique of value) in *Capital* and the until then little-known or -studied *Grundrisse*. This early work, acknowledged as a crucial source for, if also subject to critique by, the self-designating representatives of what we here designate as value-critique or *Wertkritik*, can also be traced through to the work on Marxian theory and critique of the value form associated with the *neue Marx-Lektüre* or "new reading of Marx." The latter began to emerge in the 1960s (drawing inspiration from Evgeny Pashukanis and Isaak Rubin, as well as from the German-language critical Marxist traditions) and is now probably most prominently represented by the important Marx scholarship as well as critical and polemical writings of Michael Heinrich. As can be seen from several of the texts in this collection, an intense polemic has sprung up between leading theorists associated with both current value-critical journals *Krisis* and *Exit!* and Heinrich himself, who has also become probably the most prominent of contemporary Germanophone critics of crisis theory à la *Wertkritik*. Our decision to employ the term *"Wertkritik"* in this more restricted sense is not to deny that their are interconnections between *Wertkritik* more narrowly defined and the *neue Marx-Lektüre*, but rather to recognize that within this context there exist a range of tendencies, of which *Wertkritik*, the subject of this volume, is one.

2.   Kurz distinguishes between the exoteric and the esoteric Marx. The former develops from the perspective of modernization, and is the Marx that has been dominant in the political reception of his work, most particularly by Lenin and his followers, and by social democracy, and remains dominant in what value critics tend to refer to as labor-movement or workers-movement Marxism. The esoteric Marx, which involves the development of a categorical critique of capitalism, a critique that is never brought to completion within Marx's work, remains much less accessible. For Kurz this esoteric Marx has been written out of history by Marxism's elevation of the exoteric Marx to a dogma.

3.   It is interesting to note the willingness of theory-influenced scholars in the humanities to see the force of the critique of the logic of the ("positivist") social sciences, but only very rarely to acknowledge the force of its continuation and development in Marx's critique of political economy, and the implications of this continuation for practice in the

humanities. In this of course the reduction of the first generation of the Frankfurt School's radical and potentially world-changing critique to a cultural or merely academic project mirrors long after the event the neglect of the force of Marx's critique of political economy, which was transformed into a left-wing political economy that survives today, and not only in the representatives of the transfigured image of actually-existing socialism.

4. This "thematic" sequence runs as follows: I. "value – crisis," comprising the first three selections; II. "value – gender," comprising the following two; III. "crisis and the heteronomy of politics," comprising selections six, seven, and eight; IV. "value and the critique of enlightenment," made up of nine, ten, and eleven; and V. "capitalism (and theory) at their historical limit-points," referring to the final two works, twelve and thirteen.

5. This volume, perhaps the first project since 2004 to have involved the mutually sanctioned publication of works by writers on both sides of the split, is not the place to rehearse the details of a conflict that mixed (and often conflated) political and personal disagreements. Many of the relevant documents are publicly available, and it is a story that is ultimately much less interesting than the necessarily only partial account of the theoretical resources offered by the critique of value that is told by the translations collected in this volume. Since 2004 *Exit!* — http://www.exit-online.org/ — has published eleven issues, most recently in July 2013. *Krisis* 33, the journal's last paper issue, was published in 2010; the journal recently switched to an online-only format whereby theoretical articles of often substantial length are published on the organization's website — http://www.krisis.org/ — as *Beiträge* or contributions (in line with the journal's subtitle of "Contributions to the Critique of Commodity Society") alongside more journalistic and blog-style pieces. Both organizations also organize a weekend-long public seminar involving presentations by regular contributors and occasionally invited guests, and lengthy discussion. *Streifzüge* — http://www.streifzuege.org/ — has been published in Vienna since 1997. Regular contributors to *Exit!* include Robert Kurz (until his death in 2012, although there remains a flow of posthumously published material), Roswitha Scholz, Claus-

Peter Ortlieb, Udo Winkel and, more recently, Elmar Flatschart, while frequent contributors to and editors of *Krisis* include Norbert Trenkle, Ernst Lohoff, Karl-Heinz Lewed, Peter Samol, Stefan Meretz and Julian Bierwirth. Figures associated with *Streifzüge* include Franz Schandl and Petra Ziegler.

6.   Robert Kurz, *Schwarzbuch Kapitalismus: ein Abgesang auf die Marktwirtschaft*, was first published in 1999 (Frankfurt a.M.: Eichborn) and after several re-editions an expanded, second edition was released in 2009. A PDF of a reset version of the 2002 impression is downloadable from the *Exit!* website at http://www.exit-online.org/pdf/schwarzbuch. pdf. Work is ongoing on an English translation. During his life Kurz wrote more than a dozen monographs, a writing career that began with the publication of *Der Kollaps der Modernisierung: Vom Zusammenbruch des Kasernensozialismus zur Krise der Weltökonomie* [*The Collapse of Modernization: From the Collapse of Barracks Socialism to the Crisis of the World Economy*] (Frankfurt am Main: Eichborn, 1991).

7.   Roswitha Scholz's *Das Geschlecht des Kapitalismus: Feministische Theorie und die postmoderne Metamorphose des Patriarchats* [*The Gender of Capitalism: Feminist Theory and the Postmodern Metamorphosis of Patriarchy*] (Bad Honnef: Horlemann, 2000) represents a decisive turn of the critique of value toward its implications for our understanding of the relationship between gender relations and capitalism. Scholz further develops this inquiry in "Patriarchy and Commodity Society: Gender without the Body" (123-42 in this volume). Perhaps the most significant (and certainly the most timely) collaboration between Ernst Lohoff and Norbert Trenkle is their 2012 analysis of the ongoing crisis, *Die Große Entwertung: Warum Spekulation und Staatsverschuldung nicht die Ursache der Krise sind* [*The Great Devaluation: Why Speculation and Public Borrowing are not the Causes of the Crisis*] (Münster: Unrast, 2012). See also Josh Robinson's review "Riches Beyond Value," Mediations 27.1-2 (Winter 2014) 365-68.

8.   Among them, of course, Moishe Postone ranks as the most outstanding. The fact that Postone's great work, *Time, Labor, and Social Domination*, continues, despite important critiques undertaken of the latter by both Kurz in *Exit!* and, more recently, by Lohoff in *Krisis*, to be perhaps the one

monograph-length work most carefully studied and scrupulously cited by *Wertkritik* — after Marx's *Capital* — deserves more careful assessment than has been possible in this brief introduction. Postone's work itself, although increasingly known among Anglophone readers, continues to circulate far more widely in German translation and in Germany itself than in English.

9.   Both Helmut Reichelt and Hans-Georg Backhaus studied under Adorno in Frankfurt. The appendix to the latter's account of the dialectic of the value form consists of extracts from a transcript of Adorno's seminar of summer 1962 on Marx and the fundamental concepts of sociological theory (*Dialektik der Wertform: Untersuchung zur Marxschen Ökonomiekritik* [Freiburg: Ça ira, 1997] 501–13). A translation of this transcript by Verena Erlenbusch and Chris O'Kane is forthcoming in *Historical Materialism*.

10.   See, however, internet-published translations that include a series of shorter items by Kurz that have appeared on libcom.org (at http://libcom.org/tags/robert-kurz) and a range of translations at http://principiadialectica.co.uk. It is worth noting that the former are mostly translated into English from Spanish translations (possibly themselves translated from the Portuguese) while many but by no means all of the latter come via the French of Wolfgang Kukulies and Anselm Jappe. A particularly significant contributor to this culture of freely available and widely read translations is Alexander Locascio, who has translated and published on his blog a wide range of texts from the *neue Marx-Lektüre, Wertkritk,* and from the German speaking critical Marxist left and ultra-Left more widely. His translation of Michael Heinrich's *Kritik der politischen Ökonomie: Eine Einführung* (Stuttgart, Schmetterling: 2004) was published as *An Introduction to the Three Volumes of Karl Marx's* Capital (New York: Monthly Review, 2012).

11.   For a sense of Roberto Schwarz's investment in *Wertkritik*, see "An Audacious Book," *Mediations* 27.1-2 (Winter 2014) 357-61. Schwarz has always been centrally interested in the question of combined and uneven development, which is to say in the way capitalism as a total process is experienced and indeed functions differently in diverse local contexts. See Robert Kurz, *O Colapso da Modernização: da derrocada do socialismo de*

caserna à crise da economia mundial, translated by Karen Elsabe Barbosa (Rio de Janeiro: Paz e Terra, 1991).

12. http://obeco.planetaclix.pt

13. Kurz's concept of recuperative nationalism finds its most extensive exposition in *Schwarzbuch Kapitalismus*, 206–17, in which he analyses the appeals made to German nationalism by Johann Gottlieb Fichte, Johann Gottfried Herder, and above all Friedrich List, and the persistence of these appeals both under actually existing socialism and in twentieth-century development economics. In this volume the concept is rethought and deployed in essays including Lohoff, "Violence as the Order of Things"; Lewed, "Curtains for Universalism"; and Kurz, "On the Current Global Economic Crisis" and "The Ontological Break."

14. Moishe Postone, "Anti-Semitism and National Socialism: Notes on the German Reaction to 'Holocaust,'" *New German Critique* 19 (Winter 1980) 97–115. A translation of this essay by Renate Schumacher had previously appeared in the Frankfurt am Main student journal *Diskus* 3-4 (1979) 425–37.

15. See *Die Große Entwertung*, and Trenkle's 2008 response to the earliest unfolding of this crisis in "Tremors on the Global Market," translated by Josh Robinson, online at http://www.krisis.org/2009/tremors-on-the-global-market.

16. "I mean, Karl Marx had it right, at some point capitalism can destroy itself because you cannot keep on shifting income from labor to capital without not having excess capacity and a lack of aggregate demand, and that's what's happening. We thought that markets work, they're not working, and what's individually rational: every firm wants to survive and thrive and thus slashing labor costs even more — my labor costs are somebody else's labor income and consumption. That's why it's a self-destructive process. [...] I think that there is a risk that this is the second leg of what happened in the Great Depression. We had a severe economic and financial crisis and then we kicked the can down the road with too much private debt, households, banks, governments, and you cannot resolve this problem with liquidity. At some point when there's too much debt either you grow yourself out of it, but there is not going to

be enough economic growth, it's anemic, either you save yourself out of it, but if everybody spends less and saves more in the private and public sector you have the Keynesian paradox of thrift: everybody saves more, there is less demand, you go back to recession and that ratio becomes higher. Or you can inflate yourself out of the debt problem, but that has a lot of collateral damage. So if you cannot grow yourself or save yourself or inflate yourself out of an excessive debt problem, you need debt restructure and debt reduction for households, for governments, for financial institutions, for highly leveraged institutions, and we're not doing it. We're creating zombie households, zombie banks, and zombie governments and you could have a depression." Nouriel Roubini, interview with Simon Constable, *WSJ Live*, online at http://live.wsj.com/video/nouriel-roubini-karl-marx-was-right/68EE8F89-EC24-42F8-9B9D-47B510E473B0.html. Meanwhile Catherine Rampell, writing in March 2009, charts the rise of the phrase "Great Recession," dating the rapid expansion in its use to December 2008. At the same time, she also observes how "[e]very recession of the last several decades has, at some point or another, received this special designation." "'Great Recession': A Brief Etymology" *NYT Economix* blog, March 3, 2013, online at http://economix.blogs.nytimes.com/2009/03/11/great-recession-a-brief-etymology/.

17. Readers can find full publication information immediately following the introduction.

18. Robert Kurz and Ernst Lohoff, "Der Klassenkampf-Fetisch" www.krisis.org (31 December 1989).

19. For more on Schandl's term, see 208-9n4.

Original Publication Information

Norbert Trenkle, "Was is der Wert? Was soll die Krise?" given June 1998 at University of Vienna, published www.krisis.org (27 December 1998).

Robert Kurz, "Die Krise des Tauschwerts," *Marxistische Kritik* 1 (1986) 7-48.

Claus Peter Ortlieb, "Ein Widerspruch von Stoff und Form" www.exit-online.org (12 September 2008).

Roswitha Scholz, "Das warenproduzierende Patriarchat," in *Spielregeln der Gewalt. Kulturwissenschaftliche Beiträge zur Friedens- und Geschlechterforschung*, edited by Utta Isop, Viktorija Ratkovic, Werner Wintersteiner (Bielefeld: transcript Verlag, 2009) 151-71.

Norbert Trenkle, "Aufstieg und Fall des Arbeitsmanns," www.krisis.org (23 October 2008).

Ernst Lohoff, "'Out of Area — Out of Control,'" *Streifzüge* 31 and 32 (2004).

Robert Kurz, "Weltmacht und Weltgeld," www.exit-online.org (22 January 2008).

Ernst Lohoff, "Gewaltordnung und Vernichtungslogik," Krisis 27 (2003).

Robert Kurz, "Der Alptraum der Freiheit," www.exit-online.org (19 January 2005).

Karl Heinz Lewed, "Finale des Universalismus," Krisis 32 (2008).

Robert Kurz, "Schleifung der Überkapazitäten," www.heise.de (17 and 18 July 2010).

Robert Kurz, "Der ontologische Bruch," www.exit-online.org (9 February 2005).

Value and Crisis: Basic Questions

Norbert Trenkle (1998)

The ground that I want to cover today is expansive. It stretches from the most fundamental level of the theory of value (or more precisely, from the critique of value) — that is to say, from the level of the fundamental categories of commodity-producing society: labor, value, commodity, money — to the level where these fundamental categories appear reified and fetishized, as seemingly "natural" facts of life and as "objective necessities." At this level — that of price, profit, wage, circulation, and so on — the internal contradictions of modern commodity society emerge: here such a society's ultimate historical untenability makes itself evident — in the form of the crisis. It is clear that in the limited time available today I can only sketch things out, but I hope that I can succeed in providing a clear view of the essential framework.

As a point of departure, I would like to begin with a category commonly viewed as a fully self-evident condition of human existence: "labor." Even in Marx's *Capital*, this remains largely unproblematized, and is taken to be a universally valid anthropological trait that can be found in every society in the world: "Labor, then, as the creator of use-values, as useful labor, is a condition of human existence which is independent of all forms of society; it is an eternal natural necessity which mediates the metabolism between man and nature, and therefore human life itself."[1]

It is true that for Marx, the category of "labor" is not as completely unproblematic as this quote seems to suggest. At other points, especially in the so-called early writings, he adopts far more critical tones. In a critique of German economist Friedrich List first published in the 1970s, he even goes so far as to speak of the abolition of labor as a precondition of emancipation. "'Labor' is in its very being an oppressive, inhumane, and antisocial activity that both is determined by and produces private property. The abolition of private property thus only becomes reality when it is understood as an abolition of 'labor.'"[2] Even in *Capital,* we find passages which recall this early approach. But my task here is not to trace the ambivalences around the concept of "labor" (for more on this, see Kurz); rather I would like to proceed directly to the question of the meaning of this category.[3] Is "labor" an anthropological constant? Can we use it as such to make it unproblematically into a point of departure for an analysis of commodity society? My answer is an unambiguous "no."

Marx distinguishes between abstract and concrete labor, and calls this the dual character of labor particular to commodity-producing society. He thus suggests — and also states explicitly — that it is not until the level of this doubling, or splitting, that a process of abstraction takes place. Abstract labor is abstract insofar as it moves away from the concrete material properties and particularities of the respective specific activities — for example, the work of a tailor, a carpenter, or a butcher — and is reduced to a common equivalent. But Marx overlooks here (and in any case, Marxism has yet to develop an awareness of the problem at this level) that labor as such is already such an abstraction. And not simply an abstraction in thought like a tree, animal, or plant; rather, it is a historically established, socially powerful, actually existing abstraction that violently brings people under its thumb.

Abstracting means withdrawing or withdrawing from something. In what way, then, is labor a withdrawal — that is, a withdrawal from something else? What is socially and historically specific about labor is not, of course, the fact that things are created in the first place and that social tasks are carried out. In fact, this must occur in all societies. What is specific is the form in which this takes place in capitalist society. What is essential to this form is in the first instance the fact that work is a separate sphere, cut off from the rest of its social setting. Whoever works is working and doing nothing else. Relaxing, amusing oneself, pursuing personal interests, loving, and so on — these things must take place outside labor or at least must not interfere with its thoroughly rationalized functional routines. Of course, this never fully succeeds, because despite centuries of training, it has not been possible to turn people completely into machines. But what I am talking about here is a structural principle which empirically never emerges in perfect purity — even though, at least in Central Europe, the empirical process of labor certainly seems to correspond to a great extent to this terrible model. For this reason — that is, as a result of the exclusion of all the moments of non-labor from the sphere of labor — the historical establishment of labor is accompanied by the formation of further separate spheres of society, into which all those dissociated (*abgespaltenen*) moments are banished, spheres which themselves take on an exclusive character: leisure, privacy, culture, politics, religion, and so on.

The essential structural condition for this division of social life is the modern relationship between the sexes with its dichotomous and hierarchical allocation of masculinity and femininity. The sphere of labor falls unambiguously into the realm of the "masculine," which itself is already a demonstration of the subjective demands that this makes: abstract, instrumental rationality, objectivity, formal thinking, competitive orientation — requirements that women must of course also meet if they want to get anywhere in the world of work. However, this realm of the masculine is structurally able to exist only against the background of that which has been dissociated, a sphere which is then posited as inferior — a sphere in which, ideally, the working man can regenerate, because in the ideal case the dedicated housewife takes care of his physical and emotional well being. This structural relationship, which bourgeois society has idealized and romanticized from time immemorial in countless bombastic eulogies in praise of the loving and self-sacrificial wife and mother, has over the last thirty years been analyzed more than adequately in feminist scholarship. To this extent it is possible to advance without further comment the thesis that labor and the modern system of hierarchical gender relations are inseparably linked to one another. Both are fundamental structural principles of the bourgeois social order of the commodity form.

I am unable further to pursue this relationship here in its own right, as the topic of my lecture is in fact the specific mediations and the internal contradictions within the historically and structurally male spheres of labor, commodity, and value. I should thus like to return to this matter. I remarked earlier that labor, as a specific form of activity in commodity society, is per se already abstract because it constitutes a separated sphere, withdrawn from the rest of social life. And as such, it exists only where commodity production has already become the determining form of socialization — in capitalism, that is to say, where human activity in the form of labor serves no other purpose than the valorization of value.

Human beings do not enter into the sphere of labor willingly. They do it because they were separated from the most basic means of production and existence in a long and bloody historical process, and now can survive only by selling themselves temporarily — or, more precisely, by selling their vital energy, as labor power, for an external purpose, the content of which is irrelevant. For them, labor thus primarily means a fundamental extraction of vital energy, and in this respect is thus an extremely real, actually existing abstraction. Indeed, it is precisely for this reason that the identification of labor with suffering makes sense, as the original meaning of the word *laborare* suggests.

In the end, however, abstraction in the realm of labor also reigns in the form of a highly specific rule of time that is both abstract-linear and homogeneous. What counts is objectively measurable time — in other words, the time that has been separated from the subjective sensations, feelings, and experiences of working individuals. Capital has rented them for a precisely defined time-period, in which they have to produce a maximal output of commodities or services. Each minute that they do not expend for this purpose is, from the standpoint of the purchaser of the commodity labor power, a waste. Each and every minute is valuable, insofar as it, in the literal sense, presents potential value.

Historically, the establishment of the abstract-linear and homogeneous rule of time certainly represents one of the sharpest breaks with all precapitalist social orders. It is well known that several centuries of evident compulsion and open use of violence were required before the mass of humanity had internalized this form of relationship to time, and no longer thought anything of arriving at the factory or office door punctually at a given time, giving up their lives at the factory door, and subjecting themselves for a precisely measured length of time to the metronomic rhythm of the prescribed productive and functional procedures. This well-known fact alone shows how little the form of social activity known as "labor" can be taken for granted. If labor as such, then, is not an anthropological constant, but rather is itself already an abstraction (albeit one that exerts a huge social force), how does it relate to the dual character of the labor represented in the commodity that Marx analyzes and that forms the basis of his theory of value? It is well known that Marx established that commodity-producing labor has two sides, one concrete and the other abstract. As concrete labor it creates use values — in other words, particular useful things. As abstract labor, on the other hand, it is the expenditure of labor as such, regardless of any qualitative determination. As such, it creates the value presented in commodities. But what remains beyond any qualitative determination? It is perfectly clear that the only thing that all these different sorts of labor have in common, abstracted from their material-concrete elements, is that they are different types of expenditures of abstract labor time. Abstract labor is thus the reduction of all the different forms of commodity-producing labor to a common denominator. It makes them comparable and as a result capable of being exchanged for one another, by reducing them to the pure abstract, reified quantity of elapsed time. As such, it forms the substance of value.

Virtually all Marxist theorists have adopted this not-at-all self-explanatory or obvious conception as the basic definition of an anthropological fact and quasi-natural law, and regurgitated it as such without reflection. They have never understood why Marx went to such lengths when writing the first chapter of *Capital* (which, indeed, was rewritten numerous times) and why he supposedly unnecessarily obscured what is apparently such an obvious state of affairs with recourse to a Hegelian language. Just as labor was obvious to Marxism, so too did it seem obvious to Marxism that labor quite literally creates value, in the same way that the baker bakes bread, and that in value, past labor time is preserved as dead labor time. Even in Marx it never becomes clear that abstract labor itself, both logically and historically, presupposes labor as a specific form of social activity — that it is thus the abstraction of an abstraction — or put differently, that the reduction of an activity to homogeneous units of time presupposes the existence of an abstract measure of time, which as such dominates the sphere of labor. It would never have occurred to a medieval peasant, for example, to measure the time spent harvesting his fields in hours and minutes. This is not because he did not have a watch; rather, because this activity merged with his life, and its temporal abstraction would have made no sense.

But although Marx does not adequately clarify the relationship between labor as such and abstract labor, he nonetheless leaves no doubt as to the complete insanity of a society in which human activity (that is to say, a living process) coagulates into a reified form and as such establishes itself as the dominant social power. Marx ironically questions the common belief that this was a natural fact when he remarks in response to the positivist theory of value of classical political economy, "So far, no chemist has ever discovered exchange value either in a pearl or a diamond."[4] So when Marx shows that abstract labor constitutes the substance of value, and thus also determines the mass of value by means of the labor time expended on average, he is in no way lapsing into the physiological or naturalist views of classical economics, as Michael Heinrich claims in his book *The Science of Value*. Like the better share of bourgeois thinkers since the Enlightenment, classical economics grasps bourgeois social relations to a certain degree, but only in order to declare them unceremoniously a part of the natural order. Marx criticizes this ideologization of dominant social relations by deciphering them as the fetishistic reflex of a fetishized reality. He shows that value and abstract labor are not mere figments of the imagination that people need to jettison from their heads. Rather, under the conditions of a system of labor and modern commodity production that is always presupposed and that determines their thoughts and behavior, people actually encounter their products as expressions of reified, abstract labor time, as if these products were a force of nature. For the bourgeoisie, their own social relations have become "second nature," as Marx puts it pointedly. This constitutes the fetish-character of value, commodity, and labor.

Alfred Sohn-Rethel coined the term "actually existing abstraction" for this irrational form of abstraction. By this he means a process of abstraction that is not completed in human consciousness as an act of thought, but which, as the a priori structure of social synthesis, is the presupposition of and determines human thought and action. However, for Sohn-Rethel, this actually existing abstraction is identical with the act of exchange — it governs wherever commodities confront one another in the context of the market. Only here, according to his argument, are different things made the same, are qualitatively different things reduced to a common equivalent: value, or exchange value. But in what does this common equivalent consist? If value, or exchange value, is where the different commodities are reduced to a common denominator as expressions of abstract quantities of different magnitude, one must also be able to name both the content of this ominous value and the scale by which it is measured. The answer to this is not found in Sohn-Rethel, something which we can attribute in part to his limited, almost mechanical conception of the context of commodity society.

For shortly afterwards, the sphere of labor appears as a presocial space in which private producers create their products, still untouched in any way by any determinate social form. Only afterwards do they throw these products as commodities into the sphere of circulation, where, in the act of exchange, they are abstracted from their material particularities (and thus indirectly from the concrete labor expended in their production) and thus morph into bearers of value. This perception, however, which tears the sphere of production and the sphere of circulation apart from one another and places them in superficial opposition, completely misses the inner context of the modern commodity-producing system. Sohn-Rethel systematically confuses two levels of observation: first, the necessary temporal succession between the production and sale of a single commodity; and second, the logical and real social unity of the processes of valorization and exchange, a unity which these processes always presuppose.

I would now like to explore this point of view more extensively, because it is not something that can be attributed only to Sohn-Rethel, but rather is widespread and can be found in many variations. This includes Michael Heinrich's aforementioned book, for example, where it appears at every turn. Heinrich asserts (to select just one quote of many) that commodity bodies obtain "their objectivity of value only inside the process of exchange" and then continues as follows: "In isolation, considered for itself, the commodity-body is not a commodity but merely a product."[5] It is true that Heinrich does not draw from this and many other similar statements the same theoretical conclusions as Sohn-Rethel, but they certainly lie within the logic of his own argumentation. It is only with the help of a not-particularly-convincing set of theoretical aids (by tearing the value form and the substance of value apart from one another) that he can avoid them (see Heinrich and Backhaus's and Reichelt's critique).[6]

It goes without saying that in the capitalist mode of production, it is not the case that products are innocently created and only arrive on the market a posteriori; rather, every process of production is from the outset oriented toward the valorization of capital and organized accordingly. That is to say, production occurs already in the context of a fetishized form of value, and products must fulfill a single purpose: to represent in the form of value the amount of labor time necessary for their production. It is thus the case that the sphere of circulation, the market, does not serve the exchange of commodities; it is rather the place where the value represented in the products is realized — or at least, where it is supposed to be realized. For this to succeed at all (a necessary but not sufficient condition), commodities must, as is well known, also be useful things, albeit only for the potential buyer. The concrete, material aspect of the commodity, its use value, is not the aim and purpose of production but only a more or less inevitable side effect. From the perspective of valorization, this could certainly (and gladly) be dispensed with (and in a certain respect this does in fact take place in the mass production of completely useless things or those that fall apart after a very short time), but value cannot go without a material bearer. For no one buys dead labor time as such, but rather only when it is represented in an object to which the buyer attributes a usefulness of some kind.

The concrete aspect of labor thus remains in no way untouched by the presupposed form of socialization. If abstract labor is the abstraction of an abstraction, concrete labor only represents the paradox of the concrete aspect of an abstraction — namely of the form-abstraction "labor." It is only "concrete" in the very narrow and restricted sense that the different commodities require materially different production processes: a car is made differently from, say, an aspirin tablet or a pencil sharpener. But even the behavior of these processes of production is in no way indifferent, technically or organizationally, to the presupposed goal of valorization. I hardly need elaborate at great length on how the capitalist process of production is configured in this respect: it is organized solely according to the maxim of producing the greatest possible number of products in the shortest possible time. This is then called the economic efficiency of a business. The concrete, material side of labor is thus nothing other than the tangible form in which abstract labor's diktat of time confronts the workers and forces them under its rhythm.

To this extent it is also totally correct to assert that commodities produced in the system of abstract labor also already embody value, even if they have not entered into the sphere of circulation. That the realization of value can fail — commodities can be unsellable or can only be disposed of for well below their value — is in line with the logic of the matter, but pertains to a totally different level of the problem. For in order to gain entry into the sphere of circulation, a product must already be in the fetishized form of an object of value — and since this object is as such nothing other than the representation of past abstract labor (and this always also means the representation of past abstract labor time), it necessarily always already also possesses a certain magnitude of value. For as pure form without substance (that is, without abstract labor), value cannot exist without going into a state of crisis in which it will eventually crumble.

But, as is well known, the magnitude of a commodity's value is determined not by the labor time immediately expended in its production, but rather by the average socially necessary labor time. This average, in turn, is not a fixed magnitude, but changes in accordance with the current level of productivity (that is to say, there is a secular trend for necessary labor time per commodity, and thus the quantity of value that it represents, to fall). But as the measure of value, this average is always already presupposed by every individual process of production, and it assumes power in this process as a merciless sovereign. A product thus represents a particular quantity of abstract labor time only insofar as it can stand before the judgment of the social mass of productivity. If the labor of a business is unproductive, its products do not of course represent more value than those that were made under socially average conditions. The business must therefore improve its productivity in the long term or disappear from the market altogether.

In this context it is somewhat confusing that the objectivity and magnitude of value do not appear in the individual commodity but only in the exchange of commodities — that is to say, only when they step into direct relation with other products of abstract labor. The value of one commodity then becomes visible in the other commodity. Thus, for example, the value of a dozen eggs may be expressed in four pounds of flour. In developed commodity production (and this is what is always at stake in this discussion), the place of this other commodity is assumed by a general equivalent: money, in which the value of all commodities is expressed, and which functions as a social measure of value. To claim, then, that value, in the form of exchange value, only appears at the level of circulation, already presupposes the insight that it does not come into being in the way that Sohn-Rethel and other theorists of exchange (not to mention all those representatives of the subjective theory of value) claim — the insight, in other words, that there is a difference between the essence of value and its forms of appearance.

The subjective theory of value, which in its flat empiricism is taken in by the appearance of circulation, has always lampooned the labor theory of value as metaphysics — an accusation which is once again booming, this time in postmodernist garb. Unintentionally, though, it divulges something about the fetishistic nature of commodity-producing society. If reified social relations elevate themselves to blind power over human beings, what is this if not metaphysics incarnate? The point at which both the subjective theory of value and Marxist positivism stumble is that value can in no way be nailed down empirically. For it is neither possible to filter out the substance of labor from commodities, nor consistently to derive the values of commodities from the level of empirical appearance (that is, from the level of price). "So where is this ominous value?" ask our positivist friends, only to dismiss this entire line of questioning straight away. For what is not empirically tangible and measurable does not exist in their worldview.

But this critique applies only to a crude and itself positivist variant of the labor theory of value — which is, however, typical of the greater part of Marxism. For Marxism always related positively to the category of value in two senses. Firstly, as already mentioned, value was actually understood as natural or anthropological fact. It appeared, that is, as completely self-evident that past labor or labor time could literally be preserved in the products as an object. At the very least, however, it was necessary to provide a mathematical proof of how the price of a commodity results from its value, from which it deviates. And secondly, it was then only logical to attempt to steer social production with the help of this positively construed category. A key accusation leveled against capitalism was thus that in the market, the "real values" of products are veiled and thus do not come to fruition. In socialism, by contrast, so the argument goes in Engels's famous formulation, it is easy to calculate how many labor hours are "hiding" in a ton of wheat or iron.

This was the central program of the entire project — doomed to failure — of actually existing socialism, and in diluted form also of social democracy, a program which was planned and seen through more or less critically and constructively by legions of so-called political economists. Doomed to failure because value is a non-empirical category that by its nature cannot be nailed down, but rather gains acceptance among people as a fetishistic category behind their backs, and imposes its blind laws on them. But the desire consciously to steer an unconscious relation is a contradiction. The historical punishment for such an attempt was thus inevitable.

But if I have said that value is a non-empirical category, does that also mean that it has no relevance at all for actual economic development? Of course not. It means only that value cannot be nailed down as such and must go through different levels of mediation before it appears at the economic surface in a mutated form. Marx's contribution in *Capital* is to demonstrate the logical and structural interrelation of these levels of mediation. He shows how economic surface categories such as price, profit, wage, and interest can be derived from the category of value and its internal dynamics, hence allowing them to be analyzed as such. In no way was he taken in by the illusion that these mediations could in any way be empirically calculated individually, as both economic theory and disarmed, positivist Marxism demand (without, however, being able to solve this dilemma themselves). But this is not in any way a defect of the theory of value, but merely highlights the unconscious nature of these mediations. Marx, however, never attempted to propose a positive theory that could be in any way used as an instrument of economic policy. His concern, rather, was to demonstrate the irrationality, the inner contradictions, and hence the ultimate untenability of a society based on value. At its core, his theory of value is a critique of value — it is no accident then that his magnum opus is subtitled *Critique of Political Economy* — and, at the same time, essentially a theory of crisis.

The empirical foundation of the critique of value in general and the theory of crisis in particular cannot in any way, therefore, be carried out in a quasi-scientific, mathematized form. Wherever this methodological criterion is applied a priori — as in the well-known (or infamous) value-price transformation debate of academic Marxism — the concept of value and the entire framework constructed around it is already fundamentally flawed. While it is true that the critique of value and the theory of crisis can certainly be underpinned with empirical support, the method must only comprehend the internal mediations and contradictions. What this means in concrete terms, I can at this point only suggest. Let us take, for example, the basic finding of crisis theory that since the 1970s, as a result of the worldwide, absolute displacement of living labor power from the process of valorization, capital has reached the historical limits of its power to expand, and thus also of its capacity to exist. In other words, modern commodity production has entered a fundamental process of crisis, which can only result in its downfall.

This finding is of course not based on purely logical-conceptual derivation, but is rather a result of the theoretical and empirical comprehension of the structural breakdowns in the global commodity-producing system since the end of Fordism. These include, for example, as a basic fact, the melting away of the substance of labor (that is, the diminution of the expended abstract labor time at the peak of the predominant level of production) in the productive central sectors of production for the global market as well as the continued retreat of capital from huge regions of the world that are largely cut off from the flow of commodities and investment and left to fend for themselves. Ultimately, however, the violent inflation and unleashing of the system of credit and speculation also belong to this context. That fictitious capital is being amassed to a historically unprecedented extent on one hand explains why the onset of the crisis has up until now appeared relatively mild in core regions of the world market, but on the other hints at the intense violence of the imminent wave of devaluation.

Clearly, a theory of crisis founded on the critique of value can misdiagnose individual elements, and can also fail to anticipate every way in which the crisis unfolds, even though it proves itself entirely capable in the analysis of details. But it can provide theoretical and empirical proof that there will be no more new waves of secular accumulation, and capitalism has irrevocably entered a barbaric stage of decline and disintegration. This proof necessarily coincides with the unrelenting critique of labor, commodity, value, and money, and pursues no other goal than the abolition of these fetishistic actually existing abstractions; and thus, also, its own sphere of relevance having been abolished, of the self-abolition of the theory of value.

Notes

1. Karl Marx, *Capital: A Critique of Political Economy*, Volume I, trans. Ben
    Fowkes (New York: Penguin, 1973) 133, and Karl Marx, "Über Friedrich
    Lists Buch 'Das nationale System der politischen Ökonomie,'" *Beiträge
    zur Geschichte der Arbeiterbewegung* 3 (1972) 425-446.
2. Marx, "Über Friedrich Lists Buch" 436.
3. Robert Kurz, "Postmarxismus und Arbeitsfetisch," *Krisis* 15 (1995).
4. Marx, *Capital* I 177.
5. Michael Heinrich, *The Science of Value* (Hamburg: Westfälisches
    Dampfboot, 1991) 173.
6. Heinrich, *Science*, 187; Hans Georg Backhaus and Helmut Reichelt, "Wie
    ist der Wertbegriff in der Ökonomie zu konzipieren?" *Engels' Druckfassung
    versus Marx' Manuskript zum III. Buch des "Kapital" (Beiträge zur Marx-
    Engels-Forschung Neue Folge)* (Hamburg: Argument, 1995) 60-94.

The Crisis of Exchange Value: Science as Productive Force, Productive Labor, and Capitalist Reproduction

Robert Kurz (1986)

Preliminary Remark: The Left and the Law of Value

There is really no longer a shortage of publications with more or less left-wing or Marxist — or at least emancipatory — aspirations on the concept of crisis in itself, the crisis of labor, of Marxism, of the Left, new technologies, or post-Fordist or even postindustrial society. It would not be particularly helpful to add one more text to this flood without attempting to introduce a fundamentally new or different aspect. Since it proceeds on the basis of this presupposition, the article that follows is bound to appear to have an immodest, apodictic demeanor. It is for this reason that I wish to emphasize right from the start that my aim is in no way to allude suggestively to the sophistication of my own theoretical elaboration, but rather to the fact that the left-wing media are far removed from what would be even a tolerable level of theoretical assurance and reflection on their own elementary categories. The Left's helplessness when it comes to new phenomena, and also its own political impotence, appear if nothing else to be grounded in this lack of fundamentally theoretical desire.

This thesis requires further refining.

Nothing less shall be asserted than that today's Left, in all its deep-seated factions, disposes over an understanding of the "Marxist" categories that is in no way authentic, but rather bound up with a disappearing historical stage of capital. It is ironic that the ripening objective crisis of the capital relation thus simultaneously appears as the crisis of Marxist theory itself as it is understood both by the Left and by its opponents.

While the left-wing media become more and more untheoretical, cloak themselves in the grey mantle of the shrinking modesty of the seemingly innocuous investigation of partial and superficial themes, and ultimately at least partially throw the categories of Marxian theory overboard — and sometimes, ascetically in comparison even with the positivists, completely dispense with theoretical synthesis of social totality in favor of sociological shorthand — they can only blindly walk past the central problem of their weakness. But in opposition to the general trend, becoming theoretical means, conversely, becoming fundamental again; however, as far as bourgeois society is concerned, becoming fundamental means deriving one's own essential categories from the critique of the objectivity of value — that is to say, from a concrete historical critique of the commodity fetish — in a renewed historical transition. But if it is correct — and my point is none other than this — that the conventional epigones' "Marxist" theory up until today, including that of the New Left, slips up completely as early as in the first chapter of *Capital*, then it will necessarily slip up all the more when faced with a social-economical reality that only today really begins to correspond fully to the fundamental categories of *Capital*.

As long as the law of value is understood only as the formal law of the social allocation of resources that can be influenced politically, but not as the historical determination of the essential content, the transience of which must establish itself both violently and objectively (that is to say, independently of all the political declarations of intent that refer to it), the understanding of value necessarily degenerates to the status of a category of second nature and can no longer be conceived as a fundamental contradiction. However, the determination of this contradiction at the highest level of abstraction is the determination of the relationship between matter and form, and this must be developed conceptually in order to understand the celebrated empirical or surface reality. This contradiction between the matter and the form of social reproduction, which in the logic of capitalism enters into irreconcilable opposition, can only adequately be decoded as the contradiction between productive forces and relations of production when the definition of the latter does not remain external to the commodity or value relation. The task, that is to say, would be to carve out the concepts of material production on one hand, and the value or commodity character of production on the other hand, as the essential core of the history of capital.

This is the object of this text — and its task, more narrowly defined, is to derive, by means of a categorical redefinition of the capitalist relations of value, the absolute logical and historical limit of capital in its approximate features, as a consequence of the most recent and qualitatively new stage of capitalist socialization. From the beginning we must therefore also emphasize the fact that this text will illustrate the shortcomings not only of a deeply flawed theoretical model but also of the practical politics of the Left, which, in spite of its sense of urgency, is only able to imagine social transcendence illusorily (if at all) solely in relation to what is already established and by way of value and monetary relations, which also means that it cannot but misconstrue the newly socialized productive forces as frightening intensifications of capital's might.

Use Value and Exchange Value; Productive Labor

In current "Marxist" conceptions, the contradiction between use value and exchange value appears as a static, merely terminological contradiction, which at all stages of the development of capital only ever reproduces itself inflexibly. The liberation of use value from the dictatorship of the abstraction of value, to the extent that it appears in this thinking at all, remains an external, subjective endeavor which can no longer rely on the unfolding of an objective contradiction in a concrete historical process. However, it is precisely this contradiction between use value and exchange value as it is laid out as a contradiction in the process of commodity production that makes capital into a contradiction in process, because it transforms itself under the capital relation from an apparently static relationship into a real historical process that drives toward resolution.

In order to grasp the process character of the relationship between use value and exchange value, it is, however, necessary to rediscover this contradiction within the concept of productivity or of productive labor. The Marxists' astounding and relatively prevalent dilemma consists in their inability to take this step: the contradiction between use value and exchange value remains inflexible precisely because it is no longer retained as a contradiction within the concept of productive labor. In this contradiction, rather, the material aspects ("of the nature of use value") and those that are determined by value ("of the nature of exchange value") appear to be mixed beyond differentiation, and no longer analytically distinct.

However, read against the grain of the petrified historical interpretation of Marx, it is precisely this analytical distinction in the concept of productive labor that proves itself to be essential to his work. From this point of view, productive labor must be understood as a dual concept: firstly, in relation to use value, on the material side of the process of labor as the process of the metabolism between humans and nature; but secondly, in relation to exchange value, to the process of the formation of value, as the social metabolism of humans with one another, in which labor appears to be dematerialized, as abstract human labor.

According to the first analytic definition, the concept of productivity refers exclusively to the relationship between (natural) material activity and material useful effect, a relationship which itself depends on the form and quality of the means of labor and the objects of labor, which could be termed the social extent of the domination of nature, further removed from the individual, qualitatively determined skill of the worker in handling these socially prescribed means of production. To this extent, all labor is productive labor, the content of which enters into a material relationship between activity and useful effect. But in this definition, the purely material aspect of the labor process that pertains to use value is never abandoned.

According to the second analytic definition, the concept of productivity refers exclusively to the abstract process of the formation of value, to the expenditure of abstract human labor as the fictitious substance of value, which on the surface appears reified as exchange value. From this point of view, the only productive labor is labor that is presented immediately as a social real abstraction or value-forming substance, as the expenditure of human labor per se, objectified in each and every product.

On the level of simple commodity production, this analytic distinction poses no problems. Indeed, it could even appear pointless, because productive labor, as material labor pertaining to use value, is here always immediately identical with productive labor as the social-fictional substance of the process of the formation of value. For into the product goes only the labor of the individual (artisanal) producer, seen both on the material level and on that of value. In the personal identity of the producer, the logical separation of the material labor process and the abstract process of the formation of value is suspended and as such cannot appear at all. Concrete, qualitative labor and value creation appear as one and the same, which they indeed are, because the abstract expenditure of the nerves, muscles, or brain as human labor, as such, proceeds from one and the same personal corporeality as the particular concrete, material labor process of the blacksmith, the cobbler, or the tailor.

It could appear that Marx's analytical separation of concrete, qualitatively particular labor from abstract labor were nothing other than an ingenious feat of thought that finally comes up with an appropriate term for a logic that has in fact existed for thousands of years (namely the logic of value or of commodity production). Such a conception would in any case correspond to the current Marxist understanding according to which the contradiction between use value and exchange value, and behind it the opposition between concrete and abstract labor, appears only as an inflexible definitional figure of thought, but to this extent not as a real category, as if this contradiction can no longer be retained within the concept of productive labor or productivity. However, if this contradiction is followed through logically, it is revealed that Marx's feat of thought only became possible in the first place at the point in the development of society when material and value-related production actually began to separate from one another. The capitalist mode of production set in motion a process according to which the material labor process and the process of value creation began to diverge on a progressively larger scale, and increasingly grew out of proportion with one another. The motor of this development becomes cooperation in labor as it is practiced by capital, an increased social division of labor which reaches beyond the narrow limits of the individual branches of production that until that point had been inflexible and hermetic, and thus dissolves these limits along with the immediate identity of materially productive labor and value-producing labor within the personal corporeality of the individual producer.

Total Productive Labor

The transformation of the concrete material labor process into a cooperative process, initially in the form of manufacture, and later on the basis of the factory system, appears at first simply to reproduce the identity of the concrete labor process and the process of the formation of value in an altered form: this identity is now projected onto a total productive worker, the totality of the persons active in the cooperative labor process, instead of being, as previously, united within the individual producers.

But on closer observation this identity quickly becomes untenable. In the first instance, and this aspect can only be discussed briefly, the cooperation of labor with monetary capital causes the dissociation of a variety of unproductive functions (with regard to both materiality and value). These dissociated functions — special labor processes — have neither immediate nor mediated influence on the product, yet they are contained in the nature of production as the production of commodities (commercial functions, buying and selling as such). These functions, in every respect unproductive, also already exist for the individual artisanal producers (or they are carried out by members of their families, who also perform household and subsistence labor), but they are not isolated as individual activities, and remain extremely marginal to the process of commodity production as a whole and closely related to the cultural forms of social life which cannot be reduced to the dry categories of economic analysis (market day as a feast day). Capitalist cooperation brings about the formalization of these commercial functions, their economization, and at the same time their expansion: they are no longer restricted to acts of buying and selling, but are developed into marketing, market analysis, and advertising.

Secondly, however, enigmatic functions that can no longer unambiguously be identified with either productive or unproductive labor also begin to arise within the immediate labor process: the functions of direction and control. As a cooperative process, the material labor process is not identical with the simple sum of the individual parts of the labor process, but contains the very moment of combination as a particular activity necessary for the whole process, just as the activity of the conductor belongs to the total labor of an orchestra (Marx uses this analogy on many occasions). On the other hand, in the capitalist form of cooperation this function of "conducting" is never simply a moment of the material labor process, but is always at the same time stained with the character of the labor process as a process of exploitation — that is to say, it is bound up with functions of control and oppression. The conducting function is divorced from the people involved in the directly cooperative process of labor by its exclusivity and its external character, and therefore is fundamentally loathsome to them — more so than can be said of the personifications of monetary capital itself, at whose command they toil, but which never confronts them as immediately as the "officers and NCOs" of the production process.

These functions are just as inflexible as the capitalist process of production itself, and they are revolutionized with every revolution in the material structure of the labor process. The relentless rhythm of the factory system takes on to a certain extent the task of primitive surveillance and renders human control unnecessary; but these functions, as befits the nature of production as an exploitative process, never become wholly superfluous, but also reproduce themselves on the level of the most modern technological changes brought about by microelectronics and so on and merely take on new forms. To the ambiguous content of these functions corresponds their ambiguous connection to the concept of productive labor: to the extent that they emerge as a cooperative function (the function of a conductor) from the purely material character of the labor process, they are part of the labor of immediate production and are thus productive both materially and with respect to value; but to the extent that they emerge from the hostile opposition between capital and labor as the bailiff of the command of monetary capital, they are, just like the purely commercial functions, productive neither materially nor with respect to value. The split between productive and unproductive labor similarly splits every person in half.

The problem at the heart of the divergence of matter and value under capitalism consists neither in the isolation of the commercial functions nor in the way in which the cooperative tasks of direction take on an importance in their own right, in opposition to the immediate producers. Rather, this essential core appears only when we examine a third category that is usually not perceived as a category at all, but which alone makes the contradiction between exchange value and use value, between the material labor processes and the value-forming labor process, truly manifest. At stake here are those functions which, while they apply to the material labor process within the total worker, do not do so immediately, but indirectly, in a mediated way. These functions do not arise from the commercial character of the mode of production, nor do they emerge from the formal opposition between capital and labor, but it is also the case that they do not constitute a link in the immediate cooperative labor process which is directly objectified in a product. What is at stake here are rather activities beside and beyond the immediate process of production, which without doubt become part of the material content of production, but do not straightforwardly become part of any particular product — for example, tasks of technical (rather than social) monitoring, technical project management, design, and so on.

These activities, which in the technological sense involve planning, monitoring, designing, and so on — that is to say intellectual labor in the broadest sense — were originally all united within the head of the individual producer, to the extent that they were part of his personal corporeality and not separated from the immediate manual labor. Capitalist cooperative labor involves the historical tendency to dissolve these functions from the immediate process of production, and to recompose them alongside this process.

With regard to the way in which these labors objectify value, the question arises as to whether they, as isolated functions that have been dissolved from the immediate process of production, are, nonetheless, as components of the total productive worker, still suspended in the identity of the material labor process and the abstract process of the formation of value. This is certainly the case to the extent that they, even indirectly and in a mediated form, still become part of the process of objectifying a particular total labor in a particular product; to this extent even such functions would in the end amount to no more than the collective reproduction, if in more complex forms, of the earlier individual process of production in its hermetic identity of the concrete labor process and the abstract process of value formation.

The matter no longer seems quite so unambiguous when such technological, intellectual labors that are dissociated from the immediate production process no longer flow into a particular product in any recognizable manner, but rather into a wide range of products, and thus reach well beyond the limits of cooperation or of total labor in the respective individual businesses. Even then, such labors doubtless enter, indirectly and mediatedly, the material labor process; to this extent they can unambiguously be identified as productive labor. However, as far as the process of the formation of value is concerned, a grey zone opens up: when the same activity that indirectly becomes part of the material labor process — let us take as an example the design of a control module — is not only spread across completely different products, but even (e.g., through licensing) across products of completely different participants in the market, then doubt arises as to how this labor, productive in the material sense, can objectively take on a value form.

We must not forget that value, which must appear as exchange value, does not by its nature express an in some way mythical substance inherent to things as such, as the fetish structure of exchange value suggests, but rather a social relationship between partial or private producers who are isolated from one another, whose social division of labor can only be realized by means of the sphere of circulation that has been separated from it. However, the construction of a control module that could be universally implemented is an immediately socialized task according not only to its form, but also to its content and its nature; to this extent it goes beyond the mere transformation of the process of simple production from individual to collective, cooperative production, but also begins to suspend these branches of production themselves on an ever-larger scale, by smudging the boundaries between them by means of technology. There do of course continue to exist operations specific to the production of specific products, but these become less and less characteristic of the central content of the production process, becoming rather merely an appendage to and a partial aspect of a highly socialized and networked total aggregate of immediately social labor. To the extent that a bulging, immediately social aggregate of universal, nonspecific technology pushes its way between the actual specific manufacture of a particular end product and its ideal conception, many specific branches of production also no longer relate to one another externally. Instead an integrated, technological, and social total aggregate develops arbitrarily combinable output systems of specific products as its subordinate aspects and functions. This, however, tends materially to suspend the social division of labor according to separate branches of production that have existed up until this point, and as a result commodity production itself becomes obsolete.

As long as the technological-material suspension of the isolated branches of production had not progressed particularly far, that is to say perhaps up until the end of the age of steam-powered machinery, it might have seemed to a certain extent a good idea simply to replace individual commodity producers with a collective, cooperative commodity producer, that is to say to suspend the opposition of capital and labor within the confines of commodity production itself. It is for this reason that the concept of socialism in the old workers' movement necessarily remained to a great extent confined not only within the commodity fetish, but also in the money and wage fetish, as the idea of a community of cooperative commodity producers in collectives and the like. If such thoughts are being revived today, they are certainly only reactionary, for these ideas must sink, along with the old workers' movement, not least because the process of material-technical socialization has long been left behind by capitalism. This all parenthetically.

Once it was possible to define the particular activities that were dissociated from the individual producer of the past initially either as productive or unproductive, both in the material sense and in respect to value (as an emulsion of productive and unproductive processes carried out by the officers and NCOs of the process of production). Now, however, we are confronted with an entirely new category within total labor that entails functions which may be categorized as productive labor in a material sense (insofar as they directly contribute to a labor process that is socialized on an increasingly higher technological level) but which are simultaneously unproductive with respect to the creation of value (and thus in respect to capitalist processes of valorization). At the very least, the latter category disappears into a grey zone that (as immediately social labor) is not included in the categories of the socialization of surplus value. It is thus this area of the process of reproduction, in which materially productive labor and labor that is productive with respect to value begin to diverge, that historically dissolves the former identity of the concrete and the abstract labor process.

As long as the functions of immediately social labor that emerge objectively from the context of exchange value remain on the whole marginal — that is to say, as long as they appear both quantitatively and qualitatively to be shrinking in comparison with the mass of living labor which is employed in the cooperative immediate process of production and which is still unambiguously objectified within a particular project that can appear on the market as the product of a social-partial producer (internally divided into commanding monetary capital and wage labor) — the logical contradiction of value does not yet reveal itself in its true and pure form. This does not happen until this relationship between immediate (only indirectly social) labor and mediated (directly social) labor in the material process of production is altered and ultimately overturned by the capitalist development of social productive force. Living labor is removed from the immediate production process that directly objectifies itself within a particular product. The proportion of human labor alongside and beyond this immediate process of production, which only indirectly enters the process as directly social labor, grows at the same rate.

It is true that the explosive force of this development does not become completely clear until we examine this historical divergence on the level of society as a whole, beyond the interface or grey zone in which materially productive labor and labor that is productive with respect to value begin to diverge. I have for this reason until now only cautiously spoken of a grey zone, since all determinations of the productive total worker up to this point solely developed out of capitalist cooperation on the plane of the factory or the individual business where these determinations transform into a total aggregate only at the fraying boundaries of the separate branches of production that determine immediately social labor. But if we now no longer examine the process of the material socialization of the whole apparatus of social reproduction from the bottom up (from the perspective of an individual capitalist business), but rather from the top down (from the perspective of total social reproduction), then the concept of the total productive worker must also be expanded to include this total social dimension. At this point we must deal with two levels of total labor (which both permeate each other), that of the individual business and that of society as a whole, which present themselves as reciprocally networked. On this second, expanded level of total labor the divergence of material production and value production now begins to become properly clear, and the derivation of the concept that has up until this point only been hinted at can now be fully developed.

In all precapitalist modes of production, the social network that reaches beyond the individual units of production (peasant and artisanal families) is only developed to an extremely limited extent; even the state only exists in a crude form, primarily as the armed self-organization of the ruling classes. Capitalism transforms not only the individual or familial productive units into cooperative large-scale producers that within themselves function according to the division of labor and that on a larger scale are integrated into a mechanical system, but in doing so also establishes an institutionalized social framework of conditions without which such cooperative large-scale production for the newly developing global markets would be unthinkable. The most important of these conditions consists in advanced social infrastructure (e.g., extensive and ramified transport and communication systems, energy provision, regulated and institutionalized standardization of measures, weights, and formats, and not least a comprehensive and integrated system of education and training). This framework of increasingly necessary conditions of social infrastructure must quickly be taken over and run by state-controlled or semi-state-controlled organizations — an indication that their essential character pertains to society as a whole, to the way in which they fundamentally reach beyond every concern of individual businesses. As a general framework of conditions, this infrastructure becomes part of total social production just like the natural foundations and requirements of production; it becomes a sort of material second nature (just as on the other hand value becomes an economic second nature). The general average human capacity for labor is thus for example no longer the original natural capacity, but is always already, before all productive activity, a socially produced capacity of which cultural techniques such as reading, writing, and arithmetic at the very least form a part.

All these basic conditions of social infrastructure require labor and absorb a historically increasing proportion of socially available labor power. With respect to the productivity of this labor, what was already suggested at the margins of cooperation between individual businesses in activities such as design now becomes palpable: they are productive only in terms of society as a whole as immediately social or socialized tasks. They are no longer the expression of a separation of whatever nature between partial, individual, or private social producers, but rather their exact opposite: by their nature these tasks become from the outset part of all moments of partial social production to the same extent but by different routes, and are therefore always and indeed exclusively a matter of the whole process of reproduction of society as a totality, and never of a process pertaining to an individual business. Social productive forces are here being set in motion, and all the labors that are encapsulated within them are indirectly productive at the material level. But at the same time, it is in the nature of these labors that they stand a priori outside the law of value, and cannot take on the form of objectified abstract labor in the fetish shape of value, because it is precisely as immediately social labor that they become part of all products to the same extent and at all times, and thus cannot at all appear as a moment in a process of exchange of separate units. With respect to the process of value creation they must therefore always remain unproductive, because value is nothing other than the essential core of social exchange between separated partial producers, a core which necessarily fetishizes itself, and which congeals in an apparently urgent substance.

Here we now have the new prototype of labor that is in many ways first engendered by capitalism, and with which capitalism, however, suspends the law of value and with it its own foundations according to real logic: immediately social, indirectly materially productive labor, that by its nature is unproductive with respect to value. However, with the large-scale expansion of the mechanical system of production, the social importance of this new, immediately social form of labor for the process of social reproduction grows in a historically inexorable manner, seen both in absolute and in relative terms. Logically, this also causes the law of value to become increasingly obsolete, and value-based production historically to approach an objective collapse. Marx's comments on this matter, particularly in the *Grundrisse*, are to be taken completely literally and as a concrete prognosis of the objective historical logic of the development of capital, and in no way as the subjective program of communism that is not to be realized until some distant future or other long beyond capitalism. The various tendencies of the Marxist Left might have pored over the relevant passages in Marx hundreds or even thousands of times and cited them in the most contradictory of contexts, but they have never conceptually unfolded their true logic as the logic of capital itself with reference to its actual historical unfolding; evidently not because of a fundamental lack of the capacity for abstraction, but because of a historically conditioned failure to escape the categories of exchange value, a failure that has up until the present day not been overcome.

Science as Productive Force

However, the essential determination of the content of the new, immediately social labor is that of science. That capitalism is the scientification of production is absolutely obvious and therefore beyond dispute. However, in Marxist theory this concept of the scientification of production is also used in a far-too-inflexible, ahistorical, and abstract-definitional manner — and where the actual historical development of this process of scientification is discussed at all, it is without any logical or systematic reference to the value structure of production.

There is a fundamental distinction to be made between two forms of the process of scientification, which reciprocally permeate each another and ultimately fuse into a social technology of production which by itself necessarily and wholly objectively explodes the law of value and therefore commodity production.

The first is the technological application of the natural sciences, which makes science itself into an "immediate productive force"; but the second is the science of labor or of organization, which only emerges on the basis of cooperation in the form of the capitalist division of labor. Both forms of scientification are to be discussed at first for themselves, and then in terms of the reciprocal relationship between them.

Natural science as such has existed for millennia, and arose in ancient slave-owning society. But in accordance with the economic nature of this society, natural science, as a part of philosophy, remained strictly separate from the material activity of production. It was a luxury of the ruling, slave-owning class, a decisive step forward in the history of humanity, but in the first instance did not exercise any influence on production. The idea that natural science was a product of the "inventive spirit" of the immediate producer and so forth, as can be found in some "Marxist" treatises, emerges in contrast from naïve *proletkult* ideas and from a vulgar materialism that always wishes directly to derive all social phenomena from production. It is true that, in a historically mediated form, and going all the way back to the original society of the hunter-gatherers, intellectual activities and the forms of their higher development are indeed in the first instance a direct result of material production. But the further we advance through history toward the threshold of class society as the result of the development of the productive forces, the more material production and intellectual-scientific activity (or their primitive forms) are isolated from one another and take on their own existence independently of one another. The general truth of the materialist thesis as it pertains to the process of human development as a whole, that the forms of intellectual activity have their roots in material activities of production, is no hindrance to recognizing the fact that natural science has evolved as a particular moment of this process of development in strict separation from production.

For this reason, natural science, understood as the socially abstract "love of wisdom" of luxuriant slave-owners, had in the first instance and for a long time nothing to do with the development of the social productive capacity of labor; it was an indirect result of the development of productive capacity, but conversely did not itself become a cause or motor of its further development. To the extent that the productive forces were further developed by means of improvements in the instruments and methods of production, this in fact came about as a result of the meticulous and contemplative nature of some of the immediate producers (farmers, craftsmen, fishermen), but absolutely not in a scientific manner, but purely empirically, accidentally, nonconceptually, without systematic abstraction or a sequence of logical steps that sequentially build upon one another. For this reason the process was tremendously slow and took place over very long periods of time, such that it was hardly possible to observe changes in technologies of production over many generations, and new procedures established themselves only very slowly, to the extent that they were not bound to particular natural conditions (e.g. as in the case of watermills).

In the ancient world, emerging science, with natural science as an integral component of it that had not yet developed to the status of a discipline in its own right, had already been a moment of human emancipation from religion, at least from religion in its original, naïve, unreflected, mythological form. But at the same time these beginnings of intellectual emancipation arose — and could only arise — as a luxury good produced by an idle class of slave holders who despised material production, with whose historical demise this emancipation, while it did not simply disappear, was however subordinated once more, and in a very inflexible, mechanical form, to institutionalized religion in the form of the Roman church.

The history of the new rise of science and its transformation once again into an emancipatory ideology on a higher scale is, however, since the Renaissance, nothing other than the history of bourgeois emancipation from the chains of feudalism. The renewed, more extensive separation of science from religion, the detachment of knowledge of nature from the belief in God had in the first place — and indeed for centuries — a purely ideological function: it was an ideal weapon to begin to unite the urban bourgeoisie against the feudal powers. As the founding sciences of a new secularized world picture, astronomy and cosmology (Galileo, Bruno, Kepler) were hardly suited to function as immediate productive forces. But the class that was to become the socioeconomic bearer of the modern emancipation of science from religion differed fundamentally in its economic position (and therefore also in its ways of thinking) from the ancient slave-holders who "discovered" science. The bourgeoisie understood itself in its rise and in its struggle with feudalism as a productive class, although this concept certainly remained ideologically blurred and took sustenance from its opposition to the manifestly socially parasitic classes of the feudal aristocracy and to the feudal clergy. In the bourgeoisie's understanding of itself as a productive class lay the historical ideological precondition for the productive application of the new sciences; but for this application actually to come to life, one further path must be travelled.

In the first half of the nineteenth century — that is, relatively late in the overall development of the bourgeoisie since the Renaissance — when capitalism first really began to develop by means of steam-powered machinery, this historical leap in the development of productivity was not yet in any way the result of a systematic relationship between science and production. The decisive innovations were initially still made by empirical practitioners (such as the engineer-industrialist and inventor of the spinning frame Arkwright) and not by scientists, and these innovations were made not on the basis of the socialized organization of science and technology, but individually. The development of the natural sciences since the sixteenth century was certainly a general precondition of the new technologies, and in particular of the tremendous potential of steam as a source of energy, but the technological and commercial application did not directly result from this. It essentially remained this way throughout the nineteenth century: the systematic social organization of the process of science and of its technological application and the substructure of qualifications that it requires (schools, specialist schools, the expansion of the universities, the foundation of polytechnics, the amalgamation of science and large-scale capital) only got under way gradually. As late as the *Gründerzeit* at the end of the century, the threshold to the age of imperialism, it was still inventor-capitalists such as Siemens, Daimler, or Edison in the United States who laid the decisive foundations for entire industrial branches.[1] Industry itself was still in development, the largest proportion of the working population had not yet been transformed into wage laborers, and the industrial processes themselves remained in themselves very crude and labor-intensive — the scientification of production was still in its childhood. It is perhaps necessary to bring these facts to mind in order to grasp just how extremely young the historical development of the true logic of capitalism is, the logic that Marx had already anticipated in ideal form from its beginnings through the power of abstraction, admittedly spread across a huge life's work that has remained a torso and still awaits the development that would emancipate it from the historical abbreviations of Marxism.

The scientification of production, which not only embraces the entire spectrum of the different branches of production but also reaches to the very depths of the individual labor processes, could only fully develop itself in the twentieth century — and as is the case throughout previous history, war was here, too, the father of all things. It was the two imperialist world wars that not only brought with them new inventions and technological innovations, but also the decisive breakthrough in the state and social organization of the process of science and its direct connection to material production. And after World War II, electronics, as the direct descendant of militarized research, was the basis not only on which new industries were produced out of thin air, but also on which applied natural sciences for the first time ceased to be merely the technological foundation and general prerequisite of industrial labor processes, and became the driving force of the immediate labor process itself. The resonance of this change is felt by observers in all ideological camps when they are in agreement in speaking of a new technological revolution.

The second form of the scientification of production, the science of labor as the science of the organization of the processes of production, is of an even more recent vintage than the productive application of the natural sciences, and only came into existence in the first place in the twentieth century. It will forever remain associated with the name "Taylor." It is true that the necessity of the planned organization of the process of production coincides with cooperation itself and therefore dates back to the beginnings of manufacture, but this organization remained immediate, spontaneous, and above all external to the concrete reality of the labor processes themselves, even throughout the entire nineteenth century.

The industrial system did not simply turn the worker into an appendage of the machinery straight away, but only parts of the working class (in the first instance primarily women and children), while at the same time, as a result of the machinery, new activities arose within the labor process that required certain qualifications, which looked very similar to those of the old artisanal class, and in part emerged from them. But others — technicians — must also be seen as creations of the system of machinery. These technicians possessed irreplaceable knowledge about the immediate process of production, abilities, and skills that they had acquired through practice, which left them a certain amount of room for maneuver with respect to capital. But even the unskilled workers had a certain, if smaller, latitude, by learning as it were to take advantage of the gaps in the mechanical system in order to create tiny spaces and breaks for themselves, to keep the average working speed as low as possible. Capital's attempts to bring these various instances of room for maneuver under control, along with what it saw as the squandering of valuable time, are as old as the capitalist mode of production itself, and are personified in those officers and NCOs of the process of production that with the onset of cooperation necessarily appear in particular guises. But as long as this control did not take on an objectified, operationalizable — in short, scientified — form, it had to remain external, arbitrary, and subjective.

It was not until the next stage of the development of capitalist concentration at the start of the twentieth century, which brought with it the large-scale material production that left even the most comprehensive forms of cooperation from the nineteenth century in its wake (not least in the highly organized and in part already state-directed wartime production of World War I), that the general precondition for labor science was created. Taylor himself, and it is telling that he advanced from the skilled working class (he was originally a lathe operator), combined in his own person a mixture of an almost glowing ideological defense of capitalism and the innovative fantasy of the fastidious contemplator with a bean-counting pedantry that enabled him to place the organization of the labor process itself on a scientific foundation.

The elementary principle of the science of labor over their respective immediate labor processes consists in the deindividualization and systematization of the control contained in the workers' individual personality and corporeality, and to institutionalize it as an instance of control outside the individual worker. What Taylor created can to this extent be described as a second level of cooperation: if the first level of cooperation divided the total individual labor of a branch of production into partial individual labors under a command that lies outside the partial worker and with the representative of monetary capital, then now the partial labor is itself divided into individual, standardized operations, under a control which now just as then lies outside the individual partial worker.

In the industrial labor process as Taylor found it, this new level of cooperation had, like the first before it, to turn against the worker. For the unskilled workers the consequences were devastating, for what little remained of their room to maneuver was now taken from them. The assembly line, technologically speaking, in no way a specific innovation of applied natural science, but rather a simple matter of mechanics, was, however, organizationally speaking, a decisive step in the industrial production process, and became a symbol of the new scientific torture of labor, of which the presentation in Charlie Chaplin's *Modern Times* remains unsurpassed. However, the assembly line, developed in prototypical form in the vanguard of the automobile industry, could in no way easily be applied to all branches of production at will. The principles of the new science of labor failed spectacularly when faced with the great proportion of technicians' tasks, which involved an artisanal precision that could not be dissolved into standardized and externally controlled operations. The age of Taylorism or of Fordism (named after the original image of assembly line production) thus remained an epoch characterized by perpetual struggle between the science of labor and the working class, symbolized by the despised stopwatch of the time and motion expert, whose task it was to standardize optimally the content and duration of the operations, and by the absurd consequences it brought (such as the standardization of the sequence of motions in filing a document).

We shall now consider the scientification of production under the aspect of the confluence of applied natural science and the science of labor, a process which did not start until after World War II, and is only today entering a decisive stage before our very eyes. At the beginning of the twentieth century, technologically applied natural science and the science of labor were still relatively separate disciplines; it was not until the development of electronics and the automatic processes of production control that developed out of it that they fused into a unity. This development is characterized precisely by the minimization and the tendency toward the elimination of living human labor in the immediate process of production. The gaps between the scientific organization of labor and technology are closed precisely by means of the removal of living labor itself, regardless of the place it previously occupied in immediate production.

However, this has wide-reaching consequences. From the standpoint of the money and wage fetishes, Taylor was a capitalist monster, because he wanted to redeploy the last elements of autonomy that remained in the industrial process of production outside the worker and to centralize them; from the standpoint of the money and wage fetishes, the fusion of natural-scientific technology and the science of labor must bring about another, far more hideous capitalist monstrosity, because such a fusion eliminates human labor altogether from the immediate process of production. But it is precisely in this aspect that Taylor's genius, within his capitalist constraints, becomes clear: his "science of labor" created the preconditions for automatization, as soon as applied natural sciences had become ripe for it, and with them the starting point for the suspension of commodity production itself. For the unification of technologically applied natural science and the science of labor implies a tendency toward the suspension of the partial social labor that is objectified within a particular product, and a tendency to universalize immediately social labor.

The revolutionary working class that was attacking the wage system itself ought to dedicate a monument to Taylor, for he, albeit unconsciously, and in a restricted and even sordid manner directly in accordance with the base ends of the capitalist extraction of living labor, paved the way for the ultimate suspension of that immediately productive labor that, precisely because of this direct productivity that objectifies itself within a particular product, cannot be immediately social labor and therefore remains apprehended within the socialization of exchange value. In capitalism this tendency, which is only today attaining objective maturity before our eyes, cannot be completed, because it relies on the valorization of value and therefore on the exploitation of that immediate living productive labor which it at the same time tends, according to its historical logic, to abolish.

If Marx occasionally talks of the abolition of labor but at the same time describes labor as the eternal natural condition of the metabolism between humans and nature, this apparent contradiction can now easily be accounted for: what is abolished is immediate productive labor, and with it the tendency toward the torture of labor; what is not abolished and can never wholly be abolished is mediated, indirect, productive labor alongside the immediate process of production, before and beyond this process, labor which for the most part appears to be becoming more immediately social or socialized, and therefore objectively falls outside the framework of exchange value — a historical tendency, which in capitalism can only appear as a fundamental and catastrophic crisis.

The logic of this tendency that continually works its way further into the body politic contradicts the Marxist Left, for the reason that their understanding of the capital relation is restricted to inflexible definitional determinations with which all movements within capital, including technical progress, can apparently be explained. But it becomes clear that the inflexibility of these definitions was merely the expression of an epoch of the historical development of capital itself that is now coming to an end. As applied natural science and the science of labor converge to bring about the tendency toward the automation of immediate production, the contradiction of capital as a relation that becomes its own limit is only today coming to a head. Accordingly, we now find ourselves at the start of a new epoch, in which the core of the logic of capitalist development and crisis will at last truly begin to emerge.

Because of its advanced maturity, the elimination of living labor from the immediate process of production can today be recognized as such, and it is possible to draw from this insight more fundamental and deeper-reaching conclusions than those of Marxist theory up until today. This tendency will assert itself objectively on a global scale not as a single, isolated event, but as a longer historical period in which the accumulation of capital perishes and burns out as a result of itself. The technological process of the fusion of natural science and the science of labor is still in its infancy, even if microelectronics has already provided the decisive prerequisites. The structures of material production in a great many sectors are still closing themselves off against a far-too-hasty and simple process of complete automation, even if there is a palpable tendency (as in the automobile industry, which because of its assembly-line structure is the most suited to it) for industrial robots to begin to close the gaps in the mechanical system that at the moment are still filled by people. The imperialist industrialized nations are still involved in global exchange with labor-intensive production of the countries of the Third World, from which they take control of the abstract wealth of exchange value, that spectral objectification of human labor in itself in the immediate process of production. But there can be no doubt an epoch has begun that will be defined by the necessary objective downfall of money, because the material productivity of the process of labor itself relies on direct socialization, and in doing so destroys exchange value.

It is one of the ironies of history that the Marxist and indeed non-Marxist Left has, today of all times at the beginning of this historical epoch, moved the furthest away from the concrete Marxian critique of value or of the objectivity of value, and is starting to lose what trace it had of the recollection of the objectivity of the capitalist contradiction, and is even beginning to conceive the new technological revolution as an overpowering increase of power and the potential final consolidation of capital, rather than as the beginning of its objective demolition. An essential theoretical foundation of this grotesque misunderstanding is the failure to retain in the concept of productive labor the distinction between material production and the production of value, between the immediate labor of production and directly social labor. If Marx's reference to "science as immediate productive force" is misunderstood to mean that science itself produces value, a misunderstanding that can only be based on a failure to escape the value fetish, then every new stage in the scientification of production must certainly seem to be a moment of the immortalization and consolidation of the process of the abstraction of value.[2]

While traditional Marxism had hardly touched on the problem, the New Left unfurled the question of scientification in precisely the opposite way. Michael Mauke, who was much read in the early stages of the 1968 movement, thus argued: "The shift from immediate to mediated activities has the effect that technical and scientific labor directly 'produces surplus-value for the capitalist or serves the self-valorization of capital,' that is to say it becomes productive labor in the capitalist sense."[3]

Habermas expresses this misunderstanding even more clearly when he writes:

> With the advent of large-scale industrial research, science, technology, and industrial utilisation were fused into a system. [...] Thus technology and science become a leading productive force, rendering inoperative the conditions for Marx's labor theory of value[!]. It is no longer meaningful to calculate the amount of capital investment in research and development on the basis of unskilled (simple) labor power, when scientific-technical progress has become an independent source of surplus-value, in relation to which the only source of surplus-value considered by Marx, namely the labor power of the immediate producers, plays an ever smaller role.[4]

It is writ large in the face of such proclamations that for them value has congealed into a fetish concept — but this is precisely the matter on which the Left, and Habermas with it, has failed fundamentally to reflect. These circumstances prove only that the New Left as a whole shares Habermas's fetishization of value, and that their theory and their political goals have never moved beyond this fetish, that is to say that their critique of the "traditional" workers' movement has not begun to touch on the decisive question. This becomes clear at the very latest when it is seen that the only critique of the "science as a productive force" theorem came from the *K-Gruppen*, which relied on a set of concepts that had lapsed to the petrified *proletkult* of the Third International.[5] In the very few pertinent comments from this source the problem is approached no less wrongly than by Mauke and Habermas, but merely the other way around: their insistence that science as a productive force creates no value (which is certainly by no means a result of theoretical derivation, but remains a merely dogmatic assertion of faith) thus appears immediately identical with the finding that science accordingly cannot be an immediate productive force even with respect to material production, but at most a concern that is external to the process of production.

This formulation (as well as that of Mauke, Habermas, and others that are apparently opposed to it) remains, absurdly, aconceptually and without any analytical differentiation, wedded to that historical identity of material production and the production of value which experiences a moment of real suspension precisely by capitalism's secular movement. But their respective consequences are just as opposed as their evaluations. For Habermas, at least, and the whole intellectual sphere of the Frankfurt School and indeed of the left-wing academic socialists, the result — sometimes sooner, sometimes later — was the path to obsolescence of the revolutionary subject of the working class, instead of the obsolescence of exchange value, and thus a shallow reformism on the basis of the valorization of value, presumably immortalized by means of science as a productive force. Conversely, for the *K-Gruppen* the result was once again clothed in the burlesque intellectual garb of Stalinist *proletkult*, hanging to the naïve pride in his labor of the immediate producer who boasts that he creates all value, instead of palpably abolishing value.

Relative Surplus Value and the Logic of the Development of Capital

It is now time to reveal how the divergence of material production and the production of value gradually appears in the process of the social reproduction of capital, and constitutes the historical logic of the development of the capitalist mode of production. The key concept in understanding this logic is well known to be that of relative surplus value. This concept is an analytical category found in Marx, but at the same time a real category of the total social reproduction of capital, not a surface category which would also appear in the consciousness of the representatives of monetary capital.

Presupposing the existence of an absolute physical limit (with respect both to the duration of labor time and the intensity of labor) and a relative social limit to the working day (limitations enforced by the labor movement and/or by state interventions), the valorization of value transforms itself from an absolute and extensive into a relative and intensive movement. The foundation of valorization is and remains surplus value as such — that is, the fact that the capitalist yield, apparently the output, measured in value, of the total aggregate of dead and living labor, is nothing other than the proportion of the new value that the living labor has created over and above the costs of its own reproduction. But if the capitalist share of this new value can no longer be enlarged extensively, by prolongation of the working day, its growth comes to depend on intensively and relatively increasing surplus labor, mediated through the development of the productive forces — that is, through the progressive scientification of the process of production. What presents itself with respect to a single capital as the difference between individual value and the level of social value, presents itself socially with respect to the generalization of the new productive force as a decrease in the reproduction costs of the commodity labor power. The production of relative surplus value thus necessarily becomes the prime means of capitalist accumulation. But in the movement of capital as a whole, mediated by competition, three logical historical consequences are established, the third of which is hardly discussed in either bourgeois or Marxist theory.

The first consequence consists in the fact that the increased capitalist share of the newly created value brings about an escalation of the material output of products, which in turn forces an expansion of markets and an acceleration of accumulation. Capital as it were hunts across the globe. This law of motion, as it compels an individual capital, is multiplied and politicized at the higher level of forms of state organization of national total capital, or of total capitalist blocs. Competition for higher productive capacity and over the markets takes place on all levels, on the level of the individual capital just as on the level of capitalist states and blocs of allied countries.

This process concentrates and centralizes capital within the individual states. At the same time, the world market, as the economic theater of the war over markets for commodities and capital, the war over sources of raw materials, spheres of influence, and so on, is transformed into a global political arena. The capitalist world economy gives birth to world politics, political and military power becomes a condition of economic competitiveness, to the reciprocal detriment of the economic base. Hot war, naked violence, which tends toward and in this century has actually meant world wars with millions of casualties, becomes the ultima ratio of competition. It is completely evident that in this global capitalist system known as imperialism, war is in no way the direct effect of the economic crisis, neither the crisis of overproduction nor any other, but rests on the logic of competition between capitals on the world market, and of the internal dynamic of a world politics that is itself founded on this competition. The most fundamental revolutions of this century did not result from economic crises, and to this extent not from a burning out of capitalist logic as such either, but from political crises in combination with military conflicts and defeats of the ruling classes: beginning with the Paris Commune in 1871 then the October Revolution, the German Revolution of November 1918, the Chinese Revolution in the aftermath of World War II (the specific example of anticolonial revolutions such as those in Algeria or southeast Asia ought to be given separate treatment).

Even when the capitalist world economy turns into the world-political phenomenon that takes on a dynamic of its own and engenders its own laws, the fundamental economic movement of the accumulation of relative surplus value ultimately remains the determining factor. Imperialist violence, the ultima ratio of military intervention, does not in the slightest eradicate the economic starting point of competition, nor can it solve the resulting conflicts. Competition must always reproduce itself on all levels, even if it does so in ever-new forms. The struggle over the development of productivity and over the markets is never determined or indeed ultimately resolved by mere violence, as is shown by the fulminant economic upturn in the Federal Republic of Germany and Japan during the phase of prosperity after World War II, despite their military defeats and prolonged periods of political and military weakness. The compulsion to the development of productivity is contained both in the self-determined logic of political-military competition, as is shown by the Sputnik Shock of 1957 and the subsequent technological drive in the West, and in the continued effect of purely economic competition, as is indicated today in the Federal Republic of Germany (FRG) and Western Europe by the technological race with Japan and the United States for the leading positions in microelectronics or gene technology.

The second consequence of the accumulation brought about by the increase in relative surplus value consists in the increasing tendency of the individual product to lose value — that is, in this interminable process, mediated by competition, of the development of the productive forces, the products decline in value. This tendency toward the decline in value of products allows more and more of what were previously luxury items to become available for the consumption of the masses, and creates and develops new, higher needs, which Marx with good reason reckons to be an aspect of the civilizing mission of capital. Contrary to some theoretical assertions, this tendency also develops according to its nature under imperialism, monopoly capitalism, and late capitalism — that is to say, neither the monopoly nor the state monopoly is ultimately able to render the law of value fundamentally inoperative. Even into the twentieth century, a great many products that used to be luxuries have, by means of the development of productive forces and the resultant decline in value, become objects of mass consumption (e.g., motor vehicles, electric household appliances, and so on at the start of this century; computers only more recently).

For the fact that the motor vehicle first became available to the masses in the form of the automobile and chaotic individual transport, with all its devastating consequences, is primarily the fault of the fact that this process was determined according to capitalism, for the public (that is to say communal) forms of transport were in no way developed to the same extent. But even then there is fundamentally a certain civilizing moment to the generalization of the motor vehicle: it creates a new mobility, a new mass need to travel, and thus contributes to the spasmodic broadening of the mind and to the creation of an internationalized society, even if this process in some cases engenders grotesque frictions at the same time. If the critique is directed against the universalization of the motor vehicle rather than against the fact that it is determined by its capitalist form, then the conservative and culturally pessimistic perspective of the gentleman rider can easily shine through it, a perspective that merely mourns for the privilege of the elect.

The third consequence, however — and this has hardly been brought to light in theory — consists in the fact that capital itself becomes the absolute logical and historical limit in the production of relative surplus value. Capital has no interest in and cannot be interested in the absolute creation of value; it is fixated only on surplus value in the forms in which it appears at the surface, that is to say on the relative proportion within the newly created value of the value of labor power (the costs of its reproduction) to the share of the new value that is appropriated by capital. As soon as capital can no longer increase the creation of value in absolute terms by extending the working day, but can only increase the relative size of its own share of the newly created value by means of the increase of productivity, there arises in the production of relative surplus value a countermovement, which must consume itself historically and work toward and bring about a standstill in the process of value creation. With the development of productivity, capital increases the extent of exploitation, but in doing so it undermines the foundation and the object of exploitation, the production of value as such. For the production of relative surplus value, inseparable as it is from the progressive fusion of modern science with the material process of production, includes the tendency toward the elimination of living, immediate, productive labor, as the only source of total social value creation. The same movement which increases capital's share of the new value decreases the absolute basis of value production by means of the elimination of direct living productive labor. Capital creates, necessarily and unconsciously, the immediately social labor that emerges from the value relation, the material productivity of which reduces total social labor time — but it does so only to its own end, in order to increase the rate at which it exploits the immediate producers. Capital develops social productivity for asocial ends and interests, and thus becomes entangled in a contradiction that cannot be resolved on its own foundations, the ultimate logic of which Marx sketches in the following terms:

> A development in the productive forces that would reduce the absolute number of workers, and actually enable the whole nation to accomplish its entire production in a shorter period of time would produce a revolution, since it would put the majority of the population out of action. Here we have once again the characteristic barrier to capitalist production, and we see how this is in no way an absolute form of the development of the productive forces and the creation of wealth, but rather comes into conflict with this at a certain point in its development. One aspect of this conflict is presented by the periodic crises that arise when one or another section of the working population is made superfluous in its old employment. The barrier to capitalist production is the surplus time of the workers. The absolute spare time that the society gains is immaterial to capitalist production. The development of productivity is only important to it in so far as it increases the surplus-labor time of the working class and does not just reduce the labor-time needed for material production in general; in this way it moves in a contradiction.[6]

Three questions necessarily arise from this sketch of the capitalist logic of the development of accumulation through the production of relative surplus value:

First: why has capitalism survived until today, in spite of its absolute immanent limit?

Second: why is capital, along with its theoretical advocates, blind to this tendency toward the absolute reduction of total social value creation?

Third: why has Marxist theory itself abandoned this thematic and not developed it concretely and honed it beyond Marx?

The Historical Expansion of Capital

The production of relative surplus value refers to the relationship between the capitalist share of the new value and the reproduction costs of the labor power of each individual laborer, but not to the absolute number of wage laborers employed, and therefore not to the absolute amount of surplus value, which with the absolute decrease in the creation of value is itself also necessarily decreased. This results in the situation

> that the same reasons that permit the level of exploitation of labor to increase make it impossible to exploit as much labor as before with the same total capital. These are the counter-acting tendencies which, while they act to bring about a rise in the rate of surplus-value, simultaneously lead to a fall in the mass of surplus-value produced by a given capital, hence a fall in the rate of profit.[7]

From this results the urgent necessity that capital grow as capital, that is to say that the decrease in the amount of surplus value through the increase in the rate of relative surplus value must be compensated for by the reproduction of capital not on the same scale, but on an enlarged scale, which for the first time brings about the necessity of limitless accumulation (growth). This development grows exponentially. While capital eliminates living immediate productive labor on one given level of production, it must at the same time absorb more new living immediate productive labor on a further level of production. But for this capital requires a social space, a terrain that it has not yet seized, into which it can in time grow. If this process encounters obstacles — if capital, even for a short amount of time, is unable to absorb more new living productive labor than it has eliminated by means of technological development — then periodic crises also arise when one or another section of the working population is made superfluous in its old employment. For in this case the materially and technologically mediated rise in the rate of surplus value does in fact lead to a fall in the mass of surplus value, and hence to a fall in the rate of profit — that is to say, production is no longer viable as capitalist production, and tends toward standstill, as long as it finds itself in capitalist hands. The tendency of the rate of profit to fall ought therefore only to be understood as the determination of the form of the crisis, the final content of which is founded in the material development of productivity and its absolute opposition to the value form of production in general. The crisis is only partial, periodic, and therefore transitional when capital succeeds in overcoming the obstacles in the way of its expansion, and in absorbing once again more living productive labor than it previously eliminated. In that case, the fall in the rate of profit is once again suspended. The character of this fall as a tendency must therefore not be understood as a continual process but as a historical discontinuity; this fall is fundamentally embedded in the development of productivity in the material labor process, but can again and again be suspended, as long as capital is once again able to start a new cycle of accumulation through the renewed expansion of the absolute mass of living labor employed in production.

However, the concept of capital's process of expansion remains hollow and unclear if it is only examined with respect to its value form, but not related systematically to the material content of this expansion. The process of accumulation can be understood as infinite only in the absence of a systematic relation of accumulation to its material substrate. After all, abstract wealth in the form of money is by its nature limitless and interminable, and only its material content is subject to an absolute historical limit. However, there can be no accumulation without its material bearer, however much the latter's absence would be the ideal of capital. The extended absorption of living immediate productive labor must refer to such a material content and bearer, which can be traced both historically and concretely in several respects.

First, the terrain for the expansion of capital becomes manifest in its step-by-step conquest of all branches of production that exist before it and independently of it — that is, in the transformation of subsistence and simple commodity production into capitalist production. And, again, as is taken as read in the question of the scientification of the labor process, it is necessary to remember that this process is in fact still young, and to recall how long a trajectory it would need in order to eat its way through all branches of production, starting with the textile industry. Together, the scientification of production and the transformation of, in the first instance, noncapitalist branches of production (crafts, agriculture) into capitalist branches constitute a single total process: the capitalization of noncapitalist small-scale production brings scientification in its wake, and the more branches of production are seized by capital, the greater the scale on which the total social aggregate of scientification develops. If this process is understood in inflexible definitions, as a result of the misunderstanding that the force of the Marxian abstraction had not anticipated ideally the historical logic of capital, but merely reflected an inflexible structural real logic of capital (a misunderstanding that is only possible as a result of the failure to escape the value fetish), then the temporal horizon is displaced, the process is no longer conceived as having an objective beginning and a just-as-objective end, but only as the return of the same, with this or that modification.

Even in the most-developed capitalist industrialized countries, the process of the capitalization of branches of production continued until late in the twentieth century; in Germany it did not reach its culmination until after World War II. It is possible to take the level of wage dependency within the working population as a whole as an indicator for this process (even if the category of wage labor of course also includes unproductive areas into which capitalism expands or which it has just newly created), and according to this index, capitalization does not reach saturation point in the core imperialist countries with 70 to 90 percent wage dependency until the 1960s.

Secondly, however, the elimination of human labor in the immediate process of production during the course of capitalist development was always overcome anew by the counter-absorption of living labor in new branches of production to meet new needs. Even here it is necessary to distinguish between different phases in the progression of capitalist development: World War II and the subsequent decades brought forth another new accumulation drive of capital. Particular products that before World War II were made more or less exclusively for a narrow class only entered mass production and mass consumption by means of the scientific-technological innovations of the war: cars, electric household appliances, and then electronic forms of entertainment. All these products only attained technological maturity and the phase of their true mass production in the 1950s and 1960s. At this point, a stage of scientification becomes visible in which, while the development of productivity does indeed eliminate living labor from countless older branches of production such that one or another section of the working population is made superfluous in its old employment, it nonetheless does so only in order to create new branches of production or to make those which are not yet fully developed ripe for the loss of value and for mass production; this absorbs once again great masses of living labor into capitalist production, and the labor population that has been made redundant is again incorporated into an extended level of the production of value and surplus value.

But both essential forms or moments of the process of capitalist expansion are today starting to come up against absolute material limits. The saturation point of capitalization was reached in the 1960s; this source of the absorption of living labor has come to a final standstill. At the same time, the confluence in microelectronics of natural-scientific technology and the science of labor implies a fundamentally new stage in the revolution of the material labor process. The microelectronic revolution does not eliminate living labor in immediate production only in this or that specific productive technology, but sets out on a wider front, throughout all branches of production, seizing even the unproductive areas. This process has only just started, and will not fully gain traction until the second half of the 1980s; it seems likely that it will continue until the end of the century and beyond. To the extent that new branches of production are created by means of this process, such as in the production of microelectronics itself or in gene technology, they are by their nature from the outset not very labor-intensive with respect to immediate production. This brings about the collapse of the historical compensation that has existed up until this point for the absolute immanent limit, embedded within relative surplus value, to the capitalist mode of production. The elimination on a massive scale of living productive labor as a source of the creation of value can no longer be recuperated by newly mass-produced cheap products, since this process of mass production is no longer mediated by a process of reintegrating a labor population that has been made superfluous elsewhere. This brings about a historically irreversible overturning of the relationship between the elimination of living productive labor through scientification on the one hand, and the absorption of living productive labor through processes of capitalization or through the creation of new branches of production on the other: from now on, it is inexorable that more labor is eliminated than can be absorbed. All technological innovations that are to be expected will also tend only in the direction of the further elimination of living labor, all new branches of production will from the outset come to life with less and less direct human productive labor.

Social production's objective departure from the limits of the fictitious objectivity of value must sooner or later make its presence felt clearly and with full force. The idea that a commodity, as a material product that we can see before us, is an objectivity of value, has become so commonsensical as the dominant fetish concept for the abstract individuals of commodity production that Marxists occasionally forget what value really is — namely the socially real fiction of objectified human labor in context of the immediate production process. One need only, like Habermas and company, omit the attribute "immediately" or even attribute a mystical creation of value to the directly social labor that goes into whole ranges of products only in an indirect and undifferentiated manner, in order to arrive at this fetishistic result and completely to fail to recognize the explosive force of the problem.

That the content of value is in the process of disappearing from society does not of course by a long way mean that the social forms of circulation that arise from it must themselves peter out. For the interests of the exploiters are also indissolubly dependent on them.

Capital, which has as its essential core the "miserable foundation" of wealth as the exploitation of living labor, and simultaneously dissolves this foundation through its own movement, will try — must try — with all force to maintain the value as value, that is to say, to allow the form to continue as the general form of circulation, even as it becomes empty, robbed of its social content. This must lead to catastrophic social collisions.

The new and final crisis of capitalism is fundamentally different from previous crises. All the crises that have happened up until now were crises of the growth of capital which could only temporarily interrupt the process of accumulation; the new crisis, however, reveals itself to be the end of the process of the accumulation of abstract wealth itself, because concrete material wealth can no longer be engendered within the limits of the value relation. The new crisis is thus no temporary crisis of overaccumulation or overproduction, but rather a crisis of the creation of value itself, from which there can no longer be a way out for capital.

That the crisis which in the 1970s finally ended the phase of accumulation and of general prosperity after World War II promises by its nature to become such a final crisis of capital, and differs in its fundamental characteristics from all previous crisis processes, can be confirmed today by two surface manifestations of a new kind.

First, the crisis begins to make itself visible not only as a market crisis of capital and of commodities, but as a crisis of money itself. Inflation, which even as a concept was almost unheard of before World

War I, but which erupted, above all in Germany, as a consequence of the capitalist war economy after the world wars, has meanwhile become a permanent feature both in the imperialist countries and in the Third World. The astounding process in which not only products are devalued in competition, but also money itself, across the whole society and worldwide, has a very simple cause: the fact that with the monstrous development of technological productivity, material wealth can no longer be expressed in the money commodity of gold. Until World War I there was still a universal gold standard, that is to say that the banknotes of all important industrialized countries could be directly converted into gold. Since then, material productivity has exceeded the money commodity, gold, to an ever-increasing extent. The umbilical cord of the gold standard was finally cut at the start of the 1970s with the abandonment of the Bretton Woods system — that is, even the dollar, the global currency, was irreversibly decoupled from the gold standard. But this means nothing other than the successive suspension of money as a commodity, for paper money, released in volumes with no gold backing, no longer contains any real substance of value, with the single exception of the negligible amount of labor involved in its manufacture. This has come to hold universally for paper money, and also for money that exists purely for the purposes of accounting, and all the more so for the fantastic and purely juridical creations out of nothing such as the artificial world money of the Special Drawing Rights (SDR) of the International Monetary Fund, which can only circulate between the central banks. But the disappearance of the substance value of money only reflects the overall tendency for value to disappear, the fact that material production goes beyond the limits of value.

This in no way means that the old view of the vulgar economists, castigated by Marx, of money's purely technical function had become reality, but rather that the mode of production and circulation that relies on money loses to an ever greater extent its real content, that the socially real fiction of value becomes unreal, and its fictional character begins to appear as such on the surface. Value is transformed into an empty shell that no longer measures up to the material content. Capital and the capitalist politicians and experts of course try to maintain value as value under all circumstances, and to save the abstraction of money as real abstraction whatever the cost: the currency-related and other monetary manipulations are becoming more and more intricate, complicated, and incredible. In the few years, seen from a historical perspective, since the Bretton Woods system was abandoned, the international monetary and credit systems have already been on the point of collapse on several occasions, and this collapse will emerge as a worldwide failure of the banks as the collapse of the international credit system and a wave of currency reforms leading to the effective expropriation of large swathes of the population, and will not allow itself to be postponed forever. The new dimension of a final historical crisis of capital must ultimately assert itself in all force from the monetary side, as the insoluble crisis of money, even if through many attempts by currency and credit experts to decelerate the process.

But the second fundamentally new manifestation which suggests the end of capitalist logic is the appearance since the mid-1970s of mass unemployment that is independent of the economic cycle, and has climbed relentlessly, more or less independently of the cyclical development — and its visible trend is that it will continue to climb. In the previous development of capital, it has on several occasions seemed for short periods of time that such a process was imminent, but each time it was absorbed by a new accumulation drive. On the whole, the state of unemployment followed the cycle of the accumulation of capital, the absorption and emission of living labor power in the immediate process of capitalist production. These previously valid economic laws have been rendered inoperative in all the core imperialist countries for over a decade. Even some serious bourgeois economists are seeing a relentless trend that on the basis of the financial economy will necessarily bring about apocalyptic unemployment figures and a desperate collapse of the social safety net by the end of the century. All talk on the part of bourgeois politicians of a prayed-for boom and of consolidation in the world economy must be measured against this remorseless logic.

The boom in the mid-1980s that was confined to a few countries with the highest productivity left mass unemployment almost untouched even in these countries. That at present unemployment seems stagnant and is not already noticeably higher is to be attributed more to statistical tricks and manipulations of the capitalist administration of labor, the task of which is to lead the public to accept the most favorable picture of the situation, than to an actual interruption in the process of redundancy of living immediate productive labor. And furthermore, for many branches of production, and also most of the unproductive areas, the microelectronic revolution of production still lies ahead. Every imaginable future boom for remaining sectors of capital will not put a fundamental halt to the growth in mass unemployment.

One ought now to confront the probably inescapable objection that the theory of the devaluation of value outlined here is false and potentially utopian for the reason that it presupposes as the social average the absolute and complete automation of production as a whole, the ghost factory, devoid of humans and so on. Such an objection would be naïve for the reason that it does not take into account the logic of the accumulation of capital as it is conditioned by the production of relative surplus value, but instead remains caught in inflexible definitions. The collapse of the value relation does not wait until the elimination of the last worker from immediate production before starting, but rather begins at precisely that historical point when the general relation between the elimination and the reabsorption of living immediate productive labor begins to overturn — that is, as early as the moment (and to a growing extent afterwards) when (and how) more living immediate productive labor is eliminated then is reabsorbed. This point, to the extent that it can be called a point at all, has probably already been passed, approximately in the early- to mid-1970s: it is no coincidence that both the collapse of the Bretton Woods monetary system and the start of technological mass unemployment took place within this period. And one must not, of course, imagine the collapse of the value relation as a sudden and one-off event (even though sudden declines and collapses such as bank failures and mass bankruptcies will very much be part of this collapse), but rather as a historical process, a whole epoch lasting perhaps several decades, in which the capitalist world economy can no longer escape from the maelstrom of crisis and processes of devaluation, surging mass unemployment, and the class struggles that will sooner or later inevitably follow.

It is worth noting as an aside that this development also provides the adjudication of an old debate as to the capability of capitalism to continue developing its productive forces. It is astonishing that this question was most frequently applied to the matter of whether capitalism could further propel material productivity as such; whether it could, even in its monopolistic stage, drive the process of scientification beyond a particular level. Capitalism's chances of survival were then evaluated according to the way in which this question was answered. It is not difficult to recognize by means of the conceptual definition developed above the extent of the fundamental falsity even of asking this question, how severely it misunderstands authentic Marxism and the objective logic of capital. What is in fact reached is not the limit of the development of productive forces, but the limit of the objectivity of value. It is not the case that capitalism can simply continue to develop the material forces of production: it must do so relentlessly in accordance with the logic of its own development. "The real limit of capitalist production is capital itself": that is, value. The objective failure of capital comes about as a result not of the development of material productivity itself, but of the compulsion magically to constrain the immense social potential of science and technology within the limits of value. This is the only way to understand the Marxist claim that capitalism must perish at the hand of the "development of the productive forces."

Inversion through Competition

Why can capital not see that it is historically digging its own grave due to its reliance on the production of relative surplus value by way of the development of productive forces? I have already drawn attention to the fact that the category of relative surplus value (and indeed that of surplus value itself) is no surface category that could appear in the consciousness of the representatives of self-valorizing monetary capital. The reason for this can ultimately be found in the fact that capital can never truly appear as total capital, but only ever — in whatever form — as competing individual capital. The category of value presupposes that of exchange, and thus in some form or other private producers who are in formal economic terms independent of one another. Even in highly developed forms of state capitalism in which the state appears not only as the ideal, but increasingly also as the real total capitalist, these fundamental facts cannot really be suspended. As long as the value relation exists within society at all, and with it production oriented toward the production of value, which in turn is expressed in the money form as universal form of circulation, the standpoint of the whole is in reality a practical impossibility. The state and its authorities can take up the perspective of the totality of the process of social reproduction only in a formal and external manner, but not according to its content (since the state as such is already the expression of the economic separation of social partial producers and their asociality within production). Moments of competition must therefore always develop anew and regrow like the heads of the hydra, even at the level of circulation between different states. For individual capital, the process is in its entirety only recognizable from the standpoint of participants in the struggle over markets. For the capitalist state as ideal (and increasingly real in regards to external exchange value) total capitalist, the process is only recognizable from the standpoint of the representative of a nation's total capital in the struggle over markets and spheres of influence. For an imperialist bloc, the process reveals itself from the standpoint of a coalition of different national capitals struggling for markets and political and military zones of influence against another competing bloc.

In these competitive struggles the process of the production of value in no way appears in a manner in accordance with the theoretical concept of social total reproduction, the standpoint of which is taken up by practically nobody. While the oppositional, tendentially self-cancelling movement in the production of relative surplus value is visible from the perspective of total reproduction, it is utterly invisible from the perspective of competing individual capital. In total reproduction, the production of relative surplus value appears as absurd, because it brings about an increase in the rate of surplus value at the same time as a decrease in the mass of surplus value. This holds — and not only in theory, but also in practice — exclusively for the process as a whole, but in no way for each particular capital, for which the individual increase in the rate of profit (extra profit) through an increase in productivity is not paid for in the slightest by a simultaneous decrease in the mass of profit. The logic of the development of productivity consists in the production, in the same time period, of more products with less human labor power. Considered in the abstract (that is, every individual capital taken for itself), the absurd countermovement of relative surplus value — that is, that more value is appropriated per worker, while at the same time the absolute mass of the newly created value decreases, because in total less living productive labor has been employed — would also reveal itself on this level of the individual capital. However, this consideration remains abstract for the reason that the individual capital does not of course only reproduce itself for itself, but within the competitive relationship of many capitals among themselves. The production of surplus value and its realization in circulation — that is, in processes of exchange on the market — diverge from one another. It thus becomes necessary to clarify what takes place by means of the competition relation between production and realization in circulation.

When an individual capital doubles the productivity of its total aggregate (dead labor in the form of machines and living labor are not distinct from the standpoint of capital, but both appear in the same way as input-cost factors) while at the same time reducing the amount of living labor involved in the process, this brings about in the first instance a reduction of the input costs (the amortization of the improved machinery has already been taken into account), while at the same time the amount of material products produced is increased — in this instance, doubled. However, because of the reduction in living labor, a smaller mass of value falls on this increased quantity of individual products, and therefore also on each individual product. But the absolute reduction in the mass of value thus only appears within an individual capital with the increase in its individual productivity. Each individual product of the productive capital contains less value than the corresponding social-average product, but this social average alone is valid on the market. As far as the monetary expression of the value of the commodity is concerned, and this is the only matter of practical interest, it is thus also in itself twice as high for the more productive capital, since it appears on the market with twice as great a quantity of material products that have the average social value of this product, which is still valid on the market. It is true that this monetary expression is in the first instance only the price, and not yet the realization through sale, for the doubled quantity of commodities enters a limited market with limited purchasing power. But of course, the more productive capital now has, compared with all the other participants in the market, vast room for maneuver which it can use to lower its price and to find buyers for its doubled quantity of commodities. For even if this capital must, in order to conquer the market share necessary for the doubled quantity of material products, now sell its doubled quantity of products below the average social value that holds at the time, the relationship between the absolute input costs and absolute output as yield has in any case shifted hugely in its favor.

Here the inversion of the true situation of society as a whole through the movement of competition becomes clear. In the total social reproduction of capital as a whole, the reduction of living productive labor, wherever it takes place, naturally also leads to a reduction in the total mass of value. But the very capital that achieves this reduction in living labor appropriates for itself a higher profit in doing so. The true process that appears in such an inverted form for the individual capital at the surface of the market is the fault of the liquidity of abstract exchange value, money, in comparison with the inflexibility and bulkiness of the mass of material products. The mass of value presented in material use values and the mass of the liquid money commodity stand in a perpetually oscillating compensatory relation to one another, a relation that is produced by disproportionalities, and that takes on incredibly complex forms at the level of the world market. If the German and Japanese automobile industries develop higher labor productivity than, for example, the English, this in itself means that every car produced in Germany and Japan contains a smaller amount of abstract human labor, a smaller mass of value, that is, if we take as our basis the real social fiction of the objectivity of value of things. Furthermore, it means that in absolute terms, a smaller mass of value is produced in the automobile industries of Germany and Japan than in the English industry, at any rate as long as no additional productive capacity is constructed. But on the surface of the market, this situation appears completely different: precisely because of their higher productivity, their employment of less living labor, the German and Japanese automobile capitalists produce more cost-efficiently than their English counterparts, which is the only criterion that is of interest to the vulgar, abstract bourgeois economic understanding, and can therefore offer their products on the market more affordably, and can kick the English suppliers out of the market and nonetheless record yet another extra profit at their bottom line.

In fact, what has happened is the following: in spite of the fact that they in fact produce less value, the German and Japanese automobile capitalists can capture a greater mass of the liquid money commodity in the process of realization of surplus value than their English competitors — that is, they have actually appropriated, by means of redistribution on the world market, a portion of the surplus value that is produced in England. On the surface of the market, the inversion of the true movement thus appears. The capital that reduces in absolute terms the total capitalist amount of value (which is as such the concern of no particular capital) through higher productivity and the elimination of immediate living productive labor — that saws, that is, at the bough of capitalism itself — is rewarded by extra profit and a greater market share, while at the same time the capital that employs more living productive labor (per commodity) and therefore maintains the total mass of value, and value as value, is punished by the loss of market share and the nonrealization of the surplus value that it has produced.

In the totality of this process of redistribution, the inescapable law of value is accounted for by the fact that the English automobile industry sits on a portion of its products — that these products, that is, only represent material use value, but can no longer serve as exchange values. What happens to these devalued use values is obvious: they are obviously not given to the poor, but initially stored, and then, depending on their material properties, either completely destroyed or reprocessed into raw materials and component parts: pulped, melted down, burned, thrown into the sea, whatever, but in any case destroyed as use values because they found no grace at the court of the queen of the commodities, money. All over the world, every day, every hour, use values of all kinds are thus wantonly destroyed on an ever-growing scale. Humanity sacrifices hecatombs of objectified labor torture in more and more frenzied insanity to the dark, incomprehensible god of its own socialization, the law of exchange value. The ancient families of the gods ought to explode with envy. This insanity only becomes possible by means of the divergence of production and circulation, by means of the liquidity of money and the perpetual redistribution of surplus value, mediated by competition, on the world market.

It is this inversion through competition that averts capital's gaze from the consequences of this process on the level of the reproduction of society as a whole, consequences that are fatal for capital's own mode of production. What Marx writes about capital as the process of its own objective self-abolition thus becomes clear for the first time:

> To the degree that labor time — the mere quantity of labor
> — is posited by capital as the sole determinant element, to
> that degree does direct labor and its quantity disappear as

the determinant principle of production — of the creation of use values — and is reduced both quantitatively, to a smaller proportion, and qualitatively, as an, of course, indispensable but subordinate moment, compared to general scientific labor, technological application of natural sciences, on one side, and to the general productive force arising from social combination in total production on the other side — a combination which appears as a natural fruit of social labor (although it is a historic product). Capital thus works toward its own dissolution as the form dominating production.[8]

For a short period, in the context of history, of almost a hundred years, the logic of the self-abolition of capital remained hidden, while the process of the expansion of capital still found terrain for its further development in the capitalization of noncapitalist branches of production, and the creation of new labor-intensive industries. If this process of expansion is today starting to come up against absolute limits, the inversion through competition is of course not suspended — quite the opposite, competition is accentuated, and the process of scientification is accelerated, with all the consequences it has for society as a whole. There has already existed since the beginning of the 1970s — that is, since the start of the phase that remains uncomprehended even today of the overturning of the historical logic of capital — a foreseeable trend according to which the world market's room for maneuver is beginning inexorably to shrink: a new (and, I assert on the basis of the above derivation, final) stage of the struggle over the markets has come to pass, which can be negotiated neither by economic nor by political and military means. At the periphery of the capitalist industrial societies, in countries such as Spain, Portugal, and Greece, and to an extent even in the core imperialist countries such as France, Italy, and Great Britain, the remorseless process of redistribution of surplus value, the mass of which is shrinking worldwide because of the new level of material socialization, is already leading to agony in whole branches of industry; even the FRG has not remained unaffected (viz. steel- and shipyard crisis).

The frontrunners and crisis profiteers in this process of redistribution that is becoming ever narrower — primarily Japan, the FRG, and (to a somewhat lesser extent) the United States — are trying to invoke the upturn and to deny the job-killing consequences of the new socializing technologies. In fact, the inversion through competition makes it appear on the surface as if the victors in the process, mediated through competition, of the realization and redistribution of global surplus value not only assert their position but are even able temporarily to expand their capacity for production, thus creating new jobs, and once again raising by a small amount the absolute mass of surplus value created in their country. This expansion, absolutely real for the countries and individual capitals that bring it about, is, within the total process of reproduction of world capital, only the semblance of an expansion. It is not based on a process of expansion of capital as a whole, which has reached its historical limits, but exclusively on the destruction of other capitals. The extra jobs are not created by means of microelectronics, but by the destruction of jobs, capital, and commodities in other countries and by other capitals. The situation that a capital can no longer grow by means of expansion into a historically free terrain, but can do so only at the expense of other capitals, which in previous periods of capitalist development was confined to periodic crises, now becomes a permanent normality that can no longer be suspended. In the last ages of the capital relation, the inversion through competition thus necessary leads to a spiralling cycle of ever-worsening trade wars. The provisional victories of the FRG and of Japan in the theater of war that is the world market will sooner or later have to be seen as pyrrhic victories, and indeed, to the same extent that the world market will tend to fragment through the political "iron curtain" of protectionism (which despite all the purely ideological assertions to the contrary has spread constantly since those ominous years of the early 1970s), thus to throttle the export economy, the true motor of Japan's and the FRG's economic development.

But since the character masks of capital (including a value- and wage-fetishizing trade union movement as the character mask of variable capital) are only oriented toward the surface of appearances and can thus only move within the inversions of the true process by competition on the world market, they all see only a single solution and all sound the same trumpet: Yet more rationalization! Yet more scientification! Just don't get left behind in the technological race! And they are right — save that with every small advantage that is achieved on the world market, they dig the grave of the total system of the valorization of value, this world beyond which they are neither able nor willing to think. In the last decades of the twentieth century, and at the start of the twenty-first, the nations, as character masks of the self-valorization of value, will thus present the image of a lunatic pack of wolves that tear themselves apart over an ever-smaller scrap of value. All political and potentially military conflicts of this new epoch will (increasingly) no longer be mere epiphenomena of the process of capitalist accumulation, but the immediate expression of the historical end of this accumulation — that is, the burning out of capitalist logic itself. The relation between economics and politics thus takes on a new quality.

Crisis and Theories of Crisis

To conclude, I should like now briefly to address the question of why Marxist theory has not up until now developed the true dimension of capitalist logic and its crisis that is at least implicitly contained within Marx's work. In this context, the historical rudiments of Marxist crisis theory are the first point of interest. It is well known that Marx, in accordance with the fragmentary character of his gargantuan complete works, did not leave behind a unified theory of crisis. The third volume of *Capital* and *Theories of Surplus Value*, in which the fundamental statements on crisis theory can be found, consist wholly of such fragments that have not been conclusively developed. This editorial point of departure alone has historically led to a situation in which, in the Marxist debate, individual aspects of the crisis theory left behind by Marx that were not completely developed into a system have been given existences independent of one another.

The oldest layer of interpretation of Marxist crisis theory in the Second International presents itself purely as a theory of overproduction or of underconsumption (Engels, Kautsky, Luxemburg). For this theory of overproduction, the crisis as such is really very simply a result of the contradiction between the development of productivity of labor on one hand, and the shortage of the purchasing power of the masses, restricted to the reproduction of the value of the commodity labor power, on the other. But the weakness of this apparently obvious interpretation is twofold. Firstly, it derives the crisis as a pure phenomenon of circulation, and not from the production of surplus value itself, the ancestor of the illusions of political intervention into the capitalist process of reproduction (strengthen mass purchasing power) that appear even today. But secondly, it assumes as its foundation the simple reproduction of total capital, and not the historical fact of the expansion of capital as a relation of production, mediated through the production of relative surplus value. In simple reproduction, the evidence of the contradiction between restricted mass consumption and the development of productivity would come to light immediately; even this manifest contradiction, however, would be a derived surface phenomenon that itself ought first to be attributed to the fundamental tendency of value to be suspended in immediate production. However, access to the true logic of the development of capital was first of all completely blocked by the actual expansion and continually extended reproduction of capital as a historical mechanism of compensation, and thus continued to remain hidden and inaccessible to theorists of crisis, whose crisis theory was obsessed by circulation. Only Rosa Luxemburg tried to incorporate a systematic historical moment into the theory of crisis, and to present it as the logic of the development of capital with absolute limits — unfortunately, however, in accordance with the starting point that was restricted to circulation, in a directly inverted form, as the supposed support of the capitalist realization of surplus value through non- and precapitalist producers (or consumers), rather than as the compensatory expansion of the mass of surplus value through the incorporation of living productive labor on an ever-larger scale.

There thus existed in the Second International a widespread idea as to the (potentially imminent) collapse of capitalism, but only as a vague idea that was not adequately conceptually derived, and not at all derived from the split in the concept of productive labor and the suspension of the objectivity of value itself — with the exception of Rosa Luxemburg's inverted form, the idea of collapse hardly found explicit formulation as a theory at all. The idea thus became easy prey for Bernsteinian revisionism, which could flatly appeal to the surface development of the higher level of capital expansion that was appearing at the turn of the century. Kautskyanism's insistence on orthodoxy, in contrast, remained wooden, dogmatic, and defensive, particularly concerning the question of the collapse. Whereas Bernstein had reproached Marx for his theory of collapse, admittedly without being able to give it concrete expression in concepts, and drew attention to the opposing empirical reality of (expanding) capital, Kautsky responded with the tame assertion that such a theory of collapse did not exist. Both Bernstein and Kautsky, that is, ultimately saw the surmounting of capitalism as invested only in the social action of the proletariat, not in a fundamental objective collapse of the circumstances themselves. Their positions, therefore, only differ from one another in the nuances. In the growing imperialist expansion of capital, the idea of collapse appeared as a sort of naïve belief, something like the belief among the early Christians that the messiah would soon come again and bring about the end of the world and the last judgment — and its few theoretical and political proponents such as Rosa Luxemburg were pushed to the periphery. Since then, one could speak of a reformist subjectivism, that was later complemented by a revolutionary subjectivism of Western Marxism, to an extent in the wake of the Frankfurt School.

It is easy to explain why Russian Bolshevism was unable to bring about any reversal in this respect. While it is true that Lenin defended objectivity as such, philosophically and politically, against reformist and ultra-Left insurrectionist subjectivism, he was nonetheless at least as far removed from an objective theory of crisis and collapse as the Western social democrats and revolutionaries. In his work on imperialism, crisis theory is touched on only briefly, and this is in no way a coincidence. For Russia, where capitalism was not developed in the slightest, was of course worlds removed from the burning out of the logic of capitalist accumulation, much further than Western capitalism (a fact that might well still be true today). Lenin thus found no social basis whatsoever for the conceptual derivation and further development of Marxist crisis theory. Neither in the East nor in the West, as I suggested above, did the revolutions or the revolutionary movements at the end of World War II rely in any way on any fundamental economic crises, but on the shattering of circumstances in the first instance by the war itself, by the existence for themselves of the political collisions of capital at a time as a whole still in a period of historical growth.

For this reason, Lenin's prime theoretical concern could only be the analysis of a particular, actually attained level — precisely that of imperialist, highly concentrated capital, punctuated with elements of state capitalism, which in its historical expansion as a whole had in no way come up against absolute material limits — and to present this level as the objective foundation not of a collapse of historical accumulation as such and as a whole, but of the political collision of national imperialist capital and of the resulting potential conscious political action of the working class, which the world over would be able to bring the process of capitalist development to a standstill. It was only to this extent that he could speak of imperialism as the "last and highest stage of capitalism." And to this extent the Bolshevik revolution and that within it which was specifically socialist were in the first instance politically determined, both with immediate respect to the capitalist development of Russian society and on a larger scale with respect to the worldwide, international situation of the development of capitalist logic as a whole. It was not possible to develop an adequate crisis theory on this theoretical basis of Leninism. This lack took revenge immediately in the fact that Lenin was perceptibly wrong in his assessment of the ripeness for revolution in the West. It would be downright mean to condemn him for this error (which was hardly avoidable given his starting position) with the benefit of hindsight; his rightful task as a revolutionary was to exploit all theoretical possibilities for the truly preexistent revolutionary situation.

In the Marxist debate and polemic the emphasis was on politics, the relative independence of which was exaggerated to an ever greater extent, resulting in the dogmatic reification of the political sphere and a complete conceptual divergence of economics and politics. The global economic crisis at the beginning of the 1930s thus found Marxist crisis theory in a weaker state than ever, armed only with rusted and worn-out weapons. Henryk Grossman, who had reopened the debate over Rosa Luxemburg's theory of collapse and sought critically to refound it, remained, like Paul Mattick who joined him, relatively lonely and without any real representation in the main theoretical currents. In their critique of Rosa Luxemburg, Grossman and Mattick correctly retreated from circulation to the production of surplus value itself, and determined the essence of the crisis as the overaccumulation of capital, which in the sphere of circulation can appear as overproduction, but is not essentially determined by this fact. This development in crisis theory came at the cost that it dispensed with the inverted theory of Rosa Luxemburg that remained fixated on circulation along with its fruitful account of an historically absolutely finite developmental logic of capital. The reason for this can be found in the fact that Grossman and Mattick went back to the process of production, but not to the contradiction between the development of productivity and production's objectivity of value. To this extent they therefore remained, like all previous crisis theorists, restricted and value-immanent, and thus unable to identify the contradiction in the concept of productive labor itself. Grossman's attempt to adhere to theory of collapse all the same thus remained restricted to a highly dubious value-immanent mathematical example, which (like the earlier crisis debate) took as its starting point not the conceptual derivation of value and of productive labor, but the "schemata of reproduction" of the second volume of *Capital*, and which thus remained from the start apprehended within the surface-level mediations of the market. Paul Mattick thus ultimately no more adhered to a concretely derivable theory of collapse than did Grossman.

It thus becomes clear that Marxist crisis theory, so far, has in fact not moved beyond a value-immanent mode of observation, and has not seized on the elements of a logical-historical explosion of the value relation as such are included in Marx's work. Both in theories that pertain to the realization of surplus value and in those that refer to its production, the question of the crisis is only examined within the horizon of the quantitative value relation and its analysis; the disproportionality is examined only within the quantitative logic of value, and not as a qualitative disproportionality in the relation between matter and value. In other words, it is not the value relation itself that becomes obsolete through the crisis, but only the blind mechanism of regulation by means of the market; it is not the value relation itself that collapses, but merely the relative balance of exchange value. At this point the abbreviated understanding of the law of value that was set out at the beginning of this essay reappears in the theory of the crisis debate. It would admittedly be a mistake to raise only an ahistorical and therefore abstract charge at this point. For this theoretical abbreviation is only the ideal expression (made on the basis of Marxism) of an epoch in which the capital relation is even tangibly going through crisis only within the limits of the value relation, and the threshold beyond which the value relation will begin to collapse has not yet been reached. This threshold is only being reached today with the new socializing technologies, in which applied natural science and labor science converge, and thus for the first time allow the industrial system to emerge from its crude embryonic forms. To this extent the unfortunate term "postindustrialism" completely misrecognizes the true development. Capitalism can today be historically deciphered as identical with the coarse, awkward, immature, and in every respect dirty predecessor form of the truly immediately social industry that only today is growing out of the spore of capitalism, which it thus explodes irrevocably.

The socialist and communist Left, however, is even worse prepared for the coming and in parts already visible crisis than at the start of the 1930s. The new epoch of accumulation and prosperity after World War II has completely weakened its logical force, just as it also left the practical and political old labor movement mutilated and emasculated. The thought of a theory of collapse elicits knowing winks even from so-called radicals, even though the problem has never been conceptually or theoretically explained, but has merely languished in the swamp of empirical surface reality. And questions as to the determinations in the work of Marx and Engels of a social reproduction that is not founded on value and thus functions without money still triggers at best a sheepish laugh from the Left. Marxist theorists oriented both to the Western and to the Eastern strand of the labor movement have long since repressed, forgotten, and buried the fundamental critique of the value relation — value as such is unconsciously accepted as second nature. All socialist aims, strategies, and praxes refer not to the suspension of the value relation (and thus of wage labor) but purely and simply to the form of the mechanism of social allocation through the law of value. The result is the absolutely vapid opposition between plan and market, where the concept of social planning remains subject to the value fetish. The suspension of the abstract individual of commodity production, necessarily missing from this account, must, as is demonstrated particularly repugnantly by the actually existing police socialism of the East, unthinkingly be shifted back onto the subject. It is no coincidence, then, that the alienation debate of the New Left in part leads to neoreligiosity and spiritualism. But the radical spring of the subjective political Left since 1968 has also come to an end without even a whimper. In any case, all theories and suggestions of the Left in the broadest sense that refer to the new social manifestations, regardless of whether they are orthodox Marxist or Left-wing socialist or green-alternative (Gorz) have one thing in common, that they shirk from the question of objective and subjective suspension of the value relation. But the new crisis of capital, the content of which is a development of productivity that suspends value, cannot be solved or even merely impeded either by external political state intervention (Keynesianism, state capitalism) or by naïve sociopolitical bricolages such as in the models of the dual economy (Gorz, Huber).

In saying this I do not in any way wish fundamentally to belittle the role of the subject: any true revolution must proceed by means of the subject of a social class and its political mediations. And it would be a particularly great misunderstanding to derive from the concrete delineation of an objective logic of the collapse of capital that is historically becoming a reality some sort of mechanical automatism of the transition to socialism. The opposite is rather the case. The Marxian alternative that includes the possibility of a transition to barbarism is only today becoming real, and therefore also for the first time understandable. For a collapse is precisely nothing other than a collapse: what actual circumstances develop out of it always depend and will continue to depend on the concrete actions and will of human beings. But these will not and cannot move beyond the objective circumstances that they must have understood in their objectivity in order to be able to become consciously effective.

However, no fundamental historical change has taken place that has its cause in the actual maturity of the capital relation. Even for the old labor movement, which had its point of historical culmination and its chance at the end of World War I, the objectivity of capital and of its development was the foundation and precondition of acts of political will, but in a more general sense than today. The logic of capital had not yet burned out, but could only be halted and overcome by means of social action that had been carried over this logic by highly developed consciousness. The potential for this certainly existed, but the Western labor movement, which alone could have come into consideration for this act, had not reached this height of consciousness. But history has not stood still because of this. Logic that has not been understood also remains objective and real, becomes something that can be experienced, and ultimately causes suffering — until consciousness and will turn to objectivity because it is no longer possible to do otherwise. To the extent that capitalist logic is burning out and decaying, this compulsion begins to become manifest.

It certainly matters whether proletarian action consciously brings about the end of capitalist accumulation when it is in itself not yet completely exhausted, or whether, conversely, consciousness and action on the part of the working class are driven into existence by the historical end of the possibility of accumulation that objectively becomes manifest, independent of the will of those it affects. In the first case, the organized class consciously takes advantage of temporary disproportionalities and political and military frictions of the existing order in order to topple this order. Historically, these possibilities have passed by unused, and no path leads back to this situation. In the second case — which is historically current and for the most part lies before us — this order overturns as a consequence of its own contradictions and collapses into itself without at the same time bringing about a new social formation — neither the role of the subject nor the relative independence of the political form of the contradiction is thereby suspended, but the point of departure has changed. The often cited *"hic Rhodus, hic salta!"* is irreversibly becoming reality for the Left, but not in the way it had imagined.

Notes

1. Literally "Founder Epoch" (at times translated as "promoterism"), *Gründerzeit* designates the economic period in Germany and Austria in the ninteenth century that immediately precedes the great stock market crash of 1873. [Eds.]

2. For a more detailed discussion of this point, see Karl Marx, "Chapter Fourteen: Division of Labour and Manufacture" (in particular Section Five, "The Capitalistic Character of Manufacture"), *Capital: A Critique of Political Economy*, Volume I, trans. by Ben Fowkes, (New York: Penguin, 1976) 455-491 (480-491). [Eds.]

3. Michael Mauke, *Die Klassentheorie von Marx und Engels* (Frankfurt am Main: Europäische Verlagsanstalt, 1970) 156.

4. Jürgen Habermas, 'Technology and Science as "Ideology,"' *Toward a Rational Society: Student Protest, Science, and Politics*, trans. by Jeremy J. Shapiro (Boston: Beacon Press, 1970) 104.

5. *K-Gruppen* was the label given by the media to an assortment of predominantly Maoist cadre organizations that exerted a strong influence on the New Left in the late 1960s and 1970s. [Eds.]

6. Marx, *Capital*, Volume III, trans. by David Fernbach (New York: Penguin, 1993) 372-73.

7. Marx, *Capital* III 340.

8. Marx, *Grundrisse*, trans. by Martin Nicolaus (New York: Penguin, 1973) 700.

A Contradiction between Matter and Form: On the Significance of the Production of Relative Surplus Value in the Dynamic of Terminal Crisis

Claus Peter Ortlieb (2008)

While mainstream economics is under the belief that it addresses only the material side of capitalist production, and is interested in variables such as the "real" growth of GDP or "real" income — figures that are in fact themselves mediated through monetary values — most work in economics subscribing to the labor theory of value regards itself as investigating the very same "material" process of production, only here with reference to the quantities of value and surplus value realized in its products. Both sides would appear to hold to the tacit assumption that it is a question here merely of different units of measurement of wealth as such.

Against this trend, the present work, following Marx, takes as its starting point a historically specific, dual concept of wealth within capitalism, as represented by the dual character of the commodity and of labor. As the dominant form (*Form*) of wealth in capitalism, the commodity stands opposite material wealth. And while the particular form or shape (*Gestalt*) assumed by such material wealth is irrelevant for capital, as the bearer of value it remains indispensable. However, as productivity increases, these two forms of wealth necessarily begin to diverge, and do so in a way that allowed Marx to speak of capital as "moving contradiction." It is this contradiction that is to be investigated in this essay.

In carrying out this investigation, my aim is to assess — against the background of the more serious counterarguments since formulated against it — the argument advanced by Robert Kurz in "The Crisis of Exchange Value" (see this volume), first published twenty-seven years ago (1986) and the foundation of crisis theory in the former, pre-2005 *Krisis*.[1] According to Kurz's argument, capital is heading for a terminal crisis because increasing productivity means that in the long term the total social (or global) production of surplus value can only decrease, and that the valorization of capital must ultimately grind to a halt.

With respect to this diagnosis the present work does not fundamentally differ from Kurz, but it justifies it from a somewhat different angle, with reference here to the representation of the mass of surplus value at the level of society as a whole. On one hand, this mass can be determined, as with Kurz ("Crisis of Exchange Value" and "Die Himmelfahrt des Geldes") by starting from the surplus value created by the individual worker which, when multiplied by the total number of such individuals, gives us the total surplus value created by all productive workers; but it can also be determined, as it is here, by starting from the surplus value realized in a single material unit of production which, when multiplied here by the total number of such units, results in the total surplus value realized in material production.[2] These two modes of presentation do not contradict one another, yet they do allow different aspects of the same process to come into view.

In addition, the approach chosen here makes it possible to relate the dynamics of terminal crisis to capital's tendency, analyzed by Moishe Postone, toward environmental destruction.[3]

This present work contains a small core section in which the analysis is represented in mathematical terms. Anyone who cannot stand formulae should skip over them. Of greatest importance for understanding what follows are three tables and a single graph, the qualitative meaning of which can, however, also be grasped without recourse to formulae.

The Terminal Crisis of Capital? A Controversy

The crisis theory of the original (pre-2005) *Krisis* met with numerous objections and criticisms that need not be taken seriously here insofar as they merely follow their own, well-trodden paths and do not even begin to take any real cognizance of the reasoning contained in that theory. These include the dogmatic notion that since capitalism has on each occasion raised itself from its own crises like a phoenix from the ashes, it will therefore continue to do so. Not even modern positivism dares advance such a crude inductionism. Other conceptions deny the objective side of the dynamic of capitalism altogether, and emphasize that capitalism could only be overcome by a revolution or even a "voluntaristic act." This is correct insofar as the transition to a liberated society of whatever kind presupposes conscious human action. But it does not follow from this that in the absence of such a transition capitalism can continue to function without a care: it could also end in horror.

The diagnosis that draws attention to this, first put forward by Kurz in "The Crisis of Exchange Value," argues — to summarize it in broad strokes — that capital, through the compulsive increase in productivity induced by the market, digs its own grave, because it increasingly removes labor, and thus its own substance, from the surplus-value-creating process of production. In this context an exceptional role is played by "science as productive force" in general, and the "microelectronic revolution" in particular. The text can be read as a development and actualization of a well-known Marxian observation from the fragment on machines found in the *Grundrisse*: "Capital itself is the moving contradiction, [in] that it presses to reduce labor time to a minimum, while it posits labor time, on the other side, as sole measure and source of wealth."[4]

In that same passage in the *Grundrisse*, Marx remarks that this contradiction is adequate to blow the blinkered foundation of the capitalist mode of production sky-high.

Among the critics of the thesis of an inevitable, terminal crisis of capital, Michael Heinrich plays an exceptional role insofar as, at least in part, he directly engages this thesis on the level of its logical development. Since he will not hear of any tendency of capital toward collapse, he must argue against the Marx of the *Grundrisse* and does so by playing off the latter against the Marx of *Capital*.[5] Thus Heinrich:

> The value aspect of the process [of terminal capitalist crisis], which holds that less and less labor must be expended in the process of production of the individual commodities, is analyzed in *Capital* not as a tendency toward collapse, but as the foundation of the production of relative surplus value. The apparent contradiction that so astonished Marx, that capital "presses to reduce labor time to a minimum, while it posits labor time, on the other side, as sole measure and source of wealth," even becomes for Kurz, Trenkle and other representatives of the Krisis group "capital's logical self-contradiction," of which capitalism must necessarily perish. In the first volume of *Capital*, in contrast, Marx decodes this contradiction in passing as an old riddle of political economy with which the French economist Quesnay had already tortured his opponents in the eighteenth century. This riddle, Marx argues, is easy to understand as long as one takes into consideration that what is important for the capitalist is not the absolute value of the commodity, but the surplus value (or profit) that this commodity brings him. The labor time necessary for the production of the individual commodity can by all means fall, the value of the commodity can decrease, as long as the surplus value or profit produced by his capital grows.[6]

In the first instance it must be noted that Heinrich here evidently conflates two distinct levels between which a contradiction can arise: Marx does in fact decode a riddle that appeared to the economists as a logical contradiction and was indeed a defect in their theory.

But such a decoding does not of course do away with the "moving contradiction," situated as it is on the real and not just the logical plane; at most it has the potential for explaining the contradiction even as it is left undisturbed. This contradiction consists, for the Marx of the *Grundrisse*, in the fact that capital, in its unconscious internal dynamic, seals up the well from which it draws its life. Against this, Heinrich points to Marx's argument in *Capital* that the progressive increase in productivity is what grounds the possibility of generating relative surplus value, as if this progression were not itself compatible with a tendency toward collapse. Is this the case? Does there exist an incompatibility between the production of relative surplus value and capital's tendency toward its own destruction?

Kurz, in contrast, declares that

> capital itself becomes the absolute logical and historical limit in the production of relative surplus value. Capital has no interest in and cannot be interested in the absolute creation of value; it is fixated only on surplus value in the forms in which it appears at the surface, that is to say on the relative proportion within the newly created value of the value of labor power (the costs of its reproduction) to the share of the new value that is appropriated by capital. As soon as capital can no longer go on expanding the creation of value in absolute terms by extending the working day, but can only increase the relative size of its own share of the newly created value by means of the development of productivity, there arises in the production of relative surplus value a countermovement, which must consume itself historically and work towards and bring about a standstill in the process of value creation. With the development of productivity, capital increases the extent of exploitation, but in doing so it undermines the foundation and the object of exploitation, the production of value as such. For the production of relative surplus value, inseparable as it is from the progressive fusion of modern science with the material process of production, includes the tendency toward

> the elimination of living, immediate, productive labor, as the
> only source of total social value creation.[7]

Here it is not only the case that the production of relative surplus value
is in no way in contradiction with capital's tendency toward collapse:
it is also, conversely, in fact the very tool by means of which capital
itself becomes its own "absolute logical and historical limit." But in
that case the Marx of *Capital* would not have corrected the Marx of
the *Grundrisse* at all, as Heinrich claims, but only given a more precise
justification for the "moving contradiction."

Evidently (and not entirely surprisingly) what is at stake here
is a controversy. It is possible to get to the bottom of it because the
opposing parties have a common point of departure, namely the
category, introduced by Marx into the critique of political economy,
of "relative surplus value" — from which, however, many completely
different and even mutually contradictory conclusions can be drawn.
The following attempt at a contribution to clarification must therefore
return afresh to this shared point of departure. The debate, often
mentioned in the context of debates over crisis theory, between
Norbert Trenkle and Heinrich is not suitable as a reference for this
purpose, because Trenkle's view that a final crisis is approaching does
not entail an account of surplus value.[8]

Productivity, Value, and Material Wealth

We speak of an increase in productivity when in a given labor time a
greater material output, or — and this is the same thing — when a given
quantity of commodities can be produced with lower expenditure of
labor, thus decreasing their value. Productivity is thus the proportional
relationship of the material quantity of commodities to the labor time
necessary for their production. In order to understand productivity
and the change it undergoes, it is therefore urgently necessary to
distinguish between magnitude of value and material wealth.

When Marx speaks of how capital (see above) "posits labor time
[...] as sole measure and source of wealth," what is at stake is wealth
expressed in the value form. For the Marx of the *Grundrisse*, this

historically specific form of wealth, only valid in capitalist society and characterizing its "very heart," increasingly comes into opposition with "real wealth."[9]

> But to the degree that large industry develops, the creation of real wealth comes to depend less on labor time and on the amount of labor employed than on the power of the agencies set in motion during labor time, whose "powerful effectiveness" is itself in turn out of all proportion to the direct labor time spent on their production, depending rather on the general state of science and on the progress of technology, or the application of this science to production.[10]

In *Capital* Marx speaks not of "real" but of "material wealth," which is formed of use values. This term is more appropriate for the reason that even material wealth in developed capitalist society is not the same as in noncapitalist societies: rather, the configurations in which it appears are themselves shaped by wealth in the value form. At this point it is sufficient to register that in capitalist society these two different forms of wealth must be conceptually distinguished from one another. "The wealth of societies in which the capitalist mode of production prevails appears as an 'immense collection of commodities.'"[11] And in the dual character of commodities, the fact that they are bearers both of value and use value, one can see reflected the two different forms of wealth in these societies.

Value is the predominant, nonmaterial form of wealth in capitalism — in this regard the actual character of material wealth in the value form is irrelevant. Capitalist economic activity aims solely at increasing this form of wealth (valorization of value), which finds its expression in money. Economic activity that promises no surplus value cannot continue, no matter how much material wealth it could produce. Why, indeed, should someone cast his capital into the process of production, when at the end of the process he would receive at most just as much value as he had put in?

Material wealth — according to Postone, characteristic of noncapitalist societies as their dominant form of wealth — is measured, in contrast, in use values to which society has direct access and which can serve extremely varied and completely different purposes.[12] 500 tables, 4,000 pairs of trousers, 200 hectares of land, fourteen lectures on nanotechnology, or even thirty cluster bombs would in this respect all be material wealth. Firstly, material wealth is not necessarily generated by labor, nor is it (as in the case of the air we breathe) necessarily bound to the commodity form, even if it is (as in the case of land) frequently brought into this form. Secondly, material wealth does not necessarily consist just of material goods, but can also comprise knowledge, information, other immaterial goods, and their distribution. Thirdly, it is important to guard against seeing in material wealth what is "good" as such. Although material wealth is not bound to the commodity form, and although labor is not its only source, the commodity nonetheless comprises in capitalism, conversely, the "material bearer" of value, which for its part remains bound to material wealth.[13] The aim of commodity production — that is, the accumulation of more and more surplus value — deforms as a matter of course the quality of material wealth, the producers of which are not simultaneously its consumers: the aim can never be that of maximal enjoyment in the use of material wealth, but only that of maximal microeconomic efficiency. It would not therefore be possible to overcome capitalist society if that were to consist merely in the liberation of material wealth from the compulsions of the valorization of capital; it would also, necessarily, involve the overcoming of those deformations of material wealth produced by value itself.

There is nonetheless a difference between the two forms of wealth when they are assessed in a qualitative sense. Under the material aspect, the only matter of importance is the use that can be made of things. From the perspective of wealth in the value form, in contrast, the only matter of importance as to the question of whether I, as entrepreneur, would rather produce 500 tables or thirty cluster bombs is that of the surplus value that I can obtain in each respective case.

In the concept of productivity, an abstraction takes place from the qualitative dimension of material wealth, for which reason I prefer to speak in this context of numbers of material units rather than numbers of use values. This restriction of the field of consideration here to matters of quantity is, this terminological distinction notwithstanding, still fraught with problems, because it is impossible to say whether, for example, more material wealth consists in 500 tables or in 4,000 pairs of pants — because they are qualitatively different, they are not comparable on the material level. A concept of productivity that brings both forms of wealth into relation with one another would therefore require differentiation according to the qualities which material wealth can take on: productivity in the production of tables is, or would be, different from productivity in the production of pants, and so on.

In what follows the focus is on the quantitative relationships between these two forms of wealth, both of which are created in commodity production. And while both forms are fixed in relation to each other at any give point in time, they are also, as Marx observes, in a perpetual state of flux:

> In itself, an increase in the quantity of use-values constitutes an increase in material wealth. Two coats will clothe two men, one coat will only clothe one man, etc. Nevertheless, an increase in the amount of material wealth may correspond to a simultaneous fall in the magnitude of its value. By "productivity" of course, we always mean the productivity of concrete useful labour; in reality this determines only the degree of effectiveness of productive activity directed towards a given purpose within a given period of time. Useful labour becomes, therefore, a more or less abundant source of products in direct proportion as its productivity rises or falls. As against this, however, variations in productivity have no impact whatever on the labour itself represented in value. As productivity is an attribute of labour in its concrete useful form, it naturally ceases to have any bearing on that labour as soon as we abstract from its concrete useful form. The same labour, therefore, performed for the same length of

time, always yields the same amount of value, independently of any variations in productivity. But it provides different quantities of use-values during equal periods of time; more, if productivity rises; fewer, if it falls. For this reason, the same change in productivity which increases the fruitfulness of labour, and therefore the amount of use-values produced by it, also brings about a reduction in the value of this increased total amount, if it cuts down the total amount of labour-time necessary to produce the use-values. The converse also holds.[14]

I here draw attention to this distinction between material wealth and wealth in the commodity form, the very basis upon which *Capital* is able to assume its unique propositional form and centrality to the Marxian critique of political economy, because for us, as subjects in thrall to the commodity fetish and who reproduce ourselves by means of this fetish, it cannot simply be taken as read. In our everyday life, shaped by the commodity form, each of the two forms of wealth appears as "natural" to the same extent as does the other, and indeed usually as identical. This is not only because value requires a material bearer, but also because the acquisition of use values is usually carried out by our buying them — that is, our giving out value in the money form in exchange for use values. In modern everyday life ignoring the distinction between wealth expressed in the value form and material wealth may well be unproblematic, and may well even make everyday actions easier. But any theory that papers over this distinction — or, indeed, that does not acknowledge it in the first place — will necessarily miss the historically specific core of the capitalist mode of production.

This holds — naturally, one could say — for mainstream neoclassical economic theory, for which the ahistorical aim of all economic activity consists in the maximization of individual utility, something that in turn consists in the optimal combination of "packages of goods." Abstract wealth, meanwhile, serves only as the "veil of money" that conceals the allocation of material wealth, and which therefore needs to be pulled away for the sake of greater clarity, and removed from economic theory.

The same holds for classical political economy. See David Ricardo, for example, when he writes in the preface to his major work:

> The produce of the earth — all that is derived from its surface by the united application of labor, machinery, and capital, is divided among three classes of the community; namely, the proprietor of the land, the owner of the stock or capital necessary for its cultivation, and the laborers by whose industry it is cultivated.
>
> But in different stages of society, the proportions of the whole produce of the earth which will be allotted to each of these classes, under the names of rent, profit, and wages, will be essentially different [...]
>
> To determine the laws which regulate this distribution, is the principal problem in Political Economy[.][15]

What is under discussion here is merely the distribution of material wealth, while there is no mention of the particular form of wealth in capitalism, which probably does not even come into the author's consciousness. Traditional Marxism also seems only rarely to have gone beyond this understanding. Labor, which "creates all wealth," is for traditional Marxism just as much an ahistorical natural given as the wealth which it has created. The kind of critique specific to traditional Marxism, which remains within the sphere of circulation, is only directed against the distribution of wealth as such, but not against the historically specific form of wealth in capitalism. Following Postone, it can be observed that an essential dimension of the Marxian critique of value thus remains obscured:

> [M]any arguments regarding Marx's analysis of the uniqueness of labor as the source of value do not acknowledge his distinction between "real wealth" (or "material wealth") and value. Marx's "labor theory of value," however, is not a theory of the unique properties of labor in general, but is an analysis of the historical specificity of value as a form of wealth, and of the labor that supposedly constitutes it. Consequently, it

is irrelevant to Marx's endeavour to argue for or against this theory of value as if it were intended to be a labor theory of (transhistorical) wealth — that is, as if Marx had written a political economy rather than a critique of political economy.[16]
Entire mountains of theory have been built up on this misunderstanding, criticized here by Postone, of Marx's intention. A particularly striking example is provided by Jürgen Habermas, who takes of all sources the often-cited extract from the fragment on machines from the *Grundrisse* to attribute to Marx a "revisionist notion":

> In the *Grundrisse for the Critique of Political Economy* a very interesting consideration is to be found, from which it appears that Marx himself once viewed the scientific development of the technical forces of production as a possible source of value. For here Marx limits the presupposition of the labor theory of value, that the "quantum of applied labor is the decisive factor in the production of wealth," by the following: "But as heavy industry develops the creation of real wealth depends less on labor time and on the quantity of labor utilized than on the power of mechanized agents which are set in motion during the labor time. The powerful effectiveness of these agents, in its turn, bears no relation to the immediate labor time that their labor costs. It depends rather on the general state of science and on technological progress, or the application of this science to production." [...] Marx, of course, finally dropped this "revisionist" notion: it was not incorporated in his final formulation of the labor theory of value.[17]

Completely missing Marx's point, Habermas evidently equates "real" wealth with wealth in the value form. For this is the only way in which he can imply that Marx "viewed the scientific development of the technical forces of production as a possible source of value." In doing so he deliberately overlooks the fact that in this context, a page later in the fragment on machines, Marx — as cited — speaks of capital as a "moving contradiction," which is more or less the opposite of Habermas's claim of a "revisionist notion." As Postone demonstrates, this implicit identification of wealth and value, attributed to Marx but subject to no further reflection whatsoever — and thus the ontologization of value and of labor as though they belonged to history only on the unspecified level of the human species — is the fundamental presupposition and thus results in the complete falsification that is Habermas's critique of Marx and all his attempts to go beyond Marx.[18]

Even as accomplished a value theorist as Michael Heinrich, who is thoroughly familiar with the distinction between wealth expressed in the value form and material wealth, is not always immune to the equation of these two forms of wealth. To the thesis developed by Kurz that "productive" (surplus-value-producing) labor is melting away and that the proportion of "unproductive" labor, financed by the surplus value produced by total social labor, is continually increasing, and that taken as a whole, the production of surplus value that is available to capital accumulation is sinking,[19] Heinrich objects as follows:

> increasing productivity ensures that the mass of surplus value produced by "productive" labor power grows steadily, and therefore that "productive" labor power can sustain a continually growing mass of unproductive labor.[20]

On the level of material wealth, to which alone the growing productivity of labor refers, this argument could of course, on the level of sheer possibility, turn out to be correct, but this fact has nothing to do with the "mass of surplus value produced by productive labor power," for this mass is measured simply in terms of expended labor time, on account of which the mass of surplus value produced on a single working day by labor power, however productive it is, can never be greater than this one working day.

The same mistake, perhaps borrowed from Heinrich and simply taken to extremes, can be found in the Initiative Sozialistisches Forum (ISF)'s collectively authored pamphlet "Der Theoretiker ist der Wert."[21] Here, again directed against Kurz, the possibility of a "capitalist service society" is postulated:

Let us assume that it is the case that all the "hardware" required by such a society could be produced, because of the immense productivity of labor, with minimal labor time — let us say 100,000 hours of labor in a given year X. What would prevent here the production of a mass of surplus value which would make it possible in this year X productively to cover all the money that the perhaps 10 billion service providers can save and invest at interest? Money would then concentrate in fewer hands than these 10 billion — let us say 10 million — and can be employed partly as speculative capital, but partly also as capital in competition with the producers of surplus value who work for 100,000 hours — in order in this way to secure power of disposal over society. This power of disposal over society is also a matter of importance — for in the end we still live in a class society, if also in one in which the classes, as Adorno says, have evaporated into a "super-empirical concept." The power relations in a society that is constructed in such a way still depend on — and in this society depend all the more on — the power of disposal over this "hardware"-producing labor.[22]

The question of whether or not such a society would be possible I will for the moment leave unadressed, but it is certain that there is one thing that such a society would not be, because of the impossibility of the valorization of capital, and that is capitalist. The ten million hands in which the capital would be concentrated would be allowed to exploit 100,000 working hours per year: each one, that is, one-hundredth of an hour, that is to say thirty-six seconds — nothing in comparison with a working day of perhaps eight hours, multiplied by 200 working days per year and ten billion "hands" that are fit to work. Under these conditions, why should even one of the ten million owners of capital cast his good money into the process of production? Here too, the mistake lies in the equation of the two forms of wealth: it is indeed imaginable that one day 100,000 hours of labor time per year would be sufficient to meet the needs of a population of ten billion people. But for want of a sufficient mass of surplus value, it simply will no longer pass through the eye of the needle of valorization.

It is in no way a coincidence that mistakes of this sort — made by people who should really know better — come to the surface at precisely the time when polemics are being directed at the possibility of a final crisis of capital. For the diagnosis of the necessary emergence of such a crisis essentially depends — as will presently be made clear — on the distinction between the two forms of wealth mentioned, and in the fact that they increasingly diverge from one another.

The Production of Relative Surplus Value

Marx defines as relative surplus value the surplus value that emerges as a result of the process in which, by means of the increase in the productivity of labor, and therefore the reduction in price of labor power, the necessary labor time can be shortened and the surplus labor time correspondingly increased, without lowering the real wage or lengthening the working day, as would be the case in the production of absolute surplus value.[23] The production of relative surplus value is the form of production of surplus value appropriate to developed capitalism, and is bound up with the real subsumption of labor under capital.[24]

This tendency for the productivity of labor to increase is one of the immanent laws of the capitalist mode of production, since each individual business that succeeds in raising the productivity of its own labor powers beyond the current average by the introduction of a new technology can sell its commodities for a higher profit. The consequence of this is that the new technology is universalized under the compulsive law of competition, the higher profit disappears again, and the commodity in question becomes cheaper. If this commodity belongs for its part to the supplies necessary for the reproduction of labor power — that is to say, if it is a determinant aspect of the value of labor power — its reduction in price also leads to a reduction in the price of labor power.

With the further uniform development of productivity now becoming general for all commodities (and leading to their reduction in price, including the price of the labor-power commodity itself), the necessary labor time always decreases. Yet this does not result in a reduction in the working day, but rather in a lengthening of the surplus labor time, and thus an increase in the surplus value produced on any given working day:

> Now, since relative surplus-value increases in direct proportion to the productivity of labor, while the value of commodities stands in precisely the opposite relation to the growth of productivity; since the same process both cheapens commodities and augments the surplus-value contained in them, we have here the solution to the following riddle: Why does the capitalist, whose sole concern is to produce exchange-value, continually strive to bring down the exchange-value of commodities? One of the founders of political economy, Quesnay, used to torment his opponents with this question, and they could find no answer to it.[25]

This statement by Marx, to which Heinrich (see above) also appeals, requires clarification. It is immediately obvious that the rate of surplus value and thus the proportion of surplus value in the value of a commodity increases with the productivity of labor. But the statement can also be read (and is read) as if it says that the surplus value contained within a commodity grows, although its value falls. Is this possible? And if so, is it true in the long term? It sounds at the very least improbable.

Table 1 shows a numerical example of the production of relative surplus value. It refers to a single commodity, a fixed number of material units (500 tables, 4,000 pairs of pants, or one automobile), or to a "shopping basket," an arbitrary combination of such units. The numbers represent labor time (expressed approximately in working days), by which is meant the labor time that goes into the product (including the production of the raw materials, machinery, and so on, that it requires). What is described here is the effect of a technological innovation that reduces the labor time required for production by

		value of commodity (social average) $s+v$	necessary (paid) labor v	surplus value (surplus labor) s	rate of surplus value $s'=s/v$
1	old technology	1,000	800	200	0.25
2	new technology in the individual enterprise (including extra profit)	1,000	640	360	0.5625
3	new technology across the sector (without reduction in price of labor-power)	800	640	160	0.25
4	general increase in productivity (with reduction in price of labor power)	800	512	288	0.5625

Table 1: Production of Relative Surplus Value at Low Rate

twenty percent, which is equivalent to an increase in productivity of twenty-five percent. In a working day, 125 percent of the previous quantity is produced.

With the old technology (row 1), 1,000 working days are necessary, divided into 800 working days that are necessary for the reproduction of labor power, and 200 working days that serve for the production of surplus value. A new technology is now developed in a single business (row 2), allowing the labor time required to be reduced by twenty percent, that is reduced to 640 working days. The company introduces this technology because it enables profit to be increased, and allows an advantage in innovation to be attained. As long as this technology has not been established across the entire sector, the value of the commodity remains unaffected by it, because socially average production still proceeds according to the old technology. Although the individual business can now produce the commodity twenty percent more cheaply, it can sell it at the previous price. Although only 640 days of paid labor are now employed in its production, it is still worth 1,000 working days. The individual business thus realizes an extra profit, even when it sells its commodity somewhat more cheaply than its competition in order to increase its market share.[26]

Under the compulsive laws of capitalist competition, the new technology becomes established in the entire sector (row 3) of production for the commodity in question: businesses that continued to use the old technology would become unprofitable and be driven out of the market. At the end of such a process of displacement and readjustment, all production would involve the new technology, which now corresponds to the social average. But with this the value of the commodity sinks by twenty percent, and the extra profit disappears again: compared with the previous situation, the surplus value contained in the material unit has fallen by twenty percent.

Forceably brought about by competition between individual capitals and between regional and even national economies, this counterproductive effect on the valorization of capital can be compensated for if the increase in productivity also obtains for the commodities necessary for the reproduction of labor power: if we assume an across-the-board decrease of twenty percent in the labor time necessary for commodity production (row 4), the commodity labor power also becomes cheaper by the same proportion. If wages remain constant in real terms, only 512 instead of the previous 640 working days are necessary for the reproduction of labor power, and there remain 288 working days for the production of surplus value.

The production of relative surplus value increases the rate of surplus value in every case, and in the numerical sample in Table 1 it also increases the mass of surplus value contained in a material unit, although their total value (in rows 3 and 4) decreases. There thus remains a margin for increasing wages in real terms, both in the individual business of row 2 and after the general increase in productivity in row 4, as has certainly been the case in the history

		value of commodity (social average) $s+v$	necessary (paid) labor v	surplus value (surplus labor) s	rate of surplus value $s'=s/v$
1	old technology	1,000	400	600	1.5
2	new technology in the individual enterprise (including extra profit)	1,000	320	680	2.125
3	new technology across the sector (without reduction in price of labor-power)	800	320	480	1.5
4	general increase in productivity (with reduction in price of labor power)	800	256	544	2.125

Table 2: Production of Relative Surplus Value at Higher Rate

of capital, which, in combination with the reduction in price of commodities, meant that both new innovations and what had previously been luxury goods became available for mass consumption for the first time. So, love, peace, and harmony?

Table 2 demonstrates that argumentation via numerical examples is risky, because it is impossible to generalize from such examples without doing further work. The same calculations were carried out here as in Table 1, but on the basis of a different division into necessary and surplus labor time and with a rate of surplus value of 1.5 already before the start of a process of innovation. Here too, as a result of the decrease in the labor time required for the production of the material unit, the rate of surplus value climbs starkly, but the bottom line is that the mass of surplus value contained in the commodities produced falls from 600 to 544 working days. The reason for this consists in the fact that the compensatory effect on the general decrease in the magnitude of value brought about by the simultaneous reduction in the price of labor power is only slight, because the proportion of paid labor in the value of the commodity is already low in the first place. If wages remain constant in real terms, an increase in productivity always leads to an increase in the rate of surplus value and a decrease in the value of the commodity. Against this, the mass of surplus value realized in the material unit is subject to two opposing influences: on one hand, as a fraction of the total value of the commodity, it falls in proportion to the fall in this value; on the other hand, it grows to the extent that the amount of surplus value in proportion to the total value of the commodity grows, because of the reduction in the price of labor power. What ultimately results depends on the magnitude of the proportion of paid labor at the start of the process of innovation, for it is only at the expense of this labor that the mass of surplus value can rise. So, if the rate of surplus value is low, the proportion of necessary labor correspondingly high, the mass of surplus value in the material unit increases; in contrast, if the rate of surplus value is high, and the proportion of paid labor in the total value therefore low, the mass of surplus value decreases. Since, on the basis of only two numerical examples, this assertion is still left up in the air, a more general observation is necessary, independent of the particular numerical values. This is also an opportunity to clarify where the boundary between "low" and "high" rates of surplus value lies.

In Table 3, the same calculation was carried out in a more general form, where v_1 and s_1 are the starting values for the necessary and surplus labor, and p is the factor by which the productivity increases with the introduction of the new technology in comparison with the old (in Tables 1 and 2, p was defined as 1.25). The production of relative surplus value functions by means of the fact that with a general increase in productivity by factor p (final row), the total commodity value is divided by this same factor, but the value of the necessary labor is divided by the factor p_2, because both the labor time

		value of commodity (social average) $s+v$	necessary (paid) labor v	surplus value (surplus labor) s	rate of surplus value $s'=s/v$
1	old technology	s_1+v_1	v_1	s_1	$s_1'=s_1/v_1$
2	new technology in the individual enterprise (including extra profit)	s_1+v_1	v_1/p	$s_1+v_1-v_1/p$	$s_1'p+p-1$
3	new technology across the sector (without reduction in price of labor-power)	$(s_1+v_1)/p$	v_1/p	s_1/p	s_1'
4	general increase in productivity (with reduction in price of labor power)	$(s_1+v_1)/p$	v_1/p_2	$(s_1+v_1)/p-v_1/p_2$	$s_1'p+p-1$

Table 3: Production of Relative Surplus Value in General

necessary for commodity production and the reproduction costs of the single working day have decreased by the factor $1/p$. The formulae for s and s' in the last row are of interest for the effect of an increase in productivity on the surplus value contained in a given material quantity:

$$s = \frac{s_1 + v_1}{p} - \frac{v_1}{p^2}, \ s' = p(s_1' + 1) - 1$$

Expressing p in terms of s' with the help of the second formula:

$$p = \frac{s' + 1}{s_1' + 1}$$

and if this expression is included in the formula for s, the result is

$$S = \frac{(s_1 + v_1)(s_1' + 1)}{s_1' + 1} - \frac{v_1(s_1' + 1)}{(s_1' + 1)}$$

Because $s_1 = v_1 s_1'$, the numerators of both fractions agree, and one gets

$$S = r\left(\frac{1}{s' + 1} - \frac{1}{(s' + 1)^2}\right) = r\,\frac{s}{(s' + 1)^2}$$

The constant

$$r = v_1(s_1' + 1)^2$$

can be interpreted as the labor time which can be reproduced by means of the given quantity of material wealth. It is constant because wages are here assumed to be constant in real terms. For the total value

$$S = v + s = \frac{r}{(s' + 1)^2}$$

r results precisely in the (fictitious, precapitalist) situation in which the total amount produced must be used for the reproduction of labor power, in which it is therefore impossible to extract surplus value at all.

The relationship developed here between the rate of surplus value and the amount of surplus value per unit of material wealth is presented graphically in Graph 1. The graph should not be interpreted any more than the formulae that underpin it as saying that the rate of surplus value is the independent variable, and consequently the mass of surplus value is the dependent variable. Rather, the magnitudes expressed in both variables depend on productivity: the rate of surplus value increases in direct proportion to productivity, and as long as the rate of surplus value remains below 1, the mass of surplus value also grows. It reaches its maximum when the rate of surplus value reaches 1. But with further increases in productivity and in the rate of surplus value, the surplus value falls again, and, with unlimited growth in productivity, tends, like the total value, toward zero.

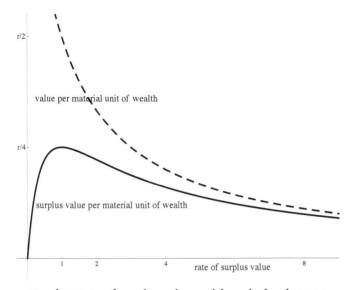

Graph 1: Rate of surplus value and (surplus) value per material unit

The relationships displayed here are not of an empirical nature: they reveal rather the logic of the production of relative surplus value in its pure form — under the assumption, that is, that the length of the working day remains constant, as do wages, in real terms, and that the change in productivity takes place uniformly in all sectors and for all products. In capitalism's immediate reality, this is of course not the case. Wages and working hours are always changing as a consequence of social struggles, and upward surges in productivity take place in an entirely asynchronous manner and to an extent that differs across different sectors.[27]

Moreover, the products themselves are always changing, and new products are always emerging, while others disappear. It is beyond doubt, for example, that productivity in the automobile industry has increased drastically in the last fifty years, but in order to quantify this increase precisely it would be necessary to find a new car that is comparatively the same as the 1950s Volkswagen Beetle — and no such car now exists. And it would not be possible to compare the production of CD players over thirty years, because thirty years ago there were no CD players, and so on.

To this extent, the calculation carried out here, along with its result as presented in Graph 1, describes nothing more than a developmental tendency, which could perhaps have been made clear without such calculation. But nevertheless, this developmental tendency really exists. It is grounded in what Marx describes as the compulsion, ceaselessly operating and induced by market competition, to reduce labor time — that is, to increase productivity. This is something that can be observed, even empirically, across all sectors and products. It is also necessarily the case that if there is unlimited growth in productivity and the value of an individual product slowly but surely disappears, the mass of surplus value realized within a unit of material wealth tends toward zero. Ultimately the mass of surplus value can never be greater than the mass of value. On the other hand it is clear that as long as productivity is no more than is sufficient for the reproduction of labor power ($s = 0$), no surplus value can be obtained (and, therefore, no capitalism is possible). It is therefore plausible even without the mathematically modeled calculation that the mass of surplus value contained in the individual product (and materialized exclusively within such products as use values or units of material wealth) has its maximum somewhere between these two values.

It is necessary to refer to this in two further ways. Firstly, the schema of Tables 1-3, with the result shown in Graph 1, is applicable not only to individual products, but also to arbitrary "shopping baskets" or even to entire national economies, such as in the case of the material wealth produced within a year — the developmental tendency derived from them is therefore of the most general kind. Secondly, the form of production of surplus value by means of perpetual growth in productivity, according to Marx the form appropriate to developed capitalism, cannot simply be switched off, even if it is the case that in the long term it works against its own "interests" insofar as it perpetually reduces the surplus value per unit of material wealth. The dynamic described here is set in motion (see transition to the second step in Tables 1-2) by competition, whether between individual businesses or between states or indeed between any "local site" that can be forced into competition with any or all others. Here the participants act entirely in accordance with their own interests, and have to do so, simply for the sake of their continued existence within capitalism. The dynamic that this sets in motion is therefore indelibly inscribed in the fact that social wealth takes on the value form. It could only be slowed down or even switched off by the abolition of value.

The Developmental Tendency of Relative Surplus Value

Because of the permanently functioning compulsion to reduce labor time it is legitimate to assume that over the course of capitalist development, productivity has always increased, even if not evenly, but in phases marked by bursts of productivity alternating with phases of only slow growth in productivity. But this means that the development, depicted in Graph 1, of the surplus value realized within a material unit as a result of growth in productivity, is also a development in the historical time of capitalism: although each increase in productivity initially led to an increase in the mass of surplus value realized in the individual commodity, in its later phases it leads to a reduction. In this sense, the history of capitalism can be divided into a phase of the rise of relative surplus value, and a phase of its fall.

Capitalism moves in a single unambiguous direction — namely, toward ever-higher productivity over the course of time. This observation is already enough to wrench the ground from underneath all conceptions that hold capitalism to be merely a process of alternation, itself unchanging, between crises and surges of accumulation — proof, as a result of its own internal dynamic, against the possibility that it could one day come to an end. Those very same investments in the streamlining and rationalization of production so widely publicized in recent years — investments intended, for example, to eliminate jobs while production output remains at the same level, to raise the productivity of the remaining job categories and increase the profitability of the individual business enterprise

— would, during the phase of increasing relative surplus value, have resulted in the growth of surplus value overall. But in the phase of declining relative surplus value production, higher productivity leads to the reduced production of surplus value overall, with life-threatening consequences for sellers of labor power who have become redundant but also with exacerbating effects on crisis conditions themselves.

Situating in precise historical terms the phase marked by the rise of relative surplus value and the phase marked by its decline, much less the tipping point between the two (at which $s' = 1$) is, to be sure, impossible — not least because of the possibility of historical discrepancies between the two. However, even without more precise historical-empirical investigations, it can be inferred that in the initial phases of the production of relative surplus value by means of cooperation and by means of the division of labor and manufacture, productivity was so low that there remained, as it were, headroom for the growth in the surplus value of each individual commodity.[28] This is perhaps too speculative, but if so it is also of no significance with respect to the question of the final crisis, for which only the late phase of capitalism plays a role, and it is clear that today we have left the tipping point where $s' = 1$ far behind us: in 2004, the net share of national income accounted for by wages in Germany was about forty percent, which corresponds to a rate of surplus value of 1.5. Here it must also be taken into account that what is important are the net wages not only of the productive (surplus-value-producing) labor powers, but also of the unproductive ones (those paid from the mass of surplus value produced by society as a whole). At this point I do not wish to attempt to provide a more precise distinction between productive and unproductive labor.[29] However, within the framework of the critique of political economy it is not disputed that all labors that involve the mere channelling of streams of money (trade, banking, insurance, but also many individual departments of business that otherwise produce surplus value) are unproductive, that is that they produce no surplus value.[30] However, this means that the net share of national income accounted for by wages must in fact be considerably lower than the forty percent mentioned, and the rate of surplus value must correspondingly be higher than 1.5.[31]

For a few decades it has already been possible to observe that capital is increasingly resorting to the production of absolute surplus value — that is, it is attempting to increase surplus value by means of the extension of the working day and by real-terms reductions in wages. This does not of course lead to the disappearance of the perpetual compulsion to increase productivity: it is impossible, therefore, to talk of relative surplus value being superseded once again by absolute surplus value — there is not sufficient opportunity to increase productivity in this way simply because of the natural limitations to the working day, the extension of which can in addition, under today's conditions, only lead to a reduction in jobs and not to more labor. Similarly, real-terms reductions in wages have a natural limit — zero — and if they approach zero it means nothing other than that the reproduction of labor power must be financed by the state, and therefore by the mass of surplus value produced by society as a whole.

According to Marx, the production of absolute surplus value belongs to an earlier form of the capitalist mode of production, in which labor was only formally subsumed under capital — that is to say, labor power was working for a capitalist, but on the material level the concrete labor was not yet bound to capital. The production of relative surplus value, in contrast, presupposes the real subsumption of labor under capital, which itself now defines the technical process of concrete labor in which labor power is employed.[32] If capital is today resorting once again to the production of absolute surplus value, this in no way means that the real subsumption of labor under capital has been suspended, but rather that what is happening is a reaction — in the long term unsuccessful — to the demise of the production of relative surplus value, a demise which, as has been shown, is final and irreversible. Against this background, it is inadequate to conclude, as Heinrich does, that capitalism is returning from the "already almost idyllic conditions" of Fordism to its "normal mode of function," by which he appears to mean the pre-Fordist phase.[33] This ignores the question of what had since happened to productivity, and in this respect simply equates qualitatively distinct phases of the development of capitalism. It is at best an argument based on forms of appearance, and it is indeed entirely possible to compare on this level the relationships of exploitation in present-day China with those of western European capitalism of the nineteenth century. However, the deep currents of the capitalist dynamic remain closed off to such a mode of observation.

It is not clear to me whether Marx took his own analysis of relative surplus value beyond the tipping point that has been identified here, as a result of which he would for the first time have been able to establish the link between the above analysis and his characterization of capital as a "moving contradiction" in the *Grundrisse*. In the corresponding chapter of *Capital* I, his argument proceeds exclusively by means of numerical examples of the sort contained in Table 1, that is to say with a low rate of surplus value (e.g., a twelve-hour working day with ten hours of necessary labor and two hours of surplus labor).[34] Heinrich appears to see the developmental tendency of relative surplus value, but because of the numerical examples he has chosen, he cannot express the this tendency in terms of its results; or, where he does get as far as to be able to point to these results, he finds ways to fend them off:

> The labor time necessary for the production of an individual commodity can certainly sink, the value of the commodity decrease, but only as long as the surplus value or profit produced by its capital increases. Whether the surplus value/ profit is distributed among a smaller number of high-value products or a greater number of low-value products is in this case irrelevant.[35]

The final sentence, which at this point serves to allow Heinrich to take up a position against the Marx of the Grundrisse and the crisis theory of the pre-2005 Krisis, is, however, at the very least extremely risky. Its consequence is that Volkswagen need not care whether, in order to realize the same surplus-value/profit, they must produce and sell four million or fifteen million cars per year. Here it is possible, particularly in markets already saturated, for a problem to arise with respect to turnover, resulting in destructive competition, as has in fact been taking place on the automobile market for years. Heinrich is certainly right in claiming that one can only speak of the surplus value produced by capital as a result of the multiplication of the surplus values of the individual commodity within the material scope of production. On one hand, this means that it is not possible to derive phases within the rise or fall of capital from those within the rise or fall of surplus value. However, on the other hand, it is precisely at this point that the contradiction — also fundamental to the argument advanced by Kurz — between material wealth and the form of value within which such wealth must be subsumed arises a "moving contradiction" that becomes greater with increased production of relative surplus value: the higher productivity, the lower the surplus value contained in the individual commodity, the greater the material output necessary for the constant production of surplus value, the more fierce the competition, the greater the compulsion to further increases in productivity, and so on.

There appears here without doubt an "absolute logical and historical limit" of capital, and the end of its capacity for accumulation thus comes into view.[36] Even if the course to be taken by the dynamics of the foreseeable crisis cannot be determined on the level of abstraction that has been taken up here, I shall nonetheless conclude by considering — including with reference to the ecological question — the in no way unambiguous directions in which the contradiction identified here between matter and form can resolve, more or less violently.

The Inner Compulsion Toward Growth, the Historical Expansion of Capital, and the Material Limits Thereof

In a society oriented solely toward material wealth — a society that merely by virtue of that fact would not be capitalist — growth in productivity would only cause a few problems, which could easily be solved technically and could unburden human life, leading to a reduction of labor but nonetheless to an increase in the number of useful goods. This is also precisely the way that the blessings of growing productivity become public knowledge, as the potential for the technical solutions to virtually all human problems. But of course such ideals, constrained within the unquestioned framework of a capitalist mode of production, would imply the belief in a capitalism that could somehow coexist with a constantly shrinking mass of surplus value.[37] This, of course, capitalism cannot do.

"When value is the form of wealth, the goal of production is necessarily surplus value. That is, the goal of capitalist production is not simply value but the constant expansion of surplus value."[38] The reason for this is the fact that in the capitalist process of production, self-valorizing capital must reproduce itself "on a progressively increasing scale," and therefore also "produce" a surplus value that is constantly growing, by incorporating and exploiting a correspondingly growing number of labor powers.[39]

As productivity increases, this compulsion to growth increases exponentially once again on the material level: if the production of more and more material wealth becomes necessary for the realization of the same surplus value, capital's material output must accordingly grow even more rapidly than the mass of surplus value. As we have seen, this holds for the phase of the fall of the production of surplus value, a phase that was reached some time ago. Now, if this movement of expansion comes up against limits, because the perpetually growing material wealth must not simply be produced, but also find a buyer, an irreversible crisis dynamic gets underway: a material output that remains constant, or even that increases, but less quickly than productivity, results in permanently shrinking production of surplus value, through which in turn the opportunities for the sale of the material output become fewer, which then has a greater effect on the fall in the mass of surplus value, and so on. It is by no means the case that such a downward movement afflicts all individual capitals uniformly: those affected are in the first instance the less productive, which must disappear from the market, culminating in the collapse of entire national economies such as, for example, in the eastern European countries at the start of the 1990s. The remaining capital can burst into the resulting empty spaces, and for the time being can expand again, which at the surface gives the impression that everything is fine for capital. This may indeed be the case for the survivors in each case — and for the moment — but it changes nothing of the character of the movement as a whole.

The growth of the mass of surplus value and — as long as productivity is increasing — the related and even stronger growth of the material output is the unconscious raison d'etre of capital and the condition sine qua non of the continued existence of the capitalist mode of production. In the past, capital has followed its compulsion to growth — that is, the necessity of its unlimited accumulation — in a process of expansion that is without historical parallel. Kurz names as its essential moments: first, the step-by-step conquering of all branches of production already existing before and independently of capital, and the concomitant condemnation of its working population to wage dependency, which also involves the conquering of geographical space (admired, though with a shudder, in the "Manifesto of the Communist Party" as the compulsion for a "constantly expanding market for its products" that "chases the bourgeoisie across the entire surface of the globe") and second, the creation of new branches of production for new needs (which themselves have first to be created), bound up, by means of mass consumption, with the additional conquering of the "dissociated," feminine realm of the reproduction of labor power, and recently the gradual suspension of the division between labor time and leisure time.[40]

The spaces into which capital has expanded are of material nature, and therefore necessarily finite and at some point, by equal necessity, bound to be full. As concerns the spatial expansionism that is capitalism's first essential moment (see above), this exhaustion of the planet itself as one, global mass of material for the valorization of capital has without doubt become a fait accompli today: there is now no spot on the earth and no branch of production that has not been delivered up to into the grip of capital. This is in no way altered even by the subsistence production that exists in some places, for this is not the remains of premodernity, but a makeshift means by which those who have fallen out of capitalist production can attempt, after a fashion, to secure their survival.

The question, in contrast, of whether the second moment of the capitalist process of expansion — the generation of new branches of production — has finally reached its end, is unresolved. This moment essentially relied on an expansion of mass consumption — which, however, is only possible if there is a sufficient real-terms rise in wages, which in turn affects the production of relative surplus value. In the high phase of Fordism after World War II — times of full employment — it was for a time even possible to implement trade union demands for wage increases of the magnitude of the growth in productivity. In the schema of wealth presented in Tables 1-3 this means in each case a transition from row 1 to row 3 (and not to row 4), with no change in the rate of surplus value, and a fall in the mass of surplus value per material unit by a factor of $1/p$ — which for a time could be compensated by the growth in mass consumption. But with perpetual further growth in productivity and the gradual saturation of the markets for the new branches of production (automobiles or household appliances, for example), this process could not be sustained in the long term. Kurz summarizes the situation as it appeared in the mid-1980s as follows:

> But both essential forms or moments of the process of capitalist expansion are today starting to come up against absolute material limits. The saturation point of capitalization was reached in the 1960s; this source of the absorption of living labor has come to a final standstill. At the same time, the confluence in microelectronics of natural-scientific technology and the science of labor implies a fundamentally new stage in the revolution of the material labor process. The microelectronic revolution does not eliminate living labor in

immediate production only in this or that specific productive technology, but sets out on a wider front, throughout all branches of production, seizing even the unproductive areas. This process has only just started, and will not fully gain traction until the second half of the 1980s; it seems likely that it will continue until the end of the century and beyond. To the extent that new branches of production are created by means of this process, such as in the production of microelectronics itself or in gene technology, they are by their nature from the outset not very labor intensive in respect to immediate production. This brings about the collapse of the historical compensation that has existed up until this point for the absolute immanent limit, embedded within relative surplus value, to the capitalist mode of production. The elimination on a massive scale of living productive labor as a source of the creation of value can no longer be recuperated by newly mass-produced cheap products, since this process of mass production is no longer mediated by a process of reintegrating a labor population that has been made superfluous elsewhere. This brings about a historically irreversible overturning of the relationship between the elimination of living productive labor through scientification on the one hand, and the absorption of living productive labor through processes of capitalization or through the creation of new branches of production on the other: from now on, it is inexorable that more labor is eliminated than can be absorbed. All technological innovations that are to be expected will also tend only in the direction of the further elimination of living labor, all new branches of production will from the outset come to life with less and less direct human productive labor.[41]

Heinrich describes, somewhat derisively, the direct reference of "Kurz's theory of collapse" to the "microelectronic revolution" as "technological determinism," which he claims is wonderfully appropriate "to the 'workers-movement Marxism' that is otherwise criticized so very fiercely by Kurz."[42] However, what is at stake here, as Heinrich is certainly aware, is not a particular individual technology, but the fact that technology is making labor to a great extent superfluous — an argument against which Heinrich marshals no argument even in his "more extensive critique."[43] But this ought really to give a theorist of value pause for thought, for a crisis of capital could in that case only fail to result if value and surplus value were not measured in labor time, but natural-scientific technology had instead replaced the application of immediate labor as a source of value, as someone like Habermas believes. But Heinrich does not go this far.

It is correct, on the other hand — and if this had been what Heinrich had said, he would have been right — that a prognosis, based on the here and now, according to which "it is inexorable that more labor is eliminated than can be absorbed," cannot be derived solely from the category, established on a more abstract level, of relative surplus value. Empirical observations are also required. These exist in great numbers, and Kurz also alludes to them. But empirical semblance can of course deceive, and capital can pull itself together once more — the question is only what the consequences would be for capital and for humanity.

This uncertainty as to the future development of the crisis dynamic changes nothing of the fact that capital must perish as a result of its own dynamic, if it is not overcome by conscious human actions before then. This results simply from the limitless compulsion to growth on one hand, and on the other hand the finitude of the human and material resources on which it depends.

Knut Hüller has already drawn attention to the fact that the total social rate of profit (rate of accumulation) must fall for no other reason than the fact that the labor power available to capital on this earth is simply finite, whereas a constant rate of profit would presuppose an exponentially growing working population.[44] And this conclusion was reached without once taking the production of relative surplus value into consideration. If one does so, it becomes clear that constant or even exponentially growing material production leads, if the rate of "real growth" is too low (under the rate of growth of productivity), to an exponential fall in the mass of surplus value (and accordingly to falls in the productively working population).

The observation that "it is inexorable that more labor is eliminated than can be absorbed" is essentially based on the presupposition that capital will no longer be able to compensate for the losses, induced by process innovations, in the production of value and surplus value, by means of product innovations. Much speaks in favor of this claim: even today, twenty-two years later, no innovations of this kind are anywhere to be found. As stated, here it is a matter not of new products and their associated needs as such, but of those whose production requires labor on such a mass scale that it would be possible at least to compensate for the streamlining potential of microelectronics. However, if this prognosis were to reveal itself to be false, the contradiction revealed here between matter and form would in no way be resolved, but would in that case result in a violent discharge in another direction.

The Inner Compulsion Toward Growth and Environmental Destruction

> Moreover, all progress in capitalist agriculture is a progress in the art, not only of robbing the worker, but of robbing the soil; all progress in increasing the fertility of the soil for a given time is a progress towards ruining the more long-lasting sources of that fertility. The more a country proceeds from large-scale industry as the background of its development, [...] the more rapid is this process of destruction. [...] Capitalist production, therefore, only develops the techniques and the degree of combination of the social process of production by simultaneously undermining the original sources of all wealth — the soil and the worker.[45]

Capital requires material wealth as the bearer of value; as such the former is indispensable, and in quantitative terms (see above) it will become even more so. But capital is not concerned with the material wealth that is freely available and that therefore does not become part of the mass of value and surplus value that is produced. In comparison with the necessity of capital accumulation, the preservation of this wealth is at best of lesser importance — or in other words, if the destruction of material wealth serves the valorization of value, then material wealth will be destroyed. It's that simple. Into this category fall all of its forms which have come into view or been mentioned over the last fifty years in the context of environmental destruction: the long-term fertility of the soil, to which Marx had already referred; air and water of a quality that they can be breathed and drunk without danger to life or limb; biodiversity and undamaged ecosystems, even merely with respect to their function as renewable sources of food; or a climate that is hospitable to human life.

The question is not, therefore, whether the environment is destroyed for the sake of the valorization of value, but at best of the extent of this destruction. And in this matter the growth of productivity, to the extent that it, as the production of relative surplus value, remains bound to value as the predominant form of wealth, plays a thoroughly sinister role because the realization of the same mass of surplus value requires an ever-greater material output and even greater consumption of resources: for the transition from old to new technologies with the purpose of reducing the labor time required is usually achieved by replacing or accelerating human labor with machines. We may assume, for example, in an ideal-typical case, that in the schema of calculation of Tables 1-3 it is possible to make 10,000 shirts in 1,000 working days by the old technology, and this production only requires cloth and labor. The new technology could consist in the reduction of the labor time necessary for the production of the same number of shirts to 500 working days, but to introduce and employ machines and additional energy which for their part could be produced in 300 working days. In the situation described in Table 2, however $(s_1' > 1)$, this would mean that in the case of the new, more profitable technique for the realization of the same surplus value as in the old, it would be necessary to produce not only more than 10,000 shirts in a capitalist manner, but also the additional machinery and energy which are used in the process of production. This means that ever-greater consumption of resources becomes necessary for the same surplus value, a consumption that is greater than, and grows even more quickly than, the required material output.

That is, if Kurz was wrong, and the accumulation of capital could continue without restriction, it would sooner or later have as its inevitable consequence the destruction not only of the material foundations of the valorization of capital, but also of human life as such.

Postone draws the following conclusion from his analysis of the contradiction between material wealth and wealth in the value form as it is brought forth by the production of relative surplus value:

> Leaving aside considerations of possible limits or barriers to capital accumulation, one consequence implied by this particular dynamic — which yields increases in material wealth far greater than those in surplus value — is the accelerating destruction of the natural environment. According to Marx, as a result of the relationship among productivity, material wealth, and surplus value, the ongoing expansion of the latter increasingly has deleterious consequences for nature as well as for humans.[46]

In explicit opposition to Horkheimer and Adorno, for whom the domination of nature is itself already the "Fall," Postone emphasises that "the growing destruction of nature should not simply be seen [...] as a consequence of increasing human control and domination of nature."[47] Such a critique is inadequate because it does not distinguish between value and material wealth, although it is the case that in capitalism nature is exploited and destroyed not because of material wealth, but because of surplus value. The increasing imbalance between the two forms of wealth leads him to come to this conclusion:

> The pattern I have outlined suggests that, in the society in which the commodity is totalized, there is an underlying tension between ecological considerations and the imperatives of value as the form of wealth and social mediation. It implies further that any attempt to respond fundamentally, within

the framework of capitalist society, to growing environmental destruction by restraining this society's mode of expansion would probably be ineffective on a long-term basis — not only because of the interests of the capitalists or state managers, but because failure to expand surplus value would indeed result in severe economic difficulties with great social costs. In Marx's analysis, the necessary accumulation of capital and the creation of capitalist society's wealth are intrinsically related. Moreover [...] because labor is determined as a necessary means of individual reproduction in capitalist society, wage laborers remain dependent on capital's "growth," even when the consequences of their labor, ecological and otherwise, are detrimental to themselves and to others. The tension between the exigencies of the commodity form and ecological requirements becomes more severe as productivity increases and, particularly during economic crises and periods of high unemployment, poses a severe dilemma. This dilemma and the tension in which it is rooted are immanent to capitalism: their ultimate resolution will be hindered so long as value remains the determining form of social wealth.[48]

The dilemma described here manifests itself in a many-faceted form. To give an example: while there is a consensus in environmental contexts that the global spread of the "American way of life" or even only of the western European lifestyle would bring with it environmental catastrophes to a degree that has not yet been seen, development organizations must nonetheless pursue precisely this goal, even if it has now become unrealistic. Or, in the terminology of this essay, the employment of labor power that would be necessary for the continued accumulation of capital, even of only half the globally available labor power, at the level of productivity that has been attained, with the corresponding material output and consumption of resources, would result in the immediate collapse of the earth's ecosystem.

This dilemma also manifests itself in the weekly walk on eggshells as to what is "ecologically necessary" and what is "economically feasible" — the two are now irreconcilable — in the political treatment of the expected climate catastrophe, which is indeed only one of many environmental problems. Politics cannot emancipate itself from capital, since it depends on successful production of surplus value even for its tax revenue and therefore its own ability to act. It already has to go against its own nature in order to pass even resolutions that remain well below the objective requirements of the problem that is to be solved, and that even then nonetheless are softened within a week under pressure from some or other lobby on behalf of what is "economically feasible." What remains is pure self-dramatization on the part of "doers" who claim still to have the objectively insoluble problems under control.

Conclusion

This present work presents a relatively meager analysis of a particular perspective that is nonetheless determinant of the capitalist dynamic — the production of relative surplus value and its consequences for the valorization of capital. The reduction of complexity necessary to carry out this analysis — and with it the occasional obscuring of all other aspects of a commodity-producing patriarchy that has entered a period of crisis — is the price to pay for a (hopefully successful) comprehensible presentation. For example, the ideological distortions that accompany the development of the crisis thus remain obscured, as does the increasing inequality with which different groups of the population bear the brunt of the crisis: women more strongly than men, and the middle class (for the moment) to a lesser extent than the majority that has already been precarized.[49]

The role of finance capital has also remained hidden — about which a few words should be said at this point, because some consider it to be the true cause of the crisis, while others believe that it could save capitalism from the ultimate collapse. Both views are false. What is true is that in late capitalism, the valorization of value would not be possible without finance capital, because the huge capitalist aggregates that are necessary at the level of productivity that has been attained today could not by a long way any longer be financed by private capital. But this makes finance capital an indispensable "lubricant," but not the "fuel" of the production of surplus value, which remains bound to the expenditure of labor. The valorization of value has not come to a standstill because capital has fled, maliciously, into the financial sector — rather, it is the other way round. Because it has already been the case for decades that the valorization of capital has come to a standstill, capital flees into the financial sector with its higher (if fictitious, seen from the perspective of the economy as a whole) yields. The effect of this flight is — in the fashion of global Keynesian deficit spending, against all neoliberal ideology — in the first instance to delay the crisis. But the longer this succeeds, the harder the impact with which the crisis must ultimately assert itself. In any case, the idea, which has its origins in the postmodern fantasy of virtuality, of a capitalism that could be "regulated" on a long-term basis by an escalating financial sector that is no longer counterbalanced by any real production of surplus value, is at least as adventitious as that of the production of surplus value without labor by means of science as productivity alone.

If, however, the production of surplus value presupposes the application of immediate labor and the production of material wealth that is bound up with it, the production of surplus value that according to Marx is appropriate to developed capitalism — that is, the production of relative surplus value — leads to the requirement of an ever-greater material output and a still greater consumption of resources for the realization of the same mass of surplus value. The capitalist process of accumulation and expansion thus comes up against absolute material limits, the observance of which must lead to the burning-out of the capitalist logic of valorization, and the disregard for which to the destruction of its material foundations and the possibility of human life as such.

The choice that this presents, between the devil of the gradual disappearance of labor and the social consequences that are, in capitalism, bound up with it, and the deep blue sea of ecological collapse, is not even an either-or choice. It seems rather that both are approaching together: falling production of surplus value at the same time as growing consumption of resources, overladen by the prospect of wars over increasingly scarce material resources, squandered in the valorization of capital, and for the chance to valorize the last remains.

Prognoses made on the basis of the investigations carried out here as to the course of such demise would therefore be pure speculation; but we ought, one way or another, to speak of the end of capitalism as a social formation — just not in the same sense as Heinrich does when he writes in relation to "Kurz's theory of collapse":

> Historically, the theory of collapse always had an exonerating function for the left: however bad the contemporary defeats, the demise of its antagonist was ultimately certain.[50]

Here, too, he is wrong. It is a matter not of the end of an "antagonist," but of our own end. Whether as a slow, lingering sickness or in a great explosion, the foreseeable demise of a social form the members of which, bound to it by means of a value form they regard as natural and thus lack any idea of what is happening to them, could at best leave its survivors to vegetate aimlessly as commodity subjects without commodities. It would merely be one more — albeit the last — defeat. And conversely, the only chance for some sort of liberated postcapitalist society presents itself to us as the overcoming of capitalism — and therefore of wealth in the value form, and of the subject form that it constitutes — brought about by conscious human action. This must come, however, before the compulsion to growth in the valorization of capital, in combination with the production of relative surplus value, leaves behind nothing other than scorched earth. Time is running out.

Notes

1. Robert Kurz, "Crisis of Exchange Value," in this volume, 17-76. For an account of the *Krisis* schism, see xlvii-xlviiin5 [Ed.].

2. Robert Kurz, "Die Himmelfahrt des Geldes," *Krisis* 16/17 (1995) 21-76.

3. Moishe Postone, *Time, Labor, and Social Domination: A Reinterpretation of Marx's Critical Theory* (Cambridge: Cambridge University Press, 1993).

4. Karl Marx, *Grundrisse: Foundations of the Critique of Political Economy*, trans. by Martin Nicolaus (London: Harmondsworth, 1973) 706.

5. Karl Marx, *Capital: A Critique of Political Economy, Volume I,* trans. Ben Fowkes (London: Harmondsworth, 1976).

6. Michael Heinrich. *Kritik der politischen Ökonomie. Eine Einführung,* (Stuttgart: Auflage, 2005) 177.

7. Kurz, "Crisis" 47-8.

8. Norbert Trenkle, "Value and Crisis: Basic Questions," in this volume, 1-16, and Michael Heinrich, "Untergang des Kapitalismus? Die Krisis und die Krise," *Streifzüge* 1 (1999) 4.

9. Marx, *Grundrisse* 704-705; compare Postone, *Time* 25.

10. *Grundrisse*, 704-705.

11. Marx, *Capital* I 125.

12. Postone, *Time* 193-94.

13. *Capital* I 126.

14. *Capital* I 136-137.

15. David Ricardo, *On the Principles of Political Economy and Taxation* (London: John Murray, 1821) v.

16. *Time* 25-26.

17. Jürgen Habermas, *Theory and Practice*, trans. by John Viertel (Boston: Beacon, 1974) 226-27.

18. *Time* 226-60.

19. See Kurz, "Himmelfahrt."

20. Heinrich, "Untergang" 4.

21. Initiative Sozialistisches Forum (ISF), *Der Theoretiker ist der Wert. Eine ideologiekritische Skizze der Wert- und Krisentheorie der Krisis-Gruppe* (Freiburg 2000).

22. ISF, 70.

23. *Capital* I 431.

24. *Capital* I 645.

25. *Capital* I 437.

26. From the point of view of a single business the process of valorization appears in the regular form $c+v+s$ with the "constant capital," c, that is to say the costs for machinery, raw materials, and so on, a factor that cannot be produced within the business itself. But c in no way alters the dynamics of innovation described here. If c was left out from the beginning, that is because it is irrelevant for an observation from the perspective of society as a whole that is the one employed here. Constant capital is also produced (somewhere else), and the magnitude of its value is the socially average labor time expended for its production, itself in turn divided into necessary and surplus labor time.

27. But the masses of surplus value obtained in individual products and therefore also the effects of increases in productivity are distributed by the adjustment of the rates of profit. Increases in productivity within individual sectors also lead by means of processes of adaptation to changes in surplus value and profit in all others. Even sectors whose products only contain "homoeopathic doses" of labor are not less profitable than others because of this fact. (For two opposing views with respect to this claim, see both Ernst Lohoff, 'Der Wert des Wissens. Grundlagen der Politische Ökonomie des Informationskapitalismus,' *Krisis* 31 (2007) 13-51; and Robert Kurz, 'Der Unwert des Unwissens. Verkürzte Wertkritik als Legitimationsideologie eines digitalen Neo-Kleinbürgertums,' *EXIT!* 5 (2008) 127-94.) With respect to the model calculation carried out here it can be said, on the other hand, that the effects of increases in productivity with respect to the mass of surplus value that is realized are more uniform than the increases in productivity themselves, and that the results of the model calculation are to this extent more realistic than the assumptions under which they are obtained.

28. *Capital* I 439 and following, and 455 and following.

29. Compare Kurz, "Crisis."

30. Compare Heinrich, *Kritik* 134.

31.   This does not of course mean that seventy percent or eighty percent of the value produced is available for the purposes of the accumulation of capital. Not only must the entire consumption of the state be financed by the surplus value that is produced, but also all the labor (wages and profits) in unproductive businesses.

32.   *Capital* I 645.

33.   "Untergang" 5.

34.   *Capital* I 645.

35.   Heinrich, *Kritik* 177-178.

36.   "Crisis" 19.

37.   In addition, unburdening human life on a global scale would require conscious planning oriented toward material wealth, that is to say more or less the opposite of an orientation toward the market. Besides, in a noncapitalist society with today's level of production it would not be a matter merely of less labor, but rather of the abolition of labor as a category.

38.   *Time* 308.

39.   *Capital* I 725 and following.

40.   Karl Marx and Friedrich Engels, "Manifesto of the Communist Party," trans. Samuel Moore, *The Marx-Engels Reader*, 2nd ed., ed. Robert C. Tucker (New York: W. W. Norton, 1978) 476, and "Crisis" 23. What is at issue here is exclusively the quantitative aspect of the objective dynamics of the valorization of capital. Under the aspect of the dissociation of value as the dark flipside of the process of disciplining the (masculine) subject so as to be fit for the valorization of value (and its necessary prerequisite, socialization in the shape of the value form), it would be worthwhile carrying out our own investigation as to whether and to what extent capital undermines its own foundations by capitalizing the "feminine," value-dissociated sphere within the social division of labor, destroying, in the process, the long-term prospects for the vital reproductive function of this sphere for the valorization of capital. The increase in mental illness and in the premature inability to work for reasons of mental health weigh in favor of this hypothesis, as do the disastrous conditions, which to a great extent have already become intolerable, in state-funded

care for children, the sick, and the elderly, once these services too have been subjected to the microeconomic time regime of capital.

41. "Crisis" 52-3.

42. *Kritik* 178.

43. "Untergang."

44. Knut Hüller, *Eine Aufwertung des Werts gegenüber dem Preis*, 2006. The so-called Okishio Theorem, which has its origin in the neo-Ricardian critique of Marx, in contrast, supposedly refutes the "law of the tendency of the rate of profit to fall": even Heinrich (*Die Wissenschaft vom Wert* [Münster: Westfälisches Dampfboot, 1991] 327 and following; *Kritik* 148) accepts this theorem as is, and likes to assert it against capital's "tendency to collapse." The Okishio Theorem says nothing more than that a particular mathematical model (a comparatively static, linear model of production, that is ridiculously laid at Marx's door), cannot demonstrate the fall of the rate of profit, but rather implies its rise. This shows nothing more than that one should not simply abstract from absolute figures and their limits, as linear models always do.

45. *Capital* I 638.

46. *Time* 311.

47. Max Horkheimer and Theodor W. Adorno, *Dialectic of Enlightenment*, trans. Edmund Jephcott (Stanford: Stanford University Press, 2002), and *Time* 312.

48. *Time* 313.

49. Compare Frank Rentschler, "Die kategoriale Abwesenheit des Geschlechts," *EXIT!* 3 (2006) 176-209; Roswitha Scholz, "Überflüssig sein und 'Mittelschichtsangst,'" *EXIT!* 5 (2008) 58-104.

50. "Untergang" 178.

Patriarchy and Commodity Society: Gender without the Body

Roswitha Scholz (2009)

In the 1980s, after the collapse of the Eastern Bloc, culturalism and theories of difference became especially prominent in women's studies courses, a discipline which has since largely developed into gender studies. Marxist feminism, which until the end of the 1980s had determined the debates in this field, retreated into the background. Recently, however, the increasing delegitimization of neoliberalism connected to the current economic crisis has produced a resurgence and increasing popularity of a diverse set of Marxisms. To date, however, these developments have barely had an impact on the fields of feminist theory or gender studies — aside from some critical globalization debates and area studies interrogating the themes of labor and money. Deconstruction is still the lead vocalist in the choir of universal feminism, especially in gender theory. Meanwhile, assertions of the necessity of a new feminism (in particular a feminism that once again includes a materialist plane of analysis) have become commonplace. The popular argument of the 1980s and 1990s that claims that we are confronted with a "confusion of the sexes" is being rapidly deflated. Instead, it is becoming clear that neither the much-professed equalization of genders nor the deconstructivist play with signifiers has yielded convincing results.

The "rediscovery" of Marxist theory on one hand and the insight that feminism is in no way anachronistic or superfluous on the other, even if it can no longer be continued in those forms that have become characteristic of the past few decades, lead me to consider a new Marxist-feminist theoretical framework, one which is able to account for recent developments since the end of actually existing socialism and the onset of the current global economic crisis. It should, of course, be clear that one cannot seamlessly connect traditional Marxist concepts and analysis with twenty-first-century problematics. Without critical innovation, a direct application is similarly impossible for those theoretical frameworks from which I will draw in what follows, such as Adorno's critical theory, even if his examinations provided us with an important basis for a patriarchy-critical theory of the present. Those feminist debates of the last twenty years that have been based on Adorno and critical theory can provide inspiration, but they must also be modified. I cannot elaborate on this here.[1] Instead, I would like to advance a few facets of my theory of gender relations, or value-dissociation theory, which I have developed via the engagement with some of the theories alluded to above. As I will show, asymmetrical gender relations today can no longer be understood in the same sense as "classical" modern gender relations; however, it is essential to base their origins in the history of modernization. Similarly, one has to account for postmodern processes of differentiation and the relevance of cultural-symbolic levels which have emerged since the 1980s. The cultural-symbolic order should here be understood as an autonomous dimension of theory. Yet, this autonomous dimension is to be thought simultaneously with value dissociation as a basic social principle without understanding Marxian theory as purely materialist. Such a theory is much better equipped to grasp the totality, insofar as the cultural-symbolic as well as the socio-psychological levels are included in the context of a social whole. Economy and culture are, therefore, neither identical (as "identity logic" that violently aims to subjugate differences to the same common denominator would suggest), nor can they be separated from each other in a dualistic sense. Rather, their identity and non-identity must be conceived as the conflictual incompatibility that shapes the commodity-producing patriarchy as such: the self-contradictory basic principle of the social form of value dissociation.

Value as Basic Social Principle

Besides the above-mentioned critical theory of Adorno, the primary theoretical benchmarks are a new, fundamental critical theory of "value" and of "abstract labor" as enhancements of the Marxist critique of political economy, whose most prominent theorists in the last decade are Robert Kurz and Moishe Postone.[2] I intend to give their texts a feminist twist.

According to this new value-critical approach, it is not surplus value itself — that is, it is not the solely externally determined exploitation of labor by capital qua legal property relations — which stands at the center of critique. Instead, critique begins at an earlier point, namely with the social character of the commodity-producing system and thus with the form of activity particular to abstract labor. Labor as abstraction develops for the first time under capitalism alongside the generalization of commodity production and must, therefore, not be ontologized. Generalized commodity production is characterized by a key contradiction: under the obligation of the valorization of value, the individuals of capitalist enterprise are highly integrated into a network while nevertheless paradoxically engaging in non-social production, as socialization proper is only established via the market and exchange. As commodities, products represent past abstract labor and, therefore, value. In other words, commodities represent a specific quantity of expenditure of human energy, recognized by the market as socially valid. This representation is, in turn, expressed by money, the universal mediator and simultaneous end in itself of the form of capital. In this way, people appear asocial and society appears to be constituted through things, which are mediated by the abstract quantity of value. The result is the alienation of members of society, as their own sociability is only bestowed upon them by commodities, dead things, thus entirely emptying sociability in its social form of representation of its concrete, sensual content. This relation can, for the time being, be expressed via the concept of fetishism, keeping in mind that this concept itself is as yet incomplete.

Opposed to this stand premodern societies, in which goods were produced under different relations of domination (personal as opposed to reified by the commodity form). Goods were produced in the agrarian field and in trades primarily for their use, determined by specific laws of guilds that precluded the pursuit of abstract profit. The very limited premodern exchange of goods was not carried out in markets and relations of competition in the modern sense. It was, therefore, not possible at this point in history to speak of a social totality in which money and value have become abstract ends in themselves. Modernity is consequently characterized by the pursuit of surplus value, by the attempt to generate more money out of money, yet not as a matter of subjective enrichment but instead as a tautological system determined by the relation of value to itself. It is in this context that Marx speaks of the "automatic subject."[3] Human needs become negligible and labor power itself is transformed into a commodity. This means that the human capacity for production has become externally determined — yet not in the sense of personal domination but in the sense of anonymous, blind mechanisms. And it is only for that reason that productive activities in modernity have become forced into the form of abstract labor. Ultimately, the development of capitalism marks life globally by means of money's self-motion and of abstract labor, which emerged only under capitalism and appears unhistorically as an ontological principle. Traditional Marxism only problematizes a part of this system of correlations, namely the legal appropriation of surplus value by the bourgeoisie, thus focusing on unequal distribution rather than commodity fetishism. Its critique of capitalism and imaginations of postcapitalist societies are consequently limited to the goal of equal distribution within the commodity-producing system in its non-suspended forms. Such critiques fail to see that the suffering resulting from capitalism emerges from its very formal relations, of which private property is merely one of many results. Accordingly, the Marxisms of the workers' movements were limited to an ideology of legitimization of system-immanent developments and social improvements. Today, this form of thought is inappropriate for a renewed critique of capitalism, as it has absorbed (and made its own) all the basic principles of capitalist socialization, in particular the categories of value and abstract labor, misunderstanding these categories as transhistorical conditions of humanity. In this context, a radical value-critical position regards past examples of actually existing socialism as the value-producing system of state-bureaucratically determined processes of recuperative (or "catch-up") modernization (*nachholende Modernisierung*) in the global East and South, which, mediated by global economic processes and the race for the development of productive forces against the West, had to collapse in the post-Fordist stage of capitalist development at the end of the 1980s. Since then the West has been engaged in the process of withdrawing social reforms in the context of crises and globalization.

Value Dissociation as Basic Social Principle

The concepts of value and abstract labor, I argue, cannot sufficiently account for capitalism's basic form as a fundamentally fetishistic relation. We have also to account for the fact that under capitalism reproductive activities emerge that are primarily carried out by women. Accordingly, value dissociation means that capitalism contains a core of female-determined reproductive activities and the affects, characteristics, and attitudes (emotionality, sensuality, and female or motherly caring) that are dissociated from value and abstract labor. Female relations of existence — that is, female reproductive activities under capitalism — are therefore of a different character from abstract labor, which is why they cannot straightforwardly be subsumed under the concept of labor. Such relations constitute a facet of capitalist societies that cannot be captured by Marx's conceptual apparatus. This facet is a necessary aspect of value, yet it also exists outside of it and is (for this very reason) its precondition. In this context I borrow from Frigga Haug the notion of a "logic of time-saving" that determines one side of modernity that is generally associated with the sphere of production, what Kurz calls the "logic of using-up (*Vernutzung*) of business administration," and a "logic of time-expenditure" that corresponds to the field of reproduction. Value and dissociation therefore stand in a dialectical relation to each other. One cannot simply be derived from the other. Rather, both simultaneously emerge out of each other. In this sense, value dissociation can be understood as the macro-theoretical framework within which the categories of the value form function micro-theoretically, allowing us to examine fetishistic socialization in its entirety instead of value alone. One must stress here, however, that the sensitivity that is usually falsely perceived as an immediate a priori in the fields of reproduction, consumption, and its related activities, as well as needs that are to be satisfied in this context, emerged historically before the backdrop of value dissociation as total process. These categories must not be misunderstood as immediate or natural, despite the fact that eating, drinking, and loving are not solely connected to symbolization (as vulgar constructivisms might claim). The traditional categories available to us for the critique of political economy, however, are also lacking in another regard. Value dissociation implies a particular socio-psychological relation. Certain undervalued qualities (sensitivity, emotionality, deficiencies in thought and character, and so forth) are associated with femininity and are dissociated from the masculine-modern subject. These gender-specific attributes are a fundamental characteristic of the symbolic order of the commodity-producing patriarchy. Such asymmetrical gender relations should, I believe, as far as theory is concerned, be examined by focusing only on modernity and postmodernity. This is not to say that these relations do not have a premodern history, but rather to insist that their universalization endowed them with an entirely new quality. The universalization of such gender relations at the beginning of modernity meant that women were now primarily responsible for the lesser-valorized (as opposed to the masculine, capital-producing) areas of reproduction, which cannot be represented in monetary terms. We must reject the understanding of gender relations under capitalism as a precapitalist residue. The small, nuclear family as we know it, for example, only emerged in the eighteenth century, just as the public and private spheres as we understand them today only emerged in modernity. What I claim here, therefore, is that the beginning of modernity not only marked the rise of capitalist commodity production, but that it also saw the emergence of a social dynamism that rests on the basis of the relations of value dissociation.

Commodity-Producing Patriarchy as Civilizational Model

Following Frigga Haug, I assume that the notion of a commodity-producing patriarchy is to be regarded as a civilizational model, yet I would like to modify her propositions by taking into account the theory of value dissociation.[4] As is well known, the symbolic order of the commodity-producing patriarchy is characterized by the following assumptions: politics and economics are associated with masculinity; male sexuality, for example, is generally described as individualized, aggressive, or violent, while women often function as pure bodies. The man is therefore regarded as human, man of intellect, and body-transcendent, while women are reduced to non-human status, to the body. War carries a masculine connotation, while women are seen as peaceful, passive, devoid of will and spirit. Men must strive for honor, bravery, and immortalizing actions. Men are thought of as heroes and capable of great deeds, which requires them to productively subjugate nature. Men stand at all times in competition with others. Women are responsible for the care for the individual as well as for humanity itself. Yet their actions remain socially undervalued and forgotten in the process of the development of theory, while their sexualization is the source of women's subordination to men and underwrites their social marginalization.

This notion also determines the idea of order underlying modern societies as a whole. Moreover, the ability and willingness to produce and the rational, economical, and effective expenditure of time also determine the civilizational model in its objective structures as a totality of relations — its mechanisms and history as much as the maxims of individual agency. A provocative formulation might suggest that the male gender should be understood as the gender of capitalism, keeping in mind that such a dualist understanding of gender is of course the dominant understanding of gender in modernity. The commodity-producing civilizational model this requires has its foundation in the oppression and marginalization of women and the simultaneous neglect of nature and the social. Subject and object, domination and subjugation, man and woman are thus typical dichotomies, antagonistic counterparts within the commodity-producing patriarchy.[5]

Yet it is important to prevent misunderstandings in this respect. Value dissociation is in this sense also to be understood as a metaconcept, since we are concerned with theoretical exegesis on a high level of abstraction. This means for the single empirical units or subjects that they are neither able to escape the socio-cultural patterns, nor able to become part of these patterns. Additionally, as we shall see, gender models are subject to historical change. It is therefore important to avoid simplified interpretations of value dissociation theory resembling, for instance, the idea of a "new femininity" associated with the difference-feminism of the 1980s or even the "Eve principle" currently being propagated by German conservatives.[6] What we must foreground in all of this is that abstract labor and domestic labor along with the known cultural patterns of masculinity and femininity determine each other simultaneously. The old "chicken or egg" question is nonsensical in this regard. Yet, such a non-dialectical approach is characteristic of deconstructivist critics who insist that masculinity and femininity initially must be produced culturally before a gendered distribution of actions can take place.[7] Frigga Haug too proceeds from the ontologizing assumption that cultural meaning attaches itself over the course of history to a previously gendered division of labor.[8]

Within the commodity-producing modern patriarchy develops, again, a public sphere, which itself comprises a number of spheres (economy, politics, science, and so on), and a private sphere. Women are primarily assigned to the private sphere. These different spheres are on one hand relatively autonomous, and on the other hand mutually determined — that is, they stand in dialectical relation to each other. It is important, then, that the private sphere not be misunderstood as an emanation of value but rather as a dissociated sphere. What is required is a sphere into which actions such as caring and loving can be deported and that stands opposed to the logic of value and time saving and its morality (competition, profit, performance). This relation between private sphere and the public sector also explains the existence of male alliances and institutions that found themselves, by means of an affective divide, against all that is female. As a consequence, the very basis of the modern state and politics, along with the principles of liberty, equality, and fraternity, rests since the eighteenth century upon the foundation of male alliances. This is not to say, however, that patriarchy resides in the spheres created by this process of dissociation. For example, women have always to an extent been active in the sphere of accumulation. Nevertheless, dissociation becomes apparent here as well, since, despite the success of Angela Merkel and others, women's existence in the public sphere is generally undervalued and women largely remain barred from upward mobility. All this indicates that value dissociation is a pervasive social formal principle that is located on a correspondingly high level of abstraction and that cannot be mechanistically separated into different spheres. This means that the effects of value dissociation pervade all spheres, including all levels of the public sphere.

Value Dissociation as Basic Social Principle and the Critique of Identity Logic

Value dissociation as critical practice disallows identity-critical approaches. That is, it does not allow for approaches that reduce analyses to the level of structures and concepts that subsume all contradictions and non-identities with regard both to the attribution of mechanisms, structures, and characteristics of the commodity-producing patriarchy to societies that do not produce commodities, and to the homogenization of different spheres and sectors within the commodity-producing patriarchy itself, disregarding qualitative differences. The necessary point of departure is not merely value, but the relation of value dissociation as a fundamental social structure that corresponds to androcentric universalist thought. After all, what is important here is not simply that it is average labor time or abstract labor that determines money as equivalent form. More important is the observation that value itself must define as less valuable and dissociate domestic labor, the non-conceptual, and everything related to non-identity, the sensuous, affective, and emotional.

Dissociation, however, is not congruent with the non-identical in Adorno. More accurately, the dissociated represents the dark underbelly of value itself. Here, dissociation must be understood as a precondition which ensures that the contingent, the irregular, the non-analytical, that which cannot be grasped by science, remains hidden and unilluminated, perpetuating classificatory thought that is unable to register and maintain particular qualities, inherent differences, ruptures, ambivalences, and asynchronies.

Inversely, this means for the "socialized society" of capitalism, to appropriate Adorno's phrase, that these levels and sectors cannot be understood in relation to each other as irreducible elements of the real, but that they also have to be examined in their objective, internal relations corresponding to the notion of value dissociation as formal principle of the social totality that constitutes a given society on the level of ontology and appearance in the first place. Yet, at every moment, value dissociation is also aware of its own limitations as theory. The self-interrogation of value dissociation theory here must go far enough to prevent positioning it as an absolute, social-form principle. That which corresponds to its concept can, after all, not be elevated to the status of main contradiction, and the theory of value dissociation can, like the theory of value, not be understood as a theory of the logic of the one. In its critique of identity logic, therefore, value dissociation theory remains true to itself and can only persist insofar as it relativizes and at times even disclaims itself. This also means that value dissociation theory must leave equal space for other forms of social disparity (including economic disparity, racism, and antisemitism).[9]

Value Dissociation as Historical Process

According to the epistemological premises of the formation of value dissociation theory, we cannot resort to linear analytical models when examining developments in a variety of global regions. Developments generally determined by the commodity form and the associated form of patriarchy did not take place in the same fashion and under the same circumstances in all societies (especially in societies that were formerly characterized by symmetrical gender relations and which have to this day not entirely adopted modernity's gender relations). Additionally, we must foreground alternative paternalistic structures and relations, which, while largely overwritten by modern, Western patriarchy in the context of global economic developments, have not entirely lost their idiosyncrasies. Further, we have to account for the fact that throughout the history of Western modernity itself ideas of masculinity and femininity have varied. Both the modern conception of labor and dualist understandings of gender are products of, and thus go hand in hand with, the specific developments that led to the dominance of capitalism. It was not until the eighteenth century that what Carol Hagemann-White calls the modern "system of dual genderedness" emerged, that led to what Karin Hausen calls a "polarization of gendered characteristics." Prior to this, women were largely regarded as just another variant of being-man, which is one of the reasons that the social and historical sciences have throughout the last fifteen years stressed the pervasiveness of the single-gender model upon which pre-bourgeois societies were based. Even the vagina was in the context of this model frequently understood as a penis, inverted and pushed into the lower body.[10] Despite the fact that women were largely regarded as inferior, prior to the development of a large-scale modern public, there still existed for them a variety of possibilities for gaining social influence. In premodern and early modern societies, man occupied a largely symbolic position of hegemony. Women were not yet exclusively confined to domestic life and motherhood, as has been the case since the eighteenth century. Women's contributions to material reproduction were in agrarian societies regarded as equally important as the contributions of men.[11] While modern gender relations and their characteristic polarization of gender roles were initially restricted to the bourgeoisie, they rapidly spread to all social spheres with the universalization of the nuclear family in the context of Fordism's rise to dominance in the 1950s.

Value dissociation is, therefore, not a static structure, as a series of sociological structuralist models claim, but should instead be understood as a process. In postmodernity, for example, value dissociation acquires a new valence. Women are now widely regarded as what Regina Becker-Schmidt calls "doubly socialized," which means that they are similarly responsible for both family and profession. What is new about this, however, is not this fact itself. After all, women have always been active in a variety of professions and trades. The characteristic particular to postmodernity in this regard is that the double socialization of women throughout the last few years has highlighted the structural contradictions that accompany this development. As indicated above, an analysis of this development must begin with a dialectical understanding of the relationship between individual and society. This means that the individual is at no point entirely subsumed within the objective structural and cultural patterns, nor can we assume that these structures stand in a purely external relation to the individual. This way, we are able to see clearly the contradictions of double socialization that are connected to the increasing differentiation of the role of women in postmodernity, which emerges alongside postmodernity's characteristic tendencies toward individualization. Current analyses of film, advertising, and literature, too, indicate that women are no longer primarily seen as mothers and housewives.

Consequently, it is not only unnecessary but in fact highly suspect to suggest that we must deconstruct the modern dualism of gender, as queer theory and its main voice, Judith Butler, claim. This strand of theory sees the internal subversion of bourgeois gender dualism via repeated parodying practice that can be found in gay and lesbian subcultures as an attempt to reveal the "radical incredulity" of modern gendered identity.[12] The problem with such an approach, however, is that those elements that are supposed to be parodied and subverted have in the capitalist sense already become obsolete. For a while now, we have been witnessing actually existing deconstruction, which becomes legible in the double socialization of women, but also when examining fashion and the changed habitus of women and men. Yet, this has happened without fundamentally eradicating the hierarchy of genders. Instead of critiquing both classically modern and the modified, flexible postmodern gendered imaginary, Butler ultimately merely affirms postmodern (gender) reality. Butler's purely culturalist approach cannot yield answers to current questions, and indeed presents to us the very problem of hierarchic gender relations in postmodernity in progressive disguise as a solution.

The Dialectic of Essence and Appearance, and the Feralization of Commodity-Producing Patriarchy in the Era of Globalization

In the attempt to analyze postmodern gender relations, it is important to insist upon the dialectic of essence and appearance. This means that changes in gender relations must be understood in relation to the mechanisms and structures of value dissociation, which determine the formal principle of all social planes. Here, it becomes apparent that in particular the development of productive forces and the market dynamic, which each rely upon value dissociation, undermine their own precondition insofar as they encourage women's development away from their traditional role. Since the 1950s, an increasing number of women were integrated into abstract labor and the process of accumulation, accompanied by a range of processes rationalizing domestic life, increased options for birth control, and the gradual equalization of access to education.[13] Consequently, the double socialization of women also underwent a change, and now resides on a higher level in the social hierarchy and similarly generates higher levels of self-valorization for women. Even though a large percentage of women have now been integrated into official society, they remain responsible for domestic life and children, they must struggle harder than men to rise up in the professional hierarchy, and their salaries are on average significantly lower than those of men. The structure of value dissociation has therefore changed, but in principle still very much exists. In this context, it may not be surprising to suggest that we appear to experience a return to a single-gender model, however with the same, familiar content: women are men, only different. Yet, since this model also moved through the classic modern process of value dissociation, it manifests itself differently than in premodern times.[14]

Traditional bourgeois gender relations are no longer appropriate for today's "turbo-capitalism" and its rigorous demands for flexibility. A range of compulsory flexible identities emerges, but these are, however, still represented as differentiated by gender.[15] The old image of woman has become obsolete and the doubly socialized woman has become the dominant role. Further, recent analyses of globalization and gender relations suggest that after a period in which it seemed as though women were finally able to enjoy greater, system-immanent freedoms, we also witnessed an increasing feralization of patriarchy. Of course, in this case, too, we have to consider a variety of social and cultural differences corresponding to a variety of global regions. Similarly, we have to note the differently situated position of women in a context in which a logic of victors and vanquished still dominates, even as the victors threaten to disappear into the abyss opened up by the current destruction of the middle class.[16] Since well situated women are able to afford the services of underpaid female immigrant laborers, we are witnessing a redistribution of, for example, personal care and nursing within the female plane of existence.

For a large part of the population, the feralization of patriarchy means that we can expect conditions similar to black ghettoes in the United States or the slums of Third World countries: women will be similarly responsible for money and survival. Women will be increasingly integrated into the world market without being given an opportunity to secure their own existence. They raise children with the help of female relatives and neighbors (another example of the redistribution of personal care and related fields of labor), while men come and go, move from job to job and from woman to woman, who may periodically have to support them. The man no longer occupies the position of provider due to the increasing precarity of employment relations and the erosion of traditional family structures.[17] Increasing individualization and atomization of social relations proceed before the backdrop of unsecured forms of existence, and continue even in times of great economic crisis without principally eradicating the traditional gender hierarchy along with the widespread eradication of the social welfare state and compulsory measures of crisis management.

Value dissociation as social formal principle consequently merely removes itself from the static, institutional confines of modernity (in particular, the family and labor). The commodity-producing patriarchy, therefore, experiences increasing feralization without leaving behind the existing relations between value (or rather, abstract labor) and the dissociated elements of reproduction. We must note here, too, that we are currently experiencing a related escalation of masculine violence, ranging from domestic violence to suicide bombers. In regards to the latter, we must further note that it is not only fundamentalist Islam that attempts to reconstruct "authentic" religious patriarchal gender relations. Indeed, it is the Western patriarchal model of civilization that should constitute the focus of our critique. Simultaneously, we are also confronted with a transition on the psychological level. In postmodernity, a "gendered code of affect" emerges that corresponds to the traditional male code of affect.[18] Nevertheless, old affective structures necessarily continue to play an important role as well, since they ensure that, even in times of postmodern single-gender relations, women continue to assume dissociated responsibilities, making possible the pervasiveness of the mother with several children who still manages to be a doctor, scientist, politician, and much more. This may occur in the form of a return to traditional female roles and ideals, particularly in times of great crisis and instability.

While turbo-capitalism demands gender-specific flexible identities, we cannot assume that corresponding postmodern gender models, such as the model of the doubly socialized woman, are permanently able to stabilize reproduction in the context of today's crisis capitalism. After all, the current stage of capitalism is characterized by the "collapse of modernization" and an associated inversion of rationalism into irrationalism.[19] The double socialization of the individualized woman should in this regard (seemingly paradoxically) be understood as serving an important, functional role for the commodity-producing patriarchy, even as the latter is slowly disintegrating. Organizations dedicated to crisis management in third world countries, for example, are frequently led by women (while one also has to recognize that reproductive activities in general are increasingly playing a subordinate role). Exemplary of the development within the West in this regard is Frank Schirrmacher (conservative journalist and coeditor of the *Frankfurter Allgemeine Zeitung*). In his 2006 book *Minimum*, he describes the "fall and re-birth of our society," in the context of which Schirrmacher wants to assign women the role of crisis managers, believing that they fulfill an important function as *Trümmerfrauen* and as cleaning and decontamination personnel.[20] In order to justify such claims, Schirrmacher mobilizes crude biological and anthropological lines of argumentation in order to account for the widespread collapse of social and gender relations and to offer so-called solutions carried out on the backs of women. In order to avoid such pseudo-solutions, it is necessary to analyze current social crises in relation to their social and historical contexts, as value dissociation theory emphasizes. From this basis, it is then also possible to ask which important theoretical and practical conclusions need to be drawn from the dilemmas of the socialization of a value dissociation that today increasingly reduces man and nature to the most basic levels of existence and that can no longer be addressed with Old Left or Keynesian reform programs. Likewise, deconstructivist and postcolonial approaches, which for example interpret racism purely culturally, are unable to address the current crisis, as are post-workerist approaches that altogether refuse to address the general problem of the socialization of value dissociation and instead seek refuge in movement-religious notions of the multitude and act as though the latter concept includes answers to racism and sexism.[21] What is required here, therefore, is a new turn toward a critique of political economy. Such a critique, however, can no longer be carried out in its traditional form that focuses on labor-ontological and androcentric-universalist methodology, but must instead include a turn toward a radical value dissociation theory and its epistemological consequences.

Conclusion

What I have attempted to show schematically in this essay is the need to think economy and culture in their contradictory identity and non-identity from the (itself contradictory) perspective of value dissociation as a basic social principle. Value dissociation, then, must also be understood not as a static structure but instead as a historically dynamic process. This approach refuses the identity-critical temptation to forcefully subsume the particular within the general. Instead, it addresses the tension between concept and differentiation (without dissolving the concept into the non-distinct, the infinite) and is thus able to speak to current processes of homogenization and differentiation in ways that can also address connected conflicts, including male violence. It is important to note that the theory of value dissociation, as far as the latter constitutes a basic social principle (and therefore is not solely concerned with gender relations in a narrow sense), must at times deny itself, insofar as it must allot next to sexism equal space to analyses of racism, antisemitism, and economic disparities, avoiding any claim toward universality. Only by relativizing its own position and function in this manner is value dissociation theory able to exist in the first place.

Notes

1. See, for instance, Scholz, *Das Geschlecht des Kapitalismus. Feministische Theorie und die postmoderne Metamorphose des Patriarchats* (Unkel: Horlemann, 2000) 61 and following, 107 and following, 184 and following, and Scholz, "Die Theorie der geschlechtlichen Abspaltung und die Kritische Theorie Adornos," *Der Alptraum der Freiheit. Perspektiven radikaler Gesellschaftskritik,* edited by Robert Kurz, Roswitha Scholz, and Jörg Ulrich (Blaubeuren: Verlag Ulmer Manuskripte, 2005).

2. Robert Kurz, *Der Kollaps der Modernisierung* (Leipzig: Reclam, 1994); Kurz, *Schwarzbuch Kapitalismus: ein Abgesang auf die Marktwirtschaft* (Frankfurt am Main: Eichborn Verlag, 1999); Moishe Postone, "Anti-Semitism and National Socialism," *Germans and Jews Since the Holocaust,* edited by Anson Rabinbach and John David Zipes (New York: Holmes and Meier, 1986); Postone, *Time, Labor, and Social Domination: A Reinterpretation of Marx's Critical Theory* (Cambridge: Cambridge University Press, 1993).

3. See Karl Marx, *Capital* Volume I, Chapter 4: "The General Formula for Capital," especially 255 [Eds.].

4. Frigga Haug, *Frauen-Politiken* (Berlin: Argument, 1996) 229 and following.

5. *ibid.*

6. Eva Herman, *Das Eva-Prinzip* (München: Pendo, 2006).

7. Regine Gildmeister and Angelika Wetterer, "Wie Geschlechter gemacht werden. Die soziale Konstruktion der Zwei-Geschlechtlichkeit und ihre Reifizierung in der Frauenforschung," *Traditionen Brüche. Entwicklungen feministischer Theorie* (Freiburg: Kore, 1992) 214 and following.

8. Haug, *Frauen-Politiken* 127 and following.

9. Since the focus of the examination at hand is on modern gender relations, I am unable to discuss these other forms of social disparity in detail. For a more substantial analysis, see Scholz, *Differenzen der Krise — Krise der Differenzen. Die neue Gesellschaftskritik im globalen Zeitalter und der Zusammenhang von "Rasse", Klasse, Geschlecht und postmoderner Individualisierung* (Unkel: Horlemann 2005).

10. Thomas Laqueur, *Making Sex: Body and Gender from the Greeks to Freud* (Cambridge: Harvard University Press, 1990) 25 and following.

11. Bettina Heintz and Claudia Honegger, "Zum Strukturwander weiblicher Widerstandsformen," *Listen der Ohnmacht. Zur Sozialgeschichte weiblicher Widerstandsformen*, edited by Bettina Heintz and Claudia Honegger (Frankfurt am Main: Europäische Verlagsanstalt, 1981) 15.

12. Judith Butler, *Gender Trouble* (London: Routeledge, 1991) 208.

13. Ulrich Beck, *Risikogesellschaft: Auf dem Wages einem andere Moderne* (Frankfurt: Suhrkampf, 1986) 174 and following.

14. Kornelia Hauser, "Die Kulturisierung der Politik. 'Anti-Political-Correctness' als Deutungskämpfe gegen den Feminismus," *Bundeszentrale für politische Bildung: Aus Politik und Zeitgeschichte* (Bomm: Beilage zur Wochenzeitung Das Parlament, 1996) 21.

15. Compare Irmgard Schultz, *Der erregende Mythos vom Geld. Die neue Verbindung von Zeit, Geld und Geschlecht im Ökologiezeitalter* (Frankfurt am Main: Campus Verlag, 1994) 198 and following, and Christa Wichterich, *Die globalisierte Frau. Berichte aus der Zukunft der Ungleichheit* (Reinbek: Rowohlt, 1998).

16. Compare Kurz, "Der letzte Stadium der Mittelklasse. Vom klassischen Kleinburgertum zum universellen Humankapital," *Der Alptraum der Freiheit, Perspectiven radikaler Gesellschaftskritik*, see 133n1.

17. Compare Schultz, *Mythos* 198 and following.

18. Compare Hauser, "Kulturisierung" 21.

19. For a more detailed account of the current stage of capitalism and its departure from the classic forms of modernity, as well as for the origins of the term "collapse of modernization," see Kurz, *Kollaps*.

20. Women who helped clear debris after World War II — literally: "rubble-women" [Eds.]. See also Christina Thürmer-Rohr, "Feminisierung der Gesellschaft. Weiblichkeit als Putz- und Entseuchungsmittel," *Vagabundinnen. Feministische Essays*, edited by Christina Thürmer-Rohr (Berlin: Orlanda Frauenverlag, 1987).

21. See Michael Hardt and Antonio Negri, *Empire* (Cambridge: Harvard University Press, 2001), and Scholz, *Differenzen* 247 and following.

The Rise and Fall of the Working Man: Toward a Critique of Modern Masculinity

Norbert Trenkle (2008)

The crisis of labor is also a crisis of modern masculinity. For in his identity, the modern bourgeois man is constituted and structured in a most fundamental way as a working man — as a someone who grapples and creates, who is target-oriented, rational, efficient, and practical, and who always wants to see a measurable result. This need not always happen "in the sweat of his brow." In this respect, modern masculine identity is very flexible. The suited man in management, consultancy, or government understands himself as a maker just as much as — or even more than — a worker in the construction industry, on the assembly line, or at the wheel of a truck. The latter have, in any case, long been outdated as models of masculine vocational orientation and are reserved to those who do not manage to jump through the social hoops on the way to the top-floor offices. However, they serve all the more as the representation of true masculinity on the symbolic level. Half-naked musclemen with heavy monkey wrenches or sledgehammers in hand, decoratively smeared with a little oil but otherwise almost aseptically stage-managed against the aestheticized backdrop of an auto workshop or a furnace, are the icons of modern masculinity.

When these men are used in advertisements for designer suits and cologne, the aim is to awaken fantasies and identificational desires that are firmly anchored in the deep structures of the construction of masculine identity. Even the pale, weedy insurance employee or corpulent, puffing sales manager of a soda firm can identify with the musclemen. On the bodily level, these are unattainable dreams. But in the psyche something else is decisive. For the musclemen and the statuesquely chiseled and hardened bodies represent the entitlement to exercise power — power over others, over the world, and over themselves. But this may be a miserable power, such as the ability to command a few employees, prevail against a rival on the market with a new kind of soda, or to have attained a rise in profits compared to the previous year. This power is also extremely precarious because it is constantly threatened and subject to revocation. For it depends not only on self-assertion in competition, which can fail at any time, but also, at the same time, on business cycles, which cannot be influenced by individuals. But it is precisely because of this uncertainty that it requires constant and aggressive self-assurance.

Modern man is thus not characterized by muscle-bound physicality as such. Rather, this symbolizes a hardness that in the first instance pertains to an inner attitude and mental (self-)punishment. A "true man" has to be hard on himself and on others. Bulging biceps are the symbol for self-mastery, discipline, and self-restraint, of the power of the will over the body. The spirit is willing, the flesh is weak — and it must therefore first be tamed if a man wants to have everything under control. Therein lies the difference from the ancient notion that a healthy spirit dwells in a healthy body. Although this idea already announces the external separation into body and mind, the aim is their balanced relationship. In the modern conception, in contrast, the domination and subjugation of the body under the mind is foregrounded. The "free will" that falsely believes itself to be independent of all sensuousness, which it must permanently fight precisely because it disowns it, and that lives in terrible fear of losing this fight, amounts to the socio-psychological core of bourgeois man.

The Labor of Desensualization

It is precisely in this respect that modern masculine identity corresponds exactly to the profile of the demands of labor in capitalist society based on universal commodity production. For labor in capitalism is by its nature a desensualized and desensualizing form of activity — in many senses. Firstly, its goal is not the manufacture of concrete, useful objects, but the production of commodities as a means of valorizing value or capital. The things that are produced thus do not count as such in their material-sensuous reality, but only so far as they are representations of value and in this form contribute to making more money out of money. From this perspective the material aspect of a commodity is a necessary evil from which one unfortunately cannot be liberated, because otherwise it would not be possible to find a buyer. This is accompanied, secondly, by a fundamental indifference toward the natural foundations of life which ultimately only count as material for valorization and even then are used up ruthlessly, despite the fact that it has for a long time been well known that this threatens the existence of millions upon millions of people. Thirdly, labor is also a desensualized activity to the extent that it takes place in a special sphere that has been detached from all other contexts of life, a sphere that is solely aimed at economic efficiency and profitability, and in which there is simply no place for other goals, needs, or feelings.

Fourthly and finally, however, labor in this form does not only represent a specific historical mode of production, but also determines the entire social context in a fundamental way — and this not only quantitatively, by means of the direct transformation of more and more areas of life into divisions of commodity production and spheres of capital investment. Labor in capitalist society represents rather the central principle of the mediation of social relations, a mediation that by its nature has an objectified, alienated form. For people do not consciously create their context by agreement or direct communication, but enter into relation with one another by the diversion of products of labor either by selling themselves as labor power or by producing commodities that are then thrown onto the market in order to realize their value. That is, in a certain way, products of labor instead of people communicate with one another, in a manner in accordance with the objectified code of the logic of valorization. Mediation through labor means subjugation of people under the presupposed laws of valorization that follow an automatized internal dynamic and that people encounter as inviolable natural laws — even though they are their own form of social relations.

The World, a Foreign Object

The almost all-encompassing establishment of this historically unique form of social activity and relation was not possible without the creation of a particular human type corresponding to it and guaranteeing that it can function adequately. For even an objectified form of relation does not produce itself independently of but through social individuals who actively produce this relation again and again. But this human type is the male-inscribed modern subject of labor and commodities, whose central essential characteristic is that the entire world becomes to him a foreign object. His relation to his social and natural context, to other people and even to his own body and his own sensuousness, is that of a relation to things — things that are supposed be processed, organized, and also treated as things — as objects of his will. The modern subject even wants to manage his feelings and correspondingly to regulate functional demands. Despite an incredible mass of self-help literature, this regularly fails, but even then the intention is by no means abandoned.

This modern form of relation to the world and to the self becomes most obvious where one sells one's labor power and thus relinquishes the power to dispose over oneself and immediately submits to the logic of valorization. But whoever works independently in no way escapes this logic but also stands under the compulsion to abstract himself from his sensuous needs and from the concrete-material characteristics of products which to him are indifferent and exchangeable means of earning his living — things of value. What is decisive, however, is that what is at stake is not an act of passive subjugation under a merely external compulsion, but that modern subjectivity is structured according to this compulsion. Only in this way can the obligation to function without rest, the obligation to objectification and self-objectification for the duration of the entire labor process, be fulfilled without a slave driver brandishing the whip. To the external pressure corresponds an internal pressure. It is precisely for this reason that the objectifying pattern of action and behavior is in no way restricted only to the spheres of labor and economy, but shapes the entire network of social relationships. But because this is intolerable in the long term (because having to act that way requires constant strain and exertion and permanently threatens to fail), the modern subject of labor and the commodity has such a fundamental hatred of all those who flounder under these pressures or even refuse them altogether.

Man Makes Woman

The Protestant work ethic first elevates this human type, which abstracts from its sensuousness and makes itself into a means of attaining an objectified success, to an ideal. At a time when the capitalist mode of production was only beginning to establish itself on a few islands in the ocean of feudal society, it already anticipated in the history of ideas the profile of requirements pertinent to a social context mediated through labor and the commodity form, and thus made a decisive contribution to its general establishment. In actually existing history, it was centuries before the human type that corresponded to these requirements was formed and had become the normal case. The entire history of early capitalism and its establishment is one of violent training and self-training of people into subjects of labor and the commodity. A history that is also one of stubborn resistance to this formation, which ultimately, however, could not be prevented.

That in this process the modern subject form was at the same time inscribed in terms of gender with the result that it corresponds to the time of modern masculine identity can be explained in the first instance historically, by means of the long prehistory of patriarchal domination on which capitalist society is based, and which it reinscribes and transforms in its own way. The identification of man with abstract reason and woman with sensuousness, which is at the same time devalued, desired, and fought against within her, follows in the wake of a long tradition that dates back at least to Greek antiquity, and which was adopted by Christianity and reinterpreted and further developed in accordance with its needs. However, in capitalist society this construction gains a new and central significance to the extent that the abstract and objectified relation to the world becomes the general mode of socialization. For this reason it combines with the basic social structure in a most fundamental way. The training of men into agents of objectification can draw on a variety of elements of the prior model of patriarchal masculinity; alongside identification with reason, this means in the first instance identification with the warrior, the violent subjugator. However, with the reification of all social relations, they are recomposed into a largely coherent and self-contained identity of "man."

However, this could not succeed without the creation of a feminine counter-identity that unites all those features that the modern subject cannot endure because they do not fit in the system of coordinates of the construction of masculine identity, and which the subject must therefore split off projectively. This is the basis for the creation of a feminine "other," the sensuous, emotional, and impulsive woman who cannot think logically or hammer a nail in the wall and is therefore charged with looking after the children, the household, and the well-being of "her" man. The invention of this "other" not only brings about the stabilization of the masculine subject's identity — at the same time, it also installs and legitimizes a gendered division of labor that is thoroughly functional for the capitalist enterprise, because it takes the load off the working man, enabling him fully to exert himself in the sphere of labor and commodity production that has been dissociated from the contexts of everyday life.

Working Man in Crisis

Now while this construct of femininity has been called into question by the wide-ranging inclusion of women in the capitalist labor process on one hand, and by the women's movement on the other, it nonetheless persists astonishingly stubbornly, and has in its core held its ground until the present day. To the extent that women have succeeded in gaining positions of social power, this has always happened at the cost of accommodating the requirements of the masculine norms of labor, competition, and abstract achievement. At the same time, seen in society as a whole, their primary responsibility for household and children remains preserved, and objectification of the female body for men's sexualized fantasies is all-pervasive, as a glance at the display of any magazine kiosk or billboard demonstrates.

This tenaciousness of polarized capitalist gender identities may at first glance seem surprising. But as long as the social context continues to be produced in the reified forms of relation of commodity, money, and labor, the male-inscribed subject-form that is proper to it survives. Even the current crisis process that catapults people out of the labor process on a massive scale or forces them into increasingly precarious working conditions in no way removes the gender identities. While it is true that the crisis process unsettles one of the basic pillars of male identity, it nonetheless at the same time leads to an intensification of competition at all levels of everyday life. However, under these conditions the classical qualities of modern masculinity such as hardness, assertiveness, and ruthlessness are more in demand than ever. It is thus no surprise that the cult of masculinity — including sexist and racist violence — is booming again today. For this reason, it is precisely under the conditions of the extensive crisis process that a fundamental critique of the modern, male-structured subject is necessary in order to open up a new perspective of social emancipation.

Off Limits, Out of Control: Commodity Society and Resistance in the Age of Deregulation and Denationalization

Ernst Lohoff (2009)

Part One: The Commodity's Final and Fatal Victory

The Heteronomy of Politics

From the end of World War I until well into the 1970s it was generally agreed that the future belonged to a market economy modified by state intervention and socially protectionist policies. This was, especially during the post-World War II boom, a perspective shared by all the dominant social and political powers within the centers of the world market. In the 1960s, this program operated in West Germany and Austria under the brand name of the "Social Market Economy" (*Soziale Marktwirtschaft*) and in the United States under that of the "Great Society." In neither instance was there any question that the state had to act as a counterweight to the free play of market forces. The welfare state in particular was regarded as a virtual synonym for modernity itself, and on both sides of the Atlantic the politics of reform meant nothing if not the robust will to build such a state.

But this scenario has, in more recent times, been radically overturned. As the leitmotif of the globalized capitalism developing since the 1980s now has it: whereever the state is, there the market shall be. The welfare state in particular, formerly the epitome of progress, has now come to stand for backwardness and ossification. Everyone knows, even in the world market centers themselves, that the very idea of such a state has ceased to play any ideological role whatsoever in mobilizing contemporary mass movements. Since the turn of the millennium, both in continental Europe and in Great Britain and, prior to that, in the United States, decades' worth of the welfare state's social accomplishments have been cast overboard with breathtaking speed.

The liquidators of the welfare state and the proponents of privatization and deregulation justify their efforts as long-overdue corrections to politically motivated errors years in the making. Government "over-regulation," which paralyzes private initiative, conspires with a welfare state that has "grown out of control" to block — so it is said — the path to growth and prosperity. On and on drone the ideological prayer wheels of market economics about the urgent need to eliminate such obstacles.

Defenders of state regulation and of the welfare state's erstwhile attempt at social redistribution see things differently. It is not the accomplishments of the welfare state but the decision to eliminate the state that produced them that amounts to the error in policy, a policy lacking any interest in the true common good of modern labor society.[1] Each of the conflicting parties arrives at a diametrically opposed assessment when it comes to diagnosing ongoing antistatist developments, but the opposing diagnoses themselves nevertheless follow the very same explanatory model. One side is no different from the other when it comes to the fact that both stubbornly treat state regulation solely as a dependent variable governed by political dissension and decision making. The trials and tribulations of political struggle are what stand out here, in the final instance, as the real causative factors for whatever priority, be it low or high, the state is to be accorded in the production and distribution of wealth in commodity society.

The Left variant of this line of argument ought to be familiar enough: labor-protection laws, reduced working hours, standardized wages, and health, accident, unemployment, and retirement/pension benefits (social security) had all been wrested from capitalism through hard-fought class struggles. Today, capital is exploiting the weakness of the organized working class to take back these concessions and reinstate the old-style capitalism of the "Manchester School."

Such a view of things gets this much right: the struggles of the workers' movement supplied the essential impetus for the process of building the welfare state. And, by the same token, its subsequent phasing out is also hardly thinkable without the fierce ideological determination of the neoliberal converts assigned the task of digging its grave. But this interpretation goes wrong by treating the decisions governing the political course of action as *prima causa*. As a result, what is essential falls by the wayside. In taking up the major political concepts at work here, we are already dealing with forms of reacting to and working through underlying structural developments that lie outside of the purview of political action itself. The architects of the welfare state were therefore only able to achieve lasting success because they added something indispensable to the implementation and universalization of the system of capitalist wealth production. And even in the case of today's purely market-ideology-driven asset strippers, we are confronted with more than an aberration owing to a politically unfavorable balance of forces; upon closer examination, such enterprises reveal themselves as part of a thoroughly logical, intracapitalist response to a deep-seated structural crisis of labor and valorization. The political paradigm shift points to a fundamental contradiction internal to the production of wealth in commodity society: both the movement toward greater statification and that toward destatification are to be grasped as historical forms of development of this internal contradiction.

A Brief Political Economy of the Public Sector

Let us begin with a clarification of the above contradictory relationship at an initially very basic level, namely with the question of what is to be generally understood, according to the logic of capitalism, by wealth. Marx provides an answer right in the two opening sentences of *Capital*: "The wealth of societies in which the capitalist mode of production prevails appears as an 'immense collection of commodities'; the individual commodity appears as its elementary form."[2] This definition can also be read in the sense of a "historical mission," i.e., an immanent historical tendency of the commodity form. Capitalist society is (in this latter sense) characterized by the drive to convert the largest possible portion of the wealth of society into commodities and to convert all producers of wealth into commodity producers. The more consistently a society achieves this, the purer the form of capitalism characterizing it.

As far as the annihilation of traditional, non-monetary forms of social reproduction is concerned, the above-described historical development has remained faithful to the very letter of the commodity's "historical mission." In the metropolitan countries at least, such non-monetary societies had either been wiped out or completely marginalized by the twentieth century at the latest. Parallel to this, meanwhile, a new actor had been taking center stage in matters of wealth production: the state. The increase in activities carried out by the state was of course itself an integral part of the larger process of the monetarization and the transformation of all socially valid activity into paid labor. Yet the state itself played no direct part in the process of commodification. The social wealth generated by state activities did not, in point of fact, consist of an additional mass of commodities produced with optimal marketability in mind. Wherever the state provides goods directly or, in the case of their commercial exchange, has its finger in the pot, what it in fact does is to cancel out the exchange of equivalents as the form of social relations subsisting between commodity owners. So what, then, could have prompted commodity society to put in place alongside itself a form of the production and distribution of wealth (the state) so at odds with its own ideal form of wealth production?

The solution to this riddle lies in the particular character that wealth takes on through its transformation into commodities. This transformation binds together in itself two contradictory moments. The elementary unit of capitalist wealth, the individual commodity, thus represents something fundamentally paradoxical, something that might be termed "asocial sociality" (*ungesellschaftliche Gesellschaftlichkeit*).[3]

Looked at from one side, the commodity's rise to dominance as a form of wealth leads to the formation of a highly socialized system with a correspondingly highly developed division of labor. The historical advance of the commodity has as its logical horizon the world market and hence the fusion of production and consumption into one planetary, interconnected whole. Individual producers and commodity subjects act as the (mutually and fully interdependent) members of a gigantic social unit.

At the same time, the reduction of wealth as such to wealth in its commodity form signifies a systematic desocialization. This is so in two respects. On one hand, desocialization is entailed by the domination of the commodity form, under which social relations exist only as relations between things. From this it also follows that, since society simply cannot function without certain directly social relationships, there can only be a place for the latter in a specialized sphere dissociated from the primary one constituted by the actual thinglike social nexus. On the other hand, however, given the metamorphosis of all the manifold relationships to material goods into what now becomes exclusively a relationship to commodities, we are concerned here with a radically desocialized relational context that tolerates no other occupant besides itself within the seemingly limitless universe of commodities. From the standpoint of the producer, the sensory-material qualities of the product together with its social effect and social reality appear totally irrelevant. Only its marketability is of any concern. From the producer's perspective there is, correspondingly, no difference whatsoever between poison gas and penny candy, or between violent video games and velvet curtains. The buyer can for her part never acquire anything more than isolated end products, the determinate origins and thus the social dimensions of which lie entirely outside her reach. In the end, the commodity subject, situated in an external relation to all commodities in general, remains utterly and completely unrelated to all commodities that she does not happen to encounter as a buyer or seller. It is only with the merest fragment of the commodity cosmos, residing within a veritable nanosphere of the latter, that the commodity subject can, via payment, enter into any relationship at all. Anyone within the commodity universe who falls out of the cycle of buying and selling immediately finds herself in the uncomfortable position of a fish out of water, cut off, within a hypersocialized world, from everything that makes up human existence.

Yet the inner contradiction between total sociability and radical asociality, thought through to its end, leads to nothing short of self-destruction. A society that actually sought to drive absolutely every expression of life through the needle's eye of the exchange of equivalents would become incapable of self-reproduction. To avoid breaking itself apart, commodity society is bound to desystematize certain components of the social production of wealth, but only so as to subsume them indirectly within the commodity form. This applies first of all to the broad palette of household activities. The indispensable processes that go into the preparation and subsequent adjustments required for personal commodity consumption, together with central aspects of basic social care giving, are relegated to a sphere dissociated from valorization proper. Commodity society relies implicitly on the fact that someone or something, as a rule feminine "invisible hands" ignored by the official bookkeepers, raise children, take care of family members, and run households.

But commodity society relies on more than just this compressed form of immediately social relations, here made up of activities that are carried out at low (or no) cost and require no large-scale or concentrated output. In order to be able to act as commodity subjects, people must find already in place certain general infrastructural preconditions without which their mode of existence is impossible. There can be no individual movement from one place to another without usable roads for these individuals' private vehicles. No labor power can enter the labor market without first passing through educational institutions and being fitted to the universal cultural standards that are deemed necessary. In order that the very preconditions for existence as a commodity subject should become universally accessible to all potential commodity subjects, these preconditions may not themselves assume commodity form. The further the development of productivity moves forward, the more profoundly, the more differentially scaled, and the more extensive this system of non-commodity infrastructural outlays becomes, to the extent that only the state as abstract universality is in any position to take its maintenance upon itself. The asocial character of commodity society imposes on the latter, as still another of its essential aspects, the formation of a second, derivative form of wealth. Were it not for the emergence of a wide-ranging sector of state-organized wealth production, the victorious onslaught of the primary commodity form of wealth could never have taken place.

In commodity society, wealth always finds social recognition in the same way, namely through its transformation into monetarized relationships. Whatever does not replace itself with the supreme commodity among commodities is an irrelevant moment of merely private satisfaction. Social significance goes wherever money flows.

The expansion of the state sector also finds its place in the larger historical process of monetarization. The state-linked, secondary, variant form of wealth, however, differs decisively from the monetarization that is synonymous with the advance of the commodity. Observed from the perspective of society as a whole, the production of marketable commodities is transparently that which increases monetary wealth. When observed from this same perspective, state-organized wealth production appears, by contrast, as consumption — that is, as consumption by the state. Commodity society's secondary (state) form of wealth must be fed by commodity wealth in its primary (private) form.

What is, overall, the deficit-like quality of this secondary form of wealth is itself indebted to a fundamental difference in the form of social mediation. Exchange relationships function strictly according to the principle of equivalence. He who wants to be in possession of a commodity must cede its counter-value to the seller, thereby realizing it as a value. In the state sector, however, this principle of equivalence is breached. Here value does not exchange itself for counter-value. Giving and receiving here diverge, at least in part. The first assumes the form of administratively and juridically established obligations to pay (taxes, levies, and so on) and the second the form of legally established claims to payment.

In the case of state activities financed exclusively by taxes and levies and available free of charge to all potential users, this decoupling of giving and receiving is complete. But even public infrastructure for which monetary payment is binding is in no way subject to the principle of equivalence. This applies not only to public utilities operating at a loss but also and just as much to those which operate at a profit. Their very infrastructural character, their focus on a comprehensive level of service, no matter the mandated area of responsibility, finds its juridical expression in a universal duty to provide such service. Public enterprises are obliged, independent of whatever the particular costs of its provision, to offer every citizen their service or product for an identical sum of payment. In lieu of price, what we have here is the charging of a fee.

Commodity society rests on the basis of one particular commodity, that of labor power. The valorization of value is a system dependent upon human material compatible with valorization. Among the general preconditions for commodity production which it is therefore the task of the state to guarantee is not only access to the commodity of labor-power, but also the maintenance of this commodity at a level of quality that matches the highest attained level of productivity.

This task coincides in part with the state's ability to supply common infrastructural needs. Current, future, and former sellers of labor power also, as do all other categories of commodity owners, make use of the educational system, of the transportation network, of cultural facilities — not to mention such things as the public water supply. But to the same extent that the owner of labor power rises to the dominant position among all other categories of commodity owners, there falls to the state as regulatory agent yet another function resulting from the special character of the dominant, labor-power commodity. It is this that obliges the state to become a social or welfare state in the narrower sense of the word.

Whoever is in possession of the commodity of labor power enjoys a twofold freedom. Like any other commodity subject she can dispose freely of her commodity and may even take her own hide to market. At the same time, the owner of this commodity is also freed of all possible modes of self-reproduction that could spare her that trip. This second freedom means nothing other than the structural compulsion to work.

The structural compulsion to work, meanwhile, does not always guarantee the possibility that the owner of labor power will be able to live off the proceeds of its sale. Existence as a seller of labor power is, it so happens, bound up with certain routine risks in the individual lives of such salespersons. The ability to work can be lost intermittently (as in the case of illness), or on a continuing basis (as in the case of old age or occupational disability), or it may, temporarily, fail to find anyone able or willing to put it to use. Against the occurrence of such risks, the welfare state and its mandatory insurance programs organize alternative revenue sources and thereby provide the displaced owners of labor power with a secondary, substitute form of access to the wonderful world of commodities. But the welfare state's socially redistributive policies have never, as a matter of principle, overridden the structural compulsion to work. On the contrary. For one thing, the duration and scope of welfare-state services are as a rule tied to wage income calculated in advance as a sum still to be generated; for another, in the case of all who are officially able to work, officially monitored readiness for work always takes the place of actual work itself. Where readiness for work begins and where it ends certainly leaves considerable room for interpretation. A certain easing of the strict compulsion to sell oneself always represents a kind of collective hedging against the dangers of existence as such for the sellers of labor power.

The Market's Pyrrhic Victory

Along with the triumphal march of commodity society in the twentieth century came the advance of the state. This was the only conceivable way that the glaring internal contradiction of "asocial sociality" could find even a provisional resolution. But this provisional resolution had a catch. It functions unproblematically only as long as the mass of value-producing labor — that is, labor in its self-objectifying, commodity form — continues to grow. But, no later than the revolution in microelectronics, a depletion of the labor substance (i.e., of the substance of value itself) becomes evident in the core industrial sectors. The discrepancy between continuous increases in the cost of maintaining necessary infrastructural supports and the shrinkage of the value-productive core itself leads to a structural crisis in the financing of the activist, "social" state. Commodity society is now threatened with being crushed by its own *faux frais*.

The crisis of labor society does not only create problems as far as financing the state's general array of public services is concerned. At the same time it undermines and renders more pliable what had until then been the statutes governing the practical services required of the state itself. The immediate and primary effect here is to raise the question of what, in any genuine sense, the welfare state now represents.

Commodity society in the age of Fordist mass labor can be described as a form of community based on repressive integration. As previously suggested in this context, the welfare state achieved its real prominence as an instrument both for making labor power fully accessible to the market and for enabling its flexibilization. Its construction was one of the indispensable preconditions for the individualizing or atomizing of universal social welfare provisions and for the suppression of precapitalist forms of reproduction resting on traditional family-based self-sufficiency. Without this protection against the routine dangers that constitute the existence of those who must sell their own labor power, people would hardly have been disposed to enter quite so willingly into this mode of existence.

In light of the crisis in Fordist labor society, more and more superfluous human material — superfluous in the capitalist sense, that is — falls under the jurisdiction of the welfare state. Yet with the change in its clientele, the respective functions of the welfare state's integrative and disciplinary mechanisms within the system of capitalist valorization begin to diverge. The welfare state's social safeguards, until now considered to be part of future as well as the current costs of enabling the productive exploitation of labor power, threaten to become, from the standpoint of capitalism as a whole, yet another of those notorious "misallocated resources." From the perspective of the local communities that begin to take the place of the national economy, the constant investment of scarce monetary resources in people from whom any corresponding return is scarcely to be expected is a "luxury." The "generosity" with which those "let go" were carried over until being rehired — under the premise that their having been let go was simply the temporarily conferred status of being a potential labor and commodity subject *honoris causa* — loses its material basis. The welfare state mutates into an authority in charge of selection and exclusion, one that must make the cut between valorizable and unvalorizable human material. If the logic of commodity society is thought through to its bitter end, there remains for the latter of these two types of human material only existence as a monetary subject without money.

The creation of fictitious capital provided the dynamic mechanism necessary to manage and carry forward the underlying crisis of post-Fordist labor society in the 1980s and 1990s. Anticipating the profitable utilization of future labor served as the substitute fuel for the flagging exploitation of actual, present-tense labor and kept the valorization machine running and, in appearance, moving forward. The hopes of casino capitalism found their material basis first and foremost in the new communications technologies. In this field, a new, additional gigantic infrastructure emerged which was supposed to generate provides for the private economic sphere.

The crash of the New Economy, however, delivered its verdict on the above, in double form. Firstly, that, over time, the trick of burning unmined coal comes to nothing. Secondly, that the attempt to turn the investment of substantial sums in the new communications infrastructure into the gold of saleable commodities has strict limits.

But of course the disaster did not herald the end of efforts to privatize the infrastructure. Prompted by the precarious financial conditions of state-held assets, what changed was more a matter of shifting the focus of the enterprise. In place of the capitalizing of unsecured future expected earnings, attention turned increasingly to another means of reheating the economy, less ephemeral than "unmined coal." What had been the state-owned and state-supplied general, material means required for all present and future social reproduction were now primed to be transformed into robustly profitable commodities. And it is the latter that now suddenly offer themselves up as combustible material ready to be thrown into the open maws of the profit engines, while whatever refuses to let go of its combustion value is ballast to be thrown overboard.

Our own present-day capitalism effaces the difference between the infrastructural preconditions of commodity production and commodity production tout court. This variant of capitalist accumulation models itself on a scene straight out of Jules Verne's *Around the World in Eighty Days*. The steamer that is to take the hero Phileas Fogg across the Atlantic and back to England runs out of coal too early. Fogg thereupon convinces the captain and crew to burn the ship itself piece by piece so that the boiler can keep up a head of steam.

What consequences does the adoption of Fogg's method have for commodity society?

The argument as it has been developed above already gives us the answer in its fullest and most fundamental sense: the commodity represents nothing other than the paradox of asocial sociality. In order that, despite this inner contradiction, the general social parameters that are the precondition of commodity society can be rendered secure, a secondary, state-organized form of wealth must take up its place alongside commodity production. But when the state's contribution to wealth production is converted into commodities, they lose the safeguard provided by the state. Here the advance of the commodity pushes society rapidly towards its own dissolution. The exclusion of those whose labor power can no longer be valorized, the dismantling of the social safety net so as gradually to turn over all responsibility for provision of care to the market — all this proves itself upon closer examination to consist of partial moments in a much more sweeping and generalized process of desocialization.

What the details of such desocialization turn out to be after a given time is dependent on the specific state-organized social programs and services, responsibility for which is currently being turned over to the market. But when it is a question of the most basic and universal infrastructural operations, such as transportation, electrical utilities, the water supply, the mail, and, above all, the further question of the infrastructural goods and services produced by such operations, a problem arises. Pure market relations are not universal but particular relations between the two separate parties to an exchange. The commodity seller never enters into relation with the entirety of all exchange partners, but rather only into as many profitable individual relationships as possible. But such relations collide with the comprehensive and generalized character of infrastructure. Privatization leads unavoidably to cherry-picking and concentration of the supply of goods within core areas of profitability. Economic logic cannot resist neglecting or shutting down lines of production that either do not pay or do so only conditionally. Coupling the privatization of infrastructure with legally stipulated commitments to provide basic care leads, under the banner of cost optimization, to a constant tendency to bid down to nothing the very meaning of basic care and social welfare.

For a functioning infrastructure, reliability of supply is worth a great deal. Such reliability is tied to reserves. The mechanism of valorization as a whole is dependent on the fact that, in the case of electrical, water, and communications infrastructure, potential can be distinguished from actually existing capacity. Maintaining such a difference, however, is a direct slap in the face for economic logic. This logic knows and wants to know only the commandment of minimizing the cost of each individual commodity. Profit maximization implies the minimization of the difference between the potential and actual efficiency of infrastructural systems. But that necessarily leads to a lack of flexibility during the fluctuations and disruptions affecting such systems. Where the market forces its logic onto infrastructure, periodic collapses are as good as preprogrammed. In this regard, the power outages in the United States during the summer of 2003, for example, demonstrated quite clearly the social price exacted by the private sector's drive to minimize costs when this drive invades infrastructural enterprises.

Using the services provided by public infrastructure has also involved and in most cases continues to involve a cost. Anyone who has water and electricity provided at home or who uses public transportation still has to pay when a public company provides these products and services. The obligation to pay here takes the form of a fee. If the same infrastructure is turned over to the market, the monetary relationship changes, and a price takes the place of the fee. What changes as a result? In the eyes of a public company that is a contractual supplier, all whom it supplies are equal. In principle, the fee does not recognize any difference between bigger and smaller consumers and it is usually constant over a longer time period. Things look different when there is a price. The latter, in principle, prefers bigger customers and shows significant fluctuations.

Privatization was and is sold to the public as a way of getting rid of bureaucracy. Competition and a profit-seeking outlook ostensibly ensure that the most customer-friendly companies with the most attractive level of service will ultimately prevail in the marketplace. Instead, competition between privatized infrastructure providers after the elimination of state monopolies is the guarantee of a hopeless tangle and confusion concerning what is for sale and what it costs. Buying infrastructural goods and services becomes a full-time job for those really interested in finding the best price. The outsourcing of various subdivisions of problem solving and compliance to subcontractors creates confusion about administrative responsibility that in retrospect makes the earlier pedantic state operation look like a refuge of transparency and efficiency — a transition that also occasionally involves life-threatening risks for its new clientele.

The commodification process also seizes hold of health insurance and old-age pensions. In answer to the financial plight inflicted upon such basic social security programs by the crisis of post-Fordist labor society the slogan of the day has become: "personal responsibility." Translation: turn over responsibility for your fate to market forces. What are the consequences of this shifting of responsibility? Two are immediately obvious. First: if what was formerly financed out of the employer's share of payroll deductions and other taxes is now to be paid out of an individual worker's wages, the costs of reproducing labor power as a commodity will, on average, go up. Second: many people are in no actual position to undertake these additional expenditures. For the younger generation in particular, the level of public provision for basic needs and of accumulated pension benefits sinks dramatically. Not only unemployment but the other two routine dangers in the typical experience of all who must sell their own labor power, old age and illness, repeat the same story: poverty.

That the advance of the market into the sphere of welfare benefits makes it harder for more and more people to have any share in them is a fact due mainly to successive changes in the mode of access to such benefits. The establishment of the welfare state meant the partial decoupling of the individual beneficiary's level of contribution from the general provision of benefits and, at the same time, the grouping together of insured individuals with different degrees of risk into what were, for monetary purposes, forms of association based on shared liability. Precisely these two aspects of the welfare state's celebrated forms of communities of solidarity were done away with by the accelerating intervention of market forces. The latter led, in the first instance, to the inevitable practice of sorting good from bad levels of risk. It became obligatory for those with a higher individual probability of claiming an insurance benefit to pay for the latter with higher individual premiums. Add to this the fact that the principle of equivalence itself disallows the practice of extending the same insurance benefit in exchange for differing premiums. Social security policies financed through worker and employer contributions were of the greatest benefit to those at lower income levels. The privileged treatment once accorded to the latter falls victim to the onslaught of the principle of equivalence.

This systemic change comes to light most noticeably in the health insurance service.In the competition between public, legally instituted and private health insurers, two opposed interpretations of equality confront each other. Public health insurance providers stand for the principle of equal access for all insured persons. "Personal responsibility," as the new slogan for private insurers in the medical field, advances the sacred principle of equivalence in its quest to achieve legitimacy. Health mutates from a universally accessible good to a commodity that one must be able to afford. The trend towards cutting people off from health care may trigger some amount of outrage; but all the while the underlying logic of such a trend can even become a kind of advertising slogan in places like this. (Delusional systems are always consistent.) At any rate, not so long ago a major German insurance company advertised with the following slogan: "It's all the same to a tooth-decay bacterium how much you earn. The same goes for a supplementary health insurance policy from Allianz."

Part Two: Fightback

What distinguishes present-day capitalism is the split between sensory-material and monetary forms of wealth. For commodity society, moreover, it is only insofar as wealth attains representational form as abstract labor that it has a right to existence. And yet this transformation itself becomes more and more problematic. Market radicalism is at the same time both an ideological reflex of and a form of processing this deep-seated, inescapable, and systemic contradiction. Yet with its widely implemented programs of commodification and deregulation, such market radicalism still cannot confront the fact that the general requirements of commodity production can now be organized only at the cost of social disruptions even more severe than the harsh demands made by contemporary commodity production itself. Capitalism had, with good reason, always assigned the task of such organization to the state as total capitalist. The market-radical concept is, by comparison, sheer hallucination when it comes to perceiving the difference — thinking again here of Phileas Fogg — between the engine itself and the fuel that it burns: for it makes what is tantamount to the structural attempt to keep the ship that is commodity society under steam a while longer through successive acts of self-combustion.

Market-Radical Ideology and Capital's Systemic Imperative

Throughout the entire history of capitalism, the ideas that have won out and gained decisive influence in conflicts over ideological orientation have been those that, after their own fashion, best reflected the overall logic of the system and the historically most advanced level of internal contradictions achieved by capitalist society at any given moment of its development. As forms of fetishized awareness, however, such dominant ideas were never simply the translation of real-time systemic imperatives onto the level of functional immediacy. No given political tendency or world view is ever exhausted in a set of purely executive functions. The same applies to the presently dominant "free market" and "every-man-for-himself" ideological frenzies. Those who proclaim the latter have, ironically, become today's most enthusiastic imitators of paleo-Marxism's erstwhile historical teleology: just as the Second International's adherents believed they had the iron necessity of history to back them up, so today's market radicals speak in swaggering tones of "unavoidable constraints" as they implement programs for dismantling the state.

Such self-understanding, however, soon becomes a diversion from what actually supplies the electrical charge for market radicalism's ideological circuitry. The "free market" and "every-man-for-himself" mania reveals itself most unmistakably, as do all ideologies, in its moments of excess, of overshooting the mark. Yet, as the present epoch's salvational religion, market radicalism takes on, over and above this, and in the worst possible sense, a visionary and utopian character that accesses reality as a whole, as though making a package deal of itself in both an ideal and a no less real sense. (In its claim to being a program for world transformation, market radicalism has almost cast itself as the rightful heir to socialism itself.) The market radicals are not mere crisis administrators. The nature of their ideology, combining social Darwinism with a work ethic so severe as to be a kind of terrorism, drives its own adherents towards its overfulfillment and hence to a completely one-sided but thereby, ironically, also a highly coherent understanding of contemporary capitalism's systemic imperatives.

Herein consists both the strength and the weakness of the market-radical project. On one hand, in its contempt for reality, market radicalism, more than almost any of the projects for world transformation that have preceded it, refuses to swerve from a path of completely foreseeable damage and destruction. Forcing its way through social reality, the steamroller of the market radicals' drive for world betterment leaves behind it one heap of rubble after another. Market radicalism's ideological overhaul of all that precedes it, however, thereby continuously brings into existence new flanks of attack and social battlefields. Not only does the project of social self-combustion as a whole show itself, even from capital's own immanent standpoint, to be made up of (to put it mildly) dysfunctional traits; the same can be said of all its individual undertakings as well.

On the other hand, the total and merciless identification with the pure logic of money positions the market radicals, as the only force still occupying the generalized ground of commodity society, as thereby also the only such force able both to provide a coherent interpretation of and perspective on the world — and the only force from which any claim to universality can be expected. (Racist ideologies, by contrast, relinquish such claims to universality.) In view of this capacity, the transitions toward outright sacrifice demanded by market radicalism's new doctrine of salvation, having formerly entered into competition with neo-Keynesian concepts of crisis management, turn into what is almost an argument in their own favor. For whatever does not at present cause any harm, can in the long run — so the market-radical logic will have it — be of no real help. With market radicalism an ideology comes into play in which, out of their own sheer, abject need, open machine-gunnings and summary executions can be sold to the slain as collateral damage that they themselves have, perforce, already accepted out of what appears to be well-understood, long-term self-interest.

This peculiar dialectic does not show the way to its own, immanent breakup. To oppose it and to occupy, in an emancipatory spirit, the many separate fields of conflict that it opens up, demands a counter-positioning that, for its part, also draws on a universal standpoint, and does so in a manner that sets forth a fundamental critique of the system.

There is no successful resistance without a vision with which to counter "free market" madness.

Commodity society makes all people into commodity and money subjects without distinction. Correspondingly, so as to wrestle over a larger share of social wealth while still resting on the ground of the existing order, all emancipatory currents had to transform themselves into or merge with existing mechanisms for asserting and enforcing banal, competitive self-interests. Striving to let go of their commodity only under the best possible conditions puts the vendors of the labor-power commodity in league with all other categories of commodity owners. In the struggle over social distribution, a recipient of social security payments is, after all, no less enamored of his money than is any given capitalist. And yet, the history of capitalism has, strictly speaking, yet to see a single struggle for improved living conditions that could be reduced to nothing more than the mere putting into effect of vulgar, competitively driven self-interests. The accomplishment of even the most modest collective achievements always presupposes a partial suspension of competition within capitalism's "human resources." All the social struggles arising from within the dominant competitive society have survived by forming an image of themselves in opposition to such a society, however vague it may have been. Yet with the fading of these counter-images they have also lost their vehement edge, and, far and wide, what was once their oppositionality loses all force.

In the age of the workers' movement, the idea of the expropriation of the expropriators — that is, the vision of seizing the great machine of labor and submitting it to the solidarity-based rule of the proletariat — served as a source of power. Yet, with the passing of that age, its corresponding image of another, different society has become profoundly exhausted. The discontent that has greeted the general offensive of market radicalism cannot transform itself into a new emancipatory countermovement until a new, more far-reaching dream takes the place of the one that has faded. The process of forming new solidarities requires that the thought of the direct appropriation of social wealth and of its productive powers becomes, itself, socially contagious. The labor and valorization machine monopolizes all resources for itself while at the same time finding less and less use for the resources of human capital, with the result that even in the metropolitan centers the more or less tolerable conditions of servitude cannot be scraped together. The adequate emancipatory response to this situation can only be the desire to dismantle the labor machine that is suffocating on its own abundance of goods. Only the counter-image arising from the radical critique of commodity society from the ground up will allow for an offensive redrawing of the social battle lines. If both the market and the mechanical demiurge of the state declare that the majority of people are superfluous, do they demonstrate anything other than their own superfluity? Society must free itself from the structural compulsion to reduce all wealth to commodity wealth and all social relations to juridical and commodity relations. For the production of goods this means the transition to a direct social reproduction oriented solely toward criteria of sensuous need, a reproduction that functions without the detours of money and state.

Needless to say, the counter-perspective cannot be translated into a mere program of ad hoc appropriation. It aims rather at profound and correspondingly long-term processes of radical upheaval. Without such a far-reaching outlook and sense of direction, however, the opponents of market radicalism not only remain at a disadvantage, but are also condemned to being worn out in blindly defensive skirmishes.

A Priori Obedience and the Paradigm of Financial Feasibility

In this respect, the current situation actually speaks a completely unambiguous language. The initial phase of grandiose neoliberal euphoria and optimism dating back to the 1980s and early 1990s has subsided.[4] However, despite — or rather, precisely because of — the crisis of casino capitalism, all the predominant social forces reveal themselves to be more committed than ever to the market-radical program. The world over, commodification and privatization are the absolute watchwords and demands of the hour. In order that growth and employment become possible again, the market and personal responsibility must finally replace the state's duty to provide across-the-board care, so it is claimed everywhere. The implementation of this program leaves in its wake a broad swathe of social devastation and provokes resistance and protests. Indeed, in a few countries, the waves of new atrocities are already bringing millions of people onto the streets. And yet the opponents of market-radical rampages remain at a disadvantage in the social array of conflicting forces, and, in the battle for public opinion, hopelessly positioned on the defensive — and this remains so the world over.

The fundamental premises of what now passes as social criticism also bear a decisive share of the responsibility for this intolerable situation. Drawing on what are essentially the nostalgic reminiscences of Fordist capitalism under the protection of the welfare state, the opponents of market radicalism assume as self-evident what also holds as self-evident for the market radicals: social reproduction can only ever be the waste product of successful valorization on all levels of society and of the accumulation of monetary wealth. And sharing just as much in the dominant market-radical consensus, market radicalism's opponents also treat monetary wealth and material wealth as coextensive. But whoever operates with these axioms performs, against his own intention, a premature act of obedience to the deadly logic of commodity society. Neo-Keynesian arguments stubbornly repeat this, as if only the proof that capitalist growth could be attained in some other manner, with many fewer victims, could legitimate opposition to market-radical rampages. By supposing that the problem of "but where are we going to find the money?" can in fact be solved by the application of its concepts, neo-Keynesianism has already allowed itself to be knocked out of the ring by market radicalism, whose arguments it has already conceded as the criterion of all criteria, thus also acknowledging the overall primacy of the logic of money and profit. It is thus always already on the road to defeat. In the struggle between what are essentially competing hallucinatory systems, the market radicals, in keeping both feet planted on the ground of this logic, will always hold the winning cards.

Commodity society is faced with two tasks that are increasingly irreconcilable with one another. As a system, it is compelled to translate all wealth into its accumulable, monetary form. At the same time, it must face the necessity for preserving the capacity for social reproduction and must prevent any relapse into a situation of lawlessness and anomie. The opposition is ill-advised to deny the structural irreconcilability of the former with the latter simply in order to uphold some putatively alternative formula for valorizing the total social capital in opposition to that of the market radicals. Instead of wasting energy on trying to pass off dubious monetary concepts as plausible, whether to themselves or to its exalted public, the opposition would be better off concentrating on questions of sensuous-material (as opposed to abstract monetary) wealth, along with the very capacity for social reproduction, and making these questions, which have been stricken from the public record by the market radicals under the aegis of a new social Darwinism, the central locus of debate. Whoever consistently works out the direct and indirect costs of market-radical spending cuts and denounces merciless, unrelenting commodification as a program for social suicide is surely under no compulsion to turn around and argue for a form of resistance to such cuts that is obliged to remain compatible with the system of self-valorizing value. The question of legitimacy ought rather to be addressed offensively from the outset. If the present-day capitalist order no longer intends to provide for social reproduction, what possible reason could there be for kowtowing before its logic?

Unlearning the four basic arithmetic operations out of respect for the sacred cow of money is not — what a surprise — the starting point of emancipatory thought, nor is fantasizing that one is the greater expert at manning the control panel of capitalism's total business operations. When confronted with the paradigm of financial feasibility ("but where are we going to find the money?") as the criterion of all criteria, emancipatory thinking begins by hitting the delete key. That social security and the general preservation of the preconditions of social reproduction itself should have ceased to be affordable can only become an argument against, say, medical care and public education in the lunatic world of market radicalism. What can be said of the notion that public infrastructure and the life prospects of millions of people must be sacrificed for the sake of a desperate attempt to balance state budgets? Only that it is madness, deserving only aggressive and purposeful incomprehension. Submitting such basic social needs to monetary calculation is tantamount to social suicide and speaks only to the need to uproot the social psychosis embedded in such grotesque procedures.

When the question of what (according to market radicalism) is and is not affordable is viewed in terms of its systematic function instead of being taken at its word, it becomes clear that it is designed to exclude all others, and has always already answered itself in the negative. The only thing that can stand up to such an over-the-top ideology is a relentless negativity ready to go double or nothing, staking everything by making the problem of wealth in its sensuous-material form — and of the social and cultural relationships that mediate sensuous-material wealth — into its single crucial and pivotal question. It must do this in such a way as, so to speak, to remain demonstratively ambivalent towards the imperatives of the existing system, going, ab initio, beyond the significance they have been accorded by commodity society. It is only under the conditions of crisis capitalism that the fundamental struggle over the question of what is actually comprehended within the category of wealth opens up a direct passage to a fully emancipatory formulation of social conflict.

The Struggle Over the Assets of a Bankrupt State

In commodity society only a single criterion separates those activities and goods that are a part of social wealth from those that are not recognized as such — that of their saleability. If paying customers are found for poison gas, its production is counted as part of social wealth; unpaid childcare, in contrast, is not. As set forth in the first part of this essay, there is only one way that commodity society can circumvent this structural blindness and ensure that the general conditions of social reproduction — indispensable, at least, for its own successful xoperation — are subsequently met: through the intervention of state power. The market-radical project has now trained its gunsights on precisely this restricted form of taking sensuous-material needs into consideration. On one hand, the barriers previously erected by state authorities against the destructive consequences of unregulated competition (environmental legislation, working conditions, regulating the hours of commercial operation) are supposed to disappear. On the other hand, with its demand for restrictions on expenditure and for universal commodification, the business of deregulation targets the redistributive power of the state, insofar as the latter, in the guise of the welfare state, attempts retrospectively to temper the results of total competition. Any opposition that posits a material-sensuous redefinition of social wealth and its corresponding forms of social relations against the dictatorship of abstract monetary wealth can only be formed in frontal opposition to this development. It cannot avoid intervening in the conflict over the power of the state to redistribute wealth, nor can it shy away from raising, in opposition to the market-radical proposal for focusing all state spending on sectors immediately relevant to valorization, demands of its own that run counter to the savaging of social needs imposed by the demands of the market. As long as the bulk of social wealth is forced through the needle's eye of money, these demands must also, inevitably, take on monetary form as well.

This could at first glance appear as a departure from the basic orientation just set forth for a fundamental critique of money and the state. But a second glance already shows that this is no longer the case. While reformist policies want to take and restore the decomposing state role of the machine operator as an ineluctable social norm, an oppositional movement that struggles for the redefinition of social wealth takes the redistributive power of the state merely as a de facto starting point. The "no" to market radicalism does not imply a "yes" to the glory of the state — in the long term, the struggle is much more concerned with its assets. Will those aspects of public infrastructure that were built up over 150 years be burned down by the market economy in a very short time, or will it be possible to keep out of the oven of valorization the moments of state infrastructure that are worth saving so that a social movement of appropriation can successively occupy and renovate them and then organize them anew, divorced from the function of the machine operator?

What Does Sustainable Mean?

For the time being, public discussion is constrained by the terms of the well-known (or infamous) paradigm of financial feasibility. Emancipatory thought can only confront the poverty of the state finances with offensive ambivalence and insist on the primacy of other criteria.

The struggle over the question of financial feasibility can also be understood as a fight over the meaning of the concept of sustainability. In the 1970s it was once said that those currently alive were abusing the future of the generations to come. What was meant was the destruction of the ecological foundations. Today, the demand "don't squander our children's future" does nothing more than legitimate restrictive fiscal policy. The demand is that current social wealth, guaranteed by the state, be sacrificed on the altar of a fictitious monetary future. High time to direct the focus of the concept of the future back on sensuous-material questions, only this time conceived more broadly.

The refusal to recognize the question of financial feasibility as the question of all questions certainly ought not to be confused with the plea for an absolute increase in state spending, and has nothing to do with any sort of orientation toward demand. This difference is already important insofar as the state that has been calibrated on competition between locations is even in times of crisis by no means fundamentally sworn to a restrictive overall fiscal policy, at least not in the centers of the world market. This is significant not only for the distant future, but also for the struggles of the coming years. In practical terms, the transition to an excessive, market-Keynesian deficit policy, also on the foundation of market radicalism, is already looming (in Europe) or has even already been implemented (in the United States). This, however, implies a change, sooner or later, including with respect to the struggle for public opinion. It is possible that soon the debate in credit-worthy states will be less concerned with whether large-scale public borrowing should be pursued, but rather to what end, and to what end the monetary means should be directed. Should the still-enormous redistributive state power in the metropolises be concentrated on areas of expenditure that are held to be relevant for the renewal of the illusions of capitalist growth? Are these societies willing to accept the huge advance costs of elite universities and futureless future industries at a time when the remaining social infrastructure is neglected?

The left-wing neo-Keynesian politics of demand does not have at its disposal any theoretically justifiable criterion for distinguishing between good and bad state expenditure. In the Keynesian framework it makes no difference, as far as growth promotion is concerned, whether the state supports demand by means of the senseless digging and filling-in of holes, increased military expenditure, or social good deeds.[5] In a situation in which the opposition also changes its opinion with respect to demand-policies under different auspices, left-wing Keynesianism necessarily begins to lose control with respect to its argumentation. At the same time, it falls into an ideal relationship of mutual liability with its opponent with respect to the foreseeable consequences of such a turn (processes of devaluation, which effect the medium of money itself). In contrast, emancipatory thought, which from the outset shifts material-sensuous questions to the center rather than treating material and immaterial goods as fundamentally exchangeable bearers of precarious growth effects, loses none of its capacity to formulate social conflict. Both the market-Keynesianism of tomorrow and the constellation of the day after tomorrow, which will probably also be essentially characterized by inflationary processes, are from the outset tailor-made for this form of critique.

Against the Standpoint State

State violence exerts a varying influence on the beautiful world of competition between commodity owners, and thus on total social reproduction, in three ways. First, as the state of command and proscription it prevents, to an extent, individualist capitalist agents from, in accordance with the logic of externalization of economic cost, summarily running workers and natural resources without regard to future cost. This it accomplishes through universal conditions and regulations such as environmental legislation and worker protection. At the same time it restricts the actors of particular commodity markets (drugs, weapons) via juridical means and prevents their free-market economic development. Secondly, the welfare state as redistribution guarantees revenue to replace and supplement earned income for groups of people defined according to particular biographical circumstances.[6] Thirdly, and finally, state authorities or state-financed institutions appear as producers of infrastructural goods (transportation networks and educational institutions).

In its polemic against these three variants of state intervention, market radicalism advances an extremely monotonous logic. Nothing has ever occurred to the hardcore theory of neoliberalism but the abolition of bureaucratic barriers and relentlessly delivering both infrastructure and the guarantee of livelihood over to the market. Market-radical practice, however, proceeds in a more nuanced manner.

It accepts, as a rule, that the prevention of public blood and thunder requires certain restrictions to market freedom, even if the perceptions of what measures are necessary for this vary from country to country.[7] Wherever state intervention in regional competition leads directly to an advantage, it is in case of doubt not only permitted, but even eagerly desired.

Even the emancipatory camp can, however, make selective reference to the previous function of the state. But the criteria according to which it will prioritize infrastructure tasks may diametrically oppose the choices at which the apologists for the market economy arrive in their refrain that "we are strengthening our competitive position." While the market radicals back massive support for elite universities, an emancipatory position will instead discover what is worthy of preservation in the idea of universal education. The market radicals forward the case for unconditional competition between all transport systems. Appropriate to this is the state-subsidized development of unmanned, energy- and land-monopolizing bullet trains, which would enter into competition with airplanes, and like them would be confined to links between large cities. From an emancipatory perspective it seems more desirable to guarantee a comparatively environmentally friendly and above all comprehensive rail system that could thus be used as an alternative to private transport.

Sensuous-Material Criteria and the Monotony of Money

Commodity society disposes over an absolute means of judging the justification for the two branches of the production of material wealth: their economic profitability. The market-radicals want to see this naïve yardstick deployed with respect to all infrastructural goods, even if this means that their comprehensive character and the assurance of supply is destroyed. The necessity of a facility can be derived from the magnitude of the yield.

A society oriented toward sensuous, material, and social needs would not recognize such an unambiguous, objectified standard. This is all the more the case for social movements which are formed in the confrontation with the insanity of commodity society. A certain provisional hierarchy might even distill itself out since completely different successes in mobilization will emerge from the struggle over a way of securing the production of wealth, which is not subjugated to the diktat of profitability. Priorities are de facto established when people show themselves either willing to commit themselves and build up social pressure together, or to let things be.

Admittedly, an abstractly more universal measure must be lacking with respect to needs, so the forms of production for which an oppositional movement of appropriation is heading cannot be reduced to a simple common denominator. A liberated society does not subordinate the organization of the production of wealth to any binding counter-principle for the sake of minimizing economic costs. Rather, it sounds out how differing aims (minimal use of resources, stimulating and low-stress conditions for the immediate producers, long-lasting final product) can best be aligned in different sectors of (re)production. A transcontinental transport network cannot be organized by the same method as local vegetable production or a cultural organization. It is ultimately the specific insanity of our current society that establishes enforced conformity as it subordinates all areas under the logic of money.

Sensuous-material differences are inevitably also expressed in struggle over the configuration of the production of wealth. It will be difficult to transfer an extended, highly complex system of infrastructure (electricity provision, transport networks) from its current state into self-organization. A social movement that opposes the insanity of the market will tend, particularly when it comes to the infrastructural services that have traditionally been organized as an activity of the state, to be content initially to make demands, while in other areas (the production of knowledge) it is already showing what it is capable of.[8] A form of state activity that, under compulsion from anti-political pressure, does not conform to competitive logic inevitably has a shimmering character. Dependent on the monetary power of the state, it remains reliant on the business of commodity society in its mobilization of resources. At the same time, anti-political pressure wants to compel the state, as a producer of wealth, to guarantee the security of particular public-universal goods independently of its role as machine operator.

Principle of Equivalence versus Free Access

It would be absurd for a social movement oriented toward sensuous-material criteria to aspire to a unified form of the production of wealth. However, with respect to the mode of access, things look somewhat different. Commodity society binds every share in social wealth to the principle of the exchange of equivalents. A horizontal movement of appropriation must thus raise in opposition the demand for free access.

Of course, the prospects of implementing this principle in the foreseeable future vary considerably from commodity to commodity. Defense is fundamentally easier than offense. Saving services which the state traditionally offers at no cost (free provision of textbooks, public streets) from commodification is one thing, the decommodification of things such as electricity, gas, or public transport quite another.

A social movement will, in resisting the market-radical ideal of the universal exchange of equivalents, have to content itself again and again with partial successes, and also for the time being to accept less-exclusionary forms of monetary access. Between the alternatives of "unaffordable for the majority" and "freely accessible" are many intermediate steps. A health-care system with income-dependent payments but comprehensive treatment provided to the same extent for everybody is certainly more desirable than the truncated insurance propagated by the neoliberals.

The advocates of free access certainly have on their side an argument that is particularly attractive because it borrows from neoliberal discourse: the rejection of bureaucracy. Nothing is as unbureaucratic and as good value to society as free access to social goods. No fences, no tollbooths. Nothing is as unclear and overcomplicated as highly individualized charges. Above all, the attempt to reintroduce a social element into an insurance system that has been restructured in the direction of the idiocy of equivalence leads to situations which make the old actually existing socialism seem in comparison a stronghold of rationality.

The orientation toward free access by no means leads to an idea of self-service which would blindly accept capitalist wealth in its material structure. The question as to what sort of production can be considered desirable in the first place must be discussed in strict separation from the conditions of access. After the automobilization of society, there are good reasons to introduce an de-automobilization. However, an emancipatory perspective can have nothing to do with the drive to maintain private transport as the preserve of better earners while the socially weak are made to walk or to get on their bike. If countries such as China or India were to catch up with the degree of motorization in the United States, it would without doubt have catastrophic consequences for the environment. But this is only an argument against automobile society as a whole, and not for the exclusion from it of these parts of the world. The acutely justified critique of high-tech medicine in no way legitimates the curtailment of medical services. The content of social standards must be investigated and determined anew. But from an emancipatory perspective, standards must always be universally accessible.

Decommodification and Guaranteed Income

Our point of departure was that contemporary capitalism is characterized by the divergence of sensuous-material and monetary wealth. In the face of this irreversible development, an emancipatory perspective on society as a whole can now only consist in the gradual decommodification and demonetarization of social relationships, and in the transition to a production of wealth that is directly socialized and that follows only sensuous-material criteria. The problem of scarcity disappears along with the needle's eye of money and exchange.

As a perspective on society as a whole, demonetarization and decommodification promise the transition to a rich society and the end of misery and poverty. However, whoever is struck individually by the fate of decommodification and demonetarization on the basis of existing society will have to deal not with a happy fate but rather with a palpable catastrophe. Anyone whose labor power is decommodified — that is, who sits on the couch unsaleably and does not find another source of money — is not rich, but markedly poor. A movement of emancipation cannot avoid taking this situation into account. As far as the production of wealth is concerned, an emancipatory perspective must protect social wealth from commodification and monetarization, and to decommodify and demonetarize commodified and monetarized wealth. However, as long as a large proportion of social wealth takes on the structure of the commodity, it must of course focus its attention of the matter of how one can attain the necessary universal equivalent, alias money, even if one is in a state of decommodification. The offensive project of the decommodification of the production of social wealth cannot be thought without a parallel defensive undertaking that secures the money supply of those who are superfluous in the capitalist sense, and enables them to have sufficient access even to commodity wealth. The question of making ends meet only decouples from income to the extent that social wealth actually becomes freely accessible, and on this basis all struggles over monetary distribution become unnecessary.

Slum Egalitarianism

This defensive undertaking draws of course on the welfare state, at least in the metropolises. Put more accurately, it can only take shape through the formation of social movements against the attacks that are currently operating at full blast on the traditional compulsory social security system.

The welfare state came into the world as an instrument to make the commodity labor power available. While it protected owners of the commodity labor power from the day-to-day risks that are bound up with their lives as sellers of labor power, it at the same time committed them to this mode of existence by rewarding them with earned entitlements. The so-called reforms of the welfare state are directed against the use of a carrot. Legal entitlements to pensions and other social security benefits are reduced as far as possible. The gradual expropriation of the rights purchased by the sale of labor power is accompanied by forms of providing for the poor that are organized along slum-egalitarian lines. These are divorced from the previous position of the claimant in labor society.

This shift in emphasis took place in recent years, first and foremost, automatically and insidiously, since, with the removal of other forms of social security, more and more people slipped down into the lowest social safety net, which had always been structured in this way. Meanwhile, however, and not only in Germany, what remains of the welfare state is increasingly being converted onto such institutions that provide the poor with a bare minimum (basic state pension, merging of unemployment benefit with welfare).

In spite of all assertions to the contrary, the transition to these slum-egalitarian fallback systems indicates that the prospect of integrating the unvalorizable into regular wage labor has evaporated. However, with the change in model, the compulsion to the availability to work that is bound up with the system of social safeguards in no way dissolves into goodwill. Quite the opposite: the weaker the prospects of actual inclusion in labor society, the more rigid the obligation to simulate labor drills. Administrative violence replaces the carrot.

Forced Labor and Time Appropriation

Given the structural weakness of struggles in pursuit of interests that operate on the basis of labor, it is conceivable that at least in Germany the struggle against the logic of exclusion will in the future have to be pursued primarily in the context of slum-egalitarian mini-incomes.

This compelled change of terrain, far-removed from the defense of earned entitlements, after a certain fashion even approaches a radical labor-critical position. There are two fields of conflict in particular that could potentially be suitable for a wide-ranging debate and mobilization. The first is the pure and simple matter of the question of the size of the planned minimal payments for the unvalorizable. This much is clear: there is no lower limit for the level of provision that results from the logic of political economy itself. Marx was right to draw attention to the fact that the value of the commodity labor power also contains a moral moment. What commodity society concedes to the unvalorizable — whether it concedes anything at all — depends, in contrast, solely on this moral moment.

Secondly, the linking of a share in this minimal provision to the performance of ritual actions that replace labor provides a rich supply of material for conflict. The delegitimation of this insanity is urgently required and leads us back to the consideration with which we started, of the redefinition of social wealth. If Marx is correct to say that the true wealth of a society consists in the time it has available, then what is at stake here is nothing but a gigantic pursuit of the annihilation of wealth, at the compulsion of the state. The content and the precondition of the appropriation of sensuous-material wealth is the appropriation of the time of life.

Notes

1. "Labor society" translates literally *"Arbeitsgesellschaft"*; that, however, has, so far as we know, no precise equivalent in English. The German here refers to a society constituted not only through the synthesizing nexus of value in the form of commodities and money but also in the form of abstract labor. In a "labor society" one works not only so as to exchange one's own labor power for commodities and money but, by virtue of this, to produce and reproduce oneself as a member of said society. [Eds.]

2. Karl Marx, *Capital: A Critique of Political Economy*, Volume I, trans. Ben Fowkes (New York: Penguin, 1976) 125.

3. The term here translated as asocial sociality, *ungesellschaftliche Gesellschaftlichkeit*, is in the original German mistakenly attributed to Marx. The origin of the term is Kant's *ungesellige Geselligkeit*, the social antagonism that consists in the fact that the human tendency to enter into society is permeated with resistances and oppositions, which at all times threaten to break this society apart, of the fourth thesis of the "Idea for a Universal History with a Cosmopolitan Aim." This concept resonates with and finds echoes in a great deal of both Hegelian and Marxian social theory. For example: "Division of labour and exchange are the two phenomena which lead the political economist to boast of the social character of his science, while in the same breath he gives unconscious expression to the contradiction of his science — the motivation of society by unsocial, particular interests" (*Marx-Engels Collected Works, Volume 3* [Moscow: International Publishers, 1973] 321). It seems likely that this compatibility led to the attribution of the Kantian expression to Marx, and that in this process Kant's idiom was transposed into the less archaic-sounding formulation that would be more consistent with a Marxian quotation. [Eds.]

4. Lohoff is writing well before the outbreak of the crisis that began in 2008. [Eds.]

5. Incidentally, I have not made up this example. It stems from Keynes, who was entirely candid in this respect. He preferred to explain the consequence of his demand-oriented model with reference to the example

of obviously futile labors. In his writings he shows a particular foible for the state construction of pyramids.

6. An example of a supplementary revenue would be a child benefit; under the rubric of replacement revenue fall welfare and the diverse social security payments.

7. Here I am thinking of the difference between the liberal American laws with respect to private gun ownership and their more restrictive equivalents in Europe.

8. Commodity society knows alarmingly little about the actual, material circumstances that it creates. Because they are organized as an appendage of the monetary flows, knowledge of material circumstances is widely strewn and always haphazard at points. A central task of this reorienting movement consists in the first instance of bringing light into the darkness. Such an investigation is not only important in order to reveal the insanity of this mode of production. It also provides an orientation for a later reorganization and also makes visible points at which the highly complex capitalism is vulnerable.

World Power and World Money: The Economic Function of the U.S. Military Machine within Global Capitalism and the Background of the New Financial Crisis

Robert Kurz (2008)

When one encounters the term "epochal break" after 1989, it usually refers to the decline of the German Democratic Republic and the end of state socialism in Russia and Eastern Europe; it also names the end of the Cold War between competing political blocs and the termination of the corresponding "hot" proxy wars in backyards of the world market. The supposed victory of capitalism, according to freedom-lovers everywhere, together with a general commitment to the "market economy" and the constitution of a singular global economic system on the Western model, was interpreted as heralding a new era of disarmament, peace, and global prosperity.

This expectation has proven to be completely naïve. Over the past seventeen years, reality has developed into the virtual opposite of that which such optimists by profession have wantonly forecast. Globalization has produced new zones of mass poverty, aimless civil wars, and a postmodern, neoreligious form of terrorism that one cannot describe as anything but barbaric. The West, led by the last world power, the United States, has responded with equally directionless "wars of world order" and precarious, planetary crisis management.

As has become obvious, the interpretation of the events following 1989 was merely superficial and therefore grasped far too little. Indeed, the break was not actually isolated only to the Eastern bloc as a "flawed system," but a similar fate befell more than a few pro-Western countries in the so-called Third World. Moreover, even in the Western core countries the postwar "economic miracle" had vanished and growth rates had long been sinking. Structural mass unemployment that has nothing to do with mere labor-market friction has subsequently developed, accompanied by underemployment and the increasing precarity of labor.[1]

Focusing instead on these tendencies, a whole other interpretation might come to the fore: namely, that it is a common crisis of the modern system of global commodity production, which includes the centers of capitalism themselves. From this perspective, the so-called "actually existing socialism" of the Eastern bloc was not a historical alternative, but a state-capitalistic system of recuperative modernization on the periphery of the world markets, and an integral component of them. After 1989, with the end of all kinds of older development regimes, this "weakest link" of the global system was broken, continuing the inexorable crisis process of direct globalization.

Many consider (not incorrectly) the third industrial revolution of microelectronics to be the deepest cause of the new world crisis. For the first time in the history of capitalism, the potential of rationalization has overtaken the possibilities of an expansion of the market. Through crisis competition, capital has melted away its own "labor substance" (Marx). The ugly underbelly of structural mass unemployment and underemployment on a global scale is the flight of capital toward the famous "financial bubble" economy, because additional real investment has become unprofitable; an index of this is the global excess capacity of production (exemplified by the auto industry) and speculative "takeover battles."[2]

This roughly sketched interpretation was in the late 1990s

considered plausible and perhaps even possible within a segment of Leftist social critique. In the meantime, however, one has become accustomed to the fact that capital is somehow able to survive even with a simulated form of financial accumulation ("jobless growth"). And doesn't the recent export industrialization in Asia, particularly in China, point to a new era of real growth — just no longer in Europe? At the same time, the wars of world order seem to have become reduced to trivial oil interests, because capitalism's combustion culture is running out of fuel. Might these circumstances not suggest a new competition between imperialist blocs — for example, between the United States, the European Union, and China? With such considerations, the Left returns (with a few modifications) largely to those old ways of thinking that characterized the times predating the epochal break. There are, however, good reasons to think that such a reinterpretation provides us with a distorted picture and that determinations appear quite different upon closer inspection. The key here is the political-economic status of the last world power, the United States, in the global crisis of capitalism.

The Crisis of Money and the World Monetary System

The world crisis of the third industrial revolution and globalization of the past two decades rests upon a much longer, simmering crisis of money that dates back to World War I. Up to that point, the nature of money as a "singled-out commodity," general equivalent with its own particular value substance, was virtually undisputed. The currencies of the major capitalist countries therefore had to be stabilized by means of gold reserves in central banks. Gold was the real world money — the lingua franca of world markets — and the sterling pound of former world power Great Britain could function as a world currency only because of its gold standard. However, the industrial war economies of the two world wars and the productive forces of the second industrial revolution (Fordist mass production, assembly line, automobilization), even with accelerated circulation, could no longer be mediated by the gold standard — which therefore had to be abolished.

In other words: the value substance of money, based on the compressed "labor substance" of rare metal gold, could not be maintained. On the level of money — the general equivalent as "king commodity" and appearance of capital — this desubstantivization was therefore perceptible already much earlier than on the level of the ordinary "commodity rabble," where it is becoming manifest only now in the third industrial revolution. The result was a "secular age of inflation" entirely unknown in the nineteenth century: the uninterrupted deflation of money, sometimes galloping (hyperinflation), sometimes creeping.

In spite of this inflationary effect, some theorists made a virtue of necessity by declaring the gold standard unnecessary and money a mere sign that could only be guaranteed by state law.[3] But the collapse of the world market in the Depression of the 1930s also had something to do with the lack of a recognized world money, after all attempts in Europe to return to the gold standard had failed. When the foundations of the economic and monetary order of the postwar period were established in Bretton Woods in 1944 under the guise of the "Pax Americana," this was done in direct orientation toward the U.S. dollar as the new currency for international trade and reserve. The basis of this was not only the paramount industrial position of the United States (due mainly to the tremendous growth spurt of the war economy), but also the fact that the dollar was the only currency that was gold-convertible. The famous Fort Knox held three-quarters of the world's gold reserves.[4]

Only on this basis — the world currency system of Bretton Woods and then the severance of the dollar from a fixed exchange rate — could the "economic miracle" of postwar history unfold in the shadow of the Cold War. But the resurgence of Europe and Japan in the prosperous world market soon began to gnaw at economic dominance of the United States and the gold substance of the dollar. In the same measure, when the share of the commodity and capital exports shifted to the detriment of the United States, the dollar also lost strength and was increasingly converted into gold. The reserves in Fort Knox melted away. In 1971, President Nixon was thus forced to cancel the gold-convertibility of the dollar.

With this, the Bretton Woods system came to an end. Exchange rates were deregulated and have since "floated" on the market, which was the starting point for a completely new kind of currency speculation founded on the fluctuation of exchange rates, with dangerous repercussions for the real economy. However, since the global currency crisis of the 1970s did not produce the great catastrophe, Left theorists, too, have considered the problem of money and currency to have been solved empirically: contrary to Marx, the character of money as singled-out commodity, with its particular and definite value substance, is said to have been disposed with.[5] But the by no means safe practice of flexible currency conditions in the brief historical period of the last decades says nothing substantial about the essential durability of the new constellation, especially with respect to the currency crises on the peripheries throughout Asia in the 1990s and Argentina after the turn of the century, which both point to a long-smoldering issue.

From Gold Dollar to Arms Dollar

The global currency crisis of the 1970s can be considered to have been mild for the sole reason that, in spite of the loss of its convertibility into gold, the U.S. dollar was able to retain its function as world trade and reserve currency in the absence of a viable alternative. If this had not been the case, the result would have been a repetition of the disaster of the 1930s, but on a greater scale — without the dollar's function as global currency, the world market could only implode. However, the reconstitution of the dollar as world currency was built on a completely new kind of foundation. World money's substance of value, which had been founded on the gold standard, was now actually based on a kind of "political" guarantee — not a formal-legal but essentially a military one. The currency of the world power or "superpower" of the Western hemisphere now took on its world-money function now purely on the basis of this power.

This gave rise to a peculiar reciprocal process: to the same degree that the economic position of the United States deteriorated within the "regular" world market of commodity and capital flows (a process that continues up to today), there was a continuous growth in what President Eisenhower described as the "military-industrial complex." The exorbitant growth rates of the military industry during World War II continued in the form of the much-discussed "permanent war economy." Against this background, the impact of the third industrial revolution of microelectronics was reflected in ever-new high-tech weapons systems, marking the path from industrialization to the computerization of war. With the development of one generation of weaponry after another, the United States moved into a position in arms that was increasingly unassailable by the rest of the world. President Reagan pushed this tendency even further. While the Soviet Union, the opposing world power of recuperative modernization, was in part undone by its own internal contradictions as a planned capitalist economy, it was also armed to death and could win the race neither economically nor militarily.

This extra-economic factor of the increasingly unrivaled U.S. military machine transformed it into a mighty economic power. The cautioners and warners in the United States who voiced opposition to the unstoppable trend towards the permanent war economy were correct insofar as it triggered an avalanche of public debt. Reagan's tight neoliberal fiscal and monetary policy brutally cut the Keynesian social programs of his predecessors, but against his own doctrine he allowed the explosion in scale of weaponized-Keynesianism. As a result, the already bloated military-industrial complex became in many ways (also in derivative forms) the main guarantor of growth and a job machine. The U.S. economy showed nominal inner strength, although it was becoming weaker on the world market.

The United States' astronomical debt arising from this process of economic militarization could already in the 1980s no longer be funded from its own savings. But the economic power of the military machine was also reflected in foreign affairs. It was the military power of the

United States as world police that offered global financial markets a safe haven — or so it seemed. This impression was reinforced significantly by the perceived victory over the opposing Eastern (European) system. The dollar maintained its function as world currency through the mutation from the gold dollar to the arms dollar. And the strategic nature of global wars in the 1990s and turn of the century in the Middle East (in the Balkans and in Afghanistan) was directed at preserving the myth of the safe haven via the demonstration of the ability to intervene militarily on a global scale, thereby also securing the dollar as world currency. On this ultimately irrational basis, excess (that is, not profitable and investable) capital from the third industrial revolution from around the world flowed increasingly into the United States, thus indirectly financing the defense and military machine.

The Biggest Financial Bubble of All Time and the U.S. Consumer Miracle

Everywhere the internal barriers of valorization of capital in the third industrial revolution caused a flight toward the credit superstructure and finance-bubble economy. This crisis economy of financial capitalism inevitably had to be concentrated in the supposed safe haven of the dollar zone. The more excess money capital strayed around the global financial markets, the greater the suction power of the United States to attract these financial flows. In this manner there arose, in God's own country, the mother of all financial bubbles. The sale of government bonds around the world not only financed the debt-driven arms boom; parallel to this, the U.S. stock market swelled in the 1990s, and so, in turn, the U.S. real estate market after the turn of the century, thus producing the basis for a new quality of debt.

In addition to the military-industrial complex thus arose the second pillar of the, as it were, irregular apparent growth of the internal U.S. economy. Due to the very wide dispersion of share and property ownership (in comparison to Europe), a paradoxical consumption miracle could take its course. Even though average real wages had stagnated or even declined since the 1970s, consumption increasingly became the critical driver of growth.[6] Though invoked again and again, the jobs miracle was in no way the real cause of this boom. Apart from jobs in the military-industrial complex, itself hanging on the drip of public debt employment, it was mainly low-income jobs in the service sector that were created — the famous "labouring poor."[7] Due to weakness in global markets, employment in the export sector was also declining.

Today, the consumption boom is fueled not so much by regular wages but primarily by financial bubbles in the stock and property markets. It was possible to borrow against the difference gains from the fictitious increase in value of relevant property titles, and its millionfold, broad dissemination resulted in credit card and mortgage debt on an unprecedented scale. The only security for this was the very same increases in stock prizes and of real estate. The influx of excess money capital from around the world into the supposed safe haven of the dollar not only financed the indebted consumption of armaments, but was also diverted into the debt-ridden field of private consumption. It is this marvelous money machine that fed the U.S. consumption miracle.

Pacific Debt Cycle and the Global Economy

The real economic weakness of the United States on the world markets revealed itself in the form of a steadily growing trade deficit. Relatively speaking, the internal economy of the last world power, characterized by the arms industry and service sector, produced fewer and fewer industrial goods (in some areas the decline was even absolute). A significant portion of U.S. citizens, who could go into debt due to sustained increases in stocks and real estate prices, increasingly consumed goods that were manufactured elsewhere. As a result, a global deficit cycle gained momentum — one visible for the first time in the 1980s, which accelerated in the 1990s and that is beginning to run hot today. While initially it was mainly the balance of trade with Japan that slipped into the red, the trade deficit soon also rose with the smaller Asian countries and Europe, eventually escalating in the context of the immense commodity flow between the United States and the colossi India and China. Today, there are hardly any industrial regions in the world that do not sell their surpluses to the United States.

The flip side of external monetary debt created by the sucking of global money flows is, conversely, that excess global commodity flows of goods are drawn back. In other words, U.S. consumers (government and private) borrow the money with which they pay for the flood of commodities from the very same suppliers. The United States has thus become the black hole of the world economy. However, this function includes a double reciprocal dependence. If the miraculous U.S. consumers had not heroically eaten up global overproduction, the global economic crisis of the third industrial revolution would have become resoundingly manifest long ago. Moreover, these are by no means the flows of goods between separate national economies, but movements within a fully global economy. In addition to Japanese and European corporations, it is mainly U.S. corporations themselves who use China as a hub for transnational value chains because of its low wage structures, in order to supply markets in the United States and elsewhere. The corresponding investments are therefore limited to economic export zones and have nothing to do with the traditional ideas of a national economic development of China, India, and so on.

The one-way street across the Pacific of Asian exports to the United States has now turned the deficit cycle into a flywheel that powers the global economy. Just as in other regions of the world market, European industry not only supplies a portion of its surpluses to the United States itself, but simultaneously exports an ever-increasing extent of the production components for the massive Asian export systems (particularly in engineering). The widely celebrated upswing of the last few years is almost entirely a result of this voodoo economy. Periodically, the danger of the increasing global economic inequalities in the form of accumulating U.S. foreign deficits become a topic of discussion, but because everything has somehow gone so well for so long, the all-clear signal is usually not far away.

The Coming Credit- and Dollar-Crisis Scenario

Over the course of 2007, however, menacing black clouds have gathered on the global horizon. It had to happen: the U.S. housing bubble, the consumption engine's fuel in recent years, is imploding, and real estate prices are shrinking fast. As a result, subprime mortgage loans suffer en masse. What forms the financial crisis might take have already been shown over the past few months: suddenly, banks and savings institutions in many countries have come under massive pressure from asset depreciation, because U.S. debt circulates globally. However, that was just the beginning. Because cycles of credit and physical capital extend over several years, the true extent of the credit crisis will only become apparent in the years 2008-2010. If in this period U.S. consumption experiences a deep slump, there will not only be a setback in global stock markets, but also a decline in Pacific deficit circulation that will bring the world economy to a halt. No one can predict the exact magnitude, but it threatens to surpass all the crisis phenomena faced by the third industrial revolution over the past twenty years.

It's mere whistling in the dark when economic commentators now pretend to expect that the domestic economy in the European Union or China could suddenly become self-supporting and might replace the U.S. consumer as the vacuum cleaner of the excess flow of goods. Where should we expect the purchasing power in these regions to come from, if it was not already there during the booming export economy? At the same time, a dual interest rate dilemma opens up. The impact of the Asian crisis of the 1990s and the collapse of the virtual New Economy after 2000 could still be absorbed by the central banks in a rate-cut race that flooded markets with cheap money. The financial markets now expect the same from the U.S. Federal Reserve, hoping that central banks everywhere else will follow. But when dying American consumption is supposed to be reignited in this way, a renewed threat of a dollar glut can reignite the long-lurking inflationary potential of asset inflation and permit a secular age of inflation to escalate. Additionally, it is foreseeable that the flow of surplus money capital into the United States will dry up, if in the face of rising inflation the European Central Bank does not follow suit and level the interest rate differential between the United States and the European Union. The simultaneity of depression and inflation moves into the realm of possibility.

The resulting global interest-rate dilemma generated by the U.S. credit crisis is also beginning to call into question the function of the dollar as global currency. Standing behind this is ultimately the towering external deficit, which requires a drastic devaluation of the dollar and a similar appreciation of the export-surplus currencies. Although the dollar had been devalued repeatedly and in controlled fashion in the past, forcing creditor countries to pay part of the U.S. debt, now there are signs of an uncontrolled crash and a rapid loss of value, one that has started against the euro, while Asian currencies are still kept artificially low. But if the credit crisis strikes through fully, even this barrier will be broken. Then, not only the financing capacity of the military-industrial complex but also the myth of the safe haven will come to an end.

It is, however, not possible to replace the dollar with a new global currency, even if the euro is widely celebrated as containing such potential. Since neither the euro nor gold is based on armament, they will not be able to replace the dollar. The crisis of the global currency and the connected potential for inflation indicate a growing crisis of money proper. This is indicated by the constant and unavoidable rise in the price of gold which accompanies the currency crisis — the commodity character of money with its own value substance is asserting itself in this crisis. Gold, no longer simply a resource, returns to its status of "real" global currency, but it is no longer possible to mediate the productive power of the Third World via movements of the global market on the basis of gold. It would be no more plausible to attempt to drain the ocean with a teaspoon. The situation of the interwar period threatens to return — this time, however, on a much higher level of development.

World Crisis, World Ideology, and World Civil War

What is required of emancipatory social critique in this situation characterized by an internal limit of capitalism is the redefinition of socialism beyond the fetish forms of commodity, money, nation, and their associated gender relations. However, to the extent that the Left returns to its old patterns of interpretation and seeks possibilities of positively appropriating immanent power inherent in the new global constellation, it runs the risk of becoming reactionary. This critique of capitalism frequently turns into anti-Americanism and into overt or structural antisemitism. The "objective thought-forms" (Marx) of the capital fetish, which contain an inversion of reality, form (if they are not broken) the ideological basis for processing the crisis, which already led in the interwar period to devastating results. From within the globalization of capital arises a murderous world ideology. Cause and effect will be turned on their head: the credit crisis does not appear as the result of the internal degradation of real accumulation, but as the result of "finance capitalist greed" (one which for 200 years has been a stereotype associated with antisemitic ideas); the role of the United States and the arms dollar are understood not as an overarching common condition of globalized capital, but as imperial oppression of the rest of the world.

The motive for these ideological inversions today is the desperate desire to flee back to the times of Fordist prosperity and Keynesian regulation. It constitutes the radical Left's option to replace the American, unilateral version of the Empire with a "democratic" globalization led by the European Union and possibly with the euro as the new international trade and reserve currency.[8] This option is not only fully crisis-blind, but it also fails to recognize the interdependence of world capital and the character of the European Union. The phantasmal illusion of a confederation of this virtual world reform is unearthly: imagine the *Gazprom*-and-intelligence regime of a Putin, or the larger part of a transnational capital-investment Chinese export bureaucracy, incorporated into an unholy alliance between the oil-caudillismo of a Chavez and the antisemitic Islamist regime in Tehran...

Quite apart from the fact that an E.U.-centered globalization would be no better than a U.S.-centric one, it is not even possible. It is not just that the euro cannot take the place of the arms dollar, but that the European Union is not in a position to reverse the excess cash flows and absorb global overproduction. In even greater global economic dependence on this paradoxical role of the U.S. economy are Russia, Venezuela, and Iran, whose political claims against the Great Satan are nourished by the explosion in oil prices. If the flywheel of the Pacific deficit cycle comes to a halt and a world depression is triggered, the oil regimes together will be thrown to the wolves.

The ripening world crisis of the third industrial revolution, for which there is no new regulatory model in sight, will certainly not only run its economic course. Even more than in previous breaks in the history of modernization, there lurks in the looming, unmanageable global economic crisis the danger of an irrational flight forward into world war. However, based on the level of development of globalization, this will not be a national war between national-imperial power blocs for the redistribution of the world. One must rather speak of a new kind of world civil war, as suggested by the "denationalization" and wars of world order since the collapse of the Soviet Union; perhaps these were precursors to this (coming civil) war. Never before has the slogan "socialism or barbarism" been as relevant as today. But simultaneously, socialism must be reinvented at the end of the history of modernization.

Notes

1. The term "structural unemployment" is deployed here somewhat differently than in current mainstream macroeconomic discourse. "Technological mass unemployment, which by now had also been given the name of 'structural' unemployment, grew since the early 1980s in parallel with the rise of the micro-electronic revolution in an increasingly relentless manner, and displayed a characteristic that would have a most disconcerting effect on capitalist consciousness:

unemployment had become structural to the extent that it no longer increased and subsided in accordance with the economic cycle, but rather displayed continuous growth independent of the economic cycle. It was not only the case that growth had become relatively slow, but also that the cycle by this time only came to rest as the weak modulation of a mass unemployment that was growing in absolute terms, the 'base level' of which would subsequently continue to grow right through to the end of the twentieth century. This problem had emerged as the main social problem, as a perpetual global crisis, in comparison with which all other problems (when they were not, as was increasingly the case, themselves caused by this crisis) paled into insignificance." Robert Kurz, *Schwarzbuch Kapitalismus: Ein Abgesang auf die Marktwirtschaft* (Frankfurt am Main: Eichborn, 2009) 642.

2.   Robert Kurz, *Das Weltkapital. Globalisierung und innere Schranken des modernen warenproduzierenden Systems* (Berlin: Bittermann, 2005), and Kurz, *Weltordnungskrieg. Das Ende der Souveränität und die Wandlungen des Imperialismus im Zeitalter der Globalisierung* (Bad Honnef: Horlemann, 2003).

3.   Georg Friedrich Knapp, *Staatliche Theorie des Geldes* (München und Leipzig, 1905).

4.   Paul Kennedy, *Preparing for the Twenty-First Century* (New York: HarperCollins, 1993).

5.   Michael Heinrich, *Die Wissenschaft vom Wert* (Münster: Westfälisches Dampfboot, 2004).

6.   Lester Thurow, *The Future of Capitalism: How Today's Economic Forces Shape Tomorrow's World* (New York: William Morrow and Company, 1996).

7.   See Karl Marx, *Capital: A Critique of Political Economy,* Volume I, trans. Ben Fowkes (New York: Penguin, 1976) 765 [Eds.].

8.   Michael Hardt and Antonio Negri, *Multitude: War and Democracy in the Age of Empire* (New York: Penguin, 2004).

Struggle without Classes: Why There Is No Resurgence of the Proletariat in the Currently Unfolding Capitalist Crisis

Norbert Trenkle (2006)

From Class Struggle to Declassing

While living and working conditions continue to grow more precarious, affecting greater and greater segments of the population even in countries that have emerged victorious on the world market, widespread talk of a return of class society and of class struggle suggest the (re)birth of a new historical conjuncture. Given the rapid growth in social polarization, such talk can, at first glance, seem quite plausible. However, as is usually the case, resorting to the past modes of interpretation and explanation leads not to clarification, but only to greater confusion. Despite initial appearances, categories of class opposition cannot provide a basis for any adequate conception of the extreme growth in social inequality, nor are the oppositions and conflicts between social interest groups resulting from such inequality simply recurrences of what, measured by their real historical content, were once accurately conceived as instances of class struggle.

The great social conflict that, in the form of class struggle, decisively shaped capitalist society throughout the historical period of its formation and establishment was, as is well known, the conflict between capital and labor. What is at stake in the structural logic of the commodity in its process of historical formation, when considered from its objectified side, are the opposed interests corresponding to two of capitalism's functional categories: the opposition between the representatives of capital, who command and organize the process of production with the valorization of capital as their end, and the wage workers, who by their labor "create" the surplus value necessary for this process. Taken for itself, this is a purely immanent conflict arising from within the common system of relations presupposed by modern commodity production, a conflict that revolves around the manner of value production (working conditions, working hours, and the like) and the distribution of the mass of value (wages, profits, benefits, and the like). As such it is a conflict impossible to overcome as long as the capitalist mode of production, which is based on the valorization of value as a self-propelling end in itself, continues to exist. This, however, in no way means that such a conflict must always express itself as class opposition. The objectified opposition of capital and labor only developed into class opposition because a generalized social mega-subject was constituted on its foundation, and under very particular historical conditions: in the course of the struggle for their interests and for social recognition, the wage workforce developed a collective identity and a consciousness as a working class. It was the constitution of such a subject that first enabled those who sell their labor power as a commodity to shift themselves into a position from which they could endow their struggle with the necessary continuity and strength, even in the face of setbacks and defeats.[1]

Now, if over the course of the second half of the twentieth century the class struggle has increasingly lost the dynamic and force that had placed its stamp on the whole of society, this was not of course because capitalism had suddenly dispensed with the production of surplus value. The objective opposition between capital and labor, as, at the same time, categorical functions within capitalism itself, has remained and remains still, even if its concrete shape has changed over the course of the development of capitalism, as will be shown more extensively below. The working class nonetheless loses its character as collective subject to the extent that wage workers now become citizens with equal rights and thus, precisely speaking, commodity subjects absorbed into the universe of bourgeois society, and the sale of labor power becomes a generalized mode of existence. With this, the revolutionary nimbus of the working class, which had been a significant part of the cement holding its identity together, dissolved, revealing its feet of clay. For even if the idea that class struggle has an antagonistic character and thus points beyond capitalist society can in retrospect be revealed to be an illusion, it nonetheless played a thoroughly important role in class constitution, and furnished the working class with the consciousness required for it to act with its eyes trained on the horizon of a far-reaching social mission.

Ultimately, however, the opposition of capital and labor in its subjective form also emerged from its cocoon, revealing itself to be, no less than in its objective manifestation, an immanent conflict between social and economic interests internal to capitalism.[2] Despite occasional rhetorical reenactments of times past, the conduct of labor struggles today is no longer premised on the irreconcilability between the interests of the sellers of labor power and those of capital. Quite the opposite: the emphasis is always placed on their compatibility, whether in the name of productivity, of local competitiveness, or of the purchasing power of internal, domestic demand. Criticism is not leveled at capital but rather at excessively high profits, unnecessary plant closures (or relocations) or, in a more ideologically charged version, at greedy bankers pitting the parasitical needs of Wall Street against the "real" economy of Main Street.[3] Those transformed into commodity subjects, workers no less than anyone else, have long since considered it only natural and self-evident that profits must be made, capital valorized, productivity increased, and growth ensured at whatever cost. They know that their (however precarious) well-being in this society — and they can scarcely imagine any other — depends on precisely this.

The development of the struggle between labor and capital

into what more and more resembles their effective identity on the subjective level can be attributed to the systematic establishment of a fully generalized commodity society, one that has successfully invested the functional logic of capitalism with what appears to be the irrevocablility of a natural law. But there is more to it than just this. At its basis also lie quite specific changes in the relationship of capital to labor, changes that had already been introduced in the Fordist era and that were brought to completion at an accelerated rate after Fordism came to an end. These changes in no way led to the suspension of the functional opposition of labor and capital, but rather to a state of affairs in which this functional opposition itself could no longer serve as ground for the constitution of any renewed class subjectivity whatsoever. There is thus, despite — or even because of — the extreme exacerbation of social inequality, no reclassing of society taking place today; we are rather dealing with a general process of declassing, a process which is expressed in at least four trends.[4]

First, since as early as the final phase of Fordism, the labor directly applied to the product has been reduced in favor of more capital-intensive technologies of automated oversight and control and of pre- and post-production functions. This has meant not only the melting away of the actual working class in the sense of the value-producing industrial workforce and the massive upsurge of the most diverse and non-traditional categories of wage labor (in circulation, in the state apparatus, and in the various "service sectors," and so on), categories that become impossible to ascribe in any meaningful way to a given class.[5] To this has been added the integration of a substantial part of the command function of capital directly within the various activities of labor, thereby shifting the contradiction between labor and capital in its immediacy to a point within individuals themselves (a process euphemistically configured as "personal responsibility," "job enrichment," "horizontal hierarchies," and so on). This tendency has been further exacerbated under the pressure of crisis-induced hypercompetition and in the course of a general precarization of working conditions. This is most apparent in the many small-scale freelancers and "entreployees," whose welfare as well as whose woe now becomes purely a matter of taking on, under their own direction and at their own risk, the outsourced job functions of this or that company. But even within the enterprises themselves there is an increasing tendency to turn employees into "managers," both of themselves and of their respective working areas (as, for example, through the establishment of so-called "profit centers"). And, in the end, this tendency even generates the cynical ideology for administering the unemployed in which praise of "self-management" and "personal responsibility" are all the more obtrusively propagated, and thus the clearer it becomes that the labor market cannot even come close to reintegrating all those whom it has spat out like so many "self-managing" bits of refuse.

Second, and as an extension of the above, the practice of constantly changing jobs and the resulting alternation among a huge variety of activities has, increasingly since the end of Fordism, become the norm — a norm that has substantially contributed to the dissolution of any given individual's identification with specific productive functions. Individuals' relationships to their position in the process of production thus ceased to be in any way anchored in their biography or environment, and empirically became closer to what it, according to its concept, already was: an external relationship.[6] In the process the categorical imperative of flexibility now demands obedience more and more adamantly. It is well known that today there is no worse sin against the law of capitalism than continuing to adhere to a single function or activity of labor. This is not only preached by the priests of the market, but also results from the objectified compulsions of the global race to the bottom. Whoever wants to survive must be prepared perpetually to switch between the categories of wage labor and self-employment, and to identify with neither — although, of course, even this brings no guarantee.

Third, the new hierarchies and divisions cut across the categories of capitalist function rather than overlapping with them. Specifically, they are not determined by the opposition between wage labor and capital, for the social differential is just as steep within the category of wage labor as it is in society as a whole. This applies in the first instance to the businesses themselves, in which (shrinking) core workforces with (at least for the moment) permanent jobs, even with collective bargaining agreements, carry out the same work alongside a growing number of part-time and agency workers under completely different conditions. However, the differences between sectors, branches of production, and regional locations are even greater, and ultimately there are huge discrepancies with respect to income, working conditions, and status depending on one's position in the hierarchy of the global chains of valorization.

Fourth, declassing ultimately means that more and more people worldwide are falling through the grid of the functional categories, because there is no longer a place for them in the system of commodity production that can productively exploit less and less labor power. They are forced to find out that they cannot only be replaced at any time, but that they are also to a growing extent becoming superfluous in the capitalist sense. Being privileged means managing to cling to some function or other, or to switch between different functions, without coming crashing down. But since these functions are themselves becoming precarious or wholly obsolete, such a balancing act is becoming increasingly more difficult. Because the objectified functional structures are disintegrating, more and more people are also falling through their grid. How many this effect varies according to the position of a country or region in global competition, but the threat of falling into social nothingness looms over everyone. The trend is clear and unambiguous: across the world a growing segment of new underclasses has emerged, which have nothing to do with the old proletariat and which neither objectively (by their function or position within the process of production) nor subjectively (by virtue of their consciousness) constitute a new social collective (something like a "precariat"). Their relationship to the capitalist process of valorization is in the first instance a purely negative one: they are no longer required. But this forces us to formulate anew the question of the possible constitution of new emancipatory social movements.

Attempts to Save the Dead Subject

The resurrected left-wing discourse of class struggle hardly makes a contribution to the clarification of this question. While it is true that it has in some respects learned from social upheavals and transformations, and undergone a few alterations in its argumentation, it has ultimately not succeeded in freeing itself of the fundamental metaphysical patterns of traditional class-struggle Marxism. These patterns are perennially reproduced, even if the subjects to which appeals are made (or rather, which desire attempts to summon up) have changed. In the last issue of *Krisis* I attempted to show this above all in the examination of Hardt and Negri and John Holloway.[7] But here attention should in the first instance be directed toward approaches with a less obviously metaphysical leaning, since their arguments proceed more in the mode of sociology, and concentrate more strongly on the analysis of the objective aspect of social development. In course it will be shown that it is precisely the empirical results of these investigations that refute the paradigm of class that has been applied. In the attempt to save class analysis by means of all sorts of extensions they become entangled in contradictions and aporias which clearly indicate that this rescue attempt is condemned to failure and that only abandoning the traditional Marxist construct can open a glimpse of a renewed perspective of emancipatory action.

Let us first hear the Gramscian class theorist Frank Deppe. The "working class," he argues in the journal *Fantômas*,

> has by no means disappeared, capitalism is still based on the exploitation of wage labor and the natural, social and political conditions of production and appropriation of surplus value.
>
> Between 1970 and 2000 the number of workers dependent on wage labor nearly doubled, and comprises about half of the entire global population. This can be explained in the first instance by development in China and other parts of Asia, where large parts of the rural population were "set free" as a result of industrialization.
>
> In the developed capitalist countries the proportion of the

population engaged in wage labor has now reached 90% and more. [8]

What is immediately striking about this argument is that it operates with a concept of the working class that swings back and forth between at least two different meanings. At first Deppe seems to classify among the working class only those wage workers who produce surplus value in the strict sense, whose surplus labor is skimmed off directly for the valorization of capital. However, this concept of class slides seamlessly into a completely different one, one which comprises all the "workers dependent on wage labor" and thus "half of the entire global population" and in the capitalist urban centers even almost the entire population (namely over 90 percent).

In this argumentative vacillation, the class theorist's entire dilemma is expressed. If the category of the working class is interpreted in the first sense (which corresponds to Marx's theory, to which Deppe explicitly refers), then it must be conceded that what is at stake is a global minority which is losing its significance to an ever-greater extent the further the processes of rationalization in the value-producing sectors advance, and the more labor is made superfluous in immediate production. In the second meaning, however, that is to say the expansion of the category of the working class to all "workers dependent on wage-labor," it becomes a non-concept, for it no longer has any power to discriminate at all. It is then just another word for the general mode of existence and life in capitalist society, which mediates its connectedness simply by means of labor and commodity production, which for the huge majority of people presents itself as the compulsion to sell their labor power in order to survive. While this universal compulsion is an essential characteristic of capitalist society, it is by no means suitable for the determination of the working class, because all people are in principle subject to it, regardless of their positions in the social hierarchy their social status and life situation.

The aporias of the newer theory of class also become clear in the writings of the historian Marcel van der Linden, whose concept of class is even broader than that of Deppe. For him, "every bearer of labor power, whose labor power is sold or hired to another person under economic or non-economic compulsion, belongs to the working class. Whether the labor power is offered by the worker herself or himself, and whether she or he owns her or his own means of production, is irrelevant."[9] With this definition, van der Linden wants to account for the fact that in globalized commodity society there has emerged a gargantuan multitude of differentiated and hierarchized working conditions that do not (any longer) fit the classical schema of wage labor. Among these he counts different transitional forms between slavery, wage labor, self-employment, and subcontracting, but also the unpaid subsistence and reproductive labor of women. Van der Linden accordingly no longer speaks of the class of "free wage workers," but chooses the broader concept of "subaltern workers."[10] But this, however, does not solve the problem, but rather goes one step further than Deppe by inflating the concept of class so that it becomes a metacategory which fundamentally encompasses capitalist society in its entirety.

It lies within the very logic of this metacategory that it is completely devoid of shape. It presents the paradox of a concept of capitalist totality, but precisely this totality slips through its hands. For on one hand it indirectly accounts for the fact that labor is the comprehensive principle — or more accurately, the principle of mediation — of bourgeois society. On the other hand, it is precisely this that is hidden by the fixation on the category of class. Traditional Marxism had always considered the mediation of the social context by labor as the transhistorical constant of all societies, and failed to recognize that what is at stake is the historically specific essential characteristic of the capitalist formation, which is inextricably linked to generalized commodity production and the valorization of value as if an end in itself.[11] What seemed to Marxism to be specific to capitalism was rather the particular way in which surplus labor is skimmed off in the form of surplus value, the mediation via the market and private ownership of the means of production — characteristics which can all be brought together in the concept of class domination or of the class opposition between the capitalist class and the working class. This perspective was certainly ideologically compatible with the struggle of a particular segment of commodity owners for recognition within bourgeois society. But whoever wants to bring it up to date and to account for the gargantuan discrepancy in working conditions under the conditions of the globalization of the capital relation will necessary fall into irresolvable contradictions.

The idea, however, that class opposition characterizes the essence of capitalism rather than presenting a derived relationship is so deeply anchored in people's heads that it obscures the view of the formal context of society even where it reveals itself to be analytically unsuitable at every turn.[12] The very attempts to found this idea more precisely make this clear. An example of this is provided by van der Linden's attempt at least to begin to delineate his concept of class, which evidently even he finds unsatisfactory, when he asks himself "what all these completely different subalterns actually have in common," only to answer "that all subaltern workers live in the status of 'institutionalized heteronomy.'"[13] What is to be understood by this he explains with a reference to Cornelius Castoriadis: "Institutionalized heteronomy expresses an 'antagonistic division of society and with it the domination of a particular social category over the whole [...] The capitalist economy thus alienates us to the extent that it coincides with the division into proletarians and capitalists.'"[14]

It is immediately striking that Castoriadis derives "institutionalized heteronomy" immediately from the class position of the workers. This definition, abbreviated as it is, logically corresponded to the traditional Marxist theory of class with its fixation on the good old proletariat. But what remains of this theory if, like van der Linden, one extends the concept of class to infinity and subsumes more or less the whole of humanity under it? Van der Linden implicitly says nothing other than that alienation is a universal feature of bourgeois society. But at the same time he cannot provide a plausible theoretical justification of this claim, because he does not set himself free from the paradigm of traditional Marxism. Even here the attempt to save this paradigm by extending it uncovers its aporias and limitations, which the historical process had initially obscured. That alienation or fetishism cannot be directly attributed to class domination, but are essential characteristics of a society that is blindly mediated by commodity production and labor, had, as is well known, already been shown by Marx. It is quite possible that to the workers' movement in its struggle for recognition within bourgeois society, this might have appeared as idle speculation. But today there stands in the way of this insight nothing more than an anachronistic refusal to let go of the paradigm of the theory of class that repeatedly disclaims itself.

The "Class" as Positive Totality

However, the protagonists of the more recent discourse of class do not acknowledge this self-disclaimer. It is true that they cannot help but implicitly recognize the emptying that results from the inflation of the concept of class, but that does not lead to a change of perspective in their critique of capitalism, but rather ensnares them in all kinds of evasive maneuvers and attempts to blur their own tracks. Above all, the shifting of the focus of investigation onto the empirical level enables the masterpiece at once to dispose of and to retain the fixation on the class opposition as essence of capitalism and center of gravity of all radical critique ("principal contradiction"): retain because the concept of class is elevated to the metalevel of the social relation, where it ekes out a living as an abstraction, devoid of content, which can be immunized against critique precisely because of this character; and dispose of because it no longer plays any real role in the empirical analyses, but only presents a diffuse, presupposed instance of invocation — which as such, however, shapes the perspective of investigation and colors the results in a particular way.

It sounds a little like unconscious self-irony when van der Linden ends his essay with the remark "But it remains to warn against every empirically empty grand theory."[15] For this is precisely what distinguishes his approach and that of all more recent protagonists of the discourse of class: their theory remains empirically empty and their empiricism remains theoretically naked; they uphold the myth of class struggle, although no subject or a movement can any longer be found in social reality to which the class struggle could be affixed without great strain. When Deppe and van der Linden describe the social hierarchies and inequalities that are formed and sharpened in the context of global crisis capitalism, it is in some respects empirically illuminating, but by setting the headline "Fragmentation of the Working Class" at the top, a highly unfortunate turn of phrase enters the room. What is assumed is always a fundamental unity which is presupposed by all those fragmentations, even if it is not possible adequately to explain in what this unity is supposed to consist. The bridging of the oppositions of interest and the positions of competition with respect to an anticapitalist formation nonetheless appears as fundamentally prearranged.

Deppe even expands this construct to the extent that he speaks, referring to Gramsci, of a "new bloc of subalterns," which alongside the "working class" is supposed also to encompass all other social movements of the last years ("landless peasants' protests in Brazil, the uprising in Chiapas, [...] global mass-demonstrations against war and the threat of war"). This bloc, he concedes, "has not yet, however, articulated itself as a bloc, because it lacks an alternative programme and the capacity to act against neoliberalism, through which the fractions of this bloc could be welded together."[16] The "bloc," that is, already exists "in itself," but has not yet "articulated itself politically" as such. It is no accident that this is reminiscent of the violent construction of "ascribed class-consciousness," if admittedly in a sort of shrunken version which — in contrast with Lukács — does not do without a metaphysical foundation because Deppe is critically beyond such things, but because he carries it around with him unacknowledged.[17] It is only because he implicitly carries the corresponding ascription through to its conclusion and thus presupposes something like a fundamental objective congruence (of interests) of all parties that he can reduce the problem to the superficial question of an "alternative programme" that he imagines could weld together the different "factions" of that bloc.

The almost incidental manner in which the fragmentations produced by capitalism are downgraded to a sort of secondary or derivative problem with respect to the presupposed "class" indicates a further aporia, which results from the frantic adherence to the paradigm of traditional Marxism. For traditional Marxism, the working class represented by its nature the standpoint of social universality — which was thought to be identical with the standpoint of labor. It was thus supposed to inherit the legacy of the bourgeoisie, which at the times of the bourgeois revolutions was supposed to have claimed this standpoint for itself, but then to have betrayed it for the sake of the selfish private interest of profit. The revolutionary aim accordingly consisted in the creation of a social totality — a totality, namely, that was mediated through labor in a conscious manner. As Moishe Postone has shown in extensive detail, this idea amounted, in two senses, to an ideologically distorted projection of the conditions of capitalism. On one hand, it is a contradiction in itself to desire consciously to shape mediation through labor (and thus through the commodity), because labor is by its nature self-referential and self-directed — that is, it follows its own reified laws, which it forces onto people as if it were a natural law. On the other hand, the constitution of the social context as totality is also an historically quite specific characteristic of capitalist society, which in contrast with all other societies is mediated through a single principle, and for that reason naturally cannot be the vanishing point of emancipation: "The capitalist social formation, according to Marx, is unique inasmuch as it is constituted by a qualitatively homogeneous social 'substance'; hence, it exists as a social totality. Other social formations are not so totalized: their fundamental social relations are not qualitatively homogeneous. They cannot be grasped by the concept of 'substance,' cannot be unfolded from a single structuring principle, and do not display an immanent, necessary historical logic."[18] It follows as a consequence of this insight "that the historical negation of capitalism would not involve the *realization*, but the *abolition*, of the totality."[19] Now it is true that the more recent discourse of class claims to offer a critique of the false identifications of traditional Marxism, but it undoes this work itself by its continued fixation on class and its inflation to a metacategory, the tendency of which is to encompass society as a whole. The appeal to totality — and the unconscious affirmation of the form of capitalist mediation that is contained within it — of traditional Marxism is thus surpassed, and at the same time reduced to absurdity. For if almost all people are ascribed to "the class" (or to the "bloc of subalterns," or whatever), the social universality that traditional Marxism depicted as still on the horizon would already be potentially realized. But with this the theoretically justified standpoint of critique is also lost. For the totality constituted on capitalist terms could not then be criticized, but would only have to acquire consciousness of itself. Only a few say this as explicitly as Hardt and Negri, who already see communism everywhere peeking through from under the thin cover of capitalism; but this is in no way just an isolated quirk, but rather the logical consequence of the theoretical approach that they fundamentally share with all the discourse of class in its entirety.

This discourse certainly believes that it goes beyond traditional Marxism, because it has freed itself from the idea of a unified subject and instead permanently evokes the heterogeneity of the putative working class. But in this it fundamentally only reflects the inner disjointedness of commodity society, which as asocial sociality, by definition, disintegrates into countless particularities.[20] If this fragmented totality is immediately identified with the working class and appealed to positively, then the criteria necessary in order adequately to address the destructive capacities that are increasingly set free in the process of disintegration of bourgeois subjectivity are ultimately missing. This holds for racist and sexist violence as much as for antisemitic delusion and the ethnic and religious fundamentalisms that are gaining currency. From the perspective of class they cannot be decoded as inherent forms of expression of subjectivity in commodity society that present independent moments of the dynamic of capitalist crisis, because the fixation on the "fragmented class-subject" would otherwise be called into question. It is basically for this reason that they are always treated as external appearances, as a sort of disturbing factor that might be able to split the class context, but are not of essential concern. It thus ultimately remains a matter of personal taste to decide whether or not reactionary movements, be they ethno-nationalistic currents (in Spain, for example) or the so-called Second Intifada, can be included in the great consensus of anticapitalist struggles. The partition between the elements of the more recent discourse of class and the regressive decayed forms of traditional Marxism is thus extremely thin for the reason that the theoretical foundation is at heart the same.

No More Making of the Working Class

In contrast to the attempts to save the working class by overexpanding its objective determinations are those whose arguments proceed primarily from the subjective side. According to these approaches, class is not defined by position in the process of production and valorization, but always constitutes itself anew and is subject to permanent changes which are an essential result of the dynamic of class struggles. Such a perspective has the initial advantage of drawing attention to the active moments in social conflict, their process character, and the possibilities for subjective development that are contained within it, because the category of class is kept open and not codified in a definition. But the appearance of openness is deceptive. It is fundamentally limited by an axiom that is always placed in front of all specific analyses in advance, and that restricts their perspective. For it can be seen how self-evidently class struggle is presupposed as a transhistorically valid principle, from which class can then in turn be derived: "Always already present in all social relations, class struggle precedes the historical classes," so the editorial of the issue of the journal *Fantômas* that has already been cited many times in this chapter.[21] But with this the argument becomes circular. Both the concept of class and that of class struggle are defined completely arbitrarily. All social conflicts can in principle be ennobled to class struggles without differentiation, and all participants to class subjects. In this manner, the subjectivist concept of class attains in principle the same result as its objective counterpart. It is thus no wonder that these former theoretical rivals are increasingly becoming reconciled with one another and living together in peace (as, for example, is the case in that issue of *Fantômas*). For wherever all conceptual stringency is lost and the "class" can simply be anything and everything, the old differences no longer play any sort of decisive role.

What is problematic here is primarily that the concept of class struggle, once it is dissolved from the historically specific context of the workers' movement, the only context in which it made any sense, can very easily be short-circuited with a completely nonspecific concept of struggle, which corresponds more to the "war of all against all" (Hobbes) than a struggle against the conditions and impositions of capitalism. Once again, this is particularly apparent in Hardt and Negri, who transfigure even the individualized daily struggle for existence to a form of expression of class struggle, and no longer have any sort of criteria to distance themselves from outbreaks of regressive violence or even fundamentalist movements. Class struggle thus becomes an abstract and ultimately affirmative empty formula which encompasses the permanent internal state of war of capitalist society and its disintegration in crisis no less than the endeavors to oppose precisely this. Now it is true that many proponents of the subjectivist standpoint of class for good reasons do not wish to pursue this consequence to its end, but in this they end up with a fairly considerable burden of justification. For their levitating, decontextualized concept of class struggle has no conceptual set of tools available that could distinguish between the mere action of bourgeois subjectivity in its ugliest facets (whether individual or collective) and the attempts to overcome precisely this (e.g., in grassroots social movements). To save the concept of class struggle, all kinds of argumentative bolt-ons are necessary (the recourse to discourse theory, for example), which only show how little it can itself contribute to the analytical clarification of social development.

One of the most important witnesses for the case of the subjectivist theorists of class is the English social historian E.P. Thompson, who always emphasized the active moment in the emergence of the working class. In the preface to his most important historical study, which has the programmatic title *The Making of the English Working Class*, he writes "*Making*, because it is a study in an active process, which owes as much to agency as to conditioning. The working class did not rise like the sun at an appointed time. It was present at its own making."[22] However, Thompson's analyses refer — as he himself always insists — to processes in a highly specific historical situation: the capitalist drive to assert itself during the last third of the eighteenth and the first third of the nineteenth century in England. But this situation is evidently different from today's in a fundamental way. It was shaped by the repression and destruction of the comparatively heterogeneous pre- and proto-capitalist living and working conditions under the ever stronger pressure of standardization of the capitalist mode of production and of life; and this means not least by the massive creation of doubly free wage workers who were compelled to sell their labor power in order to survive. In Thompson's investigations he concentrated on the revolts and the struggles of resistance that were provoked by this process, and showed how during the course of them (and also by the experience of defeats) something like a class consciousness first began to take shape.

But while it was important to emphasize the significance of these subjective processes that had been ignored by orthodox Marxism, it was just as important that the insights gained by this process not be deleted from their historical context if they were not to become abstract in the bad sense. While the formation of a class consciousness is in no way the automatic result of the process of establishment of the valorization of capital, this subjective unification in a working class nonetheless corresponds to the simultaneous objective process of subordination of all social relations under the principle of unity of abstract labor and commodity production. The two moments devour one another in a dialectical relationship. Thompson himself emphasizes: "the class experience is largely defined by the productive relations into which men are born — or enter involuntarily. Class-consciousness is the way in which these experiences are handled in cultural terms: embodied in traditions, value-systems, ideas, and institutional forms. If the experience appears as determined, class-consciousness does not."[23]

If we transpose this claim onto the current situation, it must be acknowledged straight away that the objectively predefined context within which social experiences are made and social struggles are pursued is fundamentally different from that epoch. We are not standing today at the beginning of the process of establishment of capitalism; the main trend is not by a long way that of the extermination of noncapitalist modes of life by means of the steamroller of valorization (although this is still happening in some parts of the world). We are rather facing a situation in which the commodity-producing system has generalized itself the world over and at the same time entered a fundamental process of crisis, because it undermines its own foundations by the increasing displacement of living labor power. This development, however, which is expressed in the increasing precarization of living and working conditions and in the fact that worldwide more and more people are being made surplus to the requirements of and excluded from the valorization of capital, is directly opposed to that of the beginning of the nineteenth century. In the current direction of development of the basic logic of capitalism that has become an end in itself can be found not the formation of a (new) working class, but the increasing destruction of a society which is based on the universalized compulsion to sell oneself. People, that is to say, are not being forced into a unified social form; rather, the form of unity in which they live and by means of which they are constituted is disintegrating, and they are thus falling through its structures. However, it is possible to speak of a unification in this context to the extent that the process which I described above under the concept of declassing is a universal one. But in itself, this contains nothing of consequence. Quite the opposite: capitalist fragmentation is only the intensification of the logic of capital in the stage of its decomposition. This is true not only objectively, as exemplified by the exacerbated competition between locations, a quandary that from the beginning imposes limits upon the struggle between particular interests (for example against factory closure or wage cuts), although this does not fundamentally mean that these struggles have lost their immanent justification. At the same time, the exacerbated pressure of the struggle for existence has also made an essential contribution to the atomization and decline in solidarity and the broad-reaching establishment of the capitalist subjectivity of competition and delimitation.

This development is also expressed in the subjective forms of operation and modes of action. The movements of social resistance at the start of the nineteenth century emerged against the background of a repression of non- and proto-capitalist living conditions that were incompatible with the industrial-capitalist mode of production. In the light of this collective experience and of the tremendous imposition that was daily factory labor and the selfishness of capitalist competition, cultural patterns of interpretation and forms of practical solidarity were developed in resistance, which ultimately led to the formation of the consciousness of belonging to a class with a common fate. However, because today such a process of constitution is no longer and cannot any longer take place, the beginnings of anticapitalist resistance are overlayed and pushed back by processes of collectivization that are determined by regressive forms from the core stock of commodity-society subjectivity.[24] This is true for the formation of sects and gangs just as for the antisemitic delusion, for the racist and religious forms of identity politics of all shades no less than for outbreaks of violence for its own sake. There is no new working class emerging here; what is rather taking place is the action of people who have been formed into subjects of labor and the commodity but who can no longer ordinarily function as such.[25]

However, the fragmentation of crisis capitalism does not only set free the regressive moments of the subject form; the emancipatory impulses, ideas, and aspirations which had attached themselves to the struggle of the working class for recognition within bourgeois society have also lost their context and have to a certain extent begun to float free. The historical class struggle draws its comparative coherence from its focus on the opposition of the interests of capital and labor, an opposition which developed an integrating dynamic in the phase of the rise of capitalism. The resistance against the current wave of precarization and impoverishment, in contrast, continually exposes itself to the danger of itself reproducing the centrifugal tendencies of the unfolding capitalist crisis. It is thus faced with the difficult task of formulating and pursuing social conflicts in such a way that they counteract the intensified logic of competition and exclusion and the identity-political tendencies that accompany it. This will ultimately only succeed if different struggles and conflicts can be linked together across all borders without false proclamations of unity or hierarchies. This linking, however, cannot be derived from presupposed objective or subjective determinations (class standpoint or class struggle). It can only emerge from the conscious cooperation of such social movements that aspire to the abolition of domination in all its facets, and not only as an abstract, distant goal, but also within their own structures and relationships.

Blueprints for such movements cannot be drafted at the drawing board. Theory is unable to do anything other than formulate fundamental considerations in this direction. If we have anything to learn from Thompson's investigations, it is the significance of practical experiences for the constitution of social movements. For this reason it is important to turn our attention to those processes within which resistance to capitalist impositions turns away from hierarchical, populist, and authoritarian attempts to draw people together, and where struggles between interests are linked to the establishment of self-organized structures. While such movements (as for example the Zapatistas, the autonomous currents of the Piqueteros, and other grass-roots movements) are in many respects contradictory — and we must on no account attempt to transfigure them romantically —

they are also in a minority on a world scale, and always under the threat of marginalization and cooptation.[26] However, here can be found approaches and moments which point to the perspective of a liberation from the totality of commodity society. The future belongs not to class struggle, but to an emancipatory struggle without classes.

Notes

1. On the constitution and role of collective subjects in bourgeois society, see
    Ernst Lohoff, "Die Verzauberung der Welt," *Krisis* 29 (Münster: 2005) 13-
    60; on the importance of class opposition in the process of development
    of capitalism, see Moishe Postone, *Time, Labor, and Social Domination:
    A Reinterpretation of Marx's Critical Theory* (Cambridge: Cambridge
    University Press, 1993) 314 and following.

2. To be sure, this process of emergence was by no means devoid of
    contradiction, not least because the conviction of the participants that
    class struggle was in fact a conflict with the potential to explode the
    system itself persisted for a considerable time, and particular historical
    situations even invested class struggle with a dynamic which might
    possibly have been able to break through the objectified, structural
    development. To this extent, the subjective moments are not reducible
    to nor simply identical with the objective development.

3. It is tragic to see how the crisis process and the increasingly fierce
    competition for lower prices on the world market that accompanied it
    reinforce this affirmative attitude in an extreme manner, and how in the
    mostly hopeless struggles against closures — as in the case of AEG in
    Nuremberg — the primary argument is that the management's economic
    calculations are mistaken.

4. I take the term "declassing" (*Deklassierung*) from Franz Schandl, but my
    interpretation goes beyond his. Schandl writes: "social regression can
    no longer be described primarily with respect to the social positioning
    of classes. What is at stake is not the determination of class identity,
    but *de-classing*, which means that people are literally falling out of their
    social structures. So, for example, they are losing (as in permanently out
    of) work, but still remain the monadic subjects of work or labor as such;
    they *have* no money but must remain the *subjects* of money. De-classing
    effects not only the so-called proletariat, but is all-encompassing. Despite
    the exacerbation of social contradictions, class-contradictions are being
    defused" (Franz Schandl, "Desinteresse und Deklassierung," *Streifzüge* 3
    [Vienna: 2002] 12).

5. Accordingly, a large part of the industrial sociological discussion of the 1960s and 1970s revolved around the question "does a working class still exist?" On the left, it was in the first instance André Gorz who, with his book *Abshied vom Proletariat,* opened a crack in the discourse that was shaped by the myth of class struggle. See André Gorz, *Abschied vom Proletariat* (Frankfurt: Europäische Verlagsanstalt, 1980).

6. "The capitalist individual is no longer a class-individual, the 'aggregate of social relations' [Marx] shapes itself by and in the individual in a more complicated and more manifold manner. Its attitude cannot be attributed to the process of production, even if the investigation of circulation and consumption, even of reproduction, is extended. The concept of class melts away in our fingers. It is a concept that conceives less and less. People's communicative behaviour cannot be reduced to their class-situation, its analysis cannot even be focused on this situation" (Franz Schandl, "Kommunismus oder Klassenkampf," *Streifzüge* 3 (Vienna: 2002) 9).

7. See Norbert Trenkle, "Die metaphysischen Mucken des Klassenkampfs," *Krisis* 29 (Münster: 2005) 143-59.

8. Frank Deppe, "Der postmoderne Fürst. Arbeiterklasse und Arbeiterbewegung im 21. Jahrhundert," *Fantômas* 4 (Hamburg: 2003) 11.

9. Marcel van der Linden, "Das vielköpfige Ungeheuer. Zum Begriff der WeltarbeiterInnenklasse," *Fantômas* 4 (Hamburg: 2003) 34.

10. Van der Linden, "Ungeheuer" 31-33

11. On this see Postone, *Time* particularly 148-57.

12. On the critique of this idea in general see Postone, 314 and following.

13. "Ungeheuer" 33.

14. *ibid.*

15. "Ungeheuer" 34.

16. Deppe, "Fürst" 11.

17. For my critique, see Trenkle, "Die metaphysischen Mucken."

18. *Time* 79.

19. *ibid.*; see also 156-57.

20. For more on the term "asocial sociality," see 185n3 in this volume.

21. Redaktion *Fantômas*, "Klasse Arbeit," *Fantômas* 4 (Hamburg: 2003) 4.

22. E. P. Thompson, *The Making of the English Working Class* (London: Pantheon, 1963) 9.

23. Thompson, *English Working Class* 9-10.

24. For a more extensive discussion of this, see Lohoff, "Die Verzauberung."

25. It is thus absurd when Karl Heinz Roth, for example, in explicit reference to Thompson, claims to recognize the precursors of a possible new proletarian class subjectivity of all places in the rampantly spreading neoreligious revival movements. In this context he describes the fundamentalist pentecostal communities as "the largest social self-organizing community of the new underclasses in the world, which in Latin America and Sub-Saharan Africa alone has 100 million members" (65), in order to proceed in the following terms: "As we know from E.P. Thompson's *The Making of the English Working Class*, the millenarian sects were an important constitutive moment in the process in which the English working class and its radical movements came to find themselves. We thus do not necessarily need to grow despondent at the ambiguous messages which find their way to us from the lowest segments of the global underclasses" (69). See Karl Heinz Roth, *Der Zustand der Welt. Gegenperspektiven* (Hamburg: Verlag, 2005).

26. On this see Marco Fernandes, "Piqueteros oder Wenn Arbeitslosigkeit adelt," *Krisis* 30 (Münster: 2006).

Violence as the Order of Things and the Logic of Extermination

Ernst Lohoff (2003)

> "I have always dreamed," he mouthed fiercely, "of a band of men absolute in their resolve to discard all scruples in the choice of means, strong enough to give themselves frankly the name of destroyers, and free from the taint of that resigned pessimism which rots the world. No pity for anything on earth, including themselves, and death enlisted for good and all in the service of humanity — that's what I would have liked to see."
>
> - Joseph Conrad, *The Secret Agent*

The Great Disillusionment

The epochal break of 1989 promised — of this a victorious West was thoroughly convinced — the beginning of an age of peace. In a world unified under the banners of Democracy, Human Rights, and Globalized Markets, war and violence would become as obsolete as yesterday's newspapers. With the aim of becoming their unifying synthesis, this hope grabbed hold of two of the hoariest, bedrock assumptions of Enlightenment thought. On one hand, it repeated the widely held notion, in circulation ever since the eighteenth century, that under the sway of the founding principles of modernity — reason, freedom, and the rule of law — there could be no real place for bloodshed. Wars, if they did occur, were anomalies resulting from the actions of agents of states ungrounded in these principles of liberty, fraternity, and equality. With the final victory of the West, such forms of power supposedly vanished, transforming the world into a garden of peace. The ongoing process of globalization, on the other hand, was itself understood as a guarantee of pacification, since, with the triumph of an unbounded market totality, the state as a potential war-making power would increasingly find itself left behind by the market as a supposed force for peace. Since politics and the state increasingly lose individual significance, and are, *nolens volens*, subordinated entirely to a logic governed by the market and by one's relation to it, the argument runs, wars are becoming more and more unlikely.

The assumption that the guns fall silent where the market and its laws are the order of the day and that the triumph of economic logic is in itself the road to nonviolence has deep historical roots. Ever since Adam Smith and Immanuel Kant, this notion has belonged to the standard repertoire of liberal economics and the philosophy of the Enlightenment: "The spirit of trade cannot coexist with war, and sooner or later this spirit dominates every people."[1] It fell to Thomas Paine to give liberalism's warranty of universal peace its classical configuration. In *The Rights of Man* (1792) he not only praises the peacemaking ideals glittering in the new dawn of abstract bourgeois principle, but in the same breath also salutes the market as "a pacific system, operating to unite mankind by rendering nations, as well as individuals, useful to each other."[2] "The invention of commerce has arisen since those governments began, and is the greatest approach toward universal civilization that has yet been made by any means not immediately flowing from moral principles."[3]

But developments since 1989 have effectively frustrated the expectation that, as a result of the final victory of the West, the world would become a less violent place. This frustration can of course not solely be understood as the result of an overly optimistic prognosis resting on otherwise valid premises. It is the basic premises themselves, rooted in the deepest stratum of Enlightenment thinking, that have in fact now become untenable. They stand the real relations on their head. For a start, Liberty, Fraternity, and Equality do not, after all, form a rhyming couplet with Peace and Reconciliation. The unpleasant, sickly-sweet smell rising from these principles turns out, if we really hold our noses up close, to be an effluvium of intermingled death and murder, more overpowering and all-pervasive today than ever before.

Moreover, to equate the free market with peace and nonviolence is itself already a false step. To be sure, the initial phase of commodity-producing society was marked by an increasing tendency to turn violence and war exclusively into matters of state. But from this it scarcely follows that the processes of state disintegration currently under way are going to make war and violence disappear. In the age of capitalist crisis that is now bursting onto the scene, they merely undergo a change of form. Within the framework of globalization, what we see flourishing across wide swathes of the world is, more precisely, an outright marketization of violence itself, as the latter becomes a stage for dramatis personae of an entirely new type. With the turn to warlordism and mafia rule in vast areas of the Third World, war-spawned commercial enterprises reminiscent, in a European context, of the age of the Renaissance and of the Thirty Years' War, are staging a comeback. But in the Western metropolis as well, the state as a form of regimented violence is undergoing a metamorphosis in which, rather than dissipating, the potential for violence is simply given a freer rein.

This essay starts in the manner of an exploratory excavation of intellectual history. Via critical interrogations of Hegel, Hobbes, and Freud, here proposed as exemplifying the more general trend, the following thesis is developed: that the canon of Western values popularly called to mind by the slogan of Liberty, Fraternity, Equality is ultimately predicated on a merely temporary suspension of expressly homicidal violence. The very form of the commodity subject is built around a nucleus of violence. The essay's second part analyzes the process of bringing war and violence under the sway of the state and understands the rise of the state as sole legitimate agent of violence as a two-sided process of implanting and taming this violent nucleus. In part three the dissolution of a state-governed regimentation of violence is described. The homicidal logic underlying the modern, commodity-generated process of subject constitution that has given us Western values, having once been displaced, is now thrusting itself back into plain sight.

Part One

Liberty, Eqaulity, and Fraternity and the Violence at the Core of the Subject Form of Commodity-Producing Society

According to its own self-understanding, the canon of Western values is essentially a programmatic antidote to arbitrary rule, tyranny, and murder. Notions of contract, legality, and morality derive their legitimation from the fact that, under their rule, bloodshed and all lawless, unregulated relations are prevented. Examined more closely, of course, another picture emerges than the one painted by Western ideology. The disease that Western values are supposed to remedy is, as a rule, the product of the cure itself. Destruction, murder, and chaos are themselves constitutive of Liberty, Equality, and Fraternity. What these principles represent is in no way the opposite of destruction and violence, but rather the result of the latter's partial suspension and sublimation — the result of processes that, with the decadence of commodity-producing society, could prove themselves to be everywhere subject to reversal. Where lawless, unregulated conditions take over from the day-to-day norms of commodity-producing society, the decadence of the latter serves, if anything, only to lay bare the ugliness underlying such norms.

To the degree that the core values of the West have become, so to speak, the flesh and blood of commodity rationality, to that same degree are such values exempted from all critical reflection. The same is true of the real inner connection between the universal principles of the Enlightenment and the logic of violence and extermination underlying them. But for those whose thinking first paved the way for the values of the Enlightenment, and who produced the ideological prerequisites for their implementation, things looked otherwise. If their theoretical constructions are read against the grain, they blurt out things that their heirs would now be incapable of expressing. Even just a brief test-drilling into the foundations of Liberty, Fraternity, and Equality here dredges up such monstrosities that it becomes impossible to draw in any naively positive way on the ideas of 1789 without feelings of nausea.

Homicidal Equality

It would in no way be an exaggerated claim to locate the originating ground of all modern state and contract theory and the legitimation of the state itself in the panic-driven fear of self-created specters of violence. In the case of the progenitor of modern political thought, Thomas Hobbes, at any rate, such fear constitutes both the unmistakable point of departure and a leitmotif. Hobbes's concern is to legitimate and propagate the rule of the sovereign. But the resulting picture he draws of that sovereign is far from sympathetic. As the biblical name "Leviathan" reveals, Hobbes explicitly calls for the rule of something gigantic and terrifying enough to keep all citizens in check through the threat of its capacity for violence. But if rule by such a generalized and superior power appears unavoidable, this is precisely because Hobbes imagines the human species itself as a motley collection of notoriously antisocial, violent subjects. Only a super monster, according to *Leviathan*'s ceaselessly repeated axiom, can prevent the little monsters from constantly slitting each other's throats, and thereby put an end to the supposed state of nature proclaimed to be a "war of all against all."

The point of departure for all theories of contract is the notion of human equality. Although this idea was already known to the European Middle Ages, human equality in its Western version then referred only to the afterlife, to the equality of all mortals before God. Hobbes gets the credit for bringing the ideal of equality down from the religious sphere of the divine to earth. But this process of secularization only really steps into the spotlight when one considers just how it is that the father of contract and state theory defines human equality. Mortality as *conditio humana* is replaced in Hobbes by what might be termed the universal capacity for homicide. Men are equal insofar as all are equally capable of killing each other.

Hobbes's unremittingly empiricist understanding of equality initially rests on an "equality of hope." But this equality does not join men together in a mode of common action and conduct. On the contrary, it sets them against each other in the pursuit of "the same thing, which neverthelesse they cannot both enjoy."[4] It is precisely such "equality of hope" whereby men, finding themselves on, "the way to their End, which is principally their owne conservation, and sometimes their delectation only" are led to become "Enemies." In their "Naturall Condition," however, it is a matter of more than just distrust and the constant suspicion of one another. To the equality of hope there corresponds an "equality of ability," and this is above all to be understood as the primal ability of men to dispatch one another to the other world. For Hobbes men are equal insofar as "the weakest has strength enough to kill the strongest, either by secret machination, or by confederacy with others."[5]

Only the existence of a state power armed with all means of coercion makes possible the transformation of this homicidal primal relation into a relation between equal, contractual, and juridical subjects. The very existence of a state positing such contractual and juridical subjects must spring from the prior consent of Hobbes's natural-born killers to relinquish their naturally given right to kill each other and to confer it on a generalized super-killer.

Of course, it is not hard to discern the specific historical background from which the Hobbesian approach to Western values springs. The writing of *Leviathan* bears the imprint of the wars of state formation (Jacob Burkhardt's so-called *Staatsbildungkriege*), the wars of the sixteenth and seventeenth centuries that were to decide to whom would fall the task of sovereign rule over which western and central European territories. In view of the unprecedented horrors that accompanied this process of elimination and selection, Hobbes's wish to see the number of contenders for rule over England, France, and other countries reduced as quickly as possible to one per territory — no matter which one — has something to be said for it. But insofar as Hobbes simply projected the crimes of the early modern states *in spe* onto human nature as such, they become more than the ideological inversions needed to legitimize the absolutist states of his day. There are two respects in which Hobbes's thinking points beyond his own times. First, there is the fact that the results of his efforts at ideological projection were to be widely adopted. Just as he ascribes the brutality of early-modern military absolutism to human nature and expands the definition of an institutionalized Western reason in such a way as to make it the solution itself for all horrors connected with that process, just so has commodity rationality — the spontaneous or common-sense understanding native to commodity society — repeatedly managed to exploit the horrors, past and present, born out of its own historical genesis into means of self-legitimation. Whether it is witch hunts, National Socialism, or al-Qaeda, such commodity thought always misrecognizes as nameless, alien powers sprung out of the abysses of the human soul what are, in fact, its own products. Second, Hobbes's construct renders visible the basic relation into which human beings enter as a result of capitalism's "asocial sociality."[6] Contract and law are by no means precipitates of human cooperation but instead grow out of a sublimated praxis of violence, a violence prohibited according to the enforced norms of commodity society, but which is itself logically presupposed by it.

Freedom, Liberty, and the Fight to the Death

Hegel repeatedly and decisively stresses the interconnection between freedom and violence. Concerning mind or spirit itself, a well-known passage in the introduction to the *Phenomenology* states programmatically: "But the life of Spirit is not the life that shrinks from death and keeps itself untouched by devastation, but rather the life that endures it and maintains itself in it."[7] What this means for the free commodity subject and his self-consciousness becomes particularly evident in the "lordship and bondage" section of the *Phenomenology*. Here Hegel's point of departure on the path leading to self-consciousness and freedom is a struggle taking shape as a duel to the death between two configured abstractions, lord and bondsman. This difference here between what are also, respectively, "independence" and "dependence" is referred back to differing degrees of defiance in the face of death on the part of the two contendants. The lord is the first to rise to the occasion of a still incomplete stage of self-consciousness, given his willingness to go to extremes. The bondsman, on the other hand, fearful of risking his life at the crucial moment, is not able to tear away the bars which man must break through in order to attain the conditions both of being recognized by others and of self-consciousness. "The individual who has not risked his life [...] has not attained the truth of this recognition as an independent self-consciousness."[8]

But for the bondsman as well, the duel becomes the starting point on his path to self-consciousness. "For this consciousness has been fearful, not of this or that particular thing or just at odd moments, but its whole being has been seized with dread; for it has experienced the fear of death, the absolute Lord. In that experience it has been quite unmanned, has trembled in every fibre of its being, and everything solid and stable has been shaken to its foundations."[9] Precisely this quaking makes the bondsman ripe, through the detour of labor, for leaving behind the "natural existence" from which the master had freed himself in struggle. And yet he accomplishes this even more thoroughly than did the master when he directly scaled his way upwards into the stage of self-consciousness. The autotelic activity of labor takes on the function of the fight "to the death" and thereby becomes its heir.

In the primal scene that is the achieving of freedom and self-consciousness, the death against which the combatants must face off appears as something threefold. First, "each aims at the destruction and death of the other." Achieving self-consciousness is thus bound to the will to make one's opponent into a dead object. At the same time it includes putting one's own life on the line, that is, the willingness to turn oneself into a dead object and to adopt an indifferent attitude toward one's own fate. And finally it means the essential determination of recognition-by-others and of self-consciousness as products of struggle, the devalorizing of all that is not at home and does not discover its own original image on the battlefield. Whatever is not born so as to wager its own life is judged to be inessential and therefore, paradoxically, already dead. For Hegel, freedom and, accordingly, real life are cries heard only on the battlefield — and its surrogates — where citizens indulge in manly virtues. Or as Hegel himself puts it: "But because it is only as a citizen that he is actual and substantial, the individual, so far as he is not a citizen but belongs to the Family, is only an unreal impotent shadow. This universality which the individual as such attains is pure being, death; it is a state which has been reached immediately, in the course of Nature, not the result of an action consciously done."[10]

Hegel's verdict here is aimed primarily against that whose existence he characteristically deems unworthy of mention: dissociated femininity. A masculinized logos-cum-self-consciousness imagines itself as the source of all true life, generating all that is substantive in reality out of itself.[11] While the woman inevitably leads her existence completely inside the family and therefore in the realm of the "insubstantial shadows," the man participates as citizen and warrior in the life born out of confrontation with death. The actual delivery room in which this peculiar birthing ability realizes itself, remains for Hegel on the battlefield. Death and extermination thus by no means end with what is imagined as the primal act of one-on-one combat between master and bondsman. To prevent the regression of the self-consciousness to a creature-like state, the original duel must be periodically renewed. This, then, is the true task of war, the "duel on a large scale" (Clausewitz): "War is the Spirit and the form in which the essential moment of the ethical substance, the absolute freedom of the ethical self from every existential form, is present in its actual and authentic existence."[12]

Hegel is an apologist and propagandist for the emerging fabric of commodity society, not its critic; but he is no admirer of destruction as "an end in itself." The life-and-death struggle is justified for him solely in regard to its successful suspension, in the universalization of the self-conscious labor- and commodity subject. The possibility of "sudden death" in a duel does not shrink before its own aestheticization but rather matures into praise of the "slow death" (Baudrillard), into the self-justification of the commodity subject in its expenditure of abstract labor.

Hegel's apologetic reference to war, moreover, in no way contradicts this. If he treats war as something to be honored, what he pictures here is far from an orgy of total destruction that leaves nary a stone standing. War merely demonstrates the nullity of individual existence. While later authors celebrate looking death straight in the eye on the battlefield as an act of self-positing on the part of the individual, Hegel regards this act (and death in general) as the victory of the human species over the individual human organism. In death, freedom conceived as universality triumphs over the narrow-minded particular: "The sole work and deed of universal freedom is therefore death, a death too which has no inner significance or filling, for what is negated is the empty point of the absolutely free self. It is thus the coldest and meanest of all deaths, with no more significance than cutting off a head of cabbage or swallowing mouthful of water."[13]

On the other hand, an unshackled destruction that not only causes the individual but even the universal to tremble makes Hegel cringe. This becomes obvious in the passages of the *Philosophy of Right* in which Hegel brings up the internal connection, in relation to the state and politics, between the normativity of commodity society and pure extermination. The content of the "free will" which realizes itself at the end of history in the Prussian state to which Hegel pays homage is positively determined in its content, making reality as a whole into material for the formation of the state and for the valorization of value. Before it can reach this final stage, however, it takes on the form of a negative will that flees "from all content as a barrier." Freedom appears initially as a freedom

> of the void, which has taken actual shape, and is stirred to
> passion. [...] [B]ecoming actual it assumes both in politics
> and religion the form of a fanaticism, which would destroy

the established social order, remove all individuals suspected of desiring any kind of order, and demolish any organization which then sought to rise out of the ruins. Only in devastation does the negative will feel that it has reality. It intends, indeed, to bring to pass some positive social condition, such as universal equality or universal religious life. But in fact it does not will the positive reality of any such condition, since that would carry in its train a system, and introduce a separation by way of institutions and between individuals. But classification and objective system attain self consciousness only by destroying negative freedom. Negative freedom is actuated by a mere solitary idea, whose realization is nothing but the fury of desolation.[14]

The movement of "absolute abstraction" that, otherwise contentless, finds its content in pure destruction, was historically identified by Hegel with the horrific events of the French Revolution. Although it deeply unnerves him, Hegel ascribes the "fury of destruction" without exception to an epoch that, however necessary, has drawn to a close and that reveals itself to have been a transitional stage since superseded. In the process, the "fury of destruction" is stood on its head and becomes the legitimation of commodity society and its corresponding state form. If one cancels out Hegel's historical optimism without also deleting the inner connection he establishes between the freedom of destruction and the normality of commodity society, another, more consistent but at the same time more angst-ridden picture appears: behind what purports to be an immature form of the realm of freedom now fully overcome, what the "fury of destruction" and the "freedom of the void" show us is, in fact, the inherent logic of a possibility that is continuously inherent in the "freedom of the will" and the principles of the West. Even worse, what Hegel treats as an alleged period of transition threatens to become the vanishing point of modernity. If the normality of commodity society decays, that is, if the state form begins to deteriorate and the movement of the exploitation of labor as an end in itself loses its bonding power, then an alternative end in itself — destruction and extermination — can take its place. Reified, commodity-mediated "freedom," which loses its content with the progressive cessation of nation state building and the accumulation of abstract labor, has won for itself, *ultima instantia*, in the sheer, naked destructiveness that remains, the possibility of another content. Hobbes's horrific vision of a "war of all against all" threatens to assume reality as what Hans Magnus Enzensberger has called "molecular civil-war."

Fraternity and Extended Suicide

Hobbes and Hegel have already divulged the fact that labor, as commodity society's primary relation to nature, traces its origins even further back — to violence. In the fight to the death, furthermore, they had found the source both of self-consciousness and of the universality of the state. The principles of freedom and equality are thus derivatives of that foundational experience. Both as regards its relation to nature as well as its identity, the commodity subject rests on a bedrock of violence, and the primal encounter of this subject with its other, the originating social experience, is anything but peaceful. And yet, wide-ranging as it may already be, the matter does not end here. What remains is the question of the original social bond or, to put it in terms of the holy ideals of the bourgeois revolution: does the last part of the threefold promise — Liberty, Equality, Fraternity — conceal the same threat?

    The answer given by our third involuntary principal witness, Sigmund Freud, turns out to be quite unequivocal. At the beginning of all civilization stands the collective murder that shapes our thoughts, feelings, and culture to this very day. Initially — thus Freud in allusive reliance on Darwin — the human species had been split into presocial patriarchal hordes that only had space for the chief tyrant and his wives but not for the pubescent sons. Sociality only emerges at the moment when the ostracized brothers gang up with one another so as to undertake the act of murdering the tyrannical father — whereupon, troubled by that original collective guilt, they created a common regime: "Society was now based on complicity in the common crime; religion was based on the sense of guilt and the remorse attaching to it; while morality was based partly on the exigencies of this society and partly on the penance demanded by the sense of guilt."[15]

The inner affinity between Freud's speculations regarding the emergence of culture from the original state of mankind and the world according to Hobbes is obvious enough, if only because both presume a state of radical asociality as the starting point for the development of mankind. While Hobbes's natural-born killers are able to agree on a social contract that stipulates the transfer of their sovereignty to the state in order to bring to an end the universal threat of homicide, a direct "gentlemen's agreement" takes on the same function in Freud: "In thus guaranteeing one another's lives, the brothers were declaring that no one of them must be treated by another as their father was treated by all jointly."[16] As one follows Freud's arguments in *Totem and Taboo* it becomes apparent that they increasingly approximate those of the father of state theory and indeed prove themselves to be the reproduction of Hobbes's thinking, expanded so as to account for the question of the family and the emotional life of the murderer. The development of culture, according to Freud, does not come to a stop with the emergence of the brother-clan. Rather, society and culture represent entities grounded on a posthumous identification with paternal authority. On the level of psychology the murdered patriarch celebrates his resurrection as superego, on the level of religion as the father-god, and last but not least as the secular "father" state with a vengeance. With this last point, however, Freud touches down precisely at the juncture already reached by Hobbes several generations before.

Totem and Taboo and his later writings on culture do not win Freud many friends among more recent generations of readers. The collective murder of the father is nowadays commonly held to rest on the same wild and unfounded speculation that lead Freud to formulate, as literal truth, the theory of a "death drive" in the aftermath of the World War I, which was purported to be the world-historical event in which the drive had itself first become manifest. To be sure, the construct of a primal horde of vengeful brothers appears ridiculous in the face of all that is now known about prehistory. Similarly, the statement that "the aim of all life is death" because "inanimate things existed before living ones" at first glance appears more than a little dubious.[17] But are such necrophiliac murmurings therefore nothing but superfluous noise that need only be silenced to rescue the analytical value of Freud's approach? Or are the death drive and the fraternity of parricides in fact metapsychological constructs essential to the architecture of Freud's theory? Indeed, are they not, in point of fact, indispensable if Freud is to be able to speak at all about the violence at the core of the commodity subject without revealing its historical specificity as a phenomenon of bourgeois society?

As in Hobbes and Hegel before him, in Freud the constitutive but buried connection between violence and the commodity subject is brought into view. Like his predecessors, of course, he can only reveal this intimate relation by clouding its specific character and turning it into something transhistorical and naturally given, substituting projection for repression. The projective character of Freud's phylogenetic myth can, in truth, scarcely be ignored. But the killing of the primal father is only the tip of the iceberg in the formation of a generalized theory subject to continuous ontologization. Initially, this is true of the ontogenetic model of an ominously parricidal primal horde, but therefore just as true of the oedipally constituted male infant. This model, in a process resembling a form of repetition compulsion, reproduces the murderous original event. This, however, inverts the real relationship. The (self-)destructive tendencies developed, *in statu nascendi*, by the commodity subject do not stem from a "collective unconscious" and from dredging up old memories of even more archaic conditions liable to fall prey to primary repression. What must here be repressed are the achievements of a commodity-governed civilization. Repression is, therefore, not a primary but a secondary act, for prior to any restraint on the violence at the core of the commodity subject stands, of course, that very subject's (far from archaic) implantation.

Yet such is still not the deepest layer of Freudian ontologizing. The Oedipal problem in no way stands alone. The prohibition the father imposes on the son is imposed as the "reality principle." It is therefore only the continuation and bundling of a whole range of previously existing prohibitions. On Freud's account, every human being experiences the world from the beginning as an inhospitable place and any satisfaction whatsoever is an unmistakably precarious and ephemeral affair. For the commodity subject this is, no doubt, entirely accurate. Every enjoyment turns into a surrogate satisfaction, and he or she never reaches a goal that would ultimately be worth reaching. This restlessness and emotional undernourishment, however, appears in Freud as the *conditio humana*, as a purely endogenous problem, ultimately posited by the biology of man as a being born into scarcity. Already the introduction of the concept of the drive consolidates this false ontologization. By defining the satisfaction of drives as a relief of tension and a form of protection against external stimuli, therefore as an approximation of an inorganic state, Freud must inevitably understand the relation of man to the exterior world as a relation of frustration. Every libidinal satisfaction remains not only provisional but also a detour. Actual satisfaction and the true goal can only lie in finally entering the realm of the inorganic that absolves man of the return of the drive and tension. Although Freud introduces the "death drive" (Thanatos) and its opponent, Eros, rather late, the reason for this introduction rests in the logic of the drive, the concept it rescues theory-immanently. The counterpart of the death drive, therefore, resembles more closely the concept of the drive predicated on the "nirvana principle," and it is consequently logical that Freud ultimately opposed it drive-theoretically to Eros as the more fundamental and far-reaching emotion.

It would be inadequate to dismiss Freud's idea of an external world, always hostile to man, and its counterpart, the insatiable drive, as simply false. Social critique, more accurately, must be critical of Freud insofar as he presents a product of "second nature" as one of man's first nature, and it has to trace the theoretical inversions resulting from this. If one reconsiders Freud's approach from this perspective, the "archaic heritage," the patricidal primal horde, appears in a radically changed light. It reveals itself to be a metaconcept clad in mystical garments that encompasses all social institutions involved in the process of implanting the death drive. The homicidal desire of the primal horde with regard to the father on which Freud insists reveals itself in this context as a code for a much more common urge to destroy, and simultaneously as the negation of the actual target. Above all else, the "brother horde" represents, in full accord with the paternal command, the self-sufficient masculine principle and the fear of the woman and, moreover, of the unregulated engagement with reality as such. In the ideal of "fraternity" the commodity subjects commit themselves and everyone else to the program of "emancipation" from the material-sensuous. In the dictatorship of value and logos the aim of transforming this planet into a place that is largely immune to pleasure and satisfaction shows its clear contours. Reality is only permitted as the sensuous form of representation of abstraction. But there remains a second, direct path to complete liberation from uncontrolled reality, pleasure, and satisfaction: the destruction of the world. The alleged starting point of the development of culture, the common killing of the father, represents the only possible endpoint of modernity: the extended collective suicide of patriarchal value society.

The Violent Core of the Commodity Subject

Sexuality — or at least what modernity understands by sexuality — only emerges, as Foucault illustrates convincingly, with the prohibition of the sexual. Nothing already existing was brought under control; rather, the procedures of control constituted their very objects. A similar relationship can be reconstructed for the phenomenon of violence. Officially a peace-loving being, the commodity subject is fascinated, if not obsessed, with what it resolutely rejects in its public declarations. In its actual, masculine manifestation, one can, therefore, indeed accuse the commodity subject of maintaining an intimate relation to reality much like that characterizing the relation of the

Spanish Inquisition to lust, witchcraft, and heresy. To be sure, the propensity for violence was well known in traditional societies. As the right of force of all rulers that permeated all hierarchical structures, violence was as self-evidently present as it was a fundamental aspect of gentile order (including paternalistic right of castigation and vendetta). Purified from the medium of oppression to the medium of destruction and extermination, violence in the context of commodity society transformed itself into the foundation of all subject forms. Only the ability to degrade others to the status of object makes a subject into a subject, and this degradation, even if it assumes its sublimated form as competition, remains retroactively attached to its original image: the transmutation of the living other into a lifeless object. Against this background it appears profoundly questionable to celebrate with Norbert Elias the "process of civilization" as a process of drive control in general and the control of aggression in particular. Yet, this is not only questionable because it has failed to control the "natural beast" in man, as culture pessimists such as Freud found necessary to stress time and again. Rather, the mission itself contains a crucial contradiction. The constitution of the subject is simultaneously the implantation and formation of the violent core and its integration into content.

In the breast of the developed commodity-subject two souls emerge: that of the private market subject and that of the citizen. The violent core of the commodity subject did not simply emerge temporally alongside this bipolar structure. Rather, it has to be logically as well as historically understood as the same process. The superiority of military organization founded on "citizens in uniform" as compared to previous forms of the craft of extermination contributed significantly to the triumph of the citizen and the universalization of this figure. The impulse to include previously excluded social groups as equal subjects of law into the state community had a significant impact. From the French and American revolutionary wars to the world wars and the anticolonial movements, the willingness to risk one's own life for the national cause was the measure of the accomplished degree of citizen consciousness as a citizen. Not only this, but expanding the circle of legally equal citizens and subjects of law to include those groups of people formerly relegated to the margins was in each case a consequence of the necessity to expand the mobilization for warfare — a process, therefore, that was poignantly carried out largely independently of the political auspices under which those wars were carried out.

At the same time — and even more importantly in our context — the profile required of the armed citizen matched precisely the tensions, constitutive for commodity subjectivity, emerging from a willingness to defend that was steadily and simultaneously increased in intensity and tamed. As a result of tailoring the citizen for the virtual or actual participation in wars between states, those inner regimes of violence formed, without which the modern monad of competition and labor could not have developed. The fraternity of the national "we," the self-integration of the armed body of the people, paves the way for the commodity ego by simultaneously curbing both its self-destructive tendencies and its antisocial affinity toward autonomous, self-orchestrated killing sprees.[18] Training for the state of emergency and the identification with the national cause ennobled the participation in optimized exercises of violence and extermination, elevating them to the epitome of virtue and duty, hermetically separating "fields of honor" from the normal activities of commodity society.

Part Two: The Age of Statified Violence

Beyond Law and Contract — Camp and Front

If one examines the victory of commodity society on a macro-level, it reveals itself as unifying two fundamental processes: the successive reduction of all social relations to market relations, and the statification of social existence. The history of violence clearly corresponds to the latter process. The entire epoch of the rise of commodity society, beginning with absolutism and extending into the age of Fordism, was marked by the transformation of violence and bloodshed into an exclusive right of the state. In its developed form, the state no longer tolerates any extrastatist forms of violent practice, with the exception of rudimentary forms such as the right to self-defense.

The primitive accumulation of all legitimate means of violence into the hands of the state is not just any moment within the overall process of statification. The implementation of the monopoly on violence rather constitutes the core around which the state forms itself as abstract universality. As long as it goes without saying that masters across the spectrum of power are able to enforce at times conflicting interests whenever necessary through the use of violence, social life inevitably remains confined to the realm of individual relations of loyalty and dependence. Only the implementation of the monopoly on violence allowed the state to break up the colorful mosaic of traditional customary rights and replace it with a homogenous, universal right, equally binding for all members of society. Without the monopoly on violence, the political domination adequate to commodity society, applied to an abstract geographical space, could never have been developed.

The implementation of the state monopoly on violence — the reduction of the once-broad range of legitimate actors of violence to one new type — and the formation of the violent core of the commodity subject describe one and the same process from two perspectives: first, from the standpoint of the objectified social structure as a whole; second, from the micro-logical standpoint of the singular commodity individual. Therefore, a counterpart to the above-described dialectic of breeding and taming a violent core, constitutive for commodity subjectivity, must be developed on the macro-level. Indeed, the statification of the exercise of violence can be characterized as a double process of potentiation and potentialization. In developed commodity society, manifest physical coercion plays a notably smaller role in daily life than in many other societies. Yet, this is not, as is frequently claimed, the result of reducing aggression and destruction to an insignificant marginal force in the context of the social context of mediation. The development of statified regimes of violence, rather, coincides with the focalization, purification, and intensification of the potential for extermination in its entirety. Only in a state of exception does state power wade through pools of blood and transform the citizen into the human material of the killing machine. Precisely this state of exception, however, allows for the creation of social standards in the first place and indeed, as omnipresent possibility and ultima ratio, constitutes the logical precondition of all standards.

Commodity thought does not want to know the violent core of the subject of competition and instead celebrates it as the epitome of peace-loving humanity. Correspondingly, commodity thought also remains blind to the inner relationship between statification and the hypertrophy of violence. Although the term itself already signifies the opposite, the emergence of the state monopoly on violence is positively interpreted as gradual pacification. First, according to the narrative that has been circulating since the Enlightenment, the triumph of freedom, equality, and law clears the inner space of the state of violence. In a large second step, this judification, according to this credo, is also supposed to subsume inter-state spaces and to demilitarized international relations. The classical version of this argument goes back to Kant and has been warmed over for more than 200 years now. Violence, it is argued, is an anachronism, which will not be able to resist the advance of market and law.

Already the first part of this pacification process defies reality. In commodity society one can only speak of inner pacification if the word is taken in its Latin meaning as synonym for total subjugation. Such a society is peaceful only insofar as the individual member of society, insofar as he does not act as a functionary of state violence, is tendentially robbed of all means of violence in order to deliver him to a highly developed machine of state violence. The principle of a state of law in no way supplants this fundamental relation of omnipotence and impotence. Instead, the universality of law requires this very relation. As Giorgio Agamben has shown with reference to Benjamin and Foucault, the sovereign as instance that posits and guarantees law himself has the power to reduce human existence to "bare life."[19] The normality of the constitutional state in which all those who break the law have the right to a trial based on the tenets of legality cannot be thought without recourse to the possibility of a state of exception. Only the ability to make reference to this possibility constitutes the sovereign. But this is, of course, not merely an abstract, theoretical threat. By creating an exterritorial space, the camp, it can be absolutely realized without calling the validity of legal and contractual regulations into question for the rest of society. In the twentieth century, it is precisely this localization of the state of exception in compliance with the form of right that has become a gruesome reality on several occasions. The camp, consequently, represents the "nomos of modernity" (Agamben). Yet, one does not have to invoke the death camp of Nazi Germany or the Stalinist gulags to unveil this fundamental contradiction. Already the "normal" Western deportation prisons indicate the peaceful coexistence of law and its foundation, state power exercised over human beings reduced to prelegal biomass.

To confuse the emergence of the state monopoly on violence with pacification, however, does not only mean to ignore the incredible potential of violence on which the constitutional state is predicated and that can become manifest especially in times of crisis. In addition to the camp, the internal space that is excluded from the law, the implementation of the state monopoly on violence generates out of its own logic a second area beyond the validity of law, in which pure violence takes on, in the final instance, the function of a medium of regulation: international relations. The state monopoly on violence is always confined to its own territory. Only there, that is vis-à-vis its own population, can the sovereign enforce the relinquishing of violence and therefore posit law. For international relations the dominance of the sovereignty principle correlates ultimately with the *ius ad bellum*. Of course there have existed bilateral agreements ever since ancient times and international conventions since the nineteenth century — even martial law (*ius in bello*) was created. But these contractual agreements among sovereigns have a completely different character from law connected to the omnipotence of a single sovereign. These agreements leave untouched the possibility of international wars as ultima ratio — what is more, they presuppose these wars and their validity. After World War II and especially after the breakdown of actually existing socialism, international tribunals gained a growing importance. But because they can only dispose of borrowed means of power, voluntarily surrendered by single states the basic structure does not change one bit.

In the case of military emergency the counterpart of the camp emerges, a second exterritorial space in which the social relations turn from normal, "peaceful" competition into optimized physical violence without thereby questioning the validity of law and contract in the actual territory of a sovereign. This space is the front. While in the camp human material is administered by the national sovereign, the front covers exactly that territory in which hostile sovereigns attempt to turn foreign citizens into dead biomass. As opposed to the camp, the geographical location of this exterritorial interstitial space changes constantly throughout the course of a war. At the same time, the size of this space expands as the reach of weapons systems increases. The bombing of Guernica, the beginning of modern warfare against civilian targets, marks the moment at which in principle every location in the territory of any given party involved in the conflict could be turned into a front.

Combatant and Noncombatant

The process of the statification of violence and war creates the violent core of the commodity subject, while the corresponding violence and annihilation practices are sequestered from everyday life. This separation is connected to two key characteristics of statified warfare. The state wars between 1648 and 1989 were temporally limited. The line of demarcation between war and peace was explicitly defined. The state sovereign decided, universally and with binding validity, when exactly and for how long the duty to engage in highly efficient, collective murder replaced the obligation of the contract subject to refrain unconditionally from violence. Declaration of war, ceasefire agreements, and surrenders precisely designated the beginning and end of all military action and categorically prevented precisely those abeyances that were characteristic of early modern markets of violence and their postnational epigones. But the clear distinction between war and peace in conflicts between nation-states was not just a matter of unequivocal regulations of international law; it also had an impact on practical life.

Everyday life of people in the Middle Ages was often not greatly affected by whether or not their masters were at war. Early modern wars, which were determined by the logic of markets of violence, were already accompanied by a sudden increase in losses, both material and human. But this pertained mainly to those people who were unfortunate enough to live in those areas that were afflicted by packs of lansquenets and who consequently lost their possessions or even their lives. Compared to the number of deaths suffered by uninvolved civilians, death in battle remained a rarity in the wars of the Renaissance and even throughout the Thirty Years' War. Because they would run the risk of staking their capital, that is, their troops, the *condottieri* did not categorically seek military resolutions of disputes. In many cases the goal was to motivate hostile lansquenets to switch sides rather than to kill them.

The wars of the eighteenth and nineteenth centuries broke with this pattern. The statification of war was accompanied by the focusing of the craft of murder and extermination. As the sovereign assumed the direction of a war effort himself, the killing was widely relocated to the battlefield. While the intensity of the military actions increased and war began to be a seriously dangerous business for the troops, the category of the noncombatant emerged. Now it was no longer the civilian who paid for the war effort with his life and property, but the taxpaying civilian who paid for the war effort with a portion of his property but no longer directly with his life.

That state warlords drilled their soldiers, at times with rather drastic measures, to massacre and maraud no longer for their own benefit was, of course, not a result of humanistic impulses. Facing armies that were increasingly supplied via a centralized system utilizing state resources and training soldiers for warfare, troops for whom combat was a secondary profession were at a decided disadvantage, since they were forced to disperse at regular intervals to replenish their resources. Their ability to operate was detrimentally affected by this, and, moreover, autonomous looting and raping did not exactly boost military discipline.

It was not only for strategic reasons that the statification of war sought to assign to the unarmed foreign population the status of noncombatant, thereby allowing for social normality in wartime; above all it turned the maintenance and support of normal commodity society in the home country into a military necessity. When, beginning with the Italy campaign by Francis I in 1494, war mutated from a form of reproduction of war enterprises into a duel of war machines seeking a military decision, military expenses exploded. The monetary valuation of warfare and the recruiting of mercenary soldiers had already made national bankruptcy a constant companion of the early modern superpowers. The introduction of standing armies in particular contributed to the exponential rise of mobilizing resources for destructive purposes. Access to the goods and chattels of the unfortunate vanquished inhabitants of war-torn territories proved itself to be an insufficient foundation for war economies. Vis-à-vis the local self-supply of armies, taxation become more important than ever for states engaged in military conflict. But this required above all the implantation and maintenance of economic normality and the assurance of the abstract production of wealth in the home territory.

For the hitherto main victims — the uninvolved inhabitants of the territories beleaguered by armies — the unleashing of the military potential for extermination meant the taming of destructive violence. This dialectic is also reflected in martial law. After the end of the wars of religion, the clear distinction between combatant and noncombatant emerged. But this differentiation corresponds precisely to the above-mentioned inner regime of violence implemented by statified warfare. The respective coexistence of destruction and normality appears geographically as the antagonism of front and hinterland, and, on the personal level, in the difference between combatant and noncombatant.

The classic manifestation of the noncombatant emerges in the eighteenth and nineteenth centuries. Industrialized war discovered, in addition to opposing armies, new targets of attack, the pursuit of which indirectly influences the will and military power of the opposing sovereign: infrastructure and the working civilian population. This change rendered the distinction of combatant and noncombatant problematic. However, it neither annulled nor contradicted the concentration of warfare into the foundations of state power. Because modern warfare mobilized not only monetary resources but also the majority of social resources, the producers of wealth became indirect combatants. The distinction between civil and military targets became a matter of discretion. At least in the protection of the civil population in occupied territories, limits to the practice of extermination and the difference between combatant and noncombatant continued to exist.

In the twentieth century, limiting destruction by means of differentiating between combatant and noncombatant became problematic beyond the context of industrialized wars between capitalist protopowers. Anticolonial conflicts, the wars of state creation at the periphery of the world market, also changed their classic character. In the confrontation with superior military occupying powers, the only form of armed combat with which anti-imperialist movements were left was guerilla warfare, a form of asymmetrical warfare that consciously forces the enemy into a position in which he is no longer able to tell combatants from civilians. The military goals of both sides, of course, implicitly maintained the distinction, and in this way it continued to determine the progress of war and curbed destructive energy. The theoreticians and practitioners of anti-imperialist war emphasized that the guerilla would be only a transitional stage in the liberation battle whose final stage implied the metamorphosis into a regular army. The guerillas' need to win the support of the population precluded from the beginning the massive repression of a majority of the population. But the imperial power and its local sub-agents also had to make room for the theoretical possibility of ultimately separating combatants and peaceful civilians in their effort to maintain control over land and people. Despite all cruelties, massacres, resettlements, and carpet bombings, the imperial powers never made full use of their entire potential of destruction. Despite millions of (preferably civilian) victims and despite free-fire zones, the threshold of systematic genocide was crossed neither in Algeria nor in Indochina.

The Totalization of War

Both the development of the state regime of violence in general and the history of the statist wars in particular are to be understood as a double process of potentiation and potentialization. From the beginning of modernity to the end of the short twentieth century — that is, until 1989 — the number of years at war continually decreased. In turn, the concentration of all destructive power on the supportive hand of the territorial state multiplied these powers to an unimaginable degree. Measured by the devastation of the wars of commodity societies, all armed conflicts of premodern societies seem like pub brawls. The logical vanishing point of this development was the precarious balance of the atomic horror between the superpowers. On one hand, the power of destruction accumulated by the arms race had reached a point that did not permit another qualitative increase. If the arsenals of the two superpowers sufficed for a hundredfold or a thousandfold omnicide, it ultimately remained a question of little importance. On the other hand, it was clear at the climax of the Cold War that the line between the threat of destruction and manifest war, into which the superpowers would throw all their military weight, could only be crossed once.

The statification of warfare led to an enormous increase in the efficiency of killing. It would of course be too shortsighted to see that only as progress in the technology of weapons. No society has ever transferred a similar portion of its social and material resources to the war industry; neither has any society rationalized the craft of violence to maximized destruction to the same extent as commodity society. (The construction of the Chinese wall might be the most prominent exception. But this show of strength, paid for with famine and uprisings of farmers, was notably a defensive measure.)

The precapitalist wars were mainly "limited wars" in which the bloodshed fell far behind what was technologically conceivable. War remained the private entertainment of a small caste or, where a large part of the male population was under arms, temporally confined and ritualized to prevent too big of a disturbance of the reproduction. The conflicts between the Greek city-states are paradigmatic of this second form of limited war. In these conflicts all participants refrained from big strategic maneuvers and the military action was confined to the immediate decisive battle. (Only the Peloponnesian War diverted from that pattern. It therefore ended with the downfall of all participating powers, the whole of Greece, and the rise of Macedonia as superior power.) Those who could stand their ground already had victory in their hands. The statist war on the other hand tended towards "absolute war" (Clausewitz) and knew only one limit to the complete unleashing of destruction, namely the reconnection to political ends. But this limit, scrutinized more closely, is a precarious one.

It is not just that the practice of warfare gained in statification a rational-instrumental character, gradually transforming all material and human resources into actual or potential means of warfare; while in the Middle Ages armed conflict created its significance as a specific way of life of a special caste, modernity rendered warfare a mere means of the statist calculation of interest. A politically defined will switches the war machinery on and turns it off: war is a "true political instrument"; it is to be understood as the "continuation of political intercourse, carried on with other means."[20]

In the conventional understanding, the primacy of the political over the military guarantees reason and proportion within murderous lunacy. This connection only seems necessary against the background of an affirmative image of politics, in which politics is understood as something rational per se, and its primacy, therefore, as a reasonable, even cynical end, over an irrational instrument. But politics does not reduce itself to the process of tarring competing interests, and neither does brutal statist policy confine itself to the conquering of countries, raw materials, and working populations in the service of its own capital. Where politics itself becomes an irrational means, the alleged extinguishing agent works as an accelerant and intensifier.

The extreme example is of course National Socialism. It showed that the reduction of human life to bare, extinguishable, biological existence not only provides the foundation of political sovereignty but also that destruction became, as we still see, a political program throughout the history of the rise of commodity society; a program that ultimately suspended the reluctance to destroy and kill that is contained in military logic. First, a war of conquest that from the beginning was supposed to be boundless is incoherent. Second, the decision of the leadership of the Third Reich to continue war beyond the point of obvious complete hopelessness was politically motivated. And finally, the central point of the National Socialist murder program, the destruction of the European Jewry, fully contradicted military calculation.

The Warfare of the Commodity Society as "Absolute War"

The idea of the primacy of politics goes back to Clausewitz. But it is not the only feature of statified war that he expressed with precision. Never before and never again would the essence of the statified war be comprehended more precisely and clearly than in his main work *On War*. Already in his initial definition "absolute war" seems to be the central point of reference: "War is an act of force, and there is no logical limit to the application of that force."[21] The unleashed "absolute war" is considered by Clausewitz as an ideal type that was far from being realized by the actual wars of all ages. Unlike the thinkers of the Enlightenment who wanted to see a containment of the impact of destruction by the implementation of Western civilization, Clausewitz saw destruction as a neutral factor. But the alleged transhistorical ideal type is actually, scrutinized more closely, the logical-historical vanishing point of statified violence.[22]

War has developed towards "absolute war" in three great leaps, and Clausewitz's theory has the first as historical background. Clausewitz's formula of "absolute war" was developed in the wake of the Napoleonic wars, which represented a dramatic increase in murderous efficiency in comparison to the cabinet wars of the eighteenth century. This new quality sprung immediately from the achievements of the French Revolution and cannot be thought without the discovery of the nation. In the wars of the absolutistic sovereigns of the eighteenth century, the intensity of the slaughters was mainly limited by two factors. First, the mercenary soldiers pressed into the army were completely passive tools of destruction. The highest goal was drilling them to be obedient marionettes that executed their exercised battle program on command. In the life of the soldier-material, only one form of one's own initiative existed that was not quite compatible with the murderous goal, but was practiced massively: namely, fleeing the scene on the first possible occasion. Consequently, the eighteenth century entered military history as the "age of deserters." In the battles of the Seven Years' War, on every side one-third of the troops disappeared into the woods at the first shot. Battle discipline was primarily a matter of preventing one's own troops from running away and only secondarily of the effort to destroy the enemy army. Second, the recruitment of a sufficient number of soldiers always remained an expensive problem. Both conditions stood in the way of what Clausewitz defined as the essence of war: the concentration on the abolition of the enemy, the willingness to seek the decisive battle in the appropriate moment.

Both difficulties disappeared with the emergence of the citizen soldier. In their level of training, the voluntary troops of the French Revolution were at first inferior to the regular troops of the coalition of British, Prussians, and Austrians. Furthermore, the guillotine and the escape over the French border had decimated the old aristocratic officer corps. But the tapping of hitherto unused resources made it possible to compensate for these unfavorable conditions. The identification with the national cause provided hitherto unknown readiness that can less euphemistically be described as bloodlust and fanaticism. (The lyrics of the "Marseillaise," bristling with xenophobia and the glorification of violence, speaks of that spirit of the new bourgeois age.) At the same time the *levée en masse* and the transition to general compulsory military service allowed for the immediate (and for the state budget financially cost-effective) closure of emerging gaps. It only needed a commander that knew how to turn these new possibilities into strategy. In Napoleon, a man that boasted of sacrificing a million men without the blink of an eye and who for so much manhood was rightfully raised by Hegel to the level of the "world spirit astride a horse," the epoch found its ideal embodiment. Ill-reputed among generals of the old stripe as a slaughterer, he defied all military doctrines of the eighteenth century, always looking for the immediate decision. The new French empire could only be beaten when the enemy had adopted the new methods.

Fordism and Total War

"Absolute war" stands for the ruthless application of all military means available for the "aim of military operations," the "enemy's overthrow."[23] The logical continuation and overculmination of the focalization on the goal of destroying the enemy troops lies in the consequent mobilization of all productive potential for the war effort, the transformation of society in one gigantic machine of destruction in which all wheels turn only for victory. The industrialization of warfare in World War I marked this new quality: absolute war realizes itself in total war.[24]

Up to this point, wars strained the monetary resources of the states involved. The state — the ideal general capitalist in the nineteenth century — confined itself essentially to channeling away the necessary resources for the maintenance of the standing army from the social production of wealth. The economy of war was not particularly different from the economy of peace. At this point, the relative brevity of military conflicts rendered the transformation of production obsolete. In the great conflicts of the twentieth century, on the other hand, war had a much greater impact and affected social regulation more than ever.[25]

Heraclitus is often quoted as having said that war is the father of all things. Although this translation distorts heavily what the philosopher meant, it hits the mark for modernity. In particular, the so-called German economic miracle of the 1950s is in every aspect a child of the world war era and total war.[26]

This can be seen for instance in macroeconomic regulations. The monetary and economic-political framework created by the warfare state, in order to maximize the production of destruction, only needed to be slightly modified to optimize the production of civil abstract wealth. The interventionist state, first born from the necessities of "absolute war," became a permanent arrangement and made the Fordist take-off and the short summer of full employment and historically unique growth possible at all. With regard to the methods of production and products, it is equally obvious that Fordism is an achievement of total industrialized war. Of course civil commodity production initially had to suffer under the frictions that accompanied the alignment of industry to the statist production of destruction. But in the long run, production aligned to military ends became the model for the civil application — a condition that points to the character of commodity wealth as the continuation of destruction by other means. Not only did the standardization of the labor process emerge from war production, but the key technical innovations of Fordism also all started their career in the military field. It was not only in Germany that the automobilization of society began with the motorization of warfare.[27]

At least as important, and in our context even more revealing, is the world war's historical effort regarding mentality. If there is something like an ur-experience for the *homo fordisticus*, it is the experience of the World War I battlefronts.[28] From the trenches of the "Great War" crawled men who differed as much in their thinking and feeling from the bourgeois class of the nineteenth century as from the masses of the lower classes in the past.

The horror of industrialized warfare could not be withstood by hero nonsense or by the identification with the "national whole" that essentially bore the euphoria of the outbreak of the war. The trauma of being exposed to overwhelming destructive mechanics broke down all social bonds and values. The evasive movement was internalized. Thereby the soldier-subject adopted the kind of relation to the world that was introduced as a theoretical and epistemological program by Descartes. Descartes and Hobbes had put the thought experiment of a universal "idea of destruction" that retains nothing but the thinking subject at the beginning of their philosophies. The material battles at Somme and Verdun turned this empty self back onto itself and into a mass experience.

The psychoanalyst Sandor Ferenczi wrote about the basic mechanism of war neurosis: the "[l]ibido withdraws from the object into the ego, enhancing self-love and reducing object-love to the point of indifference."[29] But even self-love threatens to become abolished in the numbing process. To be able to function and survive in conditions of war, the soldier-subject approaches a solipsistic attitude in which connections with others dissolve as much as the subject impoverishes emotionally.

Jacques Rivière expressed not only his own war experience when he wrote: "Just as he tried to delouse himself as regularly as possible, so the combatant took care to kill in himself, one by one, as soon as they appeared, before he was bitten, every one of his feelings. Now he clearly saw that feelings were vermin, and that there was nothing to do but treat them as such."[30] The horror could only be endured in some kind of psychological rigor mortis and state that Marc Boasson accurately described by as "*automatisme anesthésiant.*"[31]

The state of radical endogenous anesthesia is certainly an exceptional state but one with a model function. The soldier's effort of abstraction, his ability to abstract his self from all feelings and desires, found civil successors. The unsensuous sensuousness of the commodity subject, however, is not to be comprehended as an awakening from soldierly anesthesia. The coolness of the postmodern competition-idiot rather repeats the death-feigning reflex of the war neurotics of the World War I, while the manic bustle of the marketing professionals and coordinators is consistent with other means of going crazy in the barrage. In both versions endogenous anesthesia lives on as a constitutive moment and with good reason: only in the state of anesthesia can a reality constantly transformed by the ravages of value logic be endured.

It would be misleading to interpret the merciless subsumption of the subject as a retraction or even an eradication of the subject form. The leading image of the Freudian theory, the autocentric individual strengthened by ego power, which is sometimes equated with the true single subject, never became a mass phenomenon; even in the classical bourgeois parts of society the ideal of the ego-sovereign, controlled from within, has probably never been realized to the degree that is often ascribed to it. Subject form and external guidance, contrary to the common understanding, are not contradictory. The developed subject form is rather a mediated form of external guidance. For the subject form to become universal it has to be somehow dictated from above as a kind of collective We-Ego. The aggrandized collective identity of soldiers plays a key role in that process. With the rapid transition to the unleashed competition and commodity subject, the slaughters of the world wars and the subsumption of the subject under the military megamachine gained the character of a mass initiation. Brought into and mediated through military formation, millions of troops were trained to adopt a type of relation to the world that the fully developed commodity subject later had to execute without the continuous reference to omnipotent intermediary powers. The holiest principles of competition society became flesh and blood for the soldiers at the front: the elimination of the other is the presupposition of self-assertion. Only he who can degrade his opponent to an object secures as a degrader his own status as subject. Only by consistently treating himself as an instrument and a machine is man able to triumph as subject.

Ernst Jünger celebrated the soldiers as those that "know how to create in a martial way."[32] This is no perversion of modern subjectivity and by no means a break with it; the negative Prometheus who creates himself by the destruction of others is rather its ugly prototype.

The Age of the Scientification of Destruction

The history of modern warfare is one of gradual total mobilization of all social resources for destruction. With the Napoleonic Wars, the essential psychological, social, and military-tactical shackles that had hitherto prevented martial potentials that already existed implicitly from being fully realized had been cut. About 100 years later "total war" means industrialized warfare, systematic and widespread appropriation of civil-society labor power for the sake of destruction. But World War II also marks a third level, namely the immediate subjugation of science and research under the warfare business, the scientification of destruction.

With regard to the application and improvement of technological innovations, the military, of course, always showed itself to be open-minded; even novelties in a nonempirical science like mathematics — one could think here of mathematical functions — had military-practical applications already in early modern times, for instance in ballistics.[33] The old *entente cordiale* between freelance inventors and scientists on one hand and the military, interested in military application on the other, was now being replaced by something qualitatively new. Military needs now determined directly the alignment, focus, and development of research, and the military hired an enormous scientific apparatus to realize it. This new quality is of course in the first place represented by the Manhattan Project.[34] But the key technology of the third industrial revolution is definitely also a child of World War II and the arms race. After the end of the Cold War too, especially in the United States, the majority of the national research budget goes through the hands of the military or institutions close to it like NASA.

In the Cold War the process of the statification of war reached its culmination. First, the dialectic of potentialization and potentiation of destruction arrived at its final state in the balance of the nuclear horror. Second, the scientification of killing increased the arms effort to such a degree that it became incompatible with the competition of many national states and the classical polycentric system. For forty years, scientific complexes sufficient to compete in the technological race could only be maintained by two superpowers. The transition into the age of globalization and digital communication that also transformed the technological basis of destruction, however, exhausted even this situation. Without even one shot fired, the Soviet empire, armed to death, had to give up. The number of armies with a profound international presence had shrunk to one, an exceptional position that would not be conceivable without the privileged access of the United States to transnational capital.[35] The absolute military superiority of one state is not just an absolute novelty in the history of modernity; with the abolition of the balance of power, a cornerstone of the international order of violence has been removed.

The scientification of warfare undermined the classical statist regime of violence. It profoundly affected the traditional agent of the core of violence of commodity society, the proud citizen in uniform. His halo began to disappear, in part due to the development of nuclear weapons which displayed a potential for destruction that made traditional Fordist armies look like military atavisms at best responsible for the preparatory phases of major military engagements. Finally, the advance of microelectronics and the associated emancipation of destruction from the need for immediate destructive labor struck the final blow to the armed citizen. Certainly, the realization of the vision of the automatic battlefield, the military counterpart to the empty factory, might be limited. But its appearance alone reveals that the military and ideological mass mobilization of destruction workers no longer fits into the historical picture and is finished. The old pacifist slogan "Suppose they gave a war and nobody came" gains a frightening new significance. To wage war in all its brutality it is no longer necessary for the masses to be there; they can consume the exploding cruise missiles from their chair in front of the TV. It suffices that the destruction specialists and the military infrastructure workers do their job. Significantly, compulsory military service is conserved only in some militarily third-class countries, while the power of all powers has long since abolished this anachronism.

Part Three: The Age of Post-Statist Violence

The Unleashing of the Violent Core

After a long process of depletion, the figure of the proud defender of the fatherland associated with compulsory military service lost, bit by bit, its significance for the identity constitution of the commodity subject. Its final hour came with the breakdown of actually existing socialism. But the violent core of the competition subject did not perish with the disappearance of its traditional carrier. A new, seemingly chaotic regime of violence has been forming since the 1990s, characterized by autonomous operators running amok, killer sects, warlords of every description, and transnational NGOs of another — terrorist — stripe. If states and states in spe proved their status as sovereigns and decided between war and peace, new competition now entered the stage. A colorful cast of post-statist agents of violence begins to take possession of the ur-ground of sovereignty, the law.

This frightening development incorporates two basic moments. First, it is to be understood as a process of unleashing. Violence, up to this point essentially a means of politics, detaches itself from its connection to political ends and palpably takes on the character of an end in itself; parallel to this the market is taking the place of the state in the universe of violence as well. Amidst the process of separation from the state, violence enters a new liaison. Violence markets emerge as a substitute and competitor for state power. With this a familiar phenomenon of early modern times returns.

No development without precursors and predecessors. This is no less true for the rise of violence as an end in itself. Already in the nineteenth century the glorification of nothingness and the worship of destruction were in vogue in parts of bohemia. The basic axiom of the necrophiliac character of philosophical vitalism goes back to

Friedrich Nietzsche: "rather will nothingness than not will" was his groundbreaking expression. His successors only took the decisive step by elevating the will to nothingness to an actual will, and war and destruction to the highest acts of creation. Filippo Tommaso Marinetti did not only speak for himself when he wrote in 1909 in "The Futurist Manifesto": "We want to glorify war — the only cure for the world — militarism, patriotism, the destructive gesture of anarchists, the beautiful ideas which kill, and contempt for woman."[36] Legions of painters and authors around the end of the nineteenth and beginning of the twentieth century indulged in bloodthirsty fantasies and revealed themselves to be absorbed by Abel Bonnard's visions of unleashed violence: "We have to encompass war in all its wild poetry. If a man throws himself into war he does not only rediscover all his instincts, but also regains his virtues. [...] In war everything is created anew."[37] War occupies a place of honor not for the sake of political ends that can be achieved by military means, but is rather celebrated for its own sake — that is, as the epitome of male self-presentation and the glory of the modern subject.

This break with Clausewitz's framework and its instrumental understanding of violence, of course, only pertained to the level of individual motives. The hope for redemption from capitalist boredom was the hope for redemption by the statist war messiah. It was his task to make such an event of salvation possible, as happened to Hermann Hesse in August 1914: "To be torn out of a dull capitalistic peace was good for many Germans and it seems to me that a genuine artist would find greater value in a nation of men who have faced death and who know the immediacy and freshness of camp life."[38]

Some high priests of violence went one step further. In the "Second Surrealist Manifesto," published in 1930, André Breton praises the murder without motive or reason as an *acte gratuite* (André Gide), as an existential deed as such: "The ultimate surrealist deed is to walk into the street with a revolver in one's hand and, without aiming, fire shots into the masses of people for as long as one can."[39]

That Breton glorifies murder and violence as such does not

distinguish his perspective from the aestheticization of horror. In this regard it is only the malignant spirit of the world war epoch speaking through him. His position, insofar as he is asking the individuals to take it into their own hands, is vanguard. In Karl Kraus's *Last Days of Mankind* it was still: "War is war, and in war one has to do some things that one previously merely wanted to do."[40] Breton dreamed of a world in which one need not wait for the right circumstances but can brace oneself every time to be master over life and death.

In the age of what Peter Klein calls "mass-affirmation," this form of murderous subjective self-determination was far from the general consciousness and way of life. But this changed fundamentally with the process of consolidation through separation and depletion of the intermediary powers like state and class, which was misunderstood as a process of individualization. Seventy years ago, artists provoked by turning random destruction and self-extermination into the epitome of self-positing. Today we witness the leap to a corresponding practice of massacre.

Of course, the vanguards of violence subjectivity are exceptional figures. Probably there can be found medical terms for people like the Oklahoma City bomber Timothy McVeigh or the Beltway snipers. This does not change the fact that their pathological acts shed, as an exaggeration, a bright light on the social normality: "Just as a mentally ill person brings to light the truth of his family, a gypsy the truth of the settled citizen, the bondsman the truth of his master, an individual running amok *ex negativo* brings to light the suppressed truth of our present society."[41] However, the application of medical categories to the leading figure of our epoch, the suicide bomber, brings with it considerable difficulties.[42] The Israeli psychologist Ariel Merari in his study of the environment and biography of fifty suicide bombers came to a frightening and unequivocal conclusion: "He could [...] ascertain neither similarities in their character-structures nor pathological personality patterns. He found no insane persons or broken individuals, no failed existences, and no monstrous souls. The most conspicuous aspect of all the perpetrators was their inconspicuousness."[43] The highest level of madness can no longer be determined as such because it is not a deviant insanity but the constitutive lunacy of the commodity subject driven to its most bitter consequence.

Old and New Terrorism

Terror is not a new phenomenon. Ever since the nineteenth century, groups tried to achieve political goals by spectacular attacks. In the age of politics and state formation, terrorism always remained a marginal factor, and that goes for its effectiveness as for the number of victims. The victims of left- and right-wing terrorism in the last 150 years might amount to those killed in one day of World War II. The restricted success of terrorist acts in political confrontations is hardly surprising insofar as it has always been an emergency strategy originating from a position of extreme weakness. The recourse to terrorism has only been taken by elitist groups that saw no possibility of gaining influence on a broader political organization, but hoped to make up for that by spectacular attacks. The "propaganda of the deed" aimed at pulling the layers of society that the terrorist claimed to represent from their lethargy so that they would stand up for the interests ascribed to them by the terrorists. With their method the terrorists dreamed of paving the way for a formation of "classes" or "nations" resting on a broader social foundation.

This concept of indirect mobilization hardly ever worked, but the underlying concept of terror as a political means had the side effect of keeping the terrorist trail of blood thin. As long as terror aimed at the mobilization of interested third parties, it had to be selective in choosing the victims of attacks. Whoever targeted high-ranking and hated functionaries could hope to gain the sympathies of those circles of the population in whose name he acted. Accidental victims were to be avoided — they undermined the basis of the terrorists' legitimation — and indiscriminate mass destruction was ruled out from the beginning.

If the new terrorism rested on the same basis as the political terrorism of the past, it would be no major threat and would be relatively easy to account for. Unfortunately it has emancipated itself fundamentally from the instrumental understanding of violence. Terrorism thus gains a new quality — namely the capacity for murderous efficiency. A marginal phenomenon threatens to turn into the dominant form of violence of the twenty-first century. Whether apocalyptic sects and fundamentalist fanatics use weapons of mass destruction is merely a question of technological feasibility; one can hardly hope that a structural limit will result from the terrorist motif as such. Far from remaining a deterrent, the ability to realize Armageddon constitutes the very attraction of the new terrorism for today's competition subject who strives for omnipotence. There is no culture that does not create its own reservoir of angry young men who, equally attracted to and repelled by their existence as commodity subjects, escape into some kind of eschatological fundamentalism. Everywhere a population ripe for recruitment: commodity subjects who see no individual and collective possibility for future development other than taking revenge for a long chain of real or imagined national or individual indignities.

The Identical Subject-Object of Destruction

War in commodity society has turned violence into an act of abstraction. The place of hand-to-hand combat has been taken first by mechanical and then by automatic destruction labor. This metamorphosis is bound up with the development of the long-range weapon. The decisive historical turning point in this regard is marked by the Battle of Agincourt in 1415, in which English longbows crushingly defeated a larger French army. The distance weapon, disregarded by feudal warriors as being dishonorable and inappropriate to their social class, triumphed over the medieval warrior. The spatial distance over which the warriors raked each other grew only slightly with the development of firearms and then more rapidly after World War I. At the end of that development are those long-range bombers that flew from U.S. territory to their mission over Baghdad, and for whom the battlefield only existed on the display of their airborne computers.

To this spatial separation corresponds a process of internal distancing. The enemy is degraded to a passive object. The challenge in the duel in which the opponents confront each other as equals is substituted in commodity society war by the separation of the destruction worker on one hand and the biomass to be killed on the other. Already the Fordist (but more than ever the scientized) war resembles pest control in its methods and no longer has anything to do with classical battle. Not only does the killing move more and more out of the visual field of the killer; killing and being killed also dissolve into independent acts, with one or the other side being exposed to the man-driven apparatus of destruction.

The new archetypal actor of violence of our time, the suicide bomber, represents the implosion of this structure. The polar oppositions into which this murderous practice split suddenly unify. The suicide bomber no longer carries a weapon; he is himself one. His body is turned into an explosive body and even the separation of killing subject and subject of killing has been rendered obsolete in a perverted way. In that identical subject-object it finds its suspension. After 600 years, the long-range weapon has been substituted by a historically new weapon, the weapon of absolute lack of distance.

Weapon and Market

Neoliberal ideology categorically dreads monopolies and the state. The exception to this generally valid rule is of course presupposed even by free-market fanatics. Few of them dare to attack the state monopoly on violence. The main asset of the state is to be left untouched by the celebrated process of destatification.

The total free market economy as it prevailed after the epochal break of 1989 proves to be more consistent in this regard than its ideologues. The catastrophic final victory of the world market over the statist developing regimes is accompanied by the dissolution and gradual disintegration of the statist monopoly on violence in the South and the East. With the loss of the ability to create the basic conditions of the valorization of value in much of its territory, state power loses both the ability to eliminate and the interest in eliminating all other actors of violence from its own entire territory. Increasingly large geographical spaces de facto elude state control. Especially where the withdrawal of regular statehood provides ideal working conditions for actors operating in illegal sectors of the world markets (drugs, smuggling, weapons, and human trafficking), those apparatuses take the place of the police. Before the historical process of transferring organized violence into the sole instrument of abstract generality in the peripheral states of the world market is completed, the entire direction of development is reversed. The structures of violence are increasingly influenced by mafia factions, which are dedicated to protecting and violently carrying out their business interests.

This shift towards markets of violence is not only brought about by the displacement of state power. The statist apparatus of violence is itself undergoing a metamorphosis during the collapse of modernization. The concept of "state business" takes on a literal meaning through the loss of a perspective of valorization, and the distinction between mafia and state becomes blurred. During the period of state ascendency, corruption meant a disturbance of the normal function and reproduction of statehood. In large swathes of the world the concept of corruption has become useless insofar as the practices that it describes must be considered the rule and have long since become the actual material basis of the reproduction of the state apparatus.

In the center of that development stand the security apparatuses. For their members it is perfectly natural to use their traditional position as guarantor of law and order, and their skills in the use of violence, as private human capital. Having the social means of violence at their disposal puts them in the position to secure access for themselves to the few goods of the breakdown regions that still have a place in the global valorization process. Some African countries have already undergone this process: the national economies of Congo or Liberia turned into pure looting economies, while the world of politics has shrunk to the dimensions of an armed fight for control of raw materials. The remnants of state power turn into the main players on the thriving markets of violence.

The Post-Statist War

The old international wars dissociated the ends of war from its means. Wars used to be waged to gain a changed position of power for peace. War appeared as a kind of investment in advance for a possible postwar world. In the military competition between sovereigns organized in nation states, the side that won knew how to mobilize most effectively all the human and material resources in its territory into a machine of destruction for the sake of defeating the enemy. Considered economically, the war economy was the alignment of social production to maximized unproductive state consumption. The material substrate of the war economy was turning as much abstract wealth as possible, siphoned off through nonmilitary means such as taxes or bond issues, into as many, and as effective, means of destruction as possible.

Our post-statist wars conform to a different pattern. The separation of the ends and means of war is invalid: the ends have turned into the means. The new masters of the state of exception themselves use violence as a means to the appropriation of wealth. The war economy no longer represents the extreme version of overall social overconsumption; rather, the war economy functions as a looting economy, as the special form of reproduction of military players who have ceased to function as abstract generality. As in the early modern conflicts, it is the task of war to nourish war. In the past, the battle of nationalisms was about which of the competitors could start the task of homogenization and modernization, and where. Questions such as whether Alsace and its inhabitants would be part of the German or French modernization machines, or if Poland is allowed to experience an autonomous process of national development, were decided by the force of arms. In the wars of disintegration in the South and the East, nationalism, having degenerated into ethnicism, again plays a central, albeit differently situated role. Ethnic differences essentially determine recruitment for competing war gangs and the preferred victims of the corporations of the looting economy.

The transition from a war economy of state consumption to a looting economy dramatically changes the face of war. In the new wars the conflict between combatants begins to retreat; military actions instead find their main targets in the goods and chattels and the lives of noncombatants. Statified wars are characterized by the effort to focus the impact of destruction on the enemy troops. If the civilian population was caught in the crosshairs, it was in the course of attacks that were indirectly aimed at the armed enemy as a result of the destruction of infrastructure and supply. Massacres of the civilian population or mass migrations of refugees were the ugly side effects of military conflicts.[44] In the contemporary wars of disintegration, massacres, looting, and "ethnic cleansing" are elevated into the actual content of military operations. The direct confrontation of competing armed powers is retreating and in many wars of disintegration it is carefully avoided by all parties involved.

The epoch of statist wars, in which the elimination of enemy troops was central, was characterized by a perpetual arms race. Its monetary effect was a permanent explosion of costs. The wars of disintegration of our times are characterized instead by being permanently low-budget wars. First, many of the new warlords can, directly or indirectly, help themselves to the leftover arsenals from the epoch of statist modernization. During the Yugoslav wars, for example, the Serbian troops basically operated with the war material of the former army, left over from the time of Tito's Yugoslavia. Second, with the change of target, cheap weapons such as machine guns, mines, and machetes take the place of tanks and planes as dominant weapons. The consequences of the actions of contemporary warlords include devastation that rivals that of the wars of state creation of the past, albeit associated with a comparably minimal financial effort. Rarely in the history of modernity has the sum of investment per casualty and displaced person been as low as in the wars of disintegration of the late-twentieth and twenty-first centuries in the South and East.

This new economy of war is also in effect where the ugliest kind of economical rationality disappears behind the pure goal of destruction. Compared to states, even al-Qaeda, run and financed by a successful businessman, gets by with remarkably modest financial means.

The history of the statist regime of violence can be described as a double movement of the potentialization of violence. The power of destruction grew dramatically whereas at the same time great manifest wars became less frequent. This development is due not least to an immense increase in the price of arms. This leads gradually to the reduction of the number of actors of violence who are able to compete on the relevant level of destruction. In the course of the microelectronic revolution this number of competitors shrank to one: the United States.[45] On the other hand, however, thousands of groups worldwide are now able to raise the means to instigate a "new" war. The transition from state wars to wars of disintegration is therefore also accompanied by the process of depotentialization, which in turn is to be understood as twofold. The nightmare of a nuclear showdown of the superpowers vanished with the end of the East-West conflict, but only to make room for the low-intensity conflicts that have been emerging and growing in numbers since the 1990s. It is frightening that even in Europe military conflicts could be waged again. Even more frightening are developments in the Third World. Not only did wars continue on the periphery of the world market even after the end of the East-West confrontation; with the transposition to a purely looting-economy basis they also took on an epidemic character.

With the transition to the age of wars of disintegration, it was not only the case that the number of armed conflicts increased; individual conflicts also often drag on. In the same arenas new players of violence emerge to fight each other in changing constellations of alliances. This new feature can also easily be placed in the context of the basic changes in the war economy. As periods of massive statist overconsumption, international wars affected or even interrupted the overall social movement of accumulation. Imperialist wars then drew their legitimation essentially from their expected results. A nation state fulfilled its task as abstract universality only when it managed to end wars successfully as soon as possible. Even for the anticolonial movements, which began their battles from a position of military weakness and therefore had to rely on strategies of attrition, the mobilization for the wars of liberation was only an unfortunate, inevitable, bloody opening for their actual "peaceful" project of modernization. Despite the invaluable significance of the anticolonial struggles as rites of passage on the way to becoming a nation, it would have occurred to no one to prolong the overture voluntarily. Where war turns into a mode of reproduction for its agents and disconnects itself from the overriding social horizon, the players of war have little reason to seek a military perspective. Left to themselves, these conflicts burn out only to the extent that the potential for economic looting and appropriation of monetary wealth is exhausted. An early end usually occurs only when the "international community" brings itself to intervene. But in such cases the precarious peace is principally predicated on the international troops' allowing local players of violence to put their looting business on a different basis, and to squeeze money out of the international institutions and aid organizations instead of the local population.

In the process of statification the regime of violence obtained a binary structure. In the first place a clear boundary emerged between domestic and international violence, a difference reflected in the institutional separation of army and police. The wars of disintegration eliminate this line of demarcation: not only to the extent that these functional distinctions lose their significance, but that respect for state borders is also alien to the new players of violence. That the warlords of Rwanda and Burundi are also playing a central role in Congo is not an isolated case. Routinely operations that target members of their own state and attacks on other aspects or institutions of communal life coincide.

To the bipolar structure of the statified orders of violence there also belonged a strict separation of war and peace. Whether one or the other state of affairs was currently in effect was legally just as clearly defined as it could be experienced unequivocally in everyday life. Abeyances that could not be comprehended as either peace or war were unknown to the universe of Clausewitz. In the world of wars of disintegration, precisely these in-between states become the rule. During the war in Bosnia the international mediators pressured the conflict parties into more than a dozen truces before the Dayton agreement. As soon as the ink with which the official representatives of Serbians, Croatians, and Muslims had signed was dry, they were broken. This was no oddity peculiar to that part of the world, but an index of the blurring of war and peace in the age of the wars of disintegration.

The dominance of commodity subjectivity is ultimately predicated on the reduction of humans to biomass approved for killing. In the statified regime of violence, this basis appeared as a special, spatially and temporally limited sphere that contradicted the domain of law and contract: a counterworld that would only become reality in the state of exception. Only in this constellation could free competition as normal social relation emerge from immediate physical force. The post-statist regime of violence destroys this limitation. The regular competition of commodity owners and the irregular competition of direct killing are visibly merging. In the breakdown regions of the fully globalized world market this merging process is already in full effect.

The Ugly Inverse of Individualization

In the centers of the world market, the domination of the territorial state can look back on a much longer history than on the periphery, and it is therefore considerably more rooted. At the same time the credit-worthiness of the Western states provides a much more solid monetary foundation for the role of the state as ideal universal capitalist. In the course of globalization, the symbiosis of the territorial state and "its" capitals becomes fragile, but still state power in the West can continue to play that part for quite some time. The very heart of state sovereignty, the state monopoly on violence, remains untouched in its core substance. Although there also exist slums and banlieues ruled by gangs in the West, and although a growing privatization of "security" can be observed — symptoms for the emerging of zones of differing "security density" — the basic supremacy of state power is not put in doubt by these phenomena. Also the elsewhere barely noticeable line between state and mafia remains, in the West, fairly clear, for the moment at least.

Long before the territorial state regimes of violence lose their monetary basis even in the West, their dissolution has already begun. One of the starting points is provided immediately by the neoliberal offensive and the advance of the total market in the capitalist centers. In a world that does not want to know society — only individuals and success at all costs — inadmissible fears are growing: the total rationalization and full economization of social relations creates a greenhouse in which their immanent opposite, irrationality, always already charged with violence, thrives. The process of individualization also touches the violent core of competition subjectivity. The lunacy from which none are spared — having to exist as a self-sufficient subject — translates itself into the crazy impulse to defend this unlivable way of existence by any means necessary, preferably with a weapon in hand, against real and above all imaginary dangers. The feeling of omnipotence and impotence that determines the commodity subject finds its most extreme expression in the age of complete subjugation to the total market. It is increasingly impossible to live out nation-statist claims of omnipotence. These find an adequate form of appearance and dissolution in pseudo-religious sects and individual Rambo-fantasies in which the released component of violence threatens the core of society.

The horrific construct with which the state theorist Hobbes once legitimized the existence of the Leviathan returns as a pattern of perception, and paranoia becomes a leading psychic disturbance in an epoch in which asocial sociality is driven to the extreme. The paranoiac "finds himself in a kind of natural state, similar to the one described by Hobbes in the *Leviathan*: he is surrounded by enemies, isolated, without connection to a society....From this perspective paranoia is simply the situation of a person [who] feels forced to live outside of society. Political paranoia is the unfortunate attempt to step into relation with others again, to form a community again."[46]

This is probably furthest developed in the United States, above all with regards to ideologically motivated violence. There, racist and Christian fundamentalist groups not only turn against the existing state but increasingly against any overarching statehood at all. The most devastating terror attack in the history of the United States up to 9/11, that of Timothy McVeigh in Oklahoma City in April 1995, targeted a building of the federal government. This choice of target is not to be comprehended as the confusion of a single person, nor does the anti-statist motif limit itself to the extreme Right and millenarian religious sects.[47] Especially in established political organizations like the NRA (National Rifle Association), this basic orientation is obvious.[48]

The World Police in the Decade of Human-Rights Paternalism

The established regime of violence in the centers of the world market is dissolved not only by the emergence of new agents of violence. In confrontation with them, the established state power also begins to bid farewell to the familiar framework of reference, finally mutating into the driving force of its own dissolution.

This process occurs in two phases. The first begins immediately after the breakdown of actually existing socialism. With the disappearance of Eastern competition, the United States and its junior partners accrued a kind of world monopoly on violence. The West was now able to intervene militarily practically everywhere in the world without having to expect serious counterstrikes from the targeted ruins of modernization. This not only led to the participation of the West, no longer used to war, in the process of depotentialization while increasingly sending its own troops to military operations in the periphery of the world market; above all, for the first time the strict separation between inner-statist and international violence was questioned, as it had developed since the Westphalian Peace of 1648. On the basis of its own superiority, the West believed it would be possible to apply the model of domestic pacification — police power assigned as the monopoly on violence — to the international stage.

The conflicts emerging in the breakdown regions since the beginning of the 1990s, mostly ethnically motivated, touched the West only indirectly. To the extent that the wars of disintegration did not involve secessionist movements that impinged on capitalist centers (Yugoslavia), they merely raised legitimation problems. The TV images of ugly bloodshed were in blatant contradiction with the Western-universalistic credo that the triumph of market and democracy would open up a wonderful and peaceful future for the planet. The Western interventions had a corresponding character, namely that of human-rights paternalism. Also where glorious competition-subjectivity could no longer maintain its "peaceful" counterpart in labor society due to a lack of developmental horizon, it was not supposed to run riot in its horrific alternative form as murder-subjectivity. Even in the de facto written-off regions of the world, security imperialism tried militarily to enforce the "right" form of respect for universal Western principles against the reality of crisis.

With human-rights paternalism the West turned "mission impossible" into a program. The well-intended drivel of a new world order has from the beginning been nothing but a label for exemplary operations. This alone already denies the claim to be the world police. Where and when the Western-dominated international community intervened (Somalia, East Timor, Kosovo, and Bosnia) it was always influenced greatly by the patterns of perception of a media-transmitted world publicity rather than by a far-reaching, sustainable plan. This limited range was, however, by no means only a question of a lack of political will or of inadequate implementation. Even the attempt to manage acute conflicts would considerably overextend the military-logistic capabilities as well as the financial potentials of the West. What faces the West is all the more Sisyphean because although the military risk of the miscellaneous "peacemaking" or "peacekeeping" actions was and is in most regions limited, the peace-sheriff was doomed to permanent patrol. This necessity springs immediately from the phantasmagorical goal. The West can here and there suspend the wars of disintegration by means of troops and the application of corresponding financial means, detaining some warlords and bribing others. Real pacification would, however, mean a break with the long-anachronistic concept of recuperative nation-building and capitalist development. Durable pacification in the age of crisis is only possible by means of exoduses and emancipatory destatification from below, as a break with the Western subject form and with the imperatives of unleashed competition. But that would be precisely the opposite of even the most well-intentioned human-rights paternalism.

Western policy towards the breakdown regions and ailing ruins of modernization incorporates the clandestine acknowledgement as well as the denial of the dissolution of the territorial-statist order. While in the construction of what amounts to a new domestic foreign policy the West defies the separation, constitutive of the territorial state, of inner-statist and international violence it simultaneously hallucinates a form of nation-building, attempting to reeducate one or another warlord faction into a state power. At the high point of the national liberation movements of the Third World, the leaders of the "free world" pregnantly denounced the emergent state power *in spe* as bandits and robbers. Today the politically tainted mafia-clan leaders are welcomed as statesmen.

This continuation of the collapsed order of the territorial state, however, is made visible only by the assemblage of friends and contacts these would-be human rights keepers choose on location. It comes into effect especially in the determination of the enemy. The crazy construct of the "rogue state" speaks volumes in this regard. Hallucinating that some ruin of modernization such as Iraq, Libya, and Cuba poses a danger to the new world order, the leading Western powers, impervious to the simplest facts, define precisely the kind of enemy that does not stand a chance.

The level of asymmetry that characterized the world-order wars of the 1990s has probably not been seen since the conquest of the Inca Empire by Pizarro. Every time the United States mobilizes its high-tech military apparatus, it is confronted with an opponent with weapons from another league. If war is understood in the strictest sense by Clausewitz, then the U.S. campaigns of the last decade no longer fit the category. If, according to Clausewitz, war does not begin with an attack but a defense, then war as a phenomenon is bound to a minimal degree of ability to defend; that is, the will and the ability of the attacked side to turn blood and thunder into a mutual event. These conditions were met neither in the Iraq campaign nor in the Kosovo intervention of 1999. In both cases the "battle," from the Western point of view, is reduced to target practice from the air on run-down Fordist armies on the ground. The Kosovo conflict can be most accurately described as the merging of two hijackings. On one side, Serbian militias and paramilitaries terrorized and displaced the Kosovo-Albanian civil population. On the other side, NATO alternately punished the population of Serbia and destroyed the infrastructure of the rest of Yugoslavia without a single NATO soldier needing to set foot in the country.

The Limits of Omnipotence

The biggest "military power of all times" will never meet an enemy that could muster even a fraction of the military resources available to the United States. Of course this asymmetry does not guarantee triumph. Everywhere the fruits of military successes are withering for the West, not only ex post facto with respect to the inner contradiction of exercising control without the ability to seize territories and begin the valorization process; the military ability to triumph at any time is also limited. The first limitation lies in the extreme costs of the high-tech military apparatus of the United States. The last remaining superpower is not merely excluded from the tendency, inherent to the "new wars," of minimizing the initial monetary costs of death and destruction; it experiences the complete opposite. In the wars of world order of the West, for the first time in military history the missiles are more expensive than the targets.

In this context it is worth taking a close look at the concept of "surgical attacks," ranking high in the U.S. military apparatus. Of course this is in the first instance errant propaganda. At the same time, as a euphemism this expression describes a special battle economy, an original exaggeration of the American way of fighting in the aftermath of human-rights paternalism. Already in the Fordist wars, the U.S. destruction apparatus was characterized by an extremely high organic composition. Whether in World War II, Korea, or Vietnam, U.S. warfare was determined to minimize its own casualties by means of material expenses. In the war on Kosovo and Iraq the enemy could for the first time participate in that relative protection. It was all about beautiful pictures and an impressive demonstration of power — the effectiveness of destruction was secondary. Never before have there been such a ratio of fireworks to the number of casualties. Considering the single applied use value (explosive force in TNT units) as well as the monetary value of each explosion, the direct victims were by far the most laboriously produced deaths in military history. The U.S. cannot afford many campaigns like the one against the Hussein regime.

Second, the force of the superpower is calibrated to a very specific type of opponent. It can with ostentation crush into the dust those enemies that depend essentially on territorial control — be it only for the purposes of economic looting — and that organize themselves as states or pseudo-states. The high-tech military machine is useless as soon as the Western centers no longer confront conflicts between states but are attacked from within the global world market society.

9/11 marks a historical cut. The attacks on the World Trade Center abruptly revealed the vulnerability of the capitalist centers, but that type of violator is appropriate to challenge Western superiority. About the fate of al-Qaeda one can only speculate; but little speculation is required about the fact that this organization will become the prototype of a new epoch of violence. With 9/11, security imperialism also entered a new phase. Facing its own vulnerability, the world police got rid of paternalism in favor of brutal repression. As in every war, also in the war on terror the opponents are beginning to resemble each other.

The State of Exception as Rule; or,
Guantánamo Is Everywhere

The war on terror and especially its second phase, the conquest of down the Ba'ath regime, have a transitory function. The choice of enemy already documents that the Western leading power is hallucinating itself back to a bygone epoch of wars between states; with the Hussein regime, the United States chose a surrogate enemy organized in a territorial state. That is, a target that can be easily overrun with a high-tech military machine rather than the actual enemy, the transnational and deterritorial network al-Qaeda. At the same time, the egomaniacal world police have kicked open a door to a new epoch that would have better remained closed.

First, with the triumph over Saddam Hussein's "rogue state" and the occupation of Iraq, the United States has landed in exactly the kind of succession conflict they hallucinated away with the concept of "rogue state." After its fast victory the superpower finds itself endlessly engaged in a low-intensity war against an ungraspable, deterritorialized enemy.[49] The U.S. troops probably will not be better off in their Iraqi protectorate than Israel, equally superior in military power, facing the never-ending al-Aqsa Intifada.

At the same time, with the war on Iraq, Western hegemony abandoned the ground of human-rights paternalism. The United States itself began acting as a transnational actor of violence that no longer knows any limits. While human-rights paternalism still reacted to anomic conditions, the leadership of the last superpower claims the primal right of all sovereignty, the declaration of the state of exception, for the global theater. The war on terror represents the self-enabling of an unleashed leviathan, equally absolved from international agreements and martial and domestic law.

The war on Iraq in 2003 illustrates this new quality. It goes beyond the referential framework of the international conflicts in a threefold fashion: structurally; with regard to the arrangements of military actions; and concerning the war's ends. Whether enforced demilitarization or regime change, the explanation for the attack on

Iraq would have been unthinkable as casus belli in the traditional universe. Not that foreign powers were never involved in the overthrow of governments: as is well known, the United States in particular has some experience in the discipline. But this time regime change enforced from the outside functioned as a highly official and emphatically proclaimed war aim. All international wars since 1648 fit the most general of Clausewitz's definitions of war: "War is thus an act of force to compel our enemy to do our will."[50] The attack on Iraq in 2003 does not fit this framework. It does not aim at the retreat of the enemy sovereign. Before the U.S. troops moved towards Baghdad they had deprived the Iraqi state of the status as subject of international law, an absolutely unprecedented process in history.[51] As sovereign the Iraqi leadership could not capitulate, since doing so would have meant to acknowledge its own non-existence as sovereign, not only regarding the future but also regarding the present and the past.[52]

The military operations of the war on Iraq reflect this in their own way. They mix elements of statist warfare with manhunts against the ruling regime that were being executed according to the slogan "wanted dead or alive." The military actions were opened for instance by a (failed) attack on the alleged location of Saddam Hussein.

The battle against the Iraqi dictator was, as in the logic of the international wars, no longer about depriving the enemy government of its military instruments and rendering it defenseless. The military event seemed more like a mafia-style retribution. More precisely, there was something to it of the procedure of the avengers in Hollywood movies. The former bearer of enemy sovereignty had turned into biomass approved for killing. The special treatment that Saddam's sons faced instead of arrest speaks volumes in this context, as does the subsequent exhibition of the bodies. When dead GIs were dragged through the streets of Mogadishu for the cameras in the early 1990s, the Western public still reacted with outrage. One decade later, the U.S. administration reveals that it is not very far removed from General Aidid's gangs. It relies on the American TV audience's having arrived at the level of the jubilating mob of the Somali capital when it stages itself as master over life and death.

Because of its democracy-missionary and security-imperialist intentions, the war on terror implies a tendency to come untethered. A war aim such as "security" is neither achievable nor objectifiable and it can be only left to the free judgment of the leviathan to define it as appropriately achieved or not. But also in its temporal and geographical structure the war on terror is not simply long and wide-ranging, but limitless. The justification of the necessity of preemptive battle against terrorism renders almost every state a possible target. What could contribute more to the unleashing of fundamentalist desperados more than the war that is to subdue them?

It is more likely that the circle will be squared than that the war on terror should end with a victorious peace for democracy. On the historical horizon there lies rather the threat that the war will discharge into an exceptional state maintained both by the leviathan and by the terrorist behemoths. The result of the war on Iraq already gives some idea of how it could continue. Rather than a state of exception limited geographically and temporally (camp and front), familiar from the epoch of the rise of commodity society, a permanent and spatially omnipresent state of exception under Western auspices begins to appear.

Initially, the parallel running-amok of the superpower and Islamic fundamentalism is sure to ravage the Middle East. But it is not necessarily in the logic of things that this will remain the full extent of the matter. The security-imperialist leviathan can ultimately only fail in its efforts to externalize violent irrationality and to wage it as an external war, and to try to contain it with police force. Whether Islamic fundamentalists carry the will to destruction, the ultima ratio of commodity subjectivity, into its Western primal home, or whether other terrorist behemoths take on the job, the security-imperialist leviathan will always find an occasion and an opportunity to do his part for the abolition of the normality of commodity society even at home. The U.S. Patriot Act, the invalidation of basic rights, the police function of the military discussed in Germany — these are all indications of the direction into which the statist regime of violence might move if its foundation is crumbling: towards the permanent state of exception.

Notes

1. Immanuel Kant, *Perpetual Peace*, trans. Ted Humphrey (Indianapolis: Hackett, 1983) 127.

2. Thomas Paine, *Rights of Man, Common Sense, and Other Political Writings* (Oxford: Oxford University Press, 1995) 265.

3. See Karl Otto Hondrich, *Lehrmeister Krieg* (Hamburg: Rowohlt Taschenbuch, 1992) 16.

4. Thomas Hobbes, *Leviathan* (New Haven: Yale University Press, 2010) 127.

5. Hobbes, *Leviathan* 126.

6. For more on the term "asocial sociality," see 185n3 in this volume.

7. Georg Wilhelm Friedrich Hegel, *Phenomenology of Spirit*, trans. A.V. Miller (Oxford: Oxford University Press, 1977) 19.

8. Hegel, *Phenomenology* 114.

9. *Phenomenology* 117.

10. *Phenomenology* 270.

11. Compare Christina von Braun, *Nichtich* (Frankfurt: Neue Kritik, 1999) 231 and following.

12. *Phenomenology* 288-289.

13. *Phenomenology* 360.

14. Hegel, *Philosophy of Right*, trans. S.W. Dyde (New York: Cosimo, 2008) xxxii.

15. Sigmund Freud, *Totem and Taboo*, trans. James Strachey (New York: W. W. Norton, 1990) 181.

16. *ibid.*

17. Freud, *Beyond the Pleasure Principle*, trans. James Strachey (New York: W. W. Norton, 1990) 38, 46.

18. Freud, *Totem* 181.

19. Giorgio Agamben, *Homo Sacer*, trans. Daniel Heller-Roazen (Stanford: Stanford University Press, 1998).

20. Carl von Clausewitz, *On War*, trans. Michael Howard and Peter Paret (Oxford: Oxford Unviersity Press, 2007) 28.

21. Clausewitz, *On War* 15.

22. Clausewitz's war theory claims absolute validity. In reality it only grasps the characteristics of the statified modern war. This, however, it does very precisely.

23. *On War* 223.

24. The term "total war" was infamously used and subsequently has been associated with Joseph Goebbels's *"Sportpalastrede,"* the speech delivered by Goebbels at the Sportpalast Berlin on 18 February 1943. The proclamation of a total war was intended to reenergize the German military and public after Germany had suffered major military setbacks. In this speech, Goebbels famously asked the audience and all of Germany: "wollt ihr den totalen Krieg" (do you want total war)?

25. Of all wars of the nineteenth century, perhaps the American Civil War anticipates the industrialization of warfare most, which might be due to its sheer duration. The wars after 1815 were rather short in comparison.

26. This quote contains an error of translation. Heraclitus does not speak of war but, very generally, of "struggle" and "conflict." See Wolfgang Schadewaldt, *Anfänge der Philosophie* (Frankfurt: Suhrkamp, 2002) 389.

27. What is true for vehicle construction also is true for the fabrication of aircraft, movies, or communications engineering.

28. This context was probably expounded most clearly by Modris Eksteins in *Rites of Spring* (Boston: Mariner, 1989).

29. Quoted in Eksteins, *Rites* 213.

30. Quoted in *Rites* 174.

31. Letter from 26 March 1917, in *Rites* 173.

32. Ernst Jünger, *Der Kampf um das Reich* (Essen: Kamp, 1929) 9.

33. Remnants of these origins seem to have lasted quite some time. Certainly, during my schooldays in Bavaria in the mid-1970s, I encountred a mathematics teacher who woukd often set "demonstrative" tasks from the field of artillery as exam questions.

34. The so-called peaceful use of nuclear energy has never been more than a waste product of military use.

35. See Robert Kurz, *Weltordnungskriege* (Bad Honnef: Horlemann, 2003) 23n.

36. Compare Sibylle Tönnies, *Pazifismus passé* (Hamburg: Rotbuch, 1997) 77.

37. Abel Bonnard, "Devant La Guerre," *La Figaro* 29 October 1912: 1.

38.   Ralph Freedman, *Hermann Hesse: Pilgrim of Crisis* (New York: Pantheon Books, 1978) 168.

39.   Compare Peter Bürger, *Ursprung des postmodernen Denkens* (Weilerswist-Metternich: Velbrück Wissenschaft, 2007) 26.

40.   Karl Kraus, *The Last Days of Mankind* (Frankfurt am Main: Suhrkamp, 1992) 34.

41.   Götz Eisenberg, *Amok-Kinder in der Kälte* (Hamburg: Rowohlt, 2000) 13.

42.   People consciously sacrificing their lives in combat are not an entirely new phenomenon. In the old Roman tradition it is represented by the figure of Devotus. The twelfth-century Islamic sect of the "Assassines" also sent people to war who did not spare a thought for their survival. The association of suicide and mass murder, the combination of the greatest murder efficiency and taking one's own life, however, is a completely new phenomenon even though the weapons-technological preconditions have existed for a long time. The first event dates back to November 1982 when a seventeen-year-old Islamist attacked the headquarters of the Israeli occupiers in the south-Lebanese Tyros.

43.   Christoph Kucklick, Hania Liczak, and Christoph Reuter, "Selbstmordattentäter — Die Macht der Ohnmächtigen," eds. Hans Frank and Kai Hirschmann, *Die weltweite Gefahr Terrorismus als internationale Herausforderung* (Berlin: Berliner Wissenschafts-Verlag, 2002) 264.

44.   Where states made "ethnic cleansing" into political goal, it was notably exercised mostly after the ending of combat actions or independently of them. One should think in this regard especially of the war of destruction in the East by Nazi Germany. In the new wars they make out the center of the military operations.

45.   This ability, as is well known, is predicated on the U.S. administration's ability to tap the international finance markets for its military program.

46.   Robert S. Robins and Jerrold M. Post, *Political Paranoia: The Psychopolitics of Hatred* (New Haven: Yale University Press, 1997) 40.

47.   The novel *The Turner Diaries*, written by William Pierce, a bestseller in the American ultra-right-wing scene, can be seen as a proof for that alignment. It melts the defense of the private possession of arms, the fight against the government, and the extermination of Jews and Blacks

to one gigantic complex. "The plot of the *Turner Diaries* is a crazy triumph phantasy. It describes America after the prohibition of every private possession of arms by the Cohen Act. The protagonist, the Arian hero Earl Turner talks about the role he played in the overthrow of the U.S. government in the Great Revolution of the '90s. Turner is a member of a secret society, the organization whose goal to reconstitute the power of all whites in the U.S. and additionally to kill all non-whites and Jews. In the last part of the book millions of the American Jews, Black Latinos and 'race traitors' are killed on the day of the 'great hanging' (Robins 277).

48. The anti-statist affection in the United States can look back on a long history. To the west of the Atlantic, blood and thunder have never been an absolute statist privilege to such a degree as in Europe or East Asia. This does not mean of course that France, Germany, or Japan are immune to this.

49. Of course Western troops cannot simply withdraw from Bosnia or other regions of crisis in which they engaged in human-rights paternalism under the flag of the UN since the 1990s; but it is not only because of problems of legitimation that remaining in the position of compulsory referee is something quite different from playing the part of an active party to the war.

50. *On War* 13.

51. The first Gulf War was still about forcing Iraq by military means to withdraw from the occupied Kuwait. As an attempt to compel Iraq, as subject of international law, represented by its government, to certain measures, this event did still fit into the pattern of the international wars.

52. Here lies the fundamental difference from the resignation of existing subjects of international law in the world of international wars of annexation. The resignation as subject of international law referred to the future. It was part of the production of legitimation of the victorious side to make, if at all possible, the former subject of international law sign the resignation himself, which would in turn acknowledge its former status. In the war on Iraq of 2003, the resignation of the subject of international law is not the result of a military act; it is rather its starting point.

The Nightmare of Freedom: The Foundations of "Western Values" and the Helplessness of Critique

Robert Kurz (2005)

It is well known that the concepts of freedom and equality form the central keywords of the Enlightenment. Liberalism has certainly not been the sole trafficker of these ideals. Paradoxically, they play just as big a part in Marxism and anarchism. They also play an important ideological role in contemporary social movements. The Left stares at the idols of freedom and equality like the rabbit stares at the snake. To avoid being blinded by the splendor of these idols, it is advisable to look for their social foundations. Marx already uncovered these foundations more than 100 years ago: the sphere of the market, capitalist circulation, commodity exchange, and universal buying and selling.

In this sphere, a fully determined sort of freedom and equality prevails, which refers solely to selling what one wants to sell — as long as a buyer is found — and buying what one wants to buy — as long as one can pay. And only in this sense does equality also prevail — the equality of money and commodity owners. Their equality has nothing to do with quantity, but only with the social form common to both. The same cannot be bought for a cent as for a dollar; but no matter whether it's a penny or a dollar, in qualitative terms the equality of the money form prevails. In buying and selling there are no masters or slaves, and nobody commands or obeys; there are only free and equal people in law. Whether man, woman, child, white, black, or brown: the customer is welcome under any circumstances. The sphere of commodity exchange is the sphere of mutual respect. Where an exchange of a commodity and money takes place, there is no violence. The bourgeois smile is always that of a salesman.

Marx's sarcasm is related to the fact that this market sphere makes up only a small fraction of modern social life. Commodity exchange or circulation has as its precondition an entirely different sphere: namely, capitalist production, the functional space of business administration and what Marx calls "abstract labor." Here, laws entirely different from those of commodity circulation apply. Here, the salesman's smile freezes into the cynical grimace of the slave driver or prison guard. When working, wrote the young Marx, the worker "isn't himself, but outside himself." The freedom in commodity production is so small that the content, sense, and purpose of what is produced there cannot be determined. Neither do the owners of capital or managers have this freedom, because they are under the pressure of competition. Production, therefore, entirely follows the principles of command and obedience. Where the business administration regime is especially efficient, workers are sometimes not even allowed the right to defecate in private. Neoliberalism, in particular, loves this wholly extraordinary productive strictness.

The freedom and equality of circulation and the dictatorship of business-administered production only appear to contradict each other. Purely formally, workers are unfree in production precisely because they exercised their freedom beforehand as commodity owners on the market. That is, they sold their labor power. Naturally, this freedom to sell one's own labor power is itself owed to compulsion and unfreedom: modernization created historical circumstances under which there is no other possibility of sustaining one's life.

One must either buy labor power and employ it for the end-in-itself of capitalist valorization, or sell one's own labor power and let it be employed for this end-in-itself. As long as there were independent producers (farmers and artisans) there was no universal market. Rather, the greater part of social relations played themselves out in other forms. The rise of the universal market proceeded alongside the fall of independent producers. All other goods come to be traded as commodities only because there is a labor market, and because human labor power has also assumed the commodity form. The sphere of freedom and equality in circulation exists only because the sphere of unfreedom has developed out of production. Universal freedom thus also takes place in the form of universal competition.

This problem persists in the area of personal reproduction or private life, where commodities are consumed and intimate social relations have their place. Here there are many activities and moments of life that are not fulfilled in commodity production (such as housekeeping, raising children, or love). In the process of modernization, women were made materially, socio-psychically, and cultural-symbolically responsible for these aspects, and they were devalued for that very reason: no "money value" is transacted in these moments of social life; thus, in the sense of capitalist valorization, they are inferior. This dissociation (in the sense of Roswitha Scholz's concept of value dissociation) is not confined to a definable secondary sphere, but seeps through the entire ensemble of social life processes. Thus, within commodity production, women are as a rule worse-paid and reach leadership positions relatively infrequently. In personal relationships there is a determinate gender code that implies for women a structurally subordinate relation, even when it is sometimes broken or modified in postmodernity. Likewise, the non-white and non-Western part of humanity was already abandoned by the philosophy of the Enlightenment to a structural subordination.

The abolition of relations of "dominion of man over man" appears solely in the sphere of circulation and the market. That hypocritical sphere of freedom and equality is not, however, based merely on structures of dependence; in an immediate sense, it is constituted as a naked function of the end-in-itself of capitalist valorization. In crass opposition to the exchange of independent products, the universal market does not serve the reciprocal satisfaction of needs. Rather, it is only a regime of accumulation or transitional stage belonging to capital itself. When sold, abstract value "realizes" itself as money, and the function of apparently free trade consists precisely in that. Original monetary capital, transformed via production into commodities, turns back into its money form multiplied by profit. The nature of capital is expressed precisely therein as an end in itself, that is, to turn money into more money with the consequent accumulation of what Marx calls "abstract wealth" in an endless process. Thus, by exercising their liberty and equality in the sphere of circulation, people achieve nothing but capital's self-mediation. That is, they transform the surplus value or profit created from the commodity form back to the money form. Therefore, the freedom and equality of circulation are nothing but a mechanism for capital's goal of realization. Each act of freedom requires the performance of an act of pump-priming that transforms capital from its commodity state into its money state.

Modern bourgeois freedom possesses a peculiar character: it is identical to a higher, abstract, and anonymous form of servitude. Social emancipation would be liberation from this kind of freedom rather than its realization. Things look no better for the concept of equality, which openly implies the threat of forcing individuals into a single form. Modernization, in a manner of speaking, sewed humanity into the uniform of monetary subjects. But relations of structural dependency are hidden beneath it. In reality, the needs, the tastes, the cultural interests, and the personal objectives of individuals are never equal; they are only subjected to the equality of the commodity form. Therefore, as Adorno said, it would be emancipatory to be able to be "unequal in peace."

Since the Enlightenment, equality has retained its false aura via the argumentative sleight of hand of bourgeois ideologues. The meaning of the concept of inequality was shifted from the simple variety of individuals to the subordination of one individual to another. That which in itself is the mere expression of individual characteristics, namely inequality, suddenly appears as the expression of domination. And vice versa: that which in itself is the expression of uniform compulsion, namely equality, suddenly appears as the expression of freedom from domination. Here, in modern ideology, we must deal with a case of Orwellian language. In reality, inequality has nothing to do with domination, and equality has nothing to do with self-determination. Rather the opposite: in modernity equality itself is a relation of domination.

The result is a permanent contradiction in modern ideology. On one side, the sphere of circulation becomes separated from the entire context of capitalist reproduction and elevated as an ideal. On the other side, the de facto dictatorship of production and of the structural devaluation of the feminine are declared unbreakable objective laws of nature. Each side must be played constantly against the other; for this reason these social relations after a certain period of time enter the realm of common sense. Freedom and equality represent exactly what Adorno called the "context of blindness." And the Left inherited this blindness along with the Enlightenment's conceptual apparatus. In particular, utopian, democratic, and libertarian socialists, anarchists, and dissidents in state socialist countries all appealed to the ideals of freedom and liberty, without recognizing that they are restricted to the sphere of circulation and without seeing through to the inner link of freedom and unfreedom in modernity.

Today, social critics fall back more than ever into the ideals of circulation. This has structural causes. The global crisis caused by the third industrial revolution drives an increasing number of people out of real production and forcibly converts them into agents of circulation. As cheap labor in the service industry, as salespeople, street dealers, or even beggars, they themselves now experience, paradoxically, the sphere of freedom and equality as the yoke of a secondary job; the dictatorship of production is extended to more and more activities of circulation, finally reaching the entrepreneurs of poverty. Freedom and unfreedom immediately coincide here; but, ideologically, that paradox is once again assimilated in terms of the ideals of circulation. Inasmuch as individuals experience themselves increasingly via their own petty-bourgeois self-conception as widely circulating "human capital," a neo-petty-bourgeois version of the utopianism of commodity exchange comes back around after the demise of labor socialism. In a society in which everyone constantly attempts to sell something to someone, and in which social relations dissolve into a universal bazaar, the growing signs of crisis are perceived through the grid of circulation. In a veritably compulsory manner, an intelligentsia of self-salespeople interprets the problems of the third industrial revolution along the lines of relations of circulation: one commodity owner meets another. Even the overcoming of commodity production is imagined according to the categories of eternal exchange.

Individuals, who do not as a rule reflect critically on their social constitution and who only seem to be independent of each other in the sphere of circulation, are asked periodically to appreciate the other's good fortune and extend goodwill instead of competing with each other; all of this is to treat the problem as if it were to be found not in social production and ways of living, but rather in an individually representable pathology that could be cured by pedagogical and therapeutic measures. The salesman's smile is interpreted as the idealism of amiable social relations that are no longer minted in competition, as if social transformation were possible via the utopian construct of personal conduct, outside the substantial mode of production and life. These utopian beliefs are rooted in the idealized sphere of circulation — where the neo-petty-bourgeois utopians appoint themselves the bedside doctors of the subject.

The ideology of circles of exchange that is propagated in many countries fails, in practice, to represent anything but a hobby economy; where it has been attempted on a large scale, as in the recent Argentine crisis, it has failed massively. The attempt (supported by the research of French ethnographer Marcel Mauss, especially in his major work, *The Gift*) to redeem "eternal exchange" from competition by using the model of so-called archaic societies and transforming it into a reciprocal exchange of gifts — that is, into a kind of permanent Christmas — seems even more insufficient. The idea of an "economy of the gift" cannot, by its essence, extend beyond immediate personal relationships; hence it ignores the scale of social productive forces and highly organized social contexts. It would be absurd for one individual to say to another: "give me a kidney transplant and, if you're very good, I'll give you a combine harvester." The problem is not how individuals might mutually "grant" each other something, but to apply our social forces (infrastructures, systems of education and science, systems of industrial and immaterial production) sensibly, not destructively.

On the contrary, utopias of circulation always look for a solution primarily on the plane of individual modes of behavior. Yet that's putting the cart before the horse. Instead of making commodity circulation and its accompanying market competition superfluous through a social revolution of production and of our way of life, such a backwards approach asks the isolated subject of circulation to realize the ontological pretension of exchange in a reformed, whitewashed form. The aim is an ethical canceling-out of competition. Social emancipation then appears as the mere consequence of a utopia consisting of the freedom and equality of the subject of circulation, supposedly realized in small groups. The matter of practical solidarity in social contexts is ideologized and made into a mendacious, pedagogical, and often psychotherapeutic idealism which can simply turn into the terror of kindness and reciprocal social control (for example, along the lines of religious sects). This neo-petty-bourgeois utopianism of human capital in circulation is, just like all earlier utopias, condemned to failure.

Curtains for Universalism: Islamism as Fundamentalism in Modern Social Form

Karl-Heinz Lewed (2008)

"Western values are Western values. Islamic values are universal values."
– Mohamad Mahatir, Former Prime Minister of Malaysia

The West has responded to the threat of Islamist terror, particularly since the attacks on the World Trade Center, in two ways: first, in practical, political terms through select campaigns of destruction in Afghanistan and Iraq, and, second, in ideological terms through the myth of what Samuel P. Huntington called a "clash of civilizations" and the fundamentalism of "Western Values." 9/11 had the effect of an ideological accelerant, which managed to inflame further an already growing culturalist firestorm. The ever increasing economic crisis in the centers of capitalism, together with the social and material insecurity of individual people, had laid the groundwork for culturalism in the 1990s. Its paradigmatic claim, that is, of a major line of confrontation between the West and "Islam," was met with an even greater deal of approval as a result of the terror attacks of Islamist groups. Since then, a stream of culturalist elaborations has continued to pour forth, and the pervasive stereotypes arising out of Western culturalism are being rearticulated with growing and pervasive vehemence.[1] "Islam" is said to have nothing to do with the history of Western civilization, its way of life, and its basic values; rather it represents a totally different culture. It is said to be premodern because its views of the world stem from religiously motivated, medieval thinking, and is therefore diametrically opposed to personal freedom, the core of the Western way of life. What "Islam" strives for, then, is continually to expand its horizons, representing a threat to "Western culture." In fact, in the confrontation between Islamism and Western cultural warriors, we find not two essentially foreign cultures standing opposite each other, but two complementary variations of dealing with a globalization marked by crisis capitalism, whose common foundation takes the modern social form of interaction through the production of commodities, abstract labor and law, as well as the attendant forms of subjectivity. If the implementation of capitalist forms of socialization in "Islamic" countries has taken on a very specific and contradictory character, a fundamental transformation of social relations already took place long ago under the guidance of the nationalist modernizing dictatorships, and continues through to modern, bourgeois social relations.[2]

With the excommunication of the "Islamic" world from the social fabric of bourgeois modernity, however, the fundamental social forms that dominate in both the capitalist core regions and the global South are totally effaced. The growing social decay in countries on the periphery, in the end the product of a recuperative modernization, is painted over, seen through a culturalist lens as something purely the result of a culture foreign to the West. Thus, the asynchronous nature of the current crisis, further polarizing the periphery and the center, appears as an existential conflict between Occident and Orient. Simultaneously, the critique of the political and ideological background in its historical context is rendered impossible, since culturalism displaces critical distance in favor of classification and identity. For culturalism, one thing is fundamentally obsolete: comprehending social contradictions and their disavowals in a historical context. Identity-based logic simplifies the historical process to a cultural fashioning of a preconceived being residing inside totally self-contained and static cultural structures. Culturalism is constituted by the construction and classification of collective identities, including the formulation of a clash between them. Thus, the real historical dimensions are effaced, as are the developments looming on the horizon. Contrary to culturalist constructions, the current situation in these regions does not result from an ostensible continuation of centuries of cultural traditions; rather it has much more to do with a crisis-laden process involving the dissolution of social formations on the basis of modern bourgeois social relations. Indeed, a fundamental transformation of social structures took place under the modernizing dictatorships. The process of this transformation had as its prerequisite both colonial domination and the disentanglement and "emancipation" from this domination. The content of the newly created frame of abstract social relations was, however, the equally abstract valorization of labor. The central contradiction that Islamism's ideology of decline attests to could and can only be found in the fact that although the framework of social networks is based on modern forms, the universalization of the production of abstract wealth failed in these forms. Islamism is the direct product of this failure. It represents a specific ideological and (post)political form of decline of recuperative modernization, participating as such in the continuity of that process. Both the genesis and the decline of the nation-state form are constitutive of the emergence of Islamism. Its orientation reflects central elements of the modern bourgeois form, which cloaked themselves in religious garb, in particular the claim to sovereignty and a single legal system for all relative to the religion-based form of law.[3] For a serious critique, the ideology of Islamism is not to be understood without reference to the level of nation-statehood and form of law — in other words, the standpoint of political generality. For this reason, I will concentrate on those forms which, in the process of the decline in the economic content, have gone through a specific reformulation, taking on a religious semblance. Thus Islamism proves to be the fundamentalism of the modern social form.

The statist movement towards a national collective occurred not simply through the rationalized cobbling together of individual units, torn from their traditional modes of living and made into a functional whole; in fact, irrational elements played a central role. These elements are part and parcel of the patriarchal form of male subjectivity and its inherent impulse to classify things into an all-encompassing sociality. The requirement for the appearance of concreteness and identification with an imagined, pure totality — like a "people" or a certain culture — finds its deep subjective foundations here. Only with the universalization of isolated individuality and its concomitant powerlessness in the face of the social does it become necessary to submit and subordinate oneself to a national or ethnic community, thereby merging into it. In a future article, I will attempt to determine the implications of this relationship at the level of subjects, and show how patriarchal structures, antisemitism, and, finally, the rendering of collective subjects are re-elaborated in Islamism as specific elements of modernity, becoming virulent as means of coming to terms with socioeconomic upheaval and its contradictions.[4]

The Generality of Self-Seeking Interest

The implementation of modern bourgeois forms of social intercourse mediated through the commodity form took place fundamentally at the level of nation state formation. The statist sovereign played a double role in this process. On one hand, he spurred the dismantling of traditional forms of social hierarchy with their "ancient hierarchical and organic forms of association."[5] On the other, state-organized violence pursued a general rationalization of the social order, replacing the established social structures with new objectified power relations. The process of implementing commodity society turned out to be an "enterprise of general uprooting" of individuals and, simultaneously, a new social cohesion taking the form of abstract mediation, a social "reconstruction according to the principles of reason."[6] The constitution of state power and the creation of new and abstract relationships between individuals went hand in hand. Exemplary of this consonance is the development of absolutist power in France, which, as Tocqueville shows, anticipated the fundamental forms of bourgeois dominance.[7] Seen in this way, political systems — from the absolutist state to bourgeois democracy and on to the modernizing dictatorships — represent different manifestations of a shared identity at the most fundamental level, an identity that lies beyond the concrete formation of the statist power apparatus that administers public business. Rousseau calls this level, which lies outside the individual organs of sovereignty, the general will.[8] The general foundation of statist praxis is expressed in the fact that state operations are legitimated not from within, but through a public interest, which simultaneously underwrites and overlaps with the state.[9] Marx aptly describes the character of this universalization in the *Grundrisse*: "The general interest is precisely the generality of self-seeking interests." "The other [the partner in the generalized exchange of commodities] is also recognized and acknowledged as one who likewise realizes his self-seeking interest, so that both know that the common interest is only...the exchanges between self-seeking interests."[10] Of course, what Marx calls "self-seeking interest" is not the abject personal character of the individual but the result of generalized social interaction between commodity owners. Social connections in commodity society are thereby fundamentally marked by the fact that labor or the commodity function as social mediators. Every individual in this kind of social relationship of mediation is included only as the owner of his commodity — and that means, generally speaking, the commodity of his own labor power. Thus, he does not work in order to manufacture a specific object, but to secure money and hence a portion of the abstract wealth of commodities. The social connection of mediation through labor thus breaks down into two elements of concrete activity for others, that is, for the anonymous social context represented in commodities and in the sphere of private, "self-seeking" interest for money. "Each [both parties in the exchange process] looks only to his own advantage. The only force bringing them together, and putting them into relation with the other, is the selfishness, the gain, and the private interest of each."[11] In a society in which labor stands at the center of social mediation, every activity becomes external to individuals and therefore merely a means. At the level of social relationships, this form of mediation expresses itself in the division into separate relationships of the will of each individual commodity owner to his product or the value represented in it; that is, in property relations.[12] This is precisely what Marx means when he uses the phrase "self-seeking interests." It is no accident, then, that in the final article of the "Declaration of the Rights of Man and of the Citizen," the founding political document of modern bourgeois society, we read that "property" is an "inviolable and sacred right," of which "no one can be deprived." Property as "sacred right" obviously does not mean a "natural" relation to an object; rather, it articulates the abstract sociality of the individual commodity monads and the standpoint of their private interests. Social generality is therefore an abstract generality, a common framework of separate, individualized monads endowed with free will.

Through the notion of law, the other side of abstract generality, separate private interests are placed in an equally abstract relationship to one another and are as such mediated. The commodity-formed individual is therefore not only constituted (in relation to his private property) as free, but simultaneously as an equal among equals related to a polity (law), which forms the abstract framework of abstract individuals. In addition to freedom belonging to commodity owners, the general will emerges — in other words, the spheres of right and law, in which all are viewed as equal. The concept of universalism expresses the universalization of the abstract private standpoint as well as the equality of abstract individuals as equal subjects before the law. There are always two souls that reside in the modern universal subject: that of free will and that of "universal law." The most advanced representative of bourgeois reason, Immanuel Kant, outlines in his Critiques precisely these two aspects of bourgeois subjectivity — free will and the universal form of law — and simultaneously formulates a program of complete submission to them. Kant is theoretically consistent insofar as his concept of the "form of law in general" is clearly not aimed at actual written laws — unlike the contemporary positivist simplified notions of "jurisprudence"— rather at the level of "law itself" underlying the statist legal system.[13] This underlying form is nothing other than one pole of the individual's abstract mediation relationship vis-à-vis the commodity. The mediation implies, on one hand, the discretionary power of commodity owners over their private property (including their own labor power) to the exclusion of all others; on the other hand, the constitution of a "generality of self-seeking interests" as right and law emerge. Abstract individuals are deeply affected by two sides of the same coin of subjectivity. Obviously, the combination of freedom and legality can be found in "Declaration of the Rights of Man and of the Citizen." Article I states that "Men are born and remain free and equal in rights," while Article VI specifically clarifies the content of social relations in the form of the generality of right: "The law is the expression of the general will." This formulation makes absolutely clear how the societal cohesion of individuals reduced to commodities can only be expressed in the form of law.

The basic form of the relation of commodity owners we have been describing must take a concrete form in the daily circulation of individuals, a form which has a dual character: the abstract relation expresses itself on one hand in the sphere of the market, in which the individual commodity owners realize their private portion of the social mass of value; on the other hand, the mediation of abstract relationships through the form of law manifests itself in a highly differentiated system of public institutions: the sphere of politics and the state. The 1791 "Declaration" explicitly highlights the requirement of external force: "The guarantee of the rights of man and of the citizen necessitates a public force."

According to an uncritical understanding of human rights, they express only the interests of individuals with respect to statist force. Contrary to this limited perspective, however, the 1791 "Declaration" formulates clearly the dual character of private relationships: individuals are free to handle their hallowed property as they please and at the same time are necessarily tied to law and the state as community. Given their basic elements, the state and the free individual stand not in opposition to each other, but form a logical and complementary unity: "the Sovereign presupposes citizens to be individuals, he as an individual needs them...and he guarantees their existence as isolated citizens. Herein lies the 'common interest': that the two spheres require each other as much as much as they differ."[14] The general form of interest is private and the statist institutionalization represents this general and abstract form. The state is therefore only the external shape of the abstract form of relations between individuals. We can in no way find the underlying conditions of right and law in the empirical "forms of expressions" of state force, or likewise in the personal decisions of individuals. The profound depth of the Kantian critique quoted above therefore resides in the formulation of free will and the form of law as "transcendentality," rather than deriving it from an empirical determination of will, in the way, say, Hobbes attempts to. The latter viewpoint leads back to the constitution of the Sovereign through a contractual relation between the isolated individuals and presupposes from the outset their monadic existence as natural "people." Opposed to that, the Kantian "form of a Law in general" is a superindividual sphere, that is, a framework of "transcendental" legality and freedom in which individuals already operate. The Marxian critique of commodity production can identify this "transcendentality" as a historically specific form of relation and, to a certain extent, bring it down from the otherworldly sphere of reason to the earthly ground of commodity relations.

Independence and National Unity Within the Horizon of the General Interest

Not only has the ideology of bourgeois society underlined the categories of abstract generality and general will; the collective actors of later nation-state formations legitimate themselves explicitly by using these categories. And even its form of decline, political Islam, refers to them when legitimating itself. All of modernity's political systems, no matter how differently they style themselves, stand fundamentally in a long and unified tradition of statist sovereignty as the standpoint of generality that stretches all the way back to the beginnings of bourgeois society, a standpoint which obliges the statist institutions of power to maintain the status of neutrality in the face of private interests. What follows from the form of law as the mediation of respective private property relationships is that the representative organs must constitute themselves as neutral and independent. Figuratively, this claim is embodied well in the figure of "Lady Justice": blind to the items on her scales — that is, the respective private interests — it is only a question of legal equilibrium, the formal balance between abstract private interests.[15] This claim to independence or rather the indifference to the specific matter at hand implies that the personnel representing the institutionalized general will, in other words the officers of the court and public administrators, are likewise forced to uphold a strict neutrality because, as functionaries of general operations, they operate in a sphere which is ideally located outside the particular interests, including their own as private persons. The infringement of this basic rule — that is, the mixing of general interests and the particular interests of public personnel — is however already implied. Officials, who are meant to take the general interest seriously, find themselves all too easily mixed up with their private interest. Broadly speaking, history shows that there is no clear correlation between the regular functioning of the sphere of private relationships (mediated by the market) and the near "disturbance-free" administration of general operations. The historical implementation of the modern forms, in which the sphere of private relationships was first created, was signaled by a mixing of the two spheres. The tendency towards the diffusion of particular interests is intensified in the crisis of commodity production such that a separation of the general operations from the outside private interest proves to be more and more difficult. In these cases it is common to speak of corrupt states, which are then ranked on a new scale created especially for them. Ultimately, this contradiction leads to the collapse of the crucial neutrality of the public sphere.[16] The gravitational pull of corruption also affects the countries where Islamism has entered into the corridors of political power: "Empowered Islam offers neither new kinds of social or economic justice. Hypocrisy is dominant: under the veil of moral conservatism, corruption is pervasive. [...] Empowerment leads to corruption, compromise, and the loss of utopia."[17]

The ideal of the formal and functional independence and neutrality of the sovereign as public authority is merely one facet of this relation. In addition, political sovereignty externally represents the national unity of private, individual relationships. In the nation, the mass of isolated individuals is coalesced into a broader constituency. So, too, does the individual, the presupposed sovereign, as the general will of private property relations, find its concrete form in an all-powerful nation. The mystical transfiguration of this submission as "devotion to the nation" (Marx) points out that the real-metaphysical quality of the abstract form is in fact a civil relationship, unconsciously produced through the mediation of money and law. The mythologically charged concept of the nation has resulted, since its first formulation, from this externalization of social relationships and the subsequent metaphysical Categorical Imperative. The sovereign is thus the extended community of the nationally defined individual, one who stands in a negative relationship with any other nation. The national whole stands only on one particular territory, one fenced in by its sovereign, ever-enclosed, and secured from the outside. And so, too, privileges (such as social benefits) only come to the members of the national community.

For both the self-image and self-legitimation of the nation as a whole, as for individuals, bourgeois social dynamics play an important role: first, the need for continuous circulation of the productive basis of wealth production; second, the dissolution of traditional relationships and forms of production; and third, permanent expansion. Material production, as the social structure that underpins the requirement of constant modernization, is turned into an ideology of universal social progress, and it finds general acceptance. The nation, now identified with this comprehensive, all-encompassing dynamic, must, as the subject of "progress," grant meaning and achieve concrete goals. This identification with the national unity, however, is mediated through an individual perspective, whereby the respective private interests are included in the promise of progress of the whole. The legitimacy of executive state power is based on two rules: first, neutrality of legal institutions regulating private property relations; second, perceiving national interests in the sense of the dynamic of its own community and in contrast to all non-national interests.

These two moments are now playing an important role in the enforcement of modern social forms — not just as a real process, but also as an ideological reference point for the mobilization of the population. This is particularly true for recuperative modernization, in which the state's sovereignty came to prominence with both the dissolution of traditional social structures and the implementation of the modern social form. In the "Islamic" countries, this development came along with the historical marks of colonialism, the subsequent national modernization regime, and finally — this regime's rejection — as political Islamism. The respective contradictions, both of the recuperative modernization regimes as well as Islamism whose appearance on the historical stage they provoked, can be illustrated alongside the previously outlined two moments of national legitimacy.

Anticolonial Liberation in the World of Abstract Domination

In the European colonies and quasi-colonies, colonial policy and colonial institutions were subjected to the economic and political interests of the centers, a practice legitimated by the racist devaluation of the colonized population. Against the system of colonial domination now stand anticolonial liberation movements in the name of the nation or the people, which attack this domination on two related levels of public interest. On one hand, this was done with the demand for independence of the newly created public authority from the colonial interests. The national liberation movements stood against the particular interests of the colonial powers for political independence and for their own sovereign, who would follow the dictates of neutrality. On the other hand, linked to this was the call for the redistribution of the abstract wealth over which state authority presided and to distribute it among nationally defined members — that is, to realize national interests for the sake of their community.

Compared with colonial and imperialist oppression and exploitation, this step is undoubtedly progressive, as is the liberation of individuals from the mechanisms of racially legitimated coercive conditions, from social exclusion, and from violence by the colonial apparatus. Last but not least, the hope that the wretched living conditions of the majority of the population would improve rallied the anticolonial struggles. Still, the legitimacy and thus the practice of the national liberation movements remained essentially within the framework of abstract political universality. The independence strived for was not only independence from colonial rule, but rather a determinate content of a specific manner — namely, the constitution of a form of law independent of private interests. Thus modern forms of domination — that is, abstract domination — replaced the repressive structures of colonialism. The right to social participation and a secure livelihood for all, rights formulated during the fight for liberation, resulted in a social structure that precisely excludes this end. And so the upheaval of social relations proceeded for the most part not towards the differentiation and expansion of a national bourgeoisie, but towards "socialist" mobilization of labor under the direct supervision of the state. In these circumstances, its function was not limited to "general development," like building public infrastructure, but also included the immediate content of this private relationship, the production of abstract social wealth. Insofar as the state appeared as the general contractor of labor-form mobilization, it manifested the "will of the people" in the triumvirate of production, expended labor, and income. The state control of recuperative modernization was based essentially on the latecomers to modernization, in the cities where the redevelopment of the national space was also driven by the industrialization program of a nation state. Exemplary here was the

Germany of the nineteenth century. Industrialization should lead to a general revolution in the productive base. Within this process, the categories of labor and money are provided, as well as the political sovereign, who was to bring about this development. Nasser did so in Egypt in the 1950s. He pointedly expressed the clear difficulties of implementing a commodity-producing system when he said in a speech to striking workers: "In any case it is impossible today to raise the standard of living of workers. In order to do that we need to give them money, and to do that it is our duty to increase production by creating industries. To offer you any other prospect would be to deceive you. The only way which permits us to raise the standard of living of the workers is construction and labor."[18] With the universalization of the production of abstract wealth, private, individual interests simultaneously and necessarily took on a universal, social form. Money and labor increasingly became the center of social mediation such that the individual was ever more relegated to the context of personal relationships.

Beneath the surface of state intervention, which increasingly placed social reproduction on the basis of labor power and income, a fundamental change took place in the social fabric that effected every aspect of life. This change was both visible and tangible in phenomena such as the rural exodus and soaring urbanization, the disintegration of traditional family relationships, and integration into objectified social functions. The colonial rulers had already partially transformed social relationships into commodified exchanges and the play of private interests. Now, modernizing dictatorships fundamentally revolutionized the social mediations. Strikingly, even the greatest thinkers of the national liberation movements refer without bias to the basic contradiction between the general interest and "selfish" interest, by presupposing both as given. This is evident from Frantz Fanon's indictment of colonial rule: namely, that it had failed to produce a bourgeoisie, which is precisely the class representative of private interests essential for further national development. The national dictatorships of modernization attempted to make up this gap as quickly as possible through a comprehensive political and economic development program: "The task is either to develop the national bourgeoisie, or, if that was too weak or too dependent on Western interests and influences, for the state to take it over. In light of this theory, the Communist parties in many former colonies — and especially in the Arab world — allied themselves with nationalist parties, representing an indigenous bourgeoisie, or even a military-bureaucratic state."[19] Everyone from nationalists to the state bureaucracy, from the socialists to the communist parties, shares a common position regarding the radical reformulation of social interaction under the guiding star of abstract universalism, namely, of the bourgeois categories of reason and labor. Freedom and equality before the law fall under the same framework as the mediation of labor and money. The anticolonial liberation movements made the enforcement of modern bourgeois forms their explicit program. Where attempts at continued social organization and the appropriation of social wealth developed (such as councils or cooperatives), they were relatively quickly suppressed or incorporated into state institutions.

The history of recuperative modernization shows how difficult it was to gain access to the economic standards of the West, especially the world market. Given the one-sided, metropole-aligned economy with minimal vertical integration and an orientation towards agriculture and raw materials, the starting conditions for producing value for the world system were very bad. The state needed not only to create the basis for a wide range of economic production (provision of necessary infrastructure from roads to communications, the expansion of public administration, creating an education system, and so on), but also, as a key economic agent, to begin the production of abstract wealth. But the concept of "import substitution," which was followed in almost all developing countries and designed to reduce dependence on foreign capital goods imports by developing their own self-supporting industry, was ultimately unsuccessful. Most industrial production was limited to simple assembly, minimally vertically integrated and lagging behind the international standard, so the dependence upon high-quality and expensive capital goods remained. At the same time, exports became more expensive due to overvalued exchange rates, such that the increasing need for foreign exchange led to a growing national debt. Even more serious was, however, that the aim of general, self-sustaining industrial production failed on its own terms. Not only did the unassailable lead in productivity of the industrial centers play a central role, but most important of all was the basic contradiction of trying to build a differentiated and complex system of production under the rule of a central planning bureaucracy. The cumbersome command economy was structurally incapable of organizing flexible manufacturing processes, such as are created almost automatically under conditions of capitalist competition, which is the dictate of the market. Overall, therefore, the modernization regime became entangled in structural contradictions that finally plummeted the nation state's politics of industrialization into crisis.

The Ruins of Modernization and the Emergence of Islamism

The dynamics of abstract wealth production in the "developing countries" increasingly lost its momentum in the 1970s and 1980s due to the lacking generalization of its industrial basis. Even the increasing oil revenues in some central "Islamic" countries could not compensate for this industrial stagnation, contributing instead to a one-sided orientation of the economy towards these sources of revenues, substantially benefiting only a minority. And so the system of abstract relationships was generalized, but not their content: not the abstract production of wealth. Islam expert Gilles Kepel dates the beginning of the "Islamic period" to the early 1970s, and more precisely to the first "oil crisis."[20] Saudi Arabia, as an ideal core country and source of material support for Islamism, rose at that time due to rising oil prices, becoming the leading power in the region. This refers in part to the last, failed attempt to develop an independent national economy. On the other hand, there is a certain irony: in spite of Islamists' anti-Western and anti-American polemics and demarcation they materially remain attached to the IV-drip of the local valorization of value due to their reliance on the shift to a petrodollar economy.

For the populace, the implementation of modern forms of socialization meant, especially in regions that were once predominantly rural, that social relations were transformed by the process of modernization: a sprawling urban migration to the cities took place; and urban ways of life prevailed. Initially, this change represents a real improvement of material conditions, because within the newly established framework of abstract forms of relationship, opportunities for advancement and participation emerged. The ideology of national progress depended explicitly on the program of universal participation in abstract wealth. This first transition, perceived as a largely positive social change, was over no later than the mid-1970s, mainly due to a sharp population increase, and a young generation who did not see material conditions improving and lost the perspective of the social whole.[21] Bernard Schmid describes the situation in the period of national progress for Algeria:

> A majority lived with the expectation that progress in the development of the country would in the long run benefit the "lower" echelons of society. This hope was in line with reality insofar as schools and transport links were all built in the seventies, and the Algerian population benefited from relatively developed social systems, such as a free health care (in 1974). Picture this: sitting in the last car, the occupants could bear hardship as long as they had the impression that the entire train — the whole of Algerian society — was going forward and so was also transporting them towards the target. But the situation becomes unbearable if the passengers in the rear wagon have the impression that they have been suspended from the rest of the train and the front of the car is going on alone. This perception intensified in the course of the eighties: social inequalities grew, corruption became ever more obvious and determined access to artificially discounted consumer goods — which are imported by state structures, but are often sold in parallel channels on a shadow sector and distributed

there.[22]

The situation in the regions with failed modernization is now felt more generally, causing economic frictions to be experienced as comprehensive social misery and the utter loss of prospects. This train of events puts the prospect of individuals participating in the blessings of the national whole ever more into question. On one hand, the system of private interests prevailed. On the other hand, the content of said system, the production of abstract wealth, remained very fragile, so that a growing proportion of the population had no access to this wealth. Islam scholar Olivier Roy in his study *The Islamic Way West* has convincingly shown the extent to which the social transformation process was generalized and the individual standpoint is now the foundation of social relations. He shows the close relationship between the "Islamic" countries and the West in key social developments. The disintegration of traditional social relations has led to a matrix of individualization, which Roy has also identified as a central feature of Islamic fundamentalism. As in the West, the situation is dominated by strategies based on professional success and individual performance.[23] He describes the current situation as a "crisis of indigenous cultures," the moment of a "process of deculturation" in that the "social authority of religion is gone," and there is a general loss of "social authority."[24] The current re-Islamization, Roy argues, has the secularized concept of the individual as its foundation. It appears from the will of the individual" and leads to the "individual reformulation of personal religiosity."[25] "Central is the self, and consequently the individual. [...] Currently taking place among Muslims is an individualization of belief and behavior, especially among those living in the West. The ego is highlighted, each strives for self-actualization and looks for an individual reconstruction of his attitude to religion. [...] Individualization is a prerequisite for the Westernization of Islam, and that's what happened."[26] In the process, Roy distinguishes between the form and the content of praxis: Westernization means something more than just the West. The content may be different, but the "form of individuality is the same."[27] The modernization of social relations within the formation of the nation state took place therefore as the transformation of relations towards the position of the abstract individual. The process of "acculturation" and the change of the "common grammar of social relations" evolved in the horizon of modern bourgeois relations on the basis of private interest and "free will."[28]

Therefore, it is anything but surprising that in these regions the generalized private subject position, in one of his main fields of activity, is the consumer. With the generalization of private interest and the individualization of living conditions, the Western consumerist attitude arrives. From the get-go, little remains of the imagined collective future or the belief in the progress of the nation as a whole. Rather, now the abstract universality of "the spirit of the people" faces the abstract privacy of the individual. This is clearly noticeable, for instance, in Algeria: "after industrial policy has been abandoned in favor of free trade and the importation of Western commodities, the predominant fascination with the colorful world of commodities is, for the time being, displayed on the shleves of specially established state supermarkets."[29] This "free will" given to the abstract individual is subject to the temptations of the increasingly colorful commodity aesthetic that makes up an essential moment in the world of modern subjectivity. But an increasingly large part of the population cannot participate in the consumer world because the experiments spawned by recuperative modernization produced not a system of mass production, mass employment, and mass consumption, but rather one of mass poverty and exclusion, where living and working conditions are increasingly precarious, and where a rapid increase in the informal sector followed.

Large parts of the population did not perceive the mechanisms of social exclusion as an expression of economic contradictions and the structural crisis of the overall system but interpreted them through their individual, biased subject positions. Thus general misery appeared to be due to corruption, that is, in the illegal mixing of "general operations" with the private interests of executives. The national *nomenklatura* procured gross benefits through their privileged access to the material resources of the public. This widespread perception was not entirely wrong, as corruption, obvious to all, grew along with the economy. However, this confuses cause and effect. For the ever-increasing diffusion of private interests in the public sector can be considered a consequence of the fact that the state was interested in erecting itself as abstract universality against particular interests, along with the failure of recuperative modernization. From the individuals' perspective, the social regression appears to be caused by the *nomenklatura*, who are responsible for the crisis. The latter have driven the sovereign into the abyss, in that they wrongly used him in terms of their selfish, individual interests, rather than as a general framework for the mediation of diverse, social, private interests, thus creating appropriate private development opportunities. The structural failure to generalize the production of abstract wealth appeared, from the perspective of their own social frame of reference, to be due to the individual misconduct of the "privileged elite" governing the country.[30]

With the national state bureaucracy the concept of the nation largely came into disrepute. The charge that the national elite oppressed and exploited the individual was, retrospectively for the entire period of nationalism (i.e., of recuperative nation building), interpretively integrated into the anticolonial period. Thus, the national phase appeared to be an extension of colonial domination and exploitation, except the bearer of this rule was now not the colonial powers, but cliques of the state bureaucracy, which were characterized as spittle-licking lackeys of foreign powers, especially the United States. And just as the colonial powers kept their colonies in a relation of economic dependency and allowed them no independent political sovereignty, the postcolonial regime undermined the social order further, thereby causing general social malaise. Because they pursued only their particular interests rather than serving the public good, the sphere of the independent sovereign itself had been discredited. The result of this is the view that nationalism is identical with the particularist position and responsible for the increasing exclusion of the population from social participation. The independent sovereign, according to this logic, broke with the principle of equality that is attached to sovereignty, which, after all, enshrines the idea of equal rights for all. The anti-imperialism and anticolonialism of the past era were now actualized against the failure of modernization and became largely identical with nationalism. In this way, Islamism was a reservoir for a new anti-imperialism, one able to give political expression to the growing social upheaval and the resulting social tensions — though not without also installing certain religious motives in this protest. This results in a general shift of the voice of social protest in a direction that had heretofore been politically marginal. A common reference point for the different Islamic movements was the criticism of the oppression of national regimes as particularistic, accomplices of the West, particularly of the United States and of Israel. The Western Hemisphere and its democratic system becomes a symbol of particularism against which Islam's universality is asserted: "Western values are Western values, Islamic values, however, are universal values."[31] As a counterpoint to the particularistic point of view of foreign rule, Islamists argue for the organization of a "just society" in which the same law (understood, however, within the meaning of "Islamic law") for all would be guaranteed through the transcendence of sovereignty, the sovereignty of God. Both the movements of political Islam in the early 1980s as well as today, especially terrorist networks, share this belief. The law as the embodiment of divine order and as the central goal to be achieved was the reference point both for the "Islamic revolution" in Iran and al-Qaeda. Before analyzing this ideological shift and showing that the reformulation of the general religious standpoint reflects the contradictions of the global crisis, I would first like to clarify some statements by Osama bin Laden, Ayman al-Zawahiri, and Sayyid Qutb.

The "Spirit of the People" According to bin Laden, Ayman al-Zawahiri, and Sayyid Qutb

We begin with three quotes from George W. Bush and Osama bin Laden:

> "These people despise freedom. It is a fight for freedom. It is a struggle, so that we can say to all lovers of freedom: We will not let them terrorize us..."[32]

> "They have declared war on us. And the United States, they are hunting. As long as I am president, we are determined to be firm and strong in our pursuit of these people who kill innocent people because they hate freedom."[33]

> "Bush said...that we hate freedom....On the contrary, we want our country to return to freedom; pursuing your freedom destroys our freedom."[34]

The last quotation is from a video release by bin Laden entitled "Message to the American People." The entire text is instructive insofar as the theoretical framework — if you want to call it that — is quite familiar: first, freedom for the people and security, but also values such as justice, humanity, work, business, and common sense. So all terms that reference the modern form of socialization. The train of thought he develops in his message to the American people reflects the tradition of anti-imperialist liberation struggles as well as the dimension of sovereignty strived for, the "spirit of the people." The dominance of the West, that is, the United States and Israel, means that Muslim countries are doomed, according to bin Laden, to suffering, injustice, and misery. Since the dominant nations are only pretending to defend freedom, the war of the oppressed peoples, the war of the Jihadist, is not offensive, but rather defensive. The United States is a repressive regime, similar to the military and neo-feudal regimes in Islamic countries who are dominated by "pride and arrogance, greed and corruption."[35] Bush, too, prevailed due to his family clan, partly by choice and partly by open fraud and lies, similar to the regimes in the "Islamic" countries. Bin Laden characterizes Bush and Bush Senior in the following: "He transferred to his son, who passed a 'Patriotic Act' under the pretext of fighting terrorism, both despotism and a contempt for freedom."[36]

Bin Laden and al-Qaeda's position is therefore not one of implacable opposition between "Islam" and the "West," or between the "Orient" and the "Occident," in the sense the Western culturalists (like Huntington) discuss the "clash of civilizations." In contrast to this, al-Qaeda's position is much closer to the abstract universality of the public interest. After all, their criticism is not directed against the "American people" as a whole, as a cultural community, but rather claims to represent their "true interests." The Patriot Act, bin Laden claims, shows the despotic rule of the Bush clan, which will be consolidated with the help of this law, and will restrict the freedom of individuals and control them. This rhetoric reproduces exactly the perspective of Islamic anti-imperialists regarding the national development regimes, which they held responsible for suppressing the "true interests" of the people. Insofar as it is a global network, al-Qaeda transcends this perspective, since it is not limited to "Islamic" countries and seeks to combat state bureaucratic cliques as well. They universalize the standpoint of a global framework, and claim to be the true representatives of all individual interests in the context of the abstract universality of the global scale. It follows therefore that they attempted to mobilize the American people against the assumed particularism of the U.S. government and the U.S. oligarchy: "The real losers are you, the American people and its economy."[37] Bin Laden refers not only to the position of abstract universality in the form of the "American people" but also that of its immanent contrary, individual freedom in the economic sphere of the market. Both moments warn against the "greed" of the private interests of the Bush clique, asserting that their policies only respond to the particular interests of private companies. The American people in turn have been manipulated by these economic cliques and have made a mistake. The end of the message reads: "Know that it is better to return to the good than to remain in error and that reasonable people sacrifice neither their safety, nor their money, nor their children for a liar in the White House."[38] Bin Laden here appeals to the private interests of isolated individuals, along with their essential attributes of money and family, which under the given situation could not be realized. Reason should assist in the effort to establish a rule where both the individual and the totality of the people would have a place — and bin Laden claims this as the rule of al-Qaeda and the global Islamist movement. They are the true representative of the universal law, he claims, being based upon Islamic law, while, on the other hand, democracy represents the rule of special interests and of private interests by certain power groups at the expense of the public. This means not only that the national modernization regimes, with their nationalism, but also that the Western democracies are representatives of vested interests.

Al-Qaeda's chief theorist, Ayman al-Zawahiri engages the dialectic of general and private interests, even more thoroughly. Just like bin Laden, he identifies democracy with the rule of special interests over the standpoint of universality. According to al-Zawahiri, in a democracy, the parliament, or, more precisely, individual parliamentarians sit in the place of the people. "In democracy, the legislature is the people, represented by a majority of seats in parliament. These delegates are men and women, Christians, communists, and secularists. What they say becomes law, that must be imposed on all, by which taxes are levied and people are executed."[39] In the parliamentary systems, deputies rule according to their own private interests, which they impose on "the people" through the law, instead of the sovereign, who represents the "real interest" of the people. In this respect, democracy is not the right form to achieve the universality of the law, but instead subjugates the people under the arbitrary will of certain private interests. The claim of universal interest thus corresponds to a basic level of common anti-imperialist argument. Al-Zawahiri thus shares the latter's total blindness regarding the general standpoint as the dominance of the abstract form of sociality. One could claim that it finally becomes crazy when this perspective, instead of criticizing a universal standpoint as such, formulates the latter in neo-religious terms: "These people, who are making laws for all in a democracy, revere idols. There are those rulers whom God [...] has mentioned, 'and do not take others as lord next to Allah.'"[40] The parliamentary system, fundamentally corrupted by individual interests, culminates in the arrogance of being the supreme sovereign. It puts the private interests of a few in the place of the public interest, a handful of idols in the place of the one God.

This conception of divine universal law was already formulated by Sayyid Qutb, the most important theorist of political Islamism. He interprets the condition, "if people worship people, and human beings claim that they, as such, have the right to be entitled obedience, and the right, as creatures of law, to set values and set rules," as the presumption of divine sovereignty. "This happens both in democracies and in dictatorships: the first divine characteristic is law [...] to be able to establish rules and doctrines, to adopt laws and regulations, to establish values, and to judge as referee. [...] To elevate terrestrial systems to this Right, in one way or another, in all cases, the case is decided by a group of people, and this group, which imposes on others their laws, values, and ideas, consists of mere terrestrial men, some of whom obey men instead of God, and allow men to claim to be divine. They worship men instead of God, even if they do not bow down before them or fall on their knees."[41] And Qutb added, "This is the difference between Muslims and those who are committed to each other instead of God. This clearly shows who the Muslims are. They are the ones who worship God alone."[42]

Transcendental Legitimacy and Divine Sovereignty

The position Islamists oppose to particular interests is the public interest understood in terms of legality and justice, but related not to the secular context of a nation, rather to a higher divine authority and metaphysical sovereignty. The enlightened, Western cultural warriors understand this orientation of the Islamists as proof of their premodern or, alternatively, regressive and totalitarian backwardness, and also use it to promote their progressive civilization on the basis of modern reason. The enlightened Westerners' preferred critique of Islam is the lack of separation between religion and politics. In return the Islamists argue for the achievement of universal law in relation to the highest divine authority. The question is whether this alleged identity between the monotheistic God and the unity of the Act is actually a premodern and archaic worldview, the expression of a premodern social structure, or whether, on the contrary, it corresponds to the forms of civic association specific to bourgeois society. Looking more closely at the position of Islamists with respect to traditional religiosity, one must first clearly state that they have vehemently fought the religious traditions and cultural heritage of Islam. "The main targets of Neofundamentalists are the so-called Muslim Cultures." They "speak against local forms of Islam, such as exist in Egypt and Morocco, and lead a relentless fight against old traditions... for example, against all the 'saints cults,' such as the 'Ziarat' in Central Asia or the 'Moussem' in North Africa, a religious pilgrimage to draw in people to pray at the graves of the local patron saint."[43] The premodern communities were — both socially and in their religious practices — the opposite of a strict standardization of social relations in general laws. Traditional Islam integrated a variety of pre-Islamic moments, such as the ancient Egyptian cult of the dead. These adaptations of pre-Islamic religiosity and diverse religious practices have been a thorn in the side to the Islamists because their perspective of the reign of eternal law requires the production of a uniform basis for all Muslims and therefore includes the task of breaking up the diversified pattern of religious and cultural life. Under premodern conditions, focusing social reality on a standard principle of statutory form and politics was unthinkable. The modern character of Islam aspires to just that. Insofar as the secular regimes of modernization have not ousted traditional social relations in favor of the system of abstract social mediation, the Islamists continue that work under the banner of "eternal law." Their struggle is thus directed not only against the national regime and its "Western backers" but also against traditional cultural and religious social structures. Both of these together, according to the Islamists, are complicit in the miserable state in which the "Islamic" countries as a whole find themselves. The resistance against neocolonialism, understood as domination by the national regime, is linked to the struggle against traditional Islamic cultural remnants, insofar as both hold responsibility for the social decline of the "Islamic" order. This idea mainly comes from the already-cited Egyptian thinker of Islam, Sayyid Qutb, who traces impoverishment and social disintegration back to the fact that the "Islamic" society is falling away from the only true social and religious practice: the focus on a single principle, one given by divine law. The heterogeneous and diverse religious heritages that exist in the "Islamic" countries appear to him as equivalent to the apostasy of the individualist form of legality, that marks the depraved and dissolute life of Western decadence.

In this, the Islamists proclaim the identity of religion and politics, discredited in the West, not through arresting the development of Islamism in the premodern and religious Middle Ages, but rather in the context of the specific standardization of the practice of life within commodified modernity. The desire to orient the social whole according to the criteria of reasonable religious legalism corresponds to the enforcement of abstract forms of relationship. The ambiguity of Enlightenment thought is that it thought itself to be antireligious and secular, but that the abstract rationality of modernity is in fact based on the transcendental nature of social mediation. The Enlightenment philosophy of Kant at least was consistent inasmuch as it formulated forms of reasons as otherworldly, as a matter of metaphysics, independent of concrete human experience and sensible practice. The actions of individuals, in accordance to the Kantian foundation of bourgeois reason, must correspond to a "transcendental" framework a priori, and only this metaphysical framework established the specific conduct of subjects. As we saw earlier, this is connected by the forms of modern rationality to a system where freedom and legal status are understood as expressions of abstract private relationships.

It is more coherent to understand the law of Islamism that is oriented at the beyond in the context of this transcendentality, rather than as an extension of "backward" social relations. The concept of sovereignty came first with modernity and its system of abstract social relations, as did the categories of the "will of the people" and the uniform statutory form. The metaphysics of the divine law of the Islamists should, therefore, be seen within the horizon of modern bourgeois relations, as formulated by Kant in *The Metaphysics of Morals*.

This connection is also plausible insofar as, in the process of crisis in its entirety, the sovereign state as the realization of the universal standpoint is eroded. The sovereign is thus no longer the authority that mediates diverse private interests and provides for the operation of the abstract whole. So, where do those who seek legitimacy, who demand, in the face of growing social polarization, "social equality," "justice," and "equal rights for all"? No longer upon the earth, a real-metaphysical sphere of the unconsciously created mesh of private relations, the nation or the state, but rather only in the imagination of a supernatural, otherworldly realm. Therefore the metaphysics of the legal form ascends to the heavens and the universality of private interest finds, as its destination, divine sovereignty. That this transcendence is assumed to be identical with the "spirit of the people" has become clear in the texts of bin Laden, al-Zawahiri, and Qutb. The transcendental foundation of the general will in Islamism seems anything but arbitrary. The positivist and flattened Enlightened perspective of today cheats these dimensions, in that it assumes its constructed counterpart to be theocracy and cultural retrogression; it thus hides the problem of its own foundations.

In the early days of the enforcement of civil commerce systems, to interpret Kant's *Critiques* explicitly, the forms of "free will" and legality were far from obvious. The transformation of social relations was so fundamental that a non-negligible interest in the self-legitimation of these forms existed. An important aspect was to resolve the apparent contradiction: how one can present the comprehensive and non-empirical general spirit in the legal form of an appropriate state representation. The problem therefore consists in the attempt to realize the "spirit of the people" in the institutions of the public sphere, or rather the resolution of the fundamental tension between the real-metaphysical universality of the form of relating, on one hand, and the concreteness of a governing, legislative body, on the other hand. In the wake of the French Revolution, this tension was expressed in the form of an opposition between the sacred and the all-encompassing nation and the respective representatives of the national whole. The distrust of the representatives of state power from the perspective of the general position of the people was, in the course of revolutionary events, ever-increasingly virulent and partly caused the radicalism that sought to end the separation of the people from state power. Robespierre's criticism of the French Constitution of 1791 zeroes in on this logic, describing a "strange, fully representative system of government, without any counter weight to the sovereignty of the people" — "such a government is the most intolerable of all despotisms."[44]

The events surrounding the year 1789 in France are now long past, but the fundamental tension between the real-metaphysical universality of the form of sociability and its concrete realization in the state legislative authority remains. And this contradiction is most apparent in the Islamic reformulation of sovereignty. It is precisely in the diffusion of private interests into the sphere of the government system in the failed national modernization regimes that the state bureaucracy is "the most intolerable of all despotisms." By contrast, Islamism was consistent and moved the standpoint of universality away from the paradigm of the nation, and gave it a new religious upholstering. In view of the canonization of the nation or people, as is characteristic of all nation-state formation processes, the reference to a religious foundation presented itself. Islamism and the "Islamic revolution" thus occur as the historical legacy of national liberation. Responding to the discrediting of the national fabric in the crisis regions, Islamism, however, reclothes the general spirit in religious terms. Central to this revival of the general spirit is the right of the excluded to participate in modern forms of socialization. This claim is asserted against the corrupt regimes of modernizing dictatorships through a religious reformulation of the ideals of equality and justice, asserted against the dictators who have been accused of increasing the social exclusion of broad sectors of the population and of particular advantages to others, thus violating constitutionally promised equality.

From the Machine of Progress to the Legislative Form

The guiding star of the national independence movements was the nation as the subject of real social progress, repressing and destroying traditional structures in favor of a new national unity of the whole. Related to this was the right to bring about the production of abstract wealth. This coincided with an emphasis on the progress and development of productive forces, which aimed to revolutionize, both technically and organizationally, the production of wealth, and to focus it on the utilization of labor power. By cranking up the state-sponsored progress machine, the idea of progress was linked to creating increasingly rich forms of sensual gratification for the individual. In Islamism, this moment of material modernization takes place only in the background. Its program for liberation from domination, identified as neocolonialism, systematically masks the plane of the conditions of wealth production. Instead, the Islamists' program is reduced to the dimension of compliance with the law given by God as shaped by Muhammad. Islamism as a political force obliges itself to enforce Islamic values and principles against "depraved" society. This is the background for the integrated politics of moralization of the Islamist movement in terms of abiding by sharia law. The real social content of the legal form, the abstract production of wealth, is, for the Islamists, only a minor problem that will be corrected by the restoration of the correct law without any further action. "If the company once again respects its religious commandments and its cultural identity," so the idea goes, "then everyone would find a place in it."[45] "The reform of the soul should precede [...] the reform of the state. Policy does not help in the purification of the soul."[46] Hence the non-concrete, porous, and cloudy provisions on specific social goals. Ultimately, the control of the individual in relation to compliance with legal statutes remains the central content of government action. In Afghanistan, when in power, the Taliban realized this program with a sort of postnational, Jacobin dictatorship of virtue. With the actual social contradictions and tensions due to the continuing deterioration of the material situation, the Islamists were distant and ultimately helpless, or rather helpless and ultimately distanced: "In power (Iran) or in the opposition (Egypt), Islamists have so far always been unable to cope with the social and economic changes in which they participate. The revolutionary social message [...] of the Islamists has faded in favor of a conservative program: the insistence on a 'sharia-ization' of constitutional law."[47] This legal orientation as the sole content of state action only reflects the ongoing crisis process. The thrust of Islamism is the defense and delimitation of the outside, so that the inside can be brought under legal order. "For the radical Islamists, the priority is more to 're-establish their own morals' in their own society so that they can be 'healthy' and can withstand the 'cultural aggression of the West.'"[48] This reduction of the task of government to upholding the law once again documents the core state function. Especially in the ongoing crisis process, the legal form excludes direct social relations and entrenches the individual in the system of abstract socialization.

Conspiracy Theory

It would therefore be too simple to characterize the religious reformulation of the legal form as a mere revival of Islamic anti-imperialism in the tradition of anticolonial movements. This emphasis on the legal form makes clear that this is a matter of the restoration of a social order that threatens to fall apart at the seams. The subjugation of the individual to divine law has to be judged as a psychosocial way to work through a crisis that involves, and to process a general hopelessness regarding the possibility of effective change. Its powerlessness regarding the structural crisis and the decomposition of abstract social connection forces out the interpretive paradigms that exceed the horizon of "classical" anticolonial resistance in the phase of national liberation. The real threat of the dissolution of social relationships is made noticeable — among other things in the ideological matrix — when one tries to explain Islamism's powerlessness in the face of social collapse. Ultimately these explanations are a projective defense mechanism that explains general misery as a result of a conspiracy, of external interventions and interests, so that it can continue to believe in the fiction of a just society. The cry of "equal rights for all" is at the same time the projection of an identity wholeness in a religious-legal collective. The subjectivity threatened by this process of social breakdown attributes that threat to the external domination of certain social groups, and creates, at the same time, an identity, a collective "grandiose self" (Heinz Kohut) in an imagined community of the faithful. Conspiracy theory thus supplements the anti-imperialist critique of the failed modernization regime as an alleged neocolonial system. This perspective informs the entirety of Islamism. Behind the disintegration of the imagined harmonious whole was not only a corrupt elite who had pushed their private interests to the fore while neglecting the overall interest of the public, or who had passed on that, but rather an authority that secretly and systematically worked on behalf of a plan. The national elites did not simply act according to their private advantage — which they were doing more effectively in the wake of the crisis — rather, they were primarily puppets of the true masterminds of the decomposition, who are identified, depending on the perspective, with the West as a whole, or at least with the United States and Israel.

In Algeria, this pattern of projecting conspiracy theories was already present in the founding manifesto of the FIS whose name — "Islamic Salvation Front" — references the sense of threat it produced. It says: "The State providing service to the colonizer, in his undertaking of war on our religion and our dignity and by questioning the unity of our country, is a clear aggression against our sovereignty and our personnalité (i.e., identity)."[49] It denounces "the existence of elements inside the state apparatus that are hostile to our religion and are the only agents of the executive from colonialist plans. [...] It is vital to thwart this plot by a purge of government institutions from all telltale elements on one hand, and resolute action to end the sabotage of the entire country, on the other hand."[50] Here the alleged close links between the strong unity of a country and its related institutional framework fade into the perspective of current Islamism, which, however, increasingly favors a vague territorial identity of spiritual community of all Muslims, known as the Ummah. At heart it is always the same: to attribute to threatening external influences or claim as already foregone the loss of the unity and order of the state, which will be recovered through the consistent application of the law. The process of disintegration of the system of the abstract form of socialization is thus explained away as due to external forces, who conspired to bring it about. These conspiracy theories, which are an antisemitic form of understanding the crisis, prove once again that Islamism is a child of modernization or a crumbling form of modernization and not a premodern phenomenon.

Conclusion

Islamism reveals a specific current that counteracts, through a religiously inverted prosecution of the sovereignty of the law, the symptoms of social decay and of the global process of exclusion from the universe of abstract wealth production through a religiously inverted prosecution of the sovereignty of the law. The contradiction between the form of social relations and the crisis of its content is resolved in the affirmation of religious reformulation of the form of the universal standpoint.

Developments in the "Islamic" countries are, however, to be valued as a kind of negative preview to the processes that began long ago in the capitalist centers, and that continue to accelerate, albeit in different concrete forms, of course. Putin as a paragovernmental "godfather" represents one pole: the resolution of the universal into the realm of individual interest. Islamism represents the other: as the revival of the standpoint of universality in the form of a dictatorship of moral values and principles. Just as the implementation and universalization of commodity production was characterized by a qualitatively new form of violent domination, so too does the universalization of exclusion represent a release and potentiation of these moments of domination and violence. To look at this more closely in all its forms and levels requires that the irrational aspect of free will, law, and the system of binding together of free agents to support a "rational" whole, be discussed more extensively than in the case here. Then one could also clarify the previous section's question — the manner in which the community becomes charged with an identity, whether the "great self" (Kohut) or the "grandiose We" which is bound up with the universal standpoint of Islamism more precisely. This "we" is the collective equivalent of the masculine subjectivity of modernity, whose obsessive goal is to reassure itself perpetually of its own perfection, and which is ultimately willing to sacrifice the world for this desired perfection. In this respect the collective subjects, as they are brought into being by Islamism, are not just its passive products, but themselves contribute to its active, propulsive moments.

Notes

1. Hamburg-based writer and publisher Ralph Giordano claims, for example, regarding the building of the Mosque in Cologne, that it is "not the Mosque, but Islam itself [that] is the problem," and adds that the integration of Muslims in Germany has totally failed and that it could never have been otherwise. In the end, these "millions of people" come from a "completely different culture." "So I wonder," he adds, "how someone can consider the Koran, this archaic charter of a sheep-herding culture, to be holy, and how it can form the basis of law....One precludes the other" (*Kölner Stadtanzeiger*, 1 June 2007).

2. One can see both how far the culturalist perspective has spread and how unquestioned it remains in the collective imagination given the terminology used to express it: from everyday speech to academic statements, people speak of "the Islamic world," of a "Muslim culture," and also, in a milder form, of the "Islamically-influenced countries" and "regions with an Islamic religious tradition," and so on. All these formulations are marked by a certain degree of culturalism and the idea of a unified culture characteristic "of Islam." To avoid this linguistic error, I will place "Islamic" in quotations marks. My goal is to take the relevance of the religious tradition in the process of modernization seriously without hypostasizing it as an independent being.

3. Of course, the universalism of equality under the law collapses in the face of the fundamental patriarchal power structures of modern social relations that are inherent in the bourgeois mode and become explicit in Islamic fundamentalism.

4. Radical social critique could find harmony here with deconstruction, if the focus were to reside only at the level of the construction of shared identities. However, the standpoint of generality remains at that level unthematized. This constructedness is valid at a general level, that is, nations and political systems are quite obviously historical products, which, as we know, did not take shape until the modern era, namely, in the last two centuries. However, they are at the same time the result of a process of mediation organized around the commodity form, a process

that takes place unbeknownst to individuals, the expression of a precise yet unwitting modern form of praxis. The state and the form of law are thus not just manipulative forms of sociality deployed symbolically through cultural structures, but result from the unconsciously executed praxis inside the system of commodity-based social relations. Nationalist state formation can therefore in no way be adequately formulated as the product or result of a simple "concept," as Benedict Anderson's constructivist formulation of "the invention of the nation" suggests. Through this conceptual idealism, nation-statehood is reduced to a matrix of semantic structures and meanings, thereby overlooking the central level of the state, justice, and nation as specific elements of commodity-formed social structures and the forms of free will constituted from it.

5. Marcel Gauchet. *Die Erklärung der Menschenrechte. Die Debatte um die bürgerlichen Freiheiten 1789* (Reinbek bei Hamburg: Rowohlt, 1991) 59.

6. Gauchet, *Menschenrechte* 19.

7. "This is about the reduction of social relations to the pure, direct opposition of the public and individual poles, which the Monarchy had promised and the 'democratic monarchy' (as Tocqueville once said) emphatically demanded" (*Menschenrechte* 51). With the dissolution of society into isolated individuals, a social relationship is constituted in which "there are no more corporations, there is henceforce the special interest of each individual and general interest. No one is permitted to grant an interest in-between these to citizens" (*ibid.*).

8. For more on this, see Peter Klein, "Das Wesen des Rechts" *Krisis* 24 (Bad Honnef: 2001) 73 and following.

9. The difference between concrete state power and the standpoint of generality continues to hold even if, in the wider sense, the "will of the people" is not always precisely separated from the explicit forms of the exercise of state power.

10. Karl Marx, *Grundrisse*, trans. Martin Nicolaus (New York: Penguin, 2005) 245, 244.

11. Marx, *Capital vol. I*. trans. Ben Fowkes (New York: Penguin, 1976) 280.

12. Sieyès makes clear in the debate over the Declaration that the core of the bourgeois constitution resides precisely in every citizen's relations of

free will over their respective property: "If we were to write a declaration for a new people....four words would suffice: equality of civil rights, that is, equal protection of each citizen in both his property and his liberty; equality of political rights, that is, the same influence in the formulation of law" (quoted in *Menschenrechte* iv).

13.   For more on this, see Klein, "Rechts" 51-64.

14.   "Rechts" 81.

15.   This illustration of the abstract form of Law in the feminine form of Lady Justice is both a euphemism and the expression of bourgeois, patriarchal projection. Kafka's Gatekeeper vividly depicts this androcentric projection and how the modern legal form represents a totally objective, unfeeling relation of violence and an insanely rational relationship marked by compulsion. For the individual units, law as the comprehensive cohesion of abstracted power means both inclusion under the spell of the legal form and the rendering impossible and exclusion of direct and consciously formed social bonds. The neutrality can also be found in Kafka, though in the generalized exclusion from authority of law conceived as neutral.

16.   In the post-Soviet states, this process has reached a remarkably mature stage: Putin (even if he is now Medvedev), the most powerful "public Godfather" to date, represents a new quality both in the spread of private interests and the pervasiveness of power. The dimensions the mafia-like penetration of the state apparatus have taken on is clearly documented in the execution of Russian journalist Anna Politkovskaya, whose journalism aimed directly at this widespread corruption. In her book, *Putin's Russia*, she shows how "Putin's new-old *nomenklatura* has taken corruption to new heights undreamed of under the Communists or Yeltsin. It is now devouring small and medium-sized businesses, and with them the middle class. It is giving big and super-big business, the monopolies and quasi-state enterprises, the opportunity to develop (in other words, they are the *nomenklatura's* preferred source of bribes). Indeed, they represent the kinds of businesses that produce the highest, most stable returns not only for their owners and managers but also for their patrons in the state administration. In Russia, big business does not exist without patrons (or 'curators') in the state administration. This misconduct has nothing to do

with market forces. Putin is trying to gain the support of the so-called *byvshie*, the *ci-devants*, who occupied leadership positions under the Soviet regime. Their hankering after old times is so strong that the ideology underpinning Putin-style capitalism is increasingly reminiscent of the thinking in the Soviet Union during the height of the period of stagnation in the late Brezhnev years — the late 1970s and early 1980s" ([New York: Owl Books, 2007] 82-83). The visibility of Putin's "patenting of the state" together with his crony and clique-economy has not, however, stopped the international political class or the public media from supporting him in this theater of self-reinvention as a trustworthy man of state. Overall, we can now speak of a period of transition, at least with respect to the capitalist centers. The trend in which private interests spread into the public sector to a such a degree, thus not only eroding the claim to state independence and neutrality but also ultimately calling it into question, is at any rate new only for these centers.

17. Olivier Roy, *The Islamic Way West* (Munich: Pantheon, 2006) 89-91.

18. Eckart Wörtz, "Die Krise der Arbeitsgesellschaft als Krise von Gewerkschaften: Die unabhängige Gewerkschaftsbewegung in Ägypten" (Diss. Friedrich-Alexander-Universität Erlangen-Nürnberg, 1991) 84.

19. Bernhard Schmid, *Algerien - Frontstaat im globalen Krieg? Neoliberalismus, soziale Bewegungen und islamistische Ideologie in einem nordafrikanischen Land* (Münster: Unrast, 2005) 75.

20. Gilles Kepel, *Das Schwarzbuch des Dschihad. Aufstieg und Niedergang des Islamismus* (München: Piper, 2002) 28 and following.

21. Kepel, *Schwarzbook* 86 and following.

22. Schmid, *Algerien* 89.

23. Roy, *Way West* 30.

24. *Way West* 38, 41 and following.

25. *Way West* 48, 43.

26. *Way West* 46.

27. *Way West* 48.

28. *Way West* 51.

29. *Algerien* 89.

30. *Algerien* 92.

31.   Mahathir, quoted in *Schwarzbuch* 120.

32.   Bush on 17 September 2001, quoted in Gilles Kepel and Jean-Pierre Milelli, *Al-Qaida. Texte des Terrors* (München: Piper, 2006) 137.

33.   *ibid.*

34.   *Al-Qaida* 129.

35.   *Al-Qaida* 132.

36.   *Al-Qaida* 133.

37.   *Al-Qaida* 134.

38.   *Al-Qaida* 136.

39.   *Al-Qaida* 329.

40.   *Al-Qaida* 330.

41.   *Al-Qaida* 332.

42.   *ibid.*

43.   *Way West* 255.

44.   Quoted in *Menschenrechte* 26.

45.   *Algerien* 127.

46.   *Way West* 244.

47.   *Way West* 84.

48.   *Algerien* 122.

49.   *Algerien* 121.

50.   *ibid.*

On the Current Global Economic Crisis: Questions and Answers

Robert Kurz (2010)

Over the course of the last three years, the economic crisis has generated three distinct phases of transformation: from the crisis of the real estate market to the crisis of the financial markets, from the crisis of the financial markets to the economic crisis, and from the economic crisis to the currency crisis. To what extent can these three phases of crisis be explained by means of your concept of a general economic crisis of capitalism?

These three phases of transformation merely constitute the surface of events. The crisis of the real estate market was the trigger for a crisis of the finance and debt systems, which had been smoldering for a long time. The latter crisis did not result from the so-called excesses of speculation that stood opposed to a presumably healthy "normal economy." Rather, the opposite was the case: the finance and debt bubbles were a consequence of a lack of actual valorization of capital. The credit superstructure has never been an external factor, but it has always been an integral component of capitalist commodity production. Over the course of the past two decades, this internal relation has been amplified into a structural dependence of the so-called real economy on the finance markets. Consequently, the financial crisis could only result in a historical collapse of short-term economic prospects.

All three phases were already contained in the close succession of crises following the first case of insolvency in Mexico in 1982. What initially only seemed to be a debt crisis on the periphery quickly reached the global capitalist centers. In the early 1990s, the Japanese real estate bubble burst and the Nikkei shrank down to a quarter of its peak level, and to this day Japan has not recovered from the resulting banking crisis and the stagnation of its national economy. In the mid-1990s the accumulated foreign currency (largely U.S.) debt of the tiger economies led to a financial collapse and resulted in currency crisis and sharp recession. Similar events occurred in the context of the Russian financial crisis at the end of the Yeltsin era and in Argentina toward the end of the twentieth century. The bursting of the dot-com bubble in 2001 resulted in the disappearance of the new markets, along with their astronomical market capitalization of small Internet and software enterprises, which led to a brief global economic recession. All of these crises had one thing in common: they were limited both to particular regions and to specific sectors and consequently seemed manageable, in particular by means of the stagnation or lowering of federal interest rates for which Japan had provided an example. This financial strategy on the part of the central banks (in particular the U.S. Federal Reserve), however, not only brought about the largest real estate bubble of all time but also further sustained a deficit economy of unexpected proportions that manifested itself primarily in the circulation of deficits between the United States and China, which was able to help support the global economy for a few years. Up until the early summer of 2008, economic institutes calculated that the boom would last for decades, despite the fact that they were well aware of the "imbalances" underlying the one-way street of Pacific exports. But the problem was strategically understated in the face of the apparent success of "finance-driven economic growth."

The bankruptcy of Lehman Brothers in the fall of 2008 revealed that the global finance bubble economy had in reality exhausted itself. The resultant global chain reaction simultaneously affected not only the large finance centers but also virtually every corner of the globe, from Iceland to Kazakhstan. The global deficit economy had run out of steam, and the collapse could no longer be prevented by additional monetary contributions from the central banks. Everywhere, the responsibility fell on state credit systems to a degree that surpassed even the war economies of the past. The bailout packages for the banking system did not fix the system but only temporarily kept it alive. Additional national economic stimulus programs were able to avert complete collapse, but ultimately the problem was merely displaced from finance bubbles onto state finances.

These consequences initially manifested themselves in the threat of Greek bankruptcy and the associated crisis of the European monetary union. Greece constitutes the weakest link in the eurozone, which in turn constituted the weakest link in the global economy, since the euro had (as an artificial currency) been based on wholly disparate national production levels and differing strengths of capital and as a result was only useful for the one-way flow of exports of a deficit economy. This currency crisis, however, is qualitatively different from those that preceded it: it is the avatar of a general crisis of state finance, which will not only affect the central E.U. states such as Germany, France, and Great Britain but also the United States and China.

Currently, we come across consolatory narratives everywhere, arguing that the bailout packages are restoring trust in a finance system in crisis and transforming the mountains of bad credit back into tradable credit, while the immense stimulus packages are providing the thrust for the development toward a new, self-sustaining global economy. This "all clear" discourse that is merely attached to the surface of things and whose life span is largely limited to the beginning of the next quarter does not, however, take into account the fundamental laws of a capitalist system. The crisis process that has been underway since 2008 not only constitutes the culmination of previous, partial signs of crisis — it is also distinct from previous economic and structural crises.

What has come to fruition here is a secular, immanent contradiction of the valorization of capital, which can be represented in two distinct stages. Initially, the development of productive forces that was a result of the necessity of competition led to a disproportionally rapid growth of fixed capital relative to labor force as a result of the increasingly scientific character of production. In order to employ even one single worker for the production of capital, it is necessary to mobilize a constantly increasing aggregate of real capital (increasing capital intensity). As a result, the "dead" advance costs of the valorization of capital increased to a degree that increasingly made it impossible to finance these costs out of the generated profit itself (machines only transfer previously generated value; they do not generate new value). The result of this was a historical expansion of the credit system that quickly encompassed all areas (corporations, the state, and private households). More and more frequently, it became necessary to draw on future surplus value (in the form of credit) in order to be able to generate actual surplus value. This contradiction was tenable as long as those credits could be paid back by means of ongoing surplus production. This compensatory mechanism, however, effectively disappeared with the onset of the third industrial revolution (microelectronics) at the end of the 1970s — labor power that generated actual surplus value was in this new historical dimension gradually rationalized out of existence. As a result, the chains of credits, which had to reach further and further into the future, threatened to break, and in fact did so in a number of areas. It is no accident, therefore, that the onset of the third industrial revolution coincides with the beginning of a series of financial, economic, and currency crises, the culmination of which we are experiencing today.

The so-called neoliberal revolution was not a subjective, political project. It was rather an escape strategy from the objective problems of a shortage of actual surplus production, based on the rapid acceleration of current processes without any change in direction.

What is now frequently naively presented as a historical error — that is, the large-scale deregulation of finance markets — was in reality the only strategy that allowed for a further deferral of the collapse of the global system. The valorization of capital was virtualized in the form of fictional capital that could no longer be matched by the actual substance of value. The debt economy mutated into a finance bubble economy (stocks and real estate) with increasingly adventurous derivatives. Over the course of two decades this relation developed into an unprecedented actual economy determined wholly by deficits. Indeed, it is necessary to refer to this kind of economic system as a deficit economy, since fictional valorization did not remain confined to the discrete sphere of finance as in previous moments in history but, in the form of the insubstantial consumer purchasing power of the middle class (alongside real-terms declines in wages), entered the real economy and thus fuelled the global boom. The millions of apparently real jobs in the one-sidedly oriented export industries are an optical illusion, since the sale of their products is based not upon real profit and wages but instead on the injections of a rotten credit superstructure and finance bubbles.

The release of large sums of money by the central banks, which completed the break with the monetaristic doctrine of neoliberalism (a limitation of the total sum of money), was itself already a desperate measure. The recent displacement of the problem onto the sphere of state credit does not solve the problem but instead only further delays it until the next expected collapse. There is no real potential for valorization for which state-sponsored bailout and stimulus programs could provide the thrust. Hence, the internal relation between financial, economic, and currency crisis reveals itself as an internal historical limit of capital on the level of the development of productive forces and the increasingly scientific character of production that it generates. The degree of negative socialization (socialization based on value and competition) that has currently been reached can no longer be contained by capitalist categories.

According to your own estimates, how high is the risk of inflation or deflation?

Inflation and deflation are merely two different forms of devaluing the aggregate relations of capital. Structural mass unemployment, increasing precarity, and dumping wages — the new global standard resulting from the third industrial revolution — already brought about a deflationary devaluing of the commodity of labor, of what Marx would call the "variable" component of capital (the only component that generates new value). The underside of this was the finance bubble economy, the development of titles and properties without substance (thus entirely fictional) as asset inflation. Because the global connections of this asset inflation touched a number of currency areas, it was able to persist for quite a while without immediately triggering a large-scale devaluation of the monetary medium in general. Such a devaluation, however, was already to be expected in the final stages of the last deficit economy when the rates of inflation in many newly industrialized countries (including China) approached twenty percent, and the United States expected a rate of six to ten percent by the end of 2008. In principle, therefore, the inflationary endgame of such a creation of purchasing power without substance via finance bubbles, despite its complex global mediation, would have been no different from the classic idea of solving the problem by printing more and more money.

The path toward this scenario, however, was disrupted by the crash of the finance markets, which in an instant eliminated trillions of dollars of fictional assets, leaving behind mountains of basically worthless certificates in the vaults of banks. The asset inflation, therefore, did not turn into a monetary inflation but gave rise to an asset deflation. After the mechanism of the deficit economy had abruptly come to a standstill, a similarly rapid reduction of global excess capacities (especially in the auto industry) should have followed, since these capacities were based upon the influx of fictional purchasing power from the debt and finance bubbles. What should have followed is thus a large-scale devaluation of real capital (the means of production) and commodity capital on markets (commodities rendered unsellable), together with an increased push toward the devaluation of labor power (massive job losses). To this day, we are witnessing a global wave of bankruptcies, yet the deflation of real and commodity capital has for the time being been slowed by means of the gigantic state programs financed through credits. Both in the finance sector and in the production sector the beloved "market clearing" was prevented, contrary to the laws of the market, since, due to the lack of potential for new valorization, such a market clearing would have left behind nothing but an economic wasteland.

However, the dismantling of excess capacities has only been delayed, and in the not-too-distant future it will be executed via the crisis of state finance. All economic stimulus and bailout packages are ultimately nonproductive state consumption, even if their effect on the surface is artificially to keep alive a variety of businesses. States would have to finance the credits for such consumption by taxing the profits and salaries resulting from the real production of surplus value. But this, of course, is circular logic, since the former effort has only become necessary in the first place because the latter process no longer occurs to a sufficient extent. The ultima ratio in such an inescapable situation is, therefore, the increased printing of money as we have come to know from war economies — now, however, this is done in order to prolong the life of capitalism and its mode of production itself.

The central banks themselves have dismantled a variety of security structures by accepting, against their own rules, toxic certificates from banks as "securities" or by acquiring potentially worthless state loans from candidates for state bankruptcy (see the practices of the European Central Bank). On one hand, the mechanisms are put in place for the development of an enormous inflation potential (meaning the devaluation of money, of the capitalist end in itself) from which all aggregate relations of capital depart and into which they must be transformed back. Since the flood of money resulting from state-sponsored bailout and stimulus packages (as opposed to the flood of money generated by the central banks for the transnational finance markets) is directly injected into the respective currency areas, the incubation period for the realization of inflationary potential is much shorter than in the case of the transnational finance bubble economy. On the other hand, we do not see any form of apprehension with respect to further increasing the amount of new money being printed. The actual, relative stabilization on a lower level than in times of a booming deficit economy would have to be permanently subsidized by the state, and this, of course, is only possibly via the creation of new money. As a result, the saving programs in fact counteract the rescue, stimulus, and bailout measures.

This dilemma is bound to continue to run its course, in particular because the back-and-forth of mutually contradictory measures cannot lead to the vanishing of deflation and inflation into thin air. Since inflation (with regard to money proper) and deflation (with regard to labor power, monetary assets, real capital, and commodity capital) are merely different forms of devaluing elements of capitalist reproduction, they could in principle occur simultaneously. This will increasingly be the case since the emergency-driven monetary and economic policies continue to oscillate between fundamentally contradictory options. Already at the end of the 1970s and at the beginning of the 1980s, we witnessed the simultaneity of deflationary stagnation and increasing inflation (what came to be known as "stagflation") resulting from a lack of real valorization. Indeed, it was precisely this stagflation that was the grounds for the neoliberal revolution, which, however, simply produced an historical deferral by means of the deregulation of the finance bubble economy. Now, the old problem returns on a much higher level of internal contradictions. As a consequence, what has become possible is a simultaneously inflationary and deflationary shock at the moment at which one of the contradictory measures is taken to its structural extreme and exhausts itself, as well as a period of stagflation with decidedly more dire consequences than thirty years ago, should both options exhaust themselves in quick succession.

With regard to the crisis of the Greek economy, critics of neoliberalism accuse German economists of misrepresenting relations and determinations, of strangling the welfare state with the IMF's saving measures, and of generally pursuing contradictory solutions. Do you agree with these critics or does their evaluation of the matter miss the core of the problem at hand?

A pure critique of neoliberalism (as advanced by ATTAC and a large portion of the Left) is abbreviated, since it does not reach the internal relations of the crisis and instead simply addresses what are seen as erroneous economic policies. Often related to this is the hope for a return to Keynesianism and the resulting return to a "good" form of capitalism characterized by investments in certain labor sectors and the gratifications of a welfare state. Yet, this is illusory and misses the core of the problem, since both the neoliberal and the Keynesian doctrine presuppose, similarly blindly, the capitalist mode of production, its categories, and its criteria. In the context of the current crisis, however, the predominant mode of production itself is the problem. Keynesianism can only return in the form of crisis and emergency management — that is, as a continuation of neoliberalism with different means — and this can only lead to a further intensification of the contradictions.

It is, however, correct to assert that German politicians misrepresent the determinations and relations of the problem at hand and merely pursue contradictory solutions — but the hope for a re-regulated Keynesian welfare state itself is a contradictory solution. After all, what is the nature of these contradictions? Alongside the large Pacific circulation of deficits there existed a smaller European system of deficit circulation for which the euro was initially designed — and in a manner directly shaped by German interests. More than forty percent of the immense German export surpluses ended up (and still do) in the European Union and in particular in the eurozone. These surpluses confront the deficits in trade balance of other (in particular southern) E.U. nations. These nations were outcompeted with the help of the euro, since the potential for equalization via the devaluation of national currencies no longer existed. Since now everywhere the relatively weak reanimation of the deficit economy is based on the displacement of the problem from the finance bubble economy onto state credit, the state deficits of the neighboring countries constitute the flip side of the German export economy.

German elites do not want to recognize this relationship and refuse to surrender their supposed export advantages. Connected to the currency union in this respect is the fact that Germany (not only since Hartz IV) supports the largest low-wage sector in Europe and that the real wages in Germany, with the help of silent unions, have dropped faster and to a greater degree than elsewhere.[1] The constantly growing export surplus on this basis has resulted in a relative capital strength of Germany. Now, however, the business foundations of this model are being questioned. Within the European Union we are witnessing a growing conflict between Germany and the deficit countries. Also on the larger scale of transnational relations the positions of economic policy have been reversed. The United States, as the biggest deficit nation, demands just like the southern European nations that Germany abandon all saving policies and instead stimulate national consumption in order to erase imbalances. We are confronted with a world that has seemingly been turned upside down: the former champions of neoliberalism now demand diametrically opposed economic policies and take on the role German unions feared to play. This may initially seems like a development in line with hopes for Keynesianism, yet it is nonsensical insofar as this would force the inflationary option. Like the IMF, the United States and members of the European Union flirt with a supposedly "controllable inflation" in order to address the dilemma — yet, given the current economic situation, such control would be lost very quickly.

There is thus no escape from this dilemma. Secretly, the elites of course know this. The spuriously explained resignations of high-ranking political functionaries, most recently German President Horst Köhler, are an indication that a severe conflict is carried out behind the veil of professional optimism. This is likely to be repeated in other nations. A classic wait-and-see strategy when confronted with problems (as per Helmut Kohl) is no longer possible. As a result, one repair program follows the next in rapid succession while still having to keep in mind the demoscopic will of the voter (if we are not to descend into a dictatorship of a state of emergency), thus resulting in general conflict and aggression. The capitalist mode of production must not be called into question, and, as a result, similar to the first stage of the financial crisis, discussions are determined by the hunt for those who are at fault. In fact, the conflict in the CDU/FDP-led government in Germany is not party-specific but instead will, given the current problem, likely occur with any given form of coalition. It is no wonder that some combatants have thrown in the towel.

In your estimation, what will happen in the foreseeable future?

Since the monetary measures and fiscal strategies of economic policy are immanently contradictory, we can expect a second wave of the global economic crisis within the next few years. This second wave could be triggered by the crisis (and potential breakdown) of the European currency union. Formally, the situation in which Greece currently finds itself is similar to that with which Argentina was faced a decade ago. But that crisis was limited to a single nation and thus largely left the global economic system unaffected. The threatening national bankruptcies in the eurozone are quite different in this respect, since they have the potential to undo the entire currency union. The collapse of European deficit circulation would shatter the German export economy, and the strength of German capital would be lost. This would not only mean that the hitherto-deferred major bankruptcies and massive job loss would also take place in Germany, but also that German state finances (which are also based on large amounts of debt) would be in a situation similar to that of Greece, in which, after the collapse of one-sided export relations, the strength of finance markets would disappear. Such a development would not only be disastrous for the European region but also, given Europe's economic importance for the world system, for the global economy.

The situation is equally dire for the large Pacific system of debt circulation between China and the United States. In this context, each side hopes that the other side creates the preconditions for further stabilization. The state-sponsored bailout and stimulus packages on the part of the United States did manage partially to halt the collapse of consumption, yet without reaching pre-crisis levels and at the cost of calling into question the United States' status as world power, since the externally financed state credit system and its role in financing the war machine and war efforts had reached their limits. The United States demands of China a long-overdue appreciation of its national currency and, as in the case of its demands directed at Germany, credit-financed strengthening of national consumption in order to reduce the imbalance of commodity flows and to strengthen the United States' own exports, which in turn is hoped to compensate for the United States' weakened national consumption. In most industrial sectors, however, the United States simply does not have the necessary export capacities, and their development would require vast investments. Conversely, China's corresponding capacities would have to be dismantled, since U.S. corporations, just as European and Japanese corporations, have invested heavily in these capacities (due to cost advantages) in order to supply their own and foreign markets.

But China shows just as little interest in surrendering its export advantages based on low wages and an artificially depreciated currency as Germany, since in both cases the entirety of the economy is oriented toward one-sided export. A change which would have to take place over the course of a year or maybe even decades, however, would quickly reach its limits, since imbalances were the very life elixir of the global economy. China has developed the largest state-sponsored economic program of all nations and all times by basing it on its gigantic fund of monetary reserves and forcing its banks to give out massive credits. But precisely for this reason it cannot allow any serious currency correction, since this would substantially devalue its accumulated monetary reserves. The Chinese economic programs strengthen national consumption only indirectly and not to the extent necessary, and China is therefore not able to lead the world economy in the same way the United States' foreign-financed consumerism did up to this point. The largest part of China's programs flows directly into additional infrastructures and the development of production capacity, which are all directed at the same goal: restarting the one-sided export machinery. If this does not succeed, China will be left sitting on a mountain of investment ruins with corresponding consequences for the financial system. Moreover, China will not be able to survive such a program and simultaneously continue to purchase U.S. government bonds to the same degree that it did in the past.

In the Pacific region, therefore, the European dilemma is repeated on a larger scale. Deficit circulation is continuing more slowly after the crash, and is flanked by arduously reanimated national economies based on state programs. If the latter run out, the entire system threatens to collapse. The second wave of the global crisis can begin in either geographic region (or possibly even in both simultaneously). All current success stories are only momentary impressions that are falsely taken as a basis for extrapolating years into the future — just as during the peak of the global deficit economy between 2007 and the summer of 2008. Yet, in this current context, the projected success and numbers are even less credible than in the past, since they assume a much lower basic level after the crash of the global economy. This seemingly unshakably positive form of thinking is heading for its next Waterloo. The only question that remains is which incubation period and which new configuration of contradictions will be necessary this time in order to undo the system. The only consolation that remains for such positive thinkers will likely be their own characteristic short-term memory, whose horizon does not extend beyond their own noses.

What forms of mediation can be established between the immanent struggles for basic conditions of survival and the critique of the basic categories of the capitalist system (commodity, value, money, abstract labor, state, politics)?

Without a doubt, extraparliamentary, organized social struggles for the material and cultural necessities of life as resistance against the brutal lowering of the level of civilization is the only alternative to the Left's political, parliamentary complicity in state-sponsored crisis administration. A newly constituted social countermovement will be equally indispensable, initially in the form of the immanent attempt to work through contradictions, which will not delegate its needs and demands to the state but instead advance autonomous demands, even if those are made of the state. Central topics here include adequate minimum wages, resistance against increasing cuts to social transfers and against the repressive chicanery and compulsory programs of labor administration, resistance against privatization and the demolition of vitally important public infrastructures (including, for example, health care). Additionally, this would involve serious engagements with the important question of funding education and the process of questioning the accepted practice of chaining education and research to capital's needs for valorization, which have become obsolete.

An important moment in the mediation of "categorical critique" consists in the ability to learn how to distinguish between progressive and affirmative forms of working out contradictions. This includes in particular the realization that a defense of the fundamental necessities of life by party-political means has become entirely illusory. The content of the alternatives has to be developed out of direct social demands on one hand and the vain hopes for new state economic programs and new capital investments on the other. The latter instantly ties social needs to the "successful" valorization of capital on the rapidly eroding basis of abstract labor and to the ability to be financed according to capitalist criteria. The former, in contrast, can lead to a negation of the terror of "financeability" and to the possibility of surpassing the value and money forms. This alternative can, if it is put into practice, also be raised within the "Left" wing of the political class, where it would lead to polarization. Elements of these alternatives already existed in the workers' movements of the past, but against the ideological backdrop of abstract labor. It was precisely for this reason that social countermovements were always transformed into state-oriented movements (in accordance with their own labor-ontological consciousness) and qua party-Marxism limited to a state-capitalist politics of intervention — after all, the state is the subsuming social entity based on abstract labor. The limits of abstract labor and real valorization of capital today force the question of the alternative of social countermovement and statism in an entirely new direction, which thus demands to be formulated with greater rigor (at a moment at which the hope for state credit does not contain any social potential and can only lead to the embarrassment of unleashing inflation).

A second moment of mediation is the critique of all forms of social segregation, whether these are articulated openly or indirectly. As long as social movements operate upon the plane of an immanent working-out of contradictions there will always be such tendencies. Already in the traditional labor movements there were at work a series of affects articulated in opposition to the unskilled lowest classes. Today, we encounter similar attitudes in an (albeit shrinking) globalized labor-aristocracy that stands opposed to those dropped by the system or to those employed in low-wage sectors, as well as in the attitude of any given "dominant culture" to its pool of migrant workers. Most important here, however, are the academic and subacademic middle classes in the capitalist centers, who, faced with the threat of their social and economic decline, attempt to save their own skin and formulate their own specific interests as "human capital" in stylized fashion in relation to the general ideal of emancipation, in truth ultimately caring little about the existence of "others." To the extent to which a social countermovement constitutes itself, one of its duties must be a categorical critique of and the attempt to analyze and oppose the various potentials for social segregation, which intersect in complex fashion.

This will only be possible if such a critique communicates that it is in fact easily possible to provide the basic necessities of life for all if we are not bound by capitalist categories. In this respect, it is the duty of social countermovements to illustrate the immense discrepancy between the potentialities for material wealth and the impossibility of continuing to limit such potentialities to capitalist forms. Even if the theoretical reflection of the actual capitalist categories — value form, commodity, surplus value, and abstract labor — and their state-political modulation are not present in mass consciousness, practical experience of the existence of capacities for the satisfaction of material, social, and cultural needs that exist practically, technically, and materially but are rendered inaccessible by capitalism can still be mobilized — in particular at the moment at which the absurd end in itself of the transformation of labor into more labor and money into more money no longer functions. As more and more people are becoming homeless while simultaneously scores of homes and apartments are left vacant, as more and more people in need of medical support and care are inadequately attended to while doctors, caretakers, and nurses become unemployed, such experiences can form the basis for a fundamental, radical critique of the commodity and value forms, which would add a theoretical dimension to already existing reflections.

Such a strategy is appropriate, too, when considering the so-called ecological problem (climate change, exploitation of nature, and the erosion of the natural basis for life). The mediation of a categorical critique consists in this case in the attempt to foreground the internal connections (and resultant limitations) of the destructive potential of the capitalist production of material wealth on one hand and the capitalist forms of social relations on the other. It is not the production of sufficient amounts of food and cultural goods itself that led to the destruction of the biosphere, but rather the rationalization of the logic of valorization via business administration that simultaneously generates poverty, robs itself of its own foundation, and destroys nature. The destructive potential of specific capitalist forms of material wealth (traffic and transportation, armaments industry, agricultural industry, and so on) must not be privileged over the socialization of necessities of life. The alternative to making everyone "auto-mobile" is not the liquidation of mobility per se but instead the development of public transportation under social control in opposition to privatization. It is particularly perfidious in this context to present people who are impoverished by capitalism and subsist merely by means of insulting emergency rations with calculations that accuse them of overconsumption and resultant damage to the environment. While only recently the "climate catastrophe" occupied a central role in public discourse and the news media, the current crisis has led to the widespread repealing of recently established ecological programs, since the capitalist form must be preserved at any cost. Yet it is, of course, entirely possible that the crisis managers will seek further social reductions and legitimate their necessity by appealing to the ecological argument. This contradiction also determines a part of the ecological ideology that corresponds to sections of the middle classes, which speaks of the limits of capitalism only in the sense of an external limit of natural resources while the internal limit of abstract labor and the valorization of value is only recognized in a foreshortened manner (the limits of economic growth), since those sections of the middle class desire to participate "ecologically" in the administration of the current crisis. From the standpoint of a developed critique of political economy this ecological reductionism must be critiqued just like the economically affirmative temptation of crisis Keynesianism.

An additional step toward the mediation of categorical critique would be the return to a discussion about social planning that refuses to be limited to abstract labor, the commodity form, and the state. As an inheritance of the previous epoch, socialism is currently more than ever equated with statification, which leads to paradoxical expressions such as "finance market socialism," which denote nothing more directly than the real paradoxes of the new relations of crisis. For a true transformation beyond capitalism, however, the main activity consists in the new organization of the global flow of material and social resources as such and in the refusal to represent it by means of the categories such as value and labor substance, which have become historically obsolete. Included in this is the problem of the moments of social reproduction that could never be contained and subsumed by the categories of abstract labor and that were historically delegated to women (child care, health and social care, domestic and affective labor, and so on). This "social mortar," too, begins to crumble as we reach the limits of the valorization of capital. Any social transformation must also reorganize these aspects anew, reject their gendered logic, and instead organize them by means of a social time fund, which has long been possible. Moreover, a broad social discussion must be started that includes a wide variety of experiences and competencies without restricting it to a single, narrow theoretical focus. Theoretical critique can only attempt to stimulate such a discussion by means of highlighting the development of crisis and to foreground the key problems in regards to social planning.

Particularly since a categorical critique of capitalist formal relations cannot, despite the historical crisis, be mediated without experiencing moments of breakage as it reaches the limits of what Marx calls the objective forms of thought corresponding to social consciousness, it must not limit itself in a bourgeois sense to a politically and economically narrowed, "objective" line of argumentation. A crucial moment of such mediation is also a radical critique of ideology. All affirmative forms of processing the crisis on the level of consciousness produce ideology (not only in statist orientations or ecological reductionism). All modern base-ideologies such as nationalism, antisemitism, antiziganism (most notably the resentment directed against the Sinti and Roma as the pariahs of modernity), and sexism are amplified and newly configured in the context of the current crisis. The backdrop of this is the aggressive defense of the respective capitalist existence of social strata engaged in violent competition. Central in this regard is the current ideology of the "new middle classes," which in the context of the crisis are engaged in a struggle for hegemony. The different elements of ideology production here often experience a process of (at times indirect) amalgamation. It is the job of categorical critique, therefore, to analyze the modulated *dispositifs* of ideology production and to explore the concept of ideology beyond traditional

Marxism in order to connect the program of social transformation to a program of ideology-critical intervention. The current "movement Left" and its theoretically disarmed focus on largely symbolic struggles is far removed from all this. It is in part for this reason that we can increasingly observe sinister conversions of left to right positions in the context of an abbreviated critique of capitalism.

What role can class struggle in the Lukácsian sense play in the process of spreading class consciousness?

A traditional understanding of class struggles can, in this new situation of a confrontation with the absolute inner limit of valorization, no longer be mobilized. Historically, the representation of the proletariat by unions and political entities was no different from the representation of self-affirmative "variable capital" and therefore the representation of abstract labor. This depended on the construction of a merely relative opposition of the putatively transhistorical, anthropological principle of labor and the juridically construed form of capitalist private property, while abstract labor and juridical private property of the means of production in reality only constitute different formal determinations within the common, overarching system of relations of the valorization of value. Marx described this overarching relation as the "automatic subject" of modern fetish society, which contains all social situations as functions of the logic of valorization. There is no ontological principle upon which social emancipation could base itself. Instead, capitalism must be surpassed solely by means of a concrete, historical critique of its basic forms. Class struggle was first and foremost a struggle for recognition based on capitalist categories. For this reason, the workers' movement adopted from Protestantism and the bourgeois ideology of the Enlightenment not only the ontology of abstract labor but also the ontology of capitalist gender relations, that is, the historically assigned categories of masculinity and femininity. That which surpassed the struggle for recognition (right to strike, freedom of coalition, freedom of assembly, right to vote, and so on) still only led to a further statification of the unsurpassed categories of capitalism. In this, the understanding of socialism within the context of class struggle exhausted itself.

In the new historical situation, the demand for the recognition of those who depend upon wages has long been granted and in fact becomes a bond and trap for the citizen-subjects of a fetish society. For better or worse, humanity is tied to valorization-compulsion. This is not only a matter of consciousness, since the social basis of the class struggle of old is also eroded objectively. Part of the conditions of the third industrial revolution is capital's inability to assemble armies of abstract labor. Since the process of individualization as a phenomenon of crisis destroys the social filters, the socially atomized subject relates directly to the global value-relation, which is simultaneously virtualized in the form of bad debts and therefore becomes obsolete. It may appear as though a variety of diffuse social situations have been created that can no longer be integrated into capitalist categories. Temporary workers, the underemployed, the transfer-dependent unemployed as objects of crisis administration, the pseudo-self-employed, and owners of impoverished small businesses do not constitute the homogeneous mass of a surplus-value-producing proletariat. The movement ideology of the 1990s adopted the notion of such "diversity" affirmatively and assembled it purely notionally under the category of the multitude. The new organization of social struggle, however, cannot consist of the desire to be recognized as surplus-producing entity, but must instead concern itself with the critique and transformation of value as category and its associated gender relations. The basis for this cannot be a predetermined capitalist organization of labor which will be dissolved and demoralized, but the self-conscious organization of a concrete, historical critique of predominant categories that emerges out of the immanent working-through of contradictions. This is, therefore, not a question of objective class constitution as the representation of variable capital but instead a question of consciousness — yet not idealistic consciousness along the lines of a moral-philosophical ethics, but a consciousness that confronts the historical limits of valorization and the deterioration of the level of civilization.

At this point it is important to return once more to the problem of the crisis of the "new middle classes." The unorganized state of the industrial armies of labor and the deterioration of the traditional labor movement coincided with the ascension of skilled middle strata during the phase of Fordist prosperity. The economic basis for this was not the immediate, actual production of surplus value but the expansion of state credit. The associated social self-consciousness consisted less in the ontology of labor as in the status of the "human capital" of higher education. The New Left that emerged since 1968 was already largely a middle-class movement, even if it sought in vain (in abstract-ideological fashion and out of a commitment to the traditional Marxist fund) a connection with the disappearing class struggle of the proletariat. In the era of finance bubble economics, the new middle classes became increasingly dependent upon the expansion of private credit and thus experienced steadily growing precarity. In particular in this process the worldview of middle-class consciousness assumed a dominant position (also on the Left). Revivals of traditional class-struggle rhetoric and in particular their derivatives in the form of the post-workerist multitude are all implicitly (and at times even explicitly) formulated from the perspective of the categorically affirmative consciousness of the middle class. Today, it is not mainly the long-eroded ontology of labor that blocks the transformation from the Marxism of labor movements to categorical critique, but the ideology of the middle class that continues to insist upon its human capital as the basis of a variety of theoretical models and movements. Since a large-scale, social countermovement must also include the middle classes, transcending this ideology is of the utmost importance.

The problem of an organization of social struggle that must integrate the desperate "diversity" of social strata beyond the class-struggle paradigm in altered fashion theoretically does not depart from ground zero. The transition to categorical critique can be found in the work of theoreticians at the boundaries of traditional Marxism such as Georg Lukács (and in a different way in Adorno). Lukács may have provided the earliest indication of this in the essay on reification. As is to be expected, given the historical situation out of which the essay emerges, he connects for the first time the implicit ontology of labor and the class standpoint that emerges out of it to the thematization of the constitution of the modern fetish that spans social strata. Of course, Lukács let himself be convinced by party Marxists that his groundbreaking insights were idealistic and returned to an explicit and rather boring ontology of abstract labor in his later work. Yet, his 1923 work has also been recognized by new approaches to a categorical critique since the 1980s, in particular with regard to the consideration of an "imputed class consciousness" and of the proletariat as "subject-object of history." A new reading of this part of Lukács' work in the context of the current situation generates surprising insights. What he collects under the category of reification constitutes a critique, unparalleled for its time, of capitalism's basic forms — indeed, some passages read like an anticipation of postmodern thought. Important here is the postulate of a critical "coming into consciousness" of the commodity form as capitalism's universal form of being, including the integration of the commodity labor. The result of this is that Lukács is able once again to approach the Marxian determination of capitalist categories as simultaneously both actual conditions of existence and objective forms of thought that had been overshadowed by labor-movement Marxism.

If one dissociates this approach from its attribution to the standpoint of labor, much can be adopted for a new categorical critique under the conditions of individualization and the deterioration of the relations of value. Of primary importance in this context is the attempt to integrate modern gender relations (which Lukács's work does not address) into the categorical plane. Furthermore, the critical relativization of proletarian class-consciousness as it is laid out in the essay on reification must today be primarily examined in relation to the middle class. Our project, in other words, is the reformulation of Lukács' insights in the context of a fundamentally different historical situation in order to energize the critical "coming into consciousness" of the commodity form for a reintegration of social struggle beyond capitalist false objectivity.

How would you define a concept of revolution suited for the current historical situation that is able to break with fetishism and with an everyday life that is completely subordinated to the reproduction of capital?

The term "revolution" is historically determined via the paradigm of the great French Revolution, the subsequent bourgeois revolutions of the nineteenth century and the revolutions of recuperative modernization at the periphery of the global market in the twentieth century (Russia, China, and the Third World). In this context, the revolution was limited to the political form of a seizure of power and in the twentieth century to the statification of capitalist categories. Consequently, the term belongs to the history of the development of abstract labor, the logic of valorization, and modern gender relations — and for this reason, the term's career appears to be over. In the context of "remainder Marxism" and movement ideology the concept no longer plays a role in the act of political transformation — but this throws out the baby with the bathwater. By retiring the concept of revolution without reworking it in relation to the current historical context, the Left has ratified the terms of its surrender to the social basis of the middle classes.

Already in his early writings, Marx criticized politically limited variants of the term "revolution." For him, a "social revolution" was qualitatively different, since it was aimed at the abolition of the political form of the state along with capitalist value relations and the commodity form. As later in Lukács, such a transformation naturally still took the shape of a proletarian revolution. Yet, precisely this paradigm has remained stuck at the stage of a politically abbreviated conception of revolution. Beyond the ontology of abstract labor, the internal limits of valorization and the question of social revolution take on a new and different quality, and the latter must be defined as the transcendence of the currently dominant social synthesis in the forms of value and capitalist gender relations. "Social synthesis" here means nothing other than the specific form of socialization in the sense of a negative totality, which can only be surpassed by means of a total social transformation.

Especially for this reason a new social movement on a transnational scale is necessary in order to begin the process of transforming the social synthesis. Occupations of factories by workers are, therefore, in no way sufficient, since these workers merely reify their status as a collective subject of capital, thereby remaining at the mercy of the synthesis via the market and competition. All past attempts at transformation (as, for example, in the case of the great crisis in Argentina) failed for this reason. Transformation is not possible on the plane of singular units of capital or particular units of reproduction. Instead, the question of synthesis and the associated forms of social planning beyond the commodity form must form the beginning (and not the endpoint) of any practical break with capitalism. Consequently, the concept "revolution" is not simply without substance, even if it no longer bears any relation to the old political definitions of the term. Critical theory as categorical critique must insist upon the point of social synthesis, also in opposition to purely symbolic movement consciousness, which refuses to address this key problem.

The post-workerist movement-Left today (including, for example, John Holloway) enjoys talking about the desire to change the world without seizing power. In this context, the critique of social synthesis is replaced with the diffuse notion of the "quotidian," which was already popular in the movement of 1968. What is frequently designated as a revolutionization of the quotidian in one way or another always accompanies social change, but, reduced to this facet, such change can also include any given cultural adaptation to capitalist dynamics. Corresponding concepts of the movement of '68 and the postmodern Left have long been absorbed into capitalist crisis management, as exemplified by the neoliberal propaganda that foregrounds individual self-responsibility. The thematization of the quotidian can neither replace real interventions on the plane of social synthesis nor is it able to render superfluous the forms of power necessary for such an intervention (such as strikes, blockades, and the disruption of capitalist nerve centers). The question of power is in no way limited to the paradigm of state power, but it must emerge with particular significance and urgency in the context of resistance against crisis management and administration. In reality, the quotidian is not itself a pool of resistance — in fact, such assertions render the latter term hollow and useless. Resistance, on the contrary, begins where individuals raise themselves out of the pool of the quotidian that is everywhere determined by capitalism and by doing so become able to organize in the first place.

The Left metaphysics of the quotidian in essence constitutes a continuation of the failed alternative movements of the 1980s as well as a continuation of attempts pragmatically or in neo-utopian fashion to legitimate "other" forms of producing and living on a small scale within particular communities. Such attempts, as in the form of so-called "local economies" or the digital open-source movement, are also unable to reach the level of social synthesis, just like occupations of factories. As pseudo-alternatives to a social resistance movement that emerges out of capitalist immanence they threaten to transform into the self-administration of poverty. As soon as even the thought of a critique of the commodity form appears, however, it is deconstructed to a form that no longer allows for such a critique without losing its decisive content and without resulting in hopeless contradictions. The supposed alternatives not only remain stuck in bourgeois contract relations, but they also solely address tiny segments of reproduction, which, as a whole, remain determined by capitalism. It is no surprise, then, that the particular "praxis projects" tend to aim for external financing through the state, be that in the form of basic income or communal sponsoring. Keynesian statism and alternative ideology are two sides of the same coin, and the common denominator is the direct or indirect orientation in the direction of state credit. This way, the disavowed dominance of middle-class consciousness shows itself once again. The Keynesian and alternative-movement lefts are forced to the same degree to deny and repress the new quality of the present crisis, since their illusions cannot survive the end of the global credit system and finance-bubble economy. They will have to confront the real limits of the predominant social synthesis at the very latest at the point at which the massive collapse of the global economy also reaches the quotidian in the capitalist centers.

Note

1.   The Hartz reforms were the proposals put forward at the recommendation of the Hartz Commission, founded by the (Social-Democratic) Schröder administration in 2002 for the reform of the German labor market, and implemented between 2003 and 2005. The last of these reforms, Hartz IV, combined unemployment and social security benefits, at the (much lower) level of the latter, on a means-tested basis. [Eds.]

The Ontological Break: Before the Beginning of a Different World History

Robert Kurz (2005)

The debate over globalization seems to have come to a point of exhaustion. This is not, however, because the underlying social process has exhausted itself — the process itself is still in its incipient stage. Rather, the forms of interpretation have prematurely run out of steam. The guild of economists and political scientists has filled entire libraries with discussions of the boundaries of national economies blown open by the globalization of capital and with discussions of the resulting dissolution of the nation state and political regulation as a frame of reference. Yet this widespread set of realizations has largely remained without consequence. The more clearly analysis shows that nation and politics have become obsolete, the more stubbornly political and theoretical discourse tries to hold on to the concepts of nation and politics. The concepts that were developed to cope with the problem correspondingly appear weak and unpersuasive.

The problem is that there are no immanent alternatives to these concepts because, just like concepts such as labor, money, and market, they represent the petrified determinations of modern capitalist ontology — and thus also represent its categories. If we understand ontology not anthropologically or transhistorically, but rather as historically contingent, then ontological concepts or categories of sociality indicate distinct historical fields; in Marxian terms: a form of society or a mode of production and a mode of living. The modern system of commodity production constitutes a historical ontology of this kind.

Within such a field there exist at any given point in time a multitude of alternatives and arguments. These, however, remain confined to and move within the same historical-ontological categories. The critique and suspension of the categories themselves appears to be unthinkable. Thus, it is possible to critique a certain politics in order to replace it with another; but within modern ontology it is impossible to critique politics in itself and replace it with another mode of social regulation. For this we lack the appropriate form of thought, and therefore all the concepts as well. Only the determinate content of politics is malleable, but not the categorical form or mode of all content. The same goes for the categories of nation, state, rights, labor, money, and market, as well as of the individual, subject, and gender relations (social masculinity and femininity). At any given point, any of these categorical forms can be modified, only in a quasi-adjectival sense. Yet the category itself and its corresponding social mode are never put up for substantial negotiation.

The analytical insight that the process of globalization renders nation and politics obsolete can therefore not be worked through with the means and methods the modern social sciences have to offer. It is today no longer the case that it is a matter of substituting a specific content with a different, new content within the same social form — say, the substitution of the dominant political constellation with another. Such strategies would, for example, propose that the world power United States could be replaced by a new Euro-Asian power bloc, or that the neoliberal political economy could be surpassed by the return to Keynesian paradigms. Rather, globalization questions the political mode and national form as such.

What this means is that contemporary analysis asserts more than it knows. With its insight into the loss of the regulatory capacity of the nation state and of politics, it involuntarily comes up against the limits of modern ontology itself. But when one category falls, all others must fall like dominoes. For the historical formation of the modern system of commodity production can only exist as a totality, in which one basic condition presupposes another and the different categories determine each other.

It is, therefore, not the case that the loss of political authority would not affect the economy or even allow it to run free. On the contrary, the political constitutes the mode of regulation of the modern system of commodity production, which cannot function economically without such regulation. Globalization itself, which blows up the frame of the national and thus destroys the political as mode of regulation, is conditioned, in turn, by the fact that abstract labor, as the form of productive value and surplus-value generating human activity within the development of productive forces, is increasingly replaced by fixed capital (*Sachkapital*). The resulting depreciation of value pushes management toward the transnational rationalization of the business economy. In the same way that scientified objective capital substitutes for labor, capital is de-substantialized and the valorization of value reaches its historical limits; the "depreciation" of nation and politics is nothing more than a product of this process. Yet, once the categorical structure of forms of production, reproduction, and regulation has been diluted, forms of individuality, of the subject, and its androcentric determination of gender, also become obsolete.

What seems at first to be a particular crisis of the political and its national limits is in reality a crisis of modern ontology. Such a categorical crisis demands in response a categorical critique. Yet, such a project currently lacks both appropriate forms of imagination and adequate concepts. Until now, critique has been immanent to dominant categories, relating only to determinate content, and not to the ontological forms and modes of the modern system of commodity production — hence the current paralysis of thought and praxis. The planetary administration of this ontological crisis cannot hold back the dissolution into barbarism of a global society defined in capitalist terms. On the contrary, it becomes instead an integral part of the descent into barbarism.

What is required here is an ontological break — from which global discourse, however, still shies away, even the radical Left. What predominates in its place are regressive ideas that seek to reverse the movement of the wheel of history in order to avoid this utterly unthinkable ontological break. While the hardliners of crisis administration want to separate the majority of humanity from their own conditions of existence, most self-styled critics of globalization seek ideally to escape to the past from the very object of their critique; they fall back on hopelessly reactionary paradigms of nation, politics, and Keynesian regulation, or journey even further back in time to the ideals of romanticized agrarian societies. An integral part of this regressive tendency is the religious madness that rages in all cultural spheres and exceeds all comparable manifestations in the breaks in the history of modernization.

In order to be able to think clearly and question modern ontology as such it would be necessary to understand this ontology as historically determined. For only in this way does the thought of its overcoming become possible. The ontological crisis of the twenty-first century can only be resolved if the history of the constitution of those apparently natural, a priori categories of modern commodity production from the sixteenth to the eighteenth century are not only newly illuminated but also fundamentally re-evaluated.

This task, however, is blocked by an ideological apparatus, which is as constitutive of modernity as the categorical totality of its social reproduction. The foundation of this ideational, and, in its ontologically affirmative character, always already ideological apparatus is constituted by Enlightenment philosophy. All modern theories are equally derived from this root, liberalism just as Marxism, as well as the bourgeois-reactionary movements of counter-Enlightenment and antimodernity. For this reason, all of these theories are equally incapable of formulating the required categorical critique and realizing the necessary ontological break.

The once world-shattering conflicts between liberalism, Marxism, and conservatism always addressed specific social, political, juridical, or ideological matters. However, they never addressed the categorical forms and ontological modes of sociality. In this sense, liberals, Marxists, conservatives, and the radical Right could equally be patriots, politicians, subjects, androcentric universalists, and statesmen, labor-, rights-, or finance-enthusiasts, and were distinguished only by nuances of content. Because of their common grounding in Enlightenment thinking, the seemingly conflicting ideologies of modernization reveal themselves in the context of the crisis of modern ontology to be one and the same ideological apparatus in the sense of a common persistence with this same ontology at any price.

The insight that can occasionally be gleaned in postmodern discourse since the 1980s — that Left, Right, and liberal ideologies have become interchangeable — points to the hidden foundation that is common to them in the same way that neoliberalism as an ideology of crisis currently determines, with only minimal variations, the entirety of the political spectrum across party lines. Postmodern thought, however, has noticed this interchangeability solely phenomenologically and superficially, and hence without questioning the underlying ontology of modernity. Instead, postmodernism seeks to sneak past the ontological problem by means of simply rejecting all theories of modernity's ontology as dogmatic and totalitarian claims — as if the problem were inherently theoretical and not in fact a problem emerging from the reality of the social mode of reproduction. In this way, the basic categories of the modern system of commodity production are certainly not criticized, but are instead only removed from the focus of the critical gaze without, however, being escapable in social practice. Postmodernism, too, thus proves to be an integral part of the total ideological apparatus and, despite assertions to the contrary, a derivative of Enlightenment philosophy.

Enlightenment thought explicitly grounded, expanded,

consolidated, and ideologically legitimated the categories of modern ontology that prior to the eighteenth century were still unstable. For this reason, the required ontological break must be accompanied by the radical critique of the Enlightenment and of all those forms of philosophy, theory, and ideology that emerged from it. In rejecting its foundations, all the rest is rejected as well. The ontological break consists precisely in this.

However, the Enlightenment did not only develop the categories of labor, value, commodity, market, law and policy, legal status, androcentric universalism, subject, and notions of abstract individuality as conceptual reflections of a social ontology of modernity that was born out of a blind historical process; the Enlightenment simultaneously placed them within a logical and historical context so as to make them sacrosanct.

Earlier agrarian social forms also possessed their own respective historical ontologies: ancient Egypt and Mesopotamia, no differently from Greco-Roman antiquity, imperial China, Islamic culture, and the Christian Middle Ages. But all of these ontologies were in a certain sense self-sufficient. They were defined in themselves, did not need to be assessed against any other ontology, and were under no pressure to justify themselves. While there existed in each case relationships with foreign cultures of the same period, these "others" were usually negatively defined as "barbarians," "unbelievers," or "pagans." Such definitions, however, were not based on historical-philosophical systems and only represented incidental limitations.

The modern system of commodity production, in contrast, needed to ground its ontology in a reflexive manner — reflexively, however, not in the sense of a critical project but rather in the sense of a project of legitimating itself as a system. Indeed, it was the compulsion to justify the new, foundational claim to the subjugation and battering of individuals that produced the Enlightenment's philosophy of history. The monstrous demands of capitalism, which directly aims to transform the process of life in its entirety into an immediate function of its logic of valorization, could no longer be based on a loose assemblage of traditions.

On one hand, it was necessary to bestow upon the specifically modern ontology the dignity of an objective natural relation. That is, it was necessary explicitly to transform an historical ontology into a transhistorical and anthropological ontology — being-human as such. On the other, this resulted in the need to establish a logical relation between this modern, now transhistorically reasoned ontology and all previous historical formations and all concurrent noncapitalist (still predominantly agrarian) cultures.

The result could not have been any other than a stamping of the mark of inferiority on the past. This not only represented a new worldview, but also a revaluation afresh of all values. In agrarian societies, people understood themselves as the children of their parents not simply in the ontogenetic sense, but in the phylogenic and socio-historical sense as well. The oldest people were celebrated in the same way as ancestors and mythic heroes of the past were. The golden age was located in the beginnings and not in the future; the unsurpassable ideal was the mythical "first time" and not the "end result" of a process of exerting effort.

Enlightenment philosophy of history did not reflect on this worldview in a critical way. Rather, it turned it on its head. Ancestors and "primitive men" were regarded as unemancipated children in an historico-phylogenic sense, who only reached adulthood in modern ontology. All previous historical periods appeared first as errors of humanity, later becoming imperfect and immature prior stages of modernity, which, in turn, went on to represent the culmination and end point of a process of maturation — the "end of history" in the ontological sense. History was then for the first time systemically defined as development — from simpler or ontological forms to higher and better ones. That is, as the progress from the primitive to the actual state of being human in the context of commodity-producing modernity.

On one hand, the specifically historical ontological categories of modernity were established transhistorically, as if they had always been there. Even the concept of ontology itself appeared to be synonymous with anthropological, transhistorical, or ahistorical circumstances. For this reason, it became impossible to seek other historical ontologies and to determine their own specificities. Instead, the Enlightenment projected its modern categories, which it constituted and legitimated, onto all of the past and the future. The only remaining questions all followed the same principle: what were "labor," the "nation," the "political," "value," the "market," "money," the "subject," and so on, like in ancient Egypt, among the Celts, or in the Christian Middle Ages; or, conversely, how will the same categories look in the future and how will they be modified? In adopting this ontologization of modern categories, Marxism, too, was merely able to formulate its "socialist alternative" in an adjectival sense, as simply another thematic accentuation or regulation within the same social and historical form.

On the other hand, from the perspective of such a projection, past societies inevitably appeared as categorically imperfect. What were, in fact, other historical ontologies were defined (and consequently disfigured) as categorically "immature," not yet sufficiently developed modern ontology. Similarly, all contemporary societies that had not yet been completely determined by modern ontology were fitted into the same schema; these were equally seen as underdeveloped, immature, and inferior. Constituted in this way, Enlightenment philosophy of history essentially served as the legitimating ideology of internal and external colonization. In the name of that philosophy of history and its schemata, the submission of society to a system of the valorization of value — as well as its associated abstract labor with intolerable and disciplinary demands — can be propagated as historically necessary and as part of a change for the better.

The concept of barbarism, borrowed from agrarian civilizations, emerged as a pejorative definition of previous or contemporary noncapitalist humanity: "barbarism" became synonymous with a lack of civility in the sense of capitalist circulation (market subjectivity and legal form) and, as such, with a lack of submission to modern ontology. We still have no other concept at our disposition to characterize destructive, violent, and destabilizing tendencies that threaten the social context. Already Marx used the concept of "barbarism" critically by relating it to the history of the formation of the system of commodity production in reference to both "primitive accumulation" and the history of the disintegration of modernity in crises of capitalism. The break with modern ontology as it is required today requires us to move beyond Marx and to reveal as barbaric (and thus to destroy the foundations of) the core of the capitalist social machine, to destroy abstract labor and its inner structure of discipline and reified human administration that is generally misunderstood as civilization.

This task of the ontological break is nonetheless complex and difficult to grasp, since the philosophy of history produced by the Enlightenment is legitimated paradoxically not simply as affirmative, but also as critical. The ideological apparatus established by the Enlightenment blocks the necessary ontological break precisely because it has been able to move within this paradox for a long time. Liberal bourgeois criticism always focused solely on the social conditions that prevented the imposition of modern ontology. Both in the sense of internal and external colonization, this was a question of the remnants left behind by agrarian formations. Among these remnants were not only previous relations of domination in the form of personal dependencies, but also certain conditions of life that detracted from the modern demands of abstract labor. In this way, the majority of religious holidays of agrarian societies were abolished to provide a clear path for the transformation of the temporality of life into the functional temporality of the valorization of capital.

The Enlightenment criticized older forms of personal dependency solely to legitimate the new forms of reified dependency of abstract labor, market, and the state. This criticism contained repressive aspects because it was linked to the propaganda of abstract diligence, discipline, and submission to the new demands of capitalism, along with destroying, together with old forms of domination, universal human achievements of agrarian relations. In fact, an older ailment was only replaced by a new, and in many ways even worse ailment. It was nevertheless possible for the liberal ideology of the Enlightenment to champion still-emergent modern relations as liberation from the feudal burden and to represent itself as shedding light on the dark superstitions of the Middle Ages. Feudal violence was condemned, while the abstract labor of modernity was "tortured into" people with an unprecedented violence, as expressed by Marx. The concept of criticism, in general, was identified by Enlightenment liberalism with the criticism of agrarian society, as capitalist modernity, with its atrocities, appeared as progress, even while in the real world it represented something very different for great masses of people.

During the late nineteenth century and even more in the twentieth, the concept of criticism shifted more and more to internal capitalist relations, after agrarian society had practically already disappeared along with its structures of personal dependency. Obviously, this was not a question of modern ontology and its categories, but only of the overcoming of old contents and structures through new structures, still founded on the same ontological ground. The system of commodity production, that is, capitalism, is inherently not a static situation, but rather a dynamic process of constant change and evolution: but it is a process that always develops in the same manner and under the same formal categories. It is a constant struggle between the new and the old, but it is at all times only the struggle between the capitalist new and the capitalist old. For the liberal understanding of criticism, the capitalist old has taken the place of the ontologically old, that is, of the now no-longer-existing feudal agrarian social relations. The ontological break between the proto-modern and the modern has been replaced by the permanent structural break internal to modernity and its ontology. This internal dynamic operates under the label "modernization." Henceforth, liberal criticism has been formulated in the sense of a modernization of modernity.

This process of permanent modernization in the ontological categories of modernity itself undergoes an additional legitimation by means of an opposite, complementary, and immanent critique, which is in turn legitimated in a romantic or reactionary manner. The supposedly good "old" is cast against the nefarious "new," without, however, subjecting the modern ontology to the slightest criticism. This is not even a defense of the actual premodern ontology present in agrarian society. Rather, the reactionary or conservative movement of antimodernity, too, is an invention of modernity and a derivative of the Enlightenment itself.

This is a bourgeois critique of bourgeois existence, which, since the end of the eighteenth century, has been loaded with images of an idealized agrarian society and with a system of pseudo-feudal values — similar to an opposing liberalism, which is loaded with the ideals and values of capitalist circulation (freedom of the autonomous subject integrated into the market, and so on). Yet pseudo-agrarian ideals were from the beginning formulated from within the categories of modern ontology, and not against it. Just as romanticism helped in the birth of modern abstract individuality, conservatism and its more radical versions of reactionary thought became propagators of modern nationalism and its ethno-ideological, racist, and antisemitic legitimation. In the Protestant work ethic and in social Darwinism, there was always a commonality between conservatives and reactionaries with liberalism that suggests their common roots in Enlightenment thinking.

The more the ideological attachment of conservative and reactionary thought to the idealized agrarian society faded, the clearer its position within the modern ontology and its dynamic needed to be. In this context, the romantic and reactionary current followed in the same path as liberalism — only with reversed polarity. Just as liberal critique stood opposed to the capitalist old in the context of a permanent, modernization of modernity interior to capitalism, thus acting as the advocate of the capitalist new, so too did conservative and reactionary countercritique operate in the name and as advocate of the respective capitalistic old in opposition to the capitalist new, which was perceived as a force of demoralization and disintegration.

Since this immanent polarity marked the same ontological field, however, their immanent opposition at the same time shielded this field from any possible metacriticism. Apart from the intolerable demands on human beings, the discomfort and destructive potential of the modern system of production created an increasing tension that could constantly be shifted to or canalized in the internal movement between progress and reaction, between liberalism and conservatism. The destructiveness of modernity should be redeemed by the ultimate impulse of modernization (progress), or, on the contrary, tamed by activism on behalf of the present situation of modernity directed against its own dynamic (conservatism or reaction). It is precisely for this reason that the critique of the social and historical ontology underlying this position was blocked.

However, the bourgeois-immanent contradiction inherent in liberalism on one hand, and conservative or romantic reaction on the other, formed far from the only obstacle for a critique of modern ontology. Instead, a second wave of criticism developed within this ontology that superimposed itself on the first. The second wave was sustained on one hand by the Western labor movement and on the other by so-called liberation movements on the periphery of the world market, including the Russian Revolution and the anticolonial movements and regimes. In all of these historical movements, a fundamental critique of capitalism, which was articulated, in many ways, by recourse to Marxist theory, was officially established. Nevertheless, this second wave was also fundamentally limited primarily to the modern ontology of the system of commodity production and, thus, to its categories. The return to Marx was limited to the components of this ontology retained by Marx himself, while all of the other moments of his theory that went beyond this remained muted or ignored.

The reason for the historical phenomenon of this second wave of affirmative criticism, which superimposes itself onto the opposition within the bourgeoisie, must be sought in the problem the social sciences call "historical noncontemporaneity." Modern ontology did not structurally or geographically develop in uniformity, but in discontinuous spurts.

In the countries of the West that gave rise to the system of commodity production, only a few categories were formed, while others remained underdeveloped. This was particularly true for the formation of the modern subject, of abstract individuality, and associated forms of law and politics. Neither the Enlightenment nor liberalism could establish these categories as abstract and general, equally legitimate for all members of society. Universalism, formulated theoretically, fell apart as a consequence of its confrontation with social limits. Enlightenment thinkers and liberals persisted in the understanding of the "man" of modern ontology solely as the male, propertied citizen, while the mass of wage laborers, male and female, were on one hand subjugated to the discipline of abstract labor, yet remained on the other both on the juridical and on the political level ontologically exterritorialized. In order to complete its process not of a subjective but of a reified form of dependence, modern ontology needed to generalize the former relation. Only by means of political and juridical integration could the categorical subjugation of man be completed.

From that constellation, the labor movement in the West assumed the specific function of a modernization of modernity that consisted in the struggle of wage laborers for recognition as integrated subjects of law, politics, and participation in the state (universal suffrage, freedom of coalition and assembly). But here categorical critique was also blocked, and instead of the ontological break, the labor movement undertook the completion of modern ontology. It assumed in part the role of liberalism in the actual, practical universalization of certain modern categories. Liberalism, in turn, proved to be incapable of such universalization, instead revealing itself as a conservative force in this respect. Consequently, the labor movement accused liberalism of betraying its own ideals and itself adopted the principal ideologemes of the Enlightenment, including the Protestant work ethic.

The modern ontology of the system of commodity production, however, also included specific gender relations insofar as all moments of life and reproduction, whether material, psychosocial, or cultural-symbolic, that were not subsumed by capitalist categories were designated as feminine and in practice delegated to women —

throughout all historical developments internal to this ontology. The recognition of female wage laborers — and, in general, of women — in bourgeois society as subjects of law and of civil society and political life, a recognition that was denied by the majority of Enlightenment philosophers, possessed only limited validity even after the second wave of value-immanent criticism: on one hand, they moved within the official spheres of society, but at the same time kept one foot "outside" because they continued to represent those dissociated moments that could not be systemically integrated. In this way, modern ontology is not a closed totality, but rather broken and self-contradictory, mediated by what Roswitha Scholz calls specifically gendered "relations of dissociation." As a result of the relation of dissociation corresponding with modern ontology, the bourgeois recognition of women had to remain correspondingly fragmented and incomplete. The abstract individual is, in reality and in its complete form, masculinized, in much the same way that abstract universalism for this reason always remains androcentric.

The positive dialectic of bourgeois recognition was repeated on a larger scale on the periphery by movements for national independence and free participation in the global market. In this case, the critique of capitalism referred to the structure of colonial and postcolonial domination in relation to the more advanced Western nations, but not to its basic social categories. Here too it was a question of a recognition perfectly situated in modern ontology rather than in its critique or overcoming. Thus, both the Russian and Chinese Revolution and subsequent liberation movements in the southern hemisphere assumed a function within the modernization of modernity, namely, the recuperative modernization of national economies and states on the periphery. Consequently, this historical movement also had to be grounded in the idealized categories of modernity and in their legitimation carried out by the Enlightenment, thus remaining confined within androcentric universalism.

The asynchrony at the heart of modern ontology produced a gap in development — geographically and within society itself — which gave rise to both the seemingly radical critique and the liberal critique of Enlightenment. The Western labor movement, the revolutions of the East, and the national liberation movements in the southern hemisphere were merely different versions of a recuperative modernization in the context of that asymmetry. These attempted to get into the system of commodity production, and not to get out of that historical ontology. That option could be taken positively as progress and development, as long as the world system as a whole still afforded a space for a subsequent modernization of modernity.

Such a space for development, however, no longer exists. In the third industrial revolution, modern ontology as such reaches its historical limit. The very same categories within which the entire process of modernization took place are becoming obsolete, as is clearly illustrated on the level of labor as well as in concepts such as nation and politics. With that, the ashynchrony internal to the system of commodity production also disappears. But this, of course, does not mean that all societies have reached the highest level of modern development or that we have surpassed situations of uneven development and reached a new situation of positive planetary contemporaneity. Rather, asynchrony ceases to exist because the system of commodity production is experiencing a large-scale ontological crisis. Whatever the level of development achieved by particular societies, they are all hit by this ontological or categorical crisis.

The different world societies still very much experience decidedly different material, social, and political structural situations. Many countries are only in the beginnings of modern "development"; others remain stuck in the intermediate stages of this development. Yet the gap between such societies no longer mobilizes a dynamic of recuperative modernization — it only mobilizes the dynamic of barbarism. The ontological crisis produces a negative contemporaneity, a doomsday of modern categories, which gradually travels across still-unequal conditions. There is no going back to the old agrarian society, but the development of modern ontological forms, inasmuch as it has taken place, has broken down. Entire industries disappear; entire continents are decoupled; and in the Western core countries, too, the growing crisis is simply managed without any prospects for change.

Everywhere and on all levels of the exhausted capitalist ontology the crisis hits not only capitalist categories, but also the gendered relations of dissociation. Gender relations are "out of control"; the increasingly fragile masculine identity corresponding to the total and one-dimensional subjectivity of abstract labor, law, politics, and so on, begins to break apart. It decomposes into a "feral" state (Roswitha Scholz), which becomes an integral component of the tendency toward barbarism and sets loose a new potential for gratuitous violence against women. Barbarism can no longer be held at bay by a simple and already-failed inherent recognition of women. Rather, it requires an ontological break with the totality of the historical field of capitalist modernity, a field in which the relations of dissociation are inherently gendered.

The same ontological crisis, however, paralyzes critique more than ever. The paradigms of socialist critique of capitalism (immanent to its categories and ontologically positive) are so deeply rooted in asynchrony that they seem unable to surpass a general paralysis of thought. The ghostly reiteration of such forms of thought remains unsuccessful, since they are unable to reach the necessary complexity of categorical critique to respond to the context of the ontological break. In a way, liberalism, conservatism, and classical Marxism have all together become reactionary. The ideologies of modernization decompose and mingle. Enlightenment and counter-Enlightenment have become identical. Today there are antisemitic communists and racist liberals, conservative Enlightenment thinkers, radical pro-market socialists, and sexist and misogynist utopians. Recent social movements have up until now proven to be impotent in the face of the problems of ontological critique and negative contemporaneity. Despite the enormous diversity of inherited conditions, these problems can be formulated and resolved only in common, as those of a planetary society.

Index

Cover and interior design by Nora Brown.
Text set in 11/14 Skolar from TypeTogether.
Headlines set in Karbon from Klim Type Foundry.

30162798R00256

Made in the USA
Charleston, SC
08 June 2014